Poverty and Public Policy

Edited by
Vincent T. Covello

Poverty and Public Policy
An Evaluation of Social Science Research

Published for the
Committee on Evaluation of Poverty Research
Assembly of Behavioral and Social Sciences
National Research Council

National Academy of Sciences

G.K. Hall & Co.   Boston, Massachusetts

Schenkman Publishing Co.   Cambridge, Massachusetts

Notice

The project that is the subject of this report was approved by the Governing Board of the
National Research Council, whose members are drawn from the Councils of the National
Academy of Sciences, the National Academy of Engineering, and the Institute of Medicine.
The members of the committee responsible for the report were chosen for their special com-
petences and with regard for appropriate balance.

This report has been reviewed by a group other than the authors according to procedures
approved by a report review committee consisting of members of the National Academy of
Sciences, the National Academy of Engineering, and the Institute of Medicine.

This work may be reproduced in whole or in part for official use of the U.S. Government.

Library of Congress Cataloging in Publication Data
Main entry under title:
Poverty and public policy.
   (University books)
   Bibliography: p.
   1. Poverty—Addresses, essays, lectures. 2. Poverty research—United
States—Addresses, essays, lectures. 3. Social policy—Addresses, essays,
lectures. I. Covello, Vincent T. II. National Research Council. Commit-
tee on Evaluation of Poverty Research.
HV91.P69   362.5'072   79-28321
ISBN 0-8161-9017-8 cloth
ISBN 0-87073-355-9 paper

This publication is printed on permanent/durable acid-free paper
MANUFACTURED IN THE UNITED STATES OF AMERICA

Contents

Part II: Theoretical and Comparative Perspectives

Preface

At the request of the Office of the Assistant Secretary for Planning and Evaluation of the U.S. Department of Health, Education, and Welfare, the National Research Council established the Committee on Evaluation of Poverty Research to assess the current status of research on poverty and its role in the formation of federal policies that affect poor people.

The committee commissioned the papers in this volume in order to explore the potential contributions of the social and behavioral sciences to future research dealing with the problems of poverty. By asking sociologists, economists, psychologists, political scientists, and anthropologists to consider promising directions for research bearing on poverty in their particular disciplines, the committee has gathered a variety of approaches to poverty research.

The papers in this volume do not cover all significant areas of research on poverty. Nonetheless, it is hoped that this collection will leave the reader with a deeper appreciation of the complexities of the issues related to poverty and of the potential of research to provide a more complete understanding of the nature, causes, and cures of poverty. More than fifteen years have passed since the war-on-poverty research effort began, and now seems to be an appropriate time to reflect on what is known with confidence, what needs to be known, and what alternative research strategies might be undertaken.

For their help on the many intellectual tasks involved in preparing this volume, sincere appreciation is due to the members of the Committee on Evaluation of Poverty Research and to David Greenberg and his associates in the Office of the Assistant Secretary for Planning and Evaluation in the Department of Health, Education, and Welfare. Christine L. McShane did outstanding editorial work on this volume, and Genie Grohman provided valuable editorial advice. Final thanks are due to Janie R. Foote, for her fine typing as well as her patience.

Poverty and Public Policy

Vincent T. Covello

Introduction

Poverty and Poverty Research

During the 1940s and 1950s poverty in America received little scholarly or public attention. In the early 1960s, however, Harrington (1962), among others, cited statistics showing that more than 20 percent of Americans were poor, of which the majority were white, urban, native-born, and less than 60 years old. Moreover, the data showed that a substantial number of families with incomes lower than the official poverty level were headed by males with full-time jobs. Poverty, in short, was still a critical national problem.

Political recognition of the seriousness of the problem came with President Johnson's State of the Union message declaring a war on poverty and with the enactment by Congress of the Equal Opportunity Act of 1964. The Equal Opportunity Act was a landmark piece of legislation, for it represented a major commitment by the government to reduce—and ultimately eliminate—poverty.

Primary responsibility for implementing the provisions of the act was given to the newly created Office of Economic Opportunity (OEO), located in the Executive Office of the President. Although OEO was designated the lead agency in the war on poverty, it shared responsibility for designing and administering major antipoverty programs with five executive departments—Health, Education, and Welfare; Housing and Urban Development; Labor; Commerce; and Agriculture.

In the first few years of the war on poverty, several antipoverty strategies were adopted, including job training, compensatory education, community economic development, and community action. In succeeding years, several additional strategies were also emphasized, including direct cash assistance, in-kind benefits (such as food, housing, and health care), and government-financed services (such as casework

[Vincent T. Covello is Study Director of the Committee on Evaluation of Poverty Research at the National Academy of Sciences.]

social services, community health clinics, child care services, and neighborhood legal services). As programs associated with each of these strategies grew in size and complexity, so did the costs. In 1965, social welfare expenditures for programs specifically directed to low-income groups amounted to $6 billion (Plotnick and Skidmore 1975, p. 11). By 1977, they totaled more than $35 billion (Carcagno and Corson 1977, p. 253)—an increase of nearly 600 percent.

Paralleling these developments, the federal government's investment in poverty research grew from negligible amounts in 1965 to nearly $90 million in 1977 (National Research Council 1979). Most of this research was closely tied to the various strategies and programs developed for combatting poverty. As a result, there now exists a substantial body of poverty research dealing with: income maintenance and transfer systems; legal, political, and administrative systems affecting the poor; status attainment, social mobility, and education; segregation and discrimination; the economic and demographic behavior of families; employment strategies and the operation of labor markets; community organization and the political mobilization of the poor; and the evaluation and implementation of antipoverty programs. In addition to support for these areas of research, the federal government has sponsored major studies on the measurement of poverty and on the extent of poverty and inequality in the United States.

The papers in this volume include discussions of each of these topics. Although the discussions overlap to some extent, each author reviews the literature in his or her field of specialization and attempts to answer the questions: What have been the major contributions of research to an understanding of the issues? What are the areas of high priority for future research?

The volume is divided into two sections. The papers in Part I critically assess the literature in eight of the most important areas of poverty research. The papers in Part II are designed to balance the more empirically oriented papers by providing broader theoretical and comparative perspectives.

Perspectives on Empirical Research

In the first paper of Part I, Gramlich discusses several unresolved problems relating to the government's principal income maintenance and transfer programs: Aid to Families with Dependent Children, Supplemental Security Income, the Comprehensive Employment and Training Act, food stamps, medicaid, unemployment insurance, and compensatory education. Among the issues he addresses are: How should poverty be defined? Who should be the beneficiaries of government programs of income support? Why are certain programs more politically appealing than others? What should be the ultimate goal of the war on poverty? How do the goals of income support programs relate to other national objectives? How is poverty perceived by those who operate income support programs as well as by the beneficiaries? What role should state and local governments play in income redistribution efforts? Although poverty researchers have produced a large body of knowledge bearing on each of these issues, Gramlich recommends that several lines of research be given greater emphasis, including research on program participation rates, public attitudes toward income support programs, the costs of youth unemployment, the impact of public service employment programs, and the trade-off between unemployment and inflation.

The paper by Morgan on economic status and inequality falls into two sections. The first section is devoted to a review and evaluation of poverty-related research on how individuals respond to change, for example, to changes in income or to changes in government policies and programs of income support. As part of his proposed agenda for future research on this question, he emphasizes the need for more research on people's goals and on their attempts to fulfill these goals. Do individuals and families, for example, value stability and security more highly than level of income? The second half of the paper discusses poverty research priorities in six major areas of decision and behavior: (1) jobs, job mobility, and the use of time; (2) family, marriage, children, and family cohesion; (3) nutrition and health care; (4) housing and home maintenance; (5) transportation choices; and (6) family finances. Morgan's analysis indicates that there are important gaps in our understanding of each of these areas and that further progress may require new efforts of data collection.

Orcutt, Nakamura, and Nakamura present in their paper a summary and critique of recent poverty research on the determinants of family income and labor supply. The paper includes a discussion of the two principal components of wage rates for married men and married women: the offered wage and the asking wage. In their review of factors affecting offered wage rates, the authors examine studies on the effects of years of formal education, vocational training, previous job experience, and local labor market conditions. In their review of factors affecting the asking wage rate, the authors examine studies on the effects of child status (e.g., the number and age of preschool children), income from other sources (e.g., unemployment insurance), and the offered wage rate itself. This review is followed by a discussion of (1) ways to improve the predictive power of labor force participation equations; (2) possible applications of a treatment-response experimental approach to the analysis of nonexperimental data; and (3) the advantages and shortcomings of planned experimentation for addressing questions concerning labor supply and demand. In their concluding remarks, Orcutt, Nakamura, and Nakamura suggest that the studies they examined provide surprisingly little practical guidance to policy makers concerned with family labor market behavior. Even more fundamentally, the authors ask ". . . how has it happened that almost all poverty research focuses on the conditions, needs, and behavior of the poor? Isn't it at least possible that some of the causes of poverty and part of the remedy for poverty have something to do with the way our entire system functions and with the role and behavior of corporations, unions, even of government itself?"

Stromsdorfer's paper also discusses research on labor force participation and the employment of the poor. In one sense, Stromsdorfer's paper is broader than the previous article, since research on labor force participation of married men and married women is included as only one part of his review. But in another sense, his paper is narrower in scope, since it focuses on labor supply research done under the auspices of the Institute for Research on Poverty at the University of Wisconsin. Nonetheless, Stromsdorfer points out that the Institute for Research on Poverty has traditionally been a leader and major producer of research on labor supply: ". . . the work of the Institute reflects the general nature and relative scientific concentration" of labor supply research, and, . . . in general, gaps in Institute analysis also reflect gaps in the relative treatment of the same issues in the profession as a whole." As part of his review, Stromsdorfer discusses the relative strengths and weaknesses of the Institute's studies on labor market behavior and employment of the poor. In particular, he assesses the Institute's research on the labor force participation of females, youth, and the elderly, the effects of tax and transfer policies on labor supply, the labor supply results of the income maintenance experiments, the demand for labor, and public service employment. Stromsdorfer concludes the paper by proposing an ambitious program of research aimed at filling the major gaps in our understanding of these issues.

McPartland and Crain's discussion of discrimination, segregation, and processes of social mobility is a critical assessment of what is currently known about overt discrimination and systemic exclusionary processes. As part of their analysis, McPartland and Crain review the literature on discrimination and segregation dealing with occupational socialization and occupational choice, job search methods, social networks of opportunity (such as job contacts and information), career strategies, and personality and achievement. On the basis of this review, the authors conclude that there is a pressing need for additional research on the ways in which discrimination and exclusionary processes impede minority achievement. In the past, researchers have concentrated on estimating the total effects of discrimination and segregation on achievement. However, this line of research has reached the point of diminishing returns, and McPartland and Crain argue that more studies are needed on how discrimination and segregation operate through specific behaviors and processes.

Hodge and Laslett pursue an important theme briefly discussed by McPartland and Crain, that is, the link between processes of status attainment and poverty. Although there are strong grounds for believing that research on these processes can contribute to an understanding of poverty, Hodge and Laslett point out that research on status attainment has largely ignored the problem of poverty, and they cite several reasons for this neglect. First, researchers concerned with status attainment have been more interested in understanding the intergenerational transmission of educational and occupational status rather than the transmission of economic status. Second, models of status attainment refer to the achievements of individuals, whereas poverty, as conceived in the literature, is defined for families. Third, "poverty among those who do work is in some measure a structural problem that cannot be understood by reference to processes of status attainment alone." Nonetheless, Hodge and Laslett argue that there are important connections between processes of status attainment and poverty that need to be explored: ". . . the success of efforts to reduce poverty will be registered in processes of status attainment. Through the study of these processes the impact of such programs is most likely to be detected and potential ways of improving them may be uncovered."

In the final paper in this part, Lipsky seeks to establish a set of research priorities concerning the effects of administrative systems on the poor. The specific focus of the paper is on "street-level bureaucracies," or "public service agencies whose workers interact directly with the poor in the course of their jobs and who exercise substantial discretion in making decisions about them." Arguing that we are just beginning to recognize the significance of street-level bureaucratic interactions, Lipsky suggests that researchers concentrate their attention on the nature of street-level policy toward the poor. In the ideal case, such studies would be based on detailed observations of interactions between clients and workers as well as on a thorough understanding of the work problems of administrators. As a guide to future research efforts, Lipsky discusses the need for studies aimed at improving client-worker interactions, including research on (1) ways to give clients greater autonomy in solving their own problems; (2) ways to make public service employees more responsive to clients; and (3) ways to make public service employees more effective advocates of the rights of the poor.

Theoretical and Comparative Perspectives

In the first paper of Part II, Pettigrew presents a comprehensive examination of how social psychological concepts and findings can be used to study poverty. On the basis of a review of the literature, Pettigrew states that there have been no major contributions of social psychological research to an understanding of poverty. Despite the clear relevance of the discipline, poverty research has been relatively neglected by social psychologists. Given the paucity of relevant work in the field, Pettigrew devotes most of his paper to a discussion of potential applications of social psychology to the problem of poverty. More specifically, he argues that recent advances in social psychological theories of deviance and labeling can be usefully applied to the study of poverty. For example, he argues that poverty can be profitably viewed as "stigmatized social deviance" and puts forward the idea that the problem of poverty may be rooted more in the attitudes and behavior of the nonpoor than among the poor themselves.

Rein and Peattie's paper is also concerned with developing a new theoretical approach to poverty research. After analyzing how poverty research is presently conducted, Rein and Peattie propose an alternative framework for thinking about poverty and poverty research. As a substitute for the conceptual frameworks currently in use, Rein and Peattie develop a new perspective centered around the "claims" that people make against the state, the firm, and the family. They argue that "claiming" includes aspects of entitlement, negotiation, litigation, and bargaining. Not only is there a rich set of researchable poverty-related issues associated with each of these aspects of claiming, but a claims perspective allows researchers to examine the political, economic, and social dimensions of poverty within a single framework. The claims perspective also leads to a more realistic understanding of why certain poverty-related topics are selected for study and others are not. As Rein and Peattie observe, poverty research is part of the political process and the questions asked by poverty researchers are, to a large extent, shaped by the information needs of competing groups of claimants.

While Rein and Peattie sketch in broad strokes a number of fundamental conceptual issues in poverty research, Peterson's paper on federalism and the Great Society surveys the literature on the division of responsibility among layers of government and discusses the implications of such work for poverty research. Using tools of analysis from both political science and economics, he criticizes previous political science research in this area and provides an explanation for many of the difficulties faced by antipoverty programs of Johnson's Great Society.

Peterson's central thesis is that "the differing responsibilities of national and local governments generate value conflicts that impede the implementation of redistributive policies." More specifically, he argues that local governments are primarily concerned with their own economic well-being, whereas the national government is more interested in achieving equality. By identifying the inherent conflict and tension between the objectives of national and local governments, Peterson is able to indicate more precisely the problems of implementing redistributive policies in a federal system of government. He concludes the paper by suggesting several questions that future research might usefully address, including: (1) What are the implications for policy of various types of intergovernmental arrangements?; and (2) How can the federal system of government be made compatible with the objective of reducing poverty and achieving a more equitable distribution of income?

Finally, Korpi's paper provides a comparative perspective, highlighting the distinctive characteristics of European and American approaches to poverty and poverty research. Although he touches on various topics in the paper, the discussion focuses on differences between Europe and the United States in how poverty is defined, how poverty is explained, how antipoverty programs are evaluated, and how poverty is combatted. As part of his analysis, Korpi makes the following points. First, American poverty researchers have tended in practice to rely on an absolute definition of poverty, whereas European researchers view poverty more as a relative phenomenon. In addition, whereas American poverty researchers have tended to rely on income for delineating and defining poverty, European poverty researchers have, in general, defined poverty in terms of command over multiple resources. Second, efforts by researchers to explain poverty and inequality in the United States have generally been sought in terms of characteristics of the poor, for example, their work motivation. In American explanations of poverty, little attention has been paid to the relatively high levels of unemployment and inequality in the United States, to conflict-oriented approaches to the study of poverty, and to the low levels of collective organization among the poor. By comparison, European explanations of poverty are often based on such approaches. Third, to a much greater extent than in Europe, American researchers have concentrated on "target efficiency" and on the proportion of people below the officially established poverty line in evaluating antipoverty programs, and "have neglected other significant aspects of antipoverty programs, such as their political consequences in inhibiting or encouraging political coalitions in support of continued efforts to reduce poverty and inequality." Finally, Korpi observes that work requirements, in-kind transfers, and means-tested programs are a relatively minor part of European welfare systems, whereas in the United States these are still major components of the welfare system. Korpi concludes the paper by observing that surprisingly little has been learned by American policy makers and poverty researchers from European experiences.

References

Carcagno, G., and Corson, W. (1977) Welfare reform. In J. Peckman, ed., *Setting National Priorities: the 1978 Budget.* Washington, D.C.: Brookings Institution.

Harrington, M. (1962) *The Other America: Poverty in the United States.* New York: Macmillan.

National Research Council (1979) *Evaluating Federal Support for Poverty Research.* Committee on Evaluation of Poverty Research, Assembly of Behavioral and Social Sciences. Washington, D.C.: National Academy of Sciences.

Plotnick, R., and Skidmore, F. (1975) *Progress Against Poverty.* New York: Academic Press.

Part I: Perspectives on Empirical Research

Edward M. Gramlich

Future Research on Poverty and Income Maintenance

For the past decade there has been a relatively large-scale research effort to study the problems of poverty. Much of this effort has been carried out at the Institute for Research on Poverty at the University of Wisconsin, but there have been other contributors as well. Largely due to these efforts, there is now a systematic body of knowledge on how to plan, conduct, and analyze social experiments related to prospective national policies; there is much greater understanding of the pros and cons of various redistributive measures, whether planned or already in existence; there is increased knowledge about the difficulties in administering these policies, about attitudes of taxpayers and recipients, about statistical and measurement issues, and so forth. It is no exaggeration to say that because of these efforts, a new and lively field of academic research has been created almost overnight.

With this success record, it may seem strange that people are even writing about directions in which the research should now go. Researchers did very well without such direction in the past decade, and they probably will continue to do so. But there are good reasons for periodic stocktaking and this particular time is probably as good as any. Even after a decade of progress, there are many gaps in the research that has been done on poverty. As with other good research, past efforts have convincingly answered some questions and raised new ones. Even more important, the path of current events has opened up a new set of research issues that would not have seemed credible to those planning poverty research in its early years. For the most part, these new issues concern complications in implementing antipoverty policies, political constraints that have eliminated certain potential policy measures from the scene and introduced substitutes, competition between antipoverty goals and other national objectives, and a possible revolt or blacklash on the part of middle-class taxpayers. The state of society has changed radically, too.

[Edward M. Gramlich is Professor of Economics and Director of the Institute for Public Policy Studies, University of Michigan.]

Even as observers were claiming that it was not feasible to transfer large sums to poor people, there was a veritable explosion in transfer-type programs—Aid to Families with Dependent Children (AFDC), food stamps, supplemental security income, medicaid, liberalization of unemployment insurance benefits, the Comprehensive Employment and Training Act, and compensatory education. These income support programs amounted to $6.2 billion, or 3.4 percent of the federal budget, in fiscal 1969; and $40.6 billion, or 8.1 percent of the federal budget, by fiscal 1979 (U.S. Office of Management and Budget 1978). In view of these rapid changes, applied poverty research should almost certainly change in character in the future.

This paper, will spend relatively little time summarizing events in the poverty field over the past ten years—something the Institute for Research on Poverty has already done very ably[1]—and much more looking at current research priorities to suggest where, if at all, the focus should be changed.

This aim is both grandiose and modest. It is grandiose in suggesting the directions in which a whole community of researchers should be headed, a judgment that is inevitably personal and unlikely to be shared by many others, or even most others. In view of the fact that a community of researchers is constantly thinking about such matters, this paper will have served a purpose if only a small number of the suggested topics strikes a responsive chord. Yet the aim is also modest in the sense that this paper simply lays out important research areas; for the most part it does not tell researcher x how to attack problem y.

The plan of the paper is straightforward. It begins by confronting the issue of whether poverty research is still relevant, given the fact that the nation is now spending so much (or really, so much more) on redistribution and the fact that other pressing national concerns have arisen. It then delves into a series of more specific issues. One issue is what is meant by poverty in the first place. Fourteen years ago the government declared a war on poverty—most people still agree with the goals of that crusade in the abstract, but legislation passed under its aegis is not abstract but specific. Discussions of what is meant by poverty are not the same as but are similar to discussions of who should be the main beneficiaries of redistribution policies, or at least how to decide who these beneficiaries should be. A second issue is how poverty should be dealt with, including the more programmatic considerations to which past research has probably contributed most. The third issue involves attitudes towards redistribution policy, those of both taxpayers and recipients. The fourth issue refers to conflicts and harmonies of antipoverty objectives with other national goals, such as macrostabilization, stable prices, economic growth, economic efficiency, and even the freedom of the private sector from excessive governmental interference. A final section deals with a somewhat narrower issue, but one that is rapidly becoming very important: what is the role, if any, of state and local governments in income distribution policy?

Is Poverty Research Still Relevant?

Both politicians and funding agencies sometimes appear to consider poverty research passé—an issue of the 1960s but not of the 1970s. It has, in a sense, been pushed off center stage by the rapid growth of income support programs on one hand, and by the supposedly greater relevance of foreign adventures, political scandals, plummeting dollars, energy crises, and inflation on the other.

This view, if seriously held by any, is entirely unconvincing. One must distinguish between the problems of policy and the values of research. In a policy sense, the nation may well decide to defer new initiatives in the war on poverty until improvements are made in the political system, the dollar is stablized, energy supplies are ensured, and taxpayers are placated. But the researchers should clearly not be forced to lay down their computers just yet. First, the rapid growth in spending for anti-poverty programs indicates only that the government is trying harder now, not that the poverty problem has been solved. Even as measured by the absolute poverty standard, the incidence of poverty since 1965 has only been cut by a third, not eliminated, and this success rate would be much lower by a variety of other standards (U.S. Bureau of the Census 1978). More broadly, one can sensibly argue that research on poverty is more relevant in this era of tight budgets, national preoccupation with other issues, and little room for new policy initiatives. Cost-effectiveness and informed choices, both logical partners of research, are much more necessary when budgets are tight than when they are easy. If many new policy initiatives will not be possible, then we had better analyze things carefully and made the best of any opportunities that do present themselves.

Of course, simply saying that poverty research in general is still relevant and worthwhile does not solve the difficult administrative problem of deciding exactly what research is to be so considered. There has always been a tension between what might be termed the Office of Economic Opportunity project review board mentality about poverty research and the academic institution mentality. The project review board approach is to define poverty research very narrowly, so that almost any project that does not try to measure exactly the amount of new spending power poor people should get is ruled out of bounds. The academic approach is to define the rules very broadly, so that they encompass whatever project a particular researcher happens to be working on at the moment. While these diverse approaches do bracket the true dividing line between what is relevant and what is not, the brackets are so wide that it is hard to find the line. My own preference, perhaps because of my experience with Office of Economic Opportunity project review boards, is to adopt a relatively conservative, narrow view of what is and what is not relevant poverty research. Poverty research is still necessary and desirable and therefore requires a precise focus. Efforts to encourage relevant poverty research should not degenerate into research on social problems generally, or into general social science research. Because individual researchers are ingenious in justifying their own projects, one must view these justifications with at least some skepticism. Not all projects have equal claim on the scarce supply of research funds.

How Poverty is Defined: The Short-Run Perspective

There is a factual and deceptively simple definition of poverty that is useful from a short-term perspective. The poverty population is that set of people living in families with incomes less than the standard of needs determined by the Bureau of the Census and the U.S. Department of Health, Education, and Welfare for a particular year. While this definition appears straightforward and operational, almost every aspect of it is open to question, and open to analysis by researchers.[2]

One problem involves defining "needs," which has always been done in a quasi-objective way by technicians asking what people "need" to live on. But poverty is in some senses a social concept, related although not equivalent to the target population for income support programs. Since such programs are legislated in the usual democratic way, might not there be some virtue in asking the American people to define poverty? Perhaps consumer expenditure surveys of what people actually spend money on at various income levels could be combined with attitudinal surveys of the population at large to see how the problem ought to be defined, or how "needs" ought to be measured. Such a strategy would also yield a potential compromise to the still-unresolved debate over relative and absolute poverty standards. The attitudinal surveys would indicate whether people feel the poverty line should be raised according to prices (the absolute standard), real income (the relative standard), something in between, or not at all over time. This new poverty line would not entirely supplant the old one developed by technicians, but it would provide valuable information in the continuing debate about redistribution policies.[3]

A second problem concerns timing. One of the great contributions of early research on poverty is the simple empirical observation that low incomes fluctuate widely (Morgan et al. 1974). There is one set of people who are poor year-in and year-out, and there is another, much larger set of people who are poor now and then. This time-wise variation in income within the year has also been discovered in the negative income tax experiments—indeed, this variation is the source of the accounting problem that now bedevils income maintenance planners (Mathematics Policy Research 1978; see also Skidmore 1975). If income varies so much over time, from month to month or from year to year, then the proper time horizon over which the income status of a family is defined becomes an important and not easily resolved issue. Should income support programs for people with low incomes, or tax policies for people with higher incomes, be aimed at income deficiencies resulting from a one-month spell of unemployment of the main breadwinner, from a six-week strike, from a three-month seasonal layoff, from a one-year cessation of some source of nonlabor income, from a transitory change in the size of the family, or from a permanent change in the size of the family?

An approach is needed for dealing with the incredible variety of changes in income status of the population: Is income support ultimately protection against the variance in income, against low permanent income, or both? Perhaps this will always be a policy disagreement, but more factual information might help resolve it. In large part, more longitudinal data are needed, particularly for periods of less than a year, stratified by age to allow any life-cycle effects to be nailed down better. But it is also important for researchers to try to distinguish unplanned drops in income relative to needs (for which the claim for transfers or tax advantages is much greater) from planned changes in income due to actions that simply take advantage of the transfer system. The focus, moreover, should be not only on income changes but also on planned and unplanned changes in family composition and inter-unit living arrangements that accomplish the same end.

A third problem regards leisure or more precisely, nonmarket time, an issue that has always fascinated economists. I believe that the world still does not understand nonmarket time very well. Regarding levels of nonmarket time valuation, implications of recent work by Garfinkel and Haveman (1977) and Vickery (1977) are that nonmarket time is valuable, that equating the status of families of equal market incomes but unequal nonmarket time, as is traditionally done, is inappropriate, and that it might make sense to value nonmarket time before determining poverty, transfer levels, or whatever. However, all consumption can be disaggregated into nondiscretionary and discretionary components, and nonmarket time is no exception. The usual procedure is to measure well-being as a positive function of discretionary consumption and to ignore nondiscretionary consumption, because it deals with the intrinsic needs of the family. Hence the Census Bureau's poverty needs standard is really an attempt to measure necessary nondiscretionary expenditures on food and other necessities, and a family's income must rise above the standard before it is adjudged to be out of the poverty population. Similarly, most researchers would not consider reimbursements from a health insurance plan as disposable income; those reimbursements are no doubt largely nondiscretionary, occasioned by unplanned health needs, and do not indicate that the family is better off.[4] So if families consume different amounts of nonmarket time, how do we know that this consumption is discretionary, making a family better off, or nondiscretionary, dealing with unsatisfactory day care arrangements, commuting requirements, or whatever?[5]

A related but different problem arises in assessing changes in people's nonmarket time. The negative income tax (NIT) experiments were designed to measure this kind of change and they did.[6] Most supporters of the negative income tax were relieved that changes in the labor supply of the male family supporters were modest, even if those of the females were larger, because the latter changes would not be viewed as socially harmful by Congress. But putting aside for the moment congressional concern, what is the popular view of the social desirability of changes in leisure time when the household head reduces hours of overtime, the spouse stays home more, and so forth? There are now data on the use of time by households (Juster and Robinson 1974, Hill and Stafford 1978). Wouldn't it be possible to analyze these data, ask pertinent questions on opinion surveys, and thus inform social judgments about the desirability of the leisure responses in the NIT experiments?

A final problem regards the inclusion of various sources of income in the definition of poverty. Recent retabulations of census data by the Congressional Budget Office (1977) confirm that adjustments for taxes paid and the full cash value of in-kind transfer reduce fairly sharply the number of people counted as poor. Further work by Smolensky et al. (1977), Smeeding (1977), Kraft and Olsen, (1974), and Clarkson (1975) shows that this conclusion is not materially changed if in-kind transfers are valued in terms of their utility to recipients, mainly because those in-kind transfers are not large relative to what recipients would ordinarily spend on the commodity. One issue that is not covered by these studies is whether it is in fact legitimate to change the numerator of the income-needs expression without also changing the denominator, a question that is difficult to deal with given the innate arbitrariness of the poverty standard. Beyond that, one could argue for making the further inclusion, on a cash or a utility basis, of the value of local public services received by families, such as public education, trash collection, and police and fire services. Casual evidence suggests that such services vary widely across place and time. Heretofore it has not been possible to allocate the benefits of local expenditures on any but a very oversimplified basis, but growing numbers of household surveys and other microdata should facilitate more careful analyses.[7] Adjusting incomes for differing values of local public services received could give added perspective on such things as changes in the lot of the poor over time, regional differences in poverty, and the impact of federal, state, and local budget policies on the distribution of income.

How Poverty is Defined: The Long-Run Perspective

In a longer-run perspective, the relevance and the value of the operational short-run definition of poverty become even more remote. One might think of the aims of the war on poverty in two ways: as giving underprivileged groups a better chance in the race for the material and psychological rewards of life, or as reducing the cross-sectional variance in rewards. The first view of the war on poverty involves equalizing opportunity and eliminating discrimination in all its subtle forms. The second view involves arranging for income maintenance to boost the consumption of the losers of the race and progressive taxation to limit that of the winners. Of course, there is no reason one cannot hold both views—that there should be both a fair race and limitation on the variance of the reward structure. Indeed, it may never be possible to run a fair race without some reduction in the amount of income inequality.

Depending on which view is predominant, there may be a sharp difference in the nature of antipoverty efforts at different times. Very broadly, in the early days of the Office of Economic Opportunity (when the Democrats were making policy), there was more stress on programs to boost equality of opportunity, such as affirmative action, community action, legal services, Head Start, and compensatory education programs. But then, as the war on poverty aged and the Republicans took over (the very same Republicans who criticize blanket "handouts"), the emphasis in policy shifted toward measures to reduce variance in income, such as the 1969 tax cut (which finally eliminated most poor people from the tax rolls), food stamps, and supplemental security income, along with a deemphasis of many of the earlier "helping hand" programs.[8]

It is not obvious what researchers can do about this change in the character of policy except to help illuminate it, but they can deal with a related problem that is fundamental to the whole antipoverty effort. Is there any relationship between variance-reducing policy and equality-of-opportunity policy? Is the former a complement to the latter in some ultra-long-run sense, or an impediment? More specifically, what is the relationship between people with low incomes today and the long-term intergenerational status of the offspring of these people? Are the sons and daughters of today's poor more likely to be poor themselves? Is the probability lowered by an income maintenance program that brings the poor family's consumption up to minimal standards? Or is it raised by the stigma of accepting income maintenance payments?[9]

An initial step in researching these questions could be made by analyzing the external effects of education, medical care, housing, and other types of in-kind redistribution. It is possible to find or infer how much less of these social externality goods present generations of people with low incomes are consuming, and then to use some variant of human capital theory to predict the ultimate effects.[10]

This question also addresses one of the leading social policy issues of the day: If high unemployment is a necessary ingredient of a credible fight against inflation, and if high unemployment in general means extremely high unemployment rates for youths, what are going to be the long-run social consequences?[11] They might, in fact, be relatively benign: youths might spend more time searching for jobs but eventually find ones just as good as in the old days; or perhaps youths need a greater number of jobs to experiment with on a trial basis. Or the consequences might be very serious, if the discouragement from an unsatisfactory and humiliating job search warps their lives, implies a permanent sacrifice of productive human capital, or leaves them with no chance of getting a desirable job. Until this quesion is answered, we will not be able to appraise the true social cost of present-day economic difficulties; indeed, we will not even be able to answer more limited questions such as how the welfare of teenagers should be compared with that of family-supporting adults when considering an increase in the minimum wage.[12]

How Should Poverty Be Dealt With?

By which of various measures, or which mixture of measures, should poverty be combatted? A reasonable way to organize a discussion of tactics might be to do a benefit-cost calculation of various programmatic ways of dealing with poverty: income maintenance, employment inducement, in-kind programs, or whatever. What kind of information would one need to make adjustments? Is that information readily available?

Basic data are needed on who would benefit from various programs. In general, recent advances in the richness of data available to researchers have helped on this score, but there are still gaps. There are now good data on family incomes as well as good data on wage rates and unemployment from the Census Bureau's *Current Population Survey*. Merging these data (the Census Bureau's March and May questionnaires) to get wage and income distribution is possible, but time-consuming and costly. Similarly, longitudinal data on income and wages for families exist, but the sample is relatively small, and for most early years the labor force data are complete only for heads of households (Morgan et al. 1974). Recent changes have corrected the second problem, but only for a few years of the longitudinal sample.

Academic researchers can do more about the form of transfer. From the recipient's standpoint, cash is obviously preferable to in-kind transfers, a finding demonstrated by studies (Kraft and Olsen 1974, Clarkson 1975, Smeeding 1977, Smolensky et al. 1977) that compute utility ratios for in-kind transfers, although the margin of superiority is surprisingly small. From the standpoint of taxpayers, it is often alleged that taxpayers favor in-kind transfers because they can better understand specific consumption deficiencies. To my knowledge, this proposition has never been demonstrated empirically, either for taxpayers or for their voting representatives. Wouldn't it be possible to conduct a survey or to analyze existing survey data to illuminate the issue? On a more subtle level, the proposition that taxpayers favor in-kind transfers becomes logically inconsistent once taxpayers understand the displacement issue. In a rational world, it would be logically impossible for recipients to value highly public housing subsidies because they can cash them out, and for taxpayers to favor them because of the externalities attendant on higher levels of housing consumption. Perhaps it would be useful to ascertain whether taxpayers and their voting representatives understand the displacement issue, if they think it is important, and if it affects their views about the form of transfer.

A more tractable issue involves the earnings side of the income equation. Does it make more sense to supplement the incomes of people with low incomes, or to supplement their employment? Can the attitudes of taxpayers about income support and employment support be compared? Will they object to the fact that employment subsidies may go to members of families with high incomes? There are also administrative questions. Does public employment cost more than income support because of capital and supervision requirements? Can this cost be offset by the increase in productivity of the public employees? How can this productivity be valued?[13] Other questions involve the on-the-job human capital component of public jobs. Are workers better off in the long run for having taken these jobs? Do they get good jobs on leaving the public employment jobs? Is there any stigma on being part of an army of the publicly employed?

These questions are obviously important today, particularly given the strength of the political coalition backing public employment. They are so important, in fact, that they should be a prime subject for future experimentation. The Institute for Research on Poverty is already involved in evaluating the supported work experiment, a public employment program for welfare mothers, ex-offenders, ex-addicts, and young dropouts (Manpower Demonstration Research Corporation 1977). Further effects seem likely to be made in connection with the Labor Department's evaluation of the Employment Opportunities Pilot Programs. These efforts are very important and should be monitored carefully.

Perhaps gratuitously, I offer some comments on how this type of study might be done. By closely watching how long the public job workers stayed on the job and what they did after their spell of public employment was over, one could measure the benefits of public employment. Other workers who applied for and didn't get public jobs, or people selected at random from the low-wage, high-unemployment work force could be used as a control group. Since unemployed workers have to select either a CETA-funded job or unemployment insurance, the unemployment insurance rolls provide a ready, if imperfect, population of control subjects. The monitoring of performance on the job could provide some measure of the social value of the output of these workers. Budgetary records of the relevant governments could allow measurement of both the cost of the program and any potential employment displacement effects. Finally, the behavior of low-wage labor markets in a community before and after CETA-funded public employment could be compared with the behavior of those markets in other communities where CETA was not as important a factor, to measure secondary labor market effects. Such a study might fill most of the blanks in a full evaluation of public employment.

A final issue that does not fit neatly anywhere involves the intersection between income maintenance policy and social insurance policy, which are both of great importance today. Consideration of this issue raises questions about the relationship of the recent explosion of disability benefits to the causes and cures of the poverty problem; about a possible redirection of the mission of social security now that supplemental security income is in place; about combinations of medicare and medicaid as the best way to deal with the health needs of low-income aged; and about the role of private pensions, and regulations on private pensions, in a general approach to income maintenance. Perhaps a general movement toward broad social insurance will remove some of the need for, and political touchiness of, the income maintenance remedy; or perhaps income maintenance will eventually allow social insurance to be just that, unencumbered by its present dual role.

Attitudes toward Dealing with Poverty

In a simple-minded view of the income redistribution process, the most important attitude would be the attitudes of those whose income is being redistributed. They, or their representatives, are legislating programs that reduce their own spending power to raise the incomes of the poor; it would make sense to study their attitudes to understand whether transfer policies are at all in keeping with their wishes.

It is first of all difficult even to identify the relevant decision makers, those responsible for the programs now in existence. Are they voters or representatives? It is then difficult to characterize attitudes, particularly when they vary so much from program to program or from approach to approach, giving very little permanence to anything being studied. One indication that these problems are being dealt with is the 1979 Institute for Research on Poverty Conference on Universal versus Income-Tested Transfer Programs. This conference may help to promote an understanding of the motivation for redistribution programs as well as potential for analyzing political attitudes in general.

There are a number of long-standing mysteries on the attitudes of taxpayers. In casually reading newspaper quotes from the person in the street, one is usually struck by both the fundamental lack of information about the technical details of redistribution policy and the impact of changes in it; and the lack of congruence between the wishes articulated by the person in the street and actual policies.

Without going into a deep political analysis, the main explanation seems to be that in the United States redistribution policy as it has emerged is the product of many technical decisions by politicians and bureaucrats, and any popular control on the part of the electorate is remote indeed. The key distinguishing features of present-day welfare policy include the level of benefits, the federal matching rate, the extent to which two-parent families are eligible for benefits, the universality of food stamps, the administration of the food stamp work requirement, and the extent to which people must buy their food stamps. Every one of these important provisions is highly technical, and every proposal for reforming the system immediately bogs down on these highly technical issues. While redistribution and welfare policy are the stuff of inflammatory political rhetoric, in practice this rhetoric gets quickly doused by a string of boring technicalities. It sometimes seems that the country has ceded a block of important political decisions to the handful of people who have taken the trouble to understand them.

Of course the wide gap between oversimplified political rhetoric and programmatic technical detail is not unique to redistribution policy—in fact, it is hard to think of an important national issue today that does not have a similar gap. Moreover, in the area of income redistribution, so many diverse needs and political aims must be satisfied that a high degree of complexity is probably inevitable. Every attempt to simplify welfare, the tax system, or anything else seems to end up making the rule book longer, not shorter. But even the presence of this big gap between popular understanding and actual policy does not make studying the collective decision-making process hopeless, as Orr (1976) has recently shown. Perhaps there are other ways of inferring attitudes from actual policies.

The attitudes of recipients are another important issue that might be very promising for poverty research. It is often assumed that utility-maximizing recipients will take whatever transfers are made available, and that their attitudes are irrelevant to the form and impact of the transfer system. Is this assumption supported by evidence?

One of the big mysteries of income support programs is the degree of participation. The explosion in caseloads for Aid to Families with Dependent Children in the late 1960s was largely due to increased participation of eligible people. Food stamp participation rates are now low, but will they increase with the recent administrative change eliminating the purchase requirement? Why has the tax credit of the Work Incentive Program (WIN) not been more lighly subscribed? Of even more relevance, what will be the degree of participation in a large-scale public jobs program? Will prospective employees "come out of the woodwork," as is predicted, or will there be undersubscription of these jobs too?

There are lots of examples of interesting questions along these lines. Two types of behavior must be explained: that of the potential recipients and that of the potential administrators. MacDonald (1975) (foodstamps), Holmer (1976) (AFDC), and Hamermesh (1978) (the WIN tax credit) have written early and interesting exploratory pieces, but much remains to be done. One promising avenue is the simple one of conducting surveys of participants, potential employees, and potential county administrators. Among other groups, the staff of the Joint Economic Committee has recently collected program participation information that could prove useful.[14] On a more theoretical level, perhaps it would be possible to develop models of the participation of beneficiaries, the actions of administrators, and the interaction of the two. At a minimum, such models ought to be developed along with the surveys to generate useful questions.

Relationships with Other National Objectives

The preceding sections have been concerned almost exclusively with poverty and income redistribution. I now broaden the focus and examine the relationship between poverty and important exogenous events, or between antipoverty and other important national goals.

The first important outside event in the inflation problem. The past decade has been one of accelerating inflation, both in the United States and in most other countries of the world. Inflation is the United States started with a species clearly of the "excess demand type" in the late 1960s, moving to a "cost-push variety" in the early 1970s, then to externally induced inflation in the mid-1970s. By the last 1970s, however, all strains seemed inextricably intertwined and inflation now appears to have elements of all three sources. The most serious difficulty, however, is that every promising cure for inflation has been tried and found wanting. Even high unemployment, that last refuge of modern "dismal scientists," came about in 1975, in much stronger doses than even these dismal scientists wanted, and made very little impact on the basic underlying rate of inflation. Most macroeconomists now believe that a necessary condition of the fight against inflation is to avoid periods of very low unemployment, but doubt is growing that periods of very high unemployment are helpful in stabilizing prices. A sharp asymmetry (known as an L-shaped Phillips curve) seems to provide all the inflationary "costs" of low unemployment but none of the supposed "benefits" of high unemployment (Okun 1977).

Four aspects of this unpleasant situation make it particularly painful for the poor:

1. Inflation is likely to be directly harmful to the poor.
2. The inevitable unemployment necessary to protect against new bursts of excess demand inflation is even more harmful to the poor.
3. In part the growing inflationary tendency of the economy may be due to humane efforts to deal with income redistribution, and terminating or modifying these efforts could be a part of an anti-inflationary program. The examples that come to mind are public employment, unemployment insurance, minimum wages, and subsidies of the consumption of scarce services such as medicaid.
4. As a result of correctly or incorrectly perceived links between budget deficits and inflation, or the general malaise leading to politically necessary middle-class tax cuts, the poor may get squeezed out of future budgetary initiatives.

The best thing that poverty researchers could do about this situation would be to find a cure for inflation. The poor would be better off, and macroeconomists would be either eternally grateful or eternally jealous. But if inflation persists, there are other types of studies that can be carried out.

The ground of the first two points above has been trod at least a few times,[15] and it is not clear that further efforts will pay large dividends. But the second two points are still wide open. Largely due to Feldstein's efforts, many have examined the link between unemployment insurance and the deteriorating inflation-unemployment trade-off; a few have done likewise on minimum wages; but little work has been done on the other programs.[16] In particular, current proposals for public employment should be studied with some care. On one hand, the public wage could directly force up some private wages, and the elimination of the last-resort fear of unemployment could enhance labor's bargaining power and make the inflation-unemployment trade-off worse. On the other hand, Baily and Tobin (1978) make a case for why public employment may improve the trade-off, but again their contention is largely unverified. There ought to be enough experience with present-day mini public employment programs to examine the general labor market effects, although maybe co-opting some CETA sites for a quasi experiment, as the Labor Department is doing, will be necessary. Incidentally, examining unemployment insurance, public employment, and medicaid to find their potential inflationary (making the Phillips curve worse) impact is not as much of a witch-hunting strategy as it seems. Inflation is one of the potential costs of these programs (allegations of this link are made daily in the *Wall Street Journal*) and the task of research is to nail the matter down. If Baily and Tobin are right, public employment may even reduce inflation; but even if it does not, finding that a suspected cost is minor should be equally important, and equally persuasive, as is identifying benefits for public employment devotees.

Regarding the fourth point above, tight budgets, while regrettable to liberals, are the stuff of program evaluation. One cannot know absolutely the benefits of income redistribution programs, but one can follow the cost-effectiveness approach of holding these benefits constant and seeing which of many programmatic approaches minimizes either budget costs or more general social efficiency costs.[17] Or one could specify a series of aggregate benefits functions and see which of a series of constant-cost programs raise it the most—one might call this type of study a benefit-effectiveness examination (Gramlich and Wolkoff 1978). There are numerous other types of applications of the burgeoning literature on evaluation to income redistribution.

Another issue, less topical than inflation but more fundamental, involves the equity-efficiency trade-off. If the inflation-unemploy-ment trade-off is the basic dilemma of macroeconomcs, the equity-efficiency trade-off is the basic dilemma both of public finance economics and development economics. Any redistribution program can be thought of as a political resolution of this issue: the interests of economic efficiency are being compromised (in the form of higher tax rates, lower savings, and "dead-weight" losses) for the sake of a more equitable distribution of income.

One interesting direction for research to take on this issue is to make cross-sectional international comparisons of different countries. Sweden, for example, is usually given as an illustration of a country that redistributes more income than the United States, but without greater loss in efficiency, at least as measured by growth rates of gross national product. Is this true? If it is so, what explains it? Might there be some ways in which efficiency and equity are complements of and not substi-tutes for one another (better educated and more productive labor force, the incentive effect of equal opportunities, etc.)? Any research along these lines should obviously investigate all the ways that both countries redistribute—money incomes, direct in-kind benefits, and indirect public good benefits. It may be, for example, that, once the relatively large sub-sidies to higher education in this country are accounted for, the United States is redistributing more than is commonly believed.

Another departure, perhaps more theoretical, would be to incorporate redistribution into the growth development literature. The growth-development literature focuses on the aggregate saving rate as an indi-cator of how society trades present for future welfare. Another dimen-sion to this issue is that present-day consumption can be high either with high tax rates and a great deal of transfer redistribution, or with low tax rates and little redistribution. Present-day redistribution must also be traded off against the welfare of future generations, raising a develop-ment question of fundamental importance. Should developing countries compromise high-saving growth policies for the sake of present-day re-distribution? To what extent have they done so?[18] Is there evidence of a trade-off or can redistribution proceed with high saving and rapid growth?

The Federal Government and States and Localities

The level of government at which redistribution efforts are carried out is another issue of concern to poverty researchers. Conventional public fi-nance reasoning has always been of two minds on this issue. One school, following the logic of Tiebout (1956), argues that state and local governments ought to be able to choose their level of redistribution and that efficiency gains are made when generous and stingy taxpayers alike move to jurisdictions whose policies they are in sympathy with. Another school points to the adverse social consequences of these moves: support levels differ across the nation, and some see horizontal inequities in that fact. Moreover, differing support levels can create migration incentives among the poor as well, which are unlikely to be propitious. Most transfer recipients tend to go to the generous communities, raising tax prices in these communities, forcing these communities to cut back spending on merit goods, and leading to socially undesirable income stratification across jurisdictions. Taking that reasoning one step further, even if taxpayers in some communities are generous, the fear that their communities may be invaded by hordes of transfer beneficiaries will nip any redistribution efforts in the bud. Hence this school argues for centralization of the redistribution function at the national level, both to prevent income stratification across communities and to make possible any redistribution at all.[19]

The reasoning of both schools has surface plausibility, but very little empirical research has been done on the matter. Despite a stream of proposals to federalize welfare from both Republican and Democratic presidents, mixed federal-state determination of AFDC benefits is alive and well. The growth of the federalized food stamp program and variations in the federal AFDC matching rate across states have cut down the statewide dispersion of benefits in recent years, but they still do differ by a factor of as much as two to one (Blechman et al. 1974). To my knowledge, it has never been established that these diverse benefit levels cause any in-migration of low-income people, but there is a popular perception that the high state-local tax rates necessary to pay for generous welfare and other programs, in New York, for example, do cause emigration (Foltman and McClelland 1977). And even the perception of emigration is enough to thwart local redistribution efforts. Regarding both the importance of the policy questions and the plethora of testable hypotheses, this general area would seem to be a promising one for research.

The widely advertised revolt of middle-class taxpayers is a related issue that is certainly exciting to many people, in either a positive or a negative sense, though it is not clear what researchers can or should do about it. This issue has developed into primarily a state-local fiscal issue. Tax limitation laws and amendments are spreading like wildfire across the country—by mid-1978, New Jersey, Tennessee, and California had already passed such amendments and forces were gathering to propose similar amendments in at least nineteen other states (*Newsweek*, June 5, 1978, p.25). Students of public finance know that revenue-financed redistribution spending takes a very modest portion of local budgets and a relatively modest portion of state government budgets, but taxpayers don't seem to know it. The typical villains in these amendments are either self-serving public employees or lazy welfare bums. One would not, of course, want to argue that the research community should be turned around by what could be a passing political fad. But the tax limitation movement may not be a fad, and it does raise a number of interesting research questions. One question regards the likely effect of these referenda: Could one estimate doubly constrained budget models in the states that have approved such referenda to see what will happen as a result? A second, more basic, possibility is to examine the apparent popularity of these limitations. Do they represent coherent, rational preferences, or are they based on uninformed frustration with recent economic difficulties? Do voters feel that efforts to redistribute income have gone too far, or is their complaint against bureaucrats? Why has the pressure expressed itself mainly at the state-local level? A question in keeping with the theme of the 1979 Institute for Research on Poverty conference is: Do these amendments indicate that there will be, for all time, or for a long time, a fixed budget constraint? Or would this constraint have been set at a different level if government programs were not perceived as just benefiting the poor?

Implications

This paper makes a number of suggestions for research, and two general themes bear emphasizing.

First, even though other events have pushed poverty and income redistribution off the front pages of the newspapers, there is still much more important and interesting research to be done. The underlying problems have not been solved, even with a much stronger governmental effort than was made a decade ago. If it is true, as certainly seems likely, that future real growth in the antipoverty budget will not be as great as in the recent past, it becomes all the more important for researchers to find the best programs and even to make convincing cases for them. The need for research on poverty still exists.

Second, to a greater extent than in the past, the most important issues seem to involve interactions between poverty research and the real world. Understanding whether perceptions about poverty and desirable levels of income support have changed, why certain programs are politically appealing and others are not, how apparently inevitable high rates of teenage unemployment will affect the income distribution, what will happen if unemployment is dealt with through public employment, and whether other humane attempts to redistribute income are at all to blame in causing the deteriorating unemployment-inflation trade-off are some of the fascinating questions that deal with these interactions.

Notes

Acknowledgement: In writing a paper in a field like this the risks of overlooking numerous contributions are great. The poverty literature is so voluminous that it is difficult for anybody to keep up with it. I ask the reader's indulgence if I have overlooked important contributions and the researcher's patience if I have suggested a study that has already been done. I also acknowledge discussions with Vincent Covello, Irwin Garfinkel, and John Palmer and their comments on an earlier draft.

1. See in particular Plotnick and Skidmore (1975) and Lampman (1971).
2. The most complete discussion of the needs standard is found in U.S. Department of Health, Education, and Welfare (1976). The conceptual underpinnings are examined in a number of papers in Moon and Smolensky (1977).
3. One early effort along these lines is Kilpatrick (1973).
4. An argument along these lines is made by Watts (1977).
5. Incidentally, a family may react strongly when the time that it must spend dealing with unsatisfactory day care arrangements is called "leisure."
6. The most complete report on the New Jersey experiment is a series of articles in the Spring 1973 edition of the *Journal of Human Resources*. The results of the rural income maintenance experiment are reported in Palmer and Pechman (1978). The Seattle-Denver results are reported in Keeley et al. (1978).
7. For a typical "conventional" allocation of expenditure benefits, see Reynolds and Smolensky (1974). A Michigan graduate student, William Palmer, recently completed a term paper in which he investigated Detroit's public expenditure in a household survey that asked, among other things, questions about the use of and satisfaction with the Detroit public services. It should be possible to use such studies as the RAND work in New York City to similar effect.
8. A complete description of the policies followed over the decade can be found in Haveman (1977).
9. The Institute for Research on Poverty and the University of Wisconsin have always been leading contributors to research on intergenerational mobility, although to my knowledge that research cannot yet answer most of the specific questions posed here. A recent major work on the topic is Duncan et al. (1972). For an economist's review of this book, see Cain (1974). Forays into the intergenerational transmission of wealth have been made by Brittain (1977) and Menchik (1977).

10. Perhaps the closest example to the type of study envisioned here is Bowles (1973). It should be possible to conduct similar studies with health, housing, and so on.
11. One of the best discussions of the teenage unemployment problem is the Congressional Budget Office (1978). A new recruit to the Institute for Research on Poverty, Mary Kay Plantes, is writing her doctoral thesis on this topic.
12. This is an issue I tried to grapple with in Gramlich (1976).
13. Haveman (1978) conducted a systematic analysis of these gains and losses in the Netherlands.
14. See the series entitled *Studies in Public Welfare* prepared by the Joint Economic Committee, 1973.
15. A recent discussion of the inflation side of the issue is by Palmer and Barth (1977). This paper updates earlier work by Hollister and Palmer (1972). The unemployment side is covered in Gramlich (1974).
16. On unemployment insurance, see Feldstein (1973) and rejoinders of sorts by Marston (1975) and Munts and Garfinkel (1974). A convenient summary of research on the employment effects of minimum wages is found in Goldfarb (1974).
17. As was done by Garfinkel and Kessleman (1975).
18. An example is Fields (1977).
19. These issues are cogently discussed by Oates (1977). The classic Tiebout article (sometimes alleged to be tongue-in-cheek) is Tiebout (1956).

References

Baily, M.N., and Tobin, J. (1978) The inflation-unemployment consequences of job creation policies. In John L. Palmer, ed., *Creating Jobs: Public Employment and Wage Subsidy Programs.* Washington, D.C.: Brookings Institution.

Blechman, B.M., Gramlich, E.M., and Hartman, R.W. (1974) *Setting National Priorities: The 1975 Budget.* Washington, D.C.: Brookings Institution.

Bowles, S. (1973) Understanding unequal economic opportunity. *American Economic Review* 63:346–356.

Brittain, J.A. (1977) *The Inheritance of Economic Status.* Washington, D.C.: Brookings Institution.

Cain, G.G. (1974) Review of socioeconomic background and achievement. *American Journal of Sociology* 79:1497–1509.

Clarkson, K. (1975) *Food Stamps and Nutrition.* Washington, D.C.: American Enterprise Institute.

Congressional Budget Office (1977) *Poverty Status of Families Under Alternative Definitions of Income.* Washington, D.C.: U.S. Government Printing Office.

Congressional Budget Office (1978) *Youth Unemployment: The Outlook and Some Policy Strategies.* Washington, D.C.: U.S. Government Printing Office.

Duncan, O.D., Featherman, D.L., and Duncan, B. (1972) *Socioeconomic Background and Achievement.* New York: Seminar Press.

Feldstein, M.S. (1973) *Lowering the Permanent Rate of Unemployment.* Prepared for the Joint Economic Committee.

Fields, G.S. (1977) Who benefits from economic development? *American Economic Review* 67:570–582.

Foltman, F.F., and McClelland, P.D. (1977) *New York State's Economic Crisis: Jobs, Income, and Economic Growth.* Ithaca: Cornell University.

Garfinkel, I., and Haveman, R.H. (1977) *Earnings Capacity, Poverty and Inequality.* IRP Analysis Series. New York: Academic Press.

Garfinkel, I., and Kessleman, J.R. (1975) *On the Efficiency of Income Testing in Tax-Transfer Programs.* IRP Discussion Paper #339. Madison, Wis.: Institute for Research on Poverty.

Gramlich, E.M. (1974) The distributional effects of higher unemployment. *Brookings Papers on Economic Activity* 2:293–341.

Gramlich, E.M. (1976) The impact of minimum wage on other wages, employment, and family incomes. *Brookings Papers on Economic Activity* 2:409–461.

Gramlich, E.M., and Wolkoff, M.L. (1979) A framework for evaluating income distributions programs. *Journal of Human Resources,* 14:319–350.

Goldfarb, R.S. (1974) The policy content of quantitative minimum wage research. In *Industrial Relations Research Association, Proceedings of the Twenty-Seventh Annual Meeting.*

Hamermesh, D.S. (1978) Subsidies for jobs in the private sector. In John John L. Palmer, ed., *Creating Jobs: Public Employment and Wage Subsidy Programs.* Washington, D.C.: Brookings Institution.

Haveman, R.H. (1977) *A Decade of Federal Antipoverty Programs.* IRP Analysis Series. New York: Academic Press.

Haveman, R.H. (1978) The Dutch social employment program. In John L. Palmer, ed., *Creating Jobs: Public Employment and Wage Subsidy Programs.* Washington, D.C.: Brookings Institution.

Hill, C.R., and Stafford, F.P. (1978) Parental Care of Children: Time Diary Estimates of Quantity, Predictability and Variety. Unpublished University of Michigan Discussion Paper.

Hollister, R.G., and Palmer, J.L. (1972) The impact of inflation on the poor. In K. Boulding and M. Pfaff, eds., *Redistribution to the Rich and the Poor: The Grants Economics of Income Distribution.*

Holmer, M.S. (1976) The Sensitivity of Transfer Payments to Changes in Economic Conditions and Public Policy. Working paper. U.S. Department of Health, Education, and Welfare.

Juster, F.T., and Robinson, J.R. (1974) Incorporating Time Use Data into Economic and Social Accounts. Unpublished paper. Institute for Social Research, University of Michigan.

Keeley, M.C.; Robins, P.K.; Spiegelman, R.G.; and West, R.W. (1978) The labor supply effects and costs of alternative negative income tax programs. *Journal of Human Resources* 13:3–36.

Kilpatrick, R.W. (1973) The income elasticity of the poverty line. *Review of Economics and Statistics* 55:327–332.

Kraft, J., and Olsen, E. (1975) The Distribution of Benefits from Public Housing. Unpublished National Bureau of Economic Research Discussion Paper.

Lampman, R.J. (1971) *Ends and Means of Reducing Income Poverty.* IRP Analysis Series. Chicago: Markham Press.

MacDonald, M. (1975) *Why Don't More Eligibles Use Food Stamps?* IRP Discussion Paper #292. Madison, Wis.: Institute for Research on Poverty.

Marston, S.T. (1975) The impact of unemployment insurance on job search. *Brookings Papers on Economic Activity* 1:13–60.

Manpower Demonstration Research Corporation (1977) *Analysis of Nine-Month Interviews for Supported Work: Results of an Early Sample.*

Mathematica Policy Research (1978) Colorado Monthly Reporting System: Design and Operations. Unpublished project report.

Menchik, P.L. (1977) *Intergenerational Transmission of Inequality: An Empirical Study of Wealth Mobility.* IRP Discussion Paper #407. Madison, Wis.: Institute for Research on Poverty.

Moon, M., and Smolensky, E. (1977) *Improving Measures of Economic Well-Being.* IRP Analysis Series. New York: Academic Press.

Morgan, J.N., ed. (1974) *Five Thousand American Families—Patterns of Economic Progress.* Vols. 1–5. Ann Arbor: University of Michigan Institute for Social Research.

Munts, R., and Garfinkel, I. (1974) *The Work Disincentive Effects of Unemployment Insurance.* Kalamazoo, Mich.: Upjohn Institute.

Oates, W.E. (1977) An economist's perspective on fiscal federalism. In W.E. Oates, ed., *The Political Economy of Fiscal Federalism.* Lexington, Mass.: Lexington Books.

Okun, A.M. (1977) The great stagflation swamp. *The Brookings Bulletin* 14:7.

Orr, L.L. (1976) Income transfers as a public good: an application to AFDC. *American Economic Review* 66:359–371.

Palmer, J.L., and Barth, M.C. (1977) The distributional effects of inflation and higher unemployment. In M. Moon and E. Smolensky, eds., *Improving Measures of Economic Well-Being.* IRP Analysis Series. New York: Academic Press.

Palmer, J.L., and Pechman, J.A. (1978) *Welfare in Rural Areas: The North Carolina, Iowa Income Maintenance Experiment.* Washington, D.C.: Brookings Institution.

Plotnick, R.D., and Skidmore, F. (1975) *Progress against Poverty: A Review of the 1964–1974 Decade.* IRP Analysis Series. New York: Academic Press.

Reynolds, M., and Smolensky, E. (1974) The post-fisc distribution: 1961 and 1970 compared. *National Tax Journal* 27:515–530.

Skidmore, F. (1975) Operational design of the experiment. In Joseph A. Pechman and P. Michael Timpane, eds., *Work Incentives and Income Guarantees*. Washington, D.C.: Brookings Institution.

Smeeding, T. (1977) The economic well-being of low income households: implications for income inequality and poverty. In M. Moon and E. Smolensky, eds., *Improving Measures of Economic Well-Being*. IRP Analysis Series. New York: Academic Press.

Smolensky, E., Stiefel, L., Schmundt, M., and Plotnick, R. (1977) In-kind transfers and the size distribution of income. In M. Moon and E. Smolensky, eds., *Improving Measures of Economic Well-Being*. IRP Analysis Series. New York: Academic Press.

Tiebout, C. (1956) A pure theory of local expenditures *Journal of Political Economy* 64:416–424.

U.S. Bureau of the Census (1978) Status of the low income population. Series P-60 in *Current Population Reports*. Washington, D.C.: U.S. Department of Commerce.

U.S. Department of Health, Education, and Welfare (1976) *The Measure of Poverty*. Report to Congress as Mandated by the Education Amendments of 1974.

U.S. Joint Economic Committee (1973) *Studies in Public Welfare*. Prepared for the use of the Subcommittee on Fiscial Policy, 93 Cong. 1 sess.

U.S. Office of Management and Budget (1978) *The Budget of the U.S. Government, Fiscal 1979*. Table 17. Washington, D.C.: U.S. Government Printing Office.

Vickery, C. (1977) The time-poor: a new look at poverty. *Journal of Human Resources* 12:27–48.

Watts, H.W. (1977) New Data on the Impact of Public Programs on Family Income and Poverty. Unpublished Columbia University paper.

James N. Morgan

Poverty Research on Economic Status and Inequality

Where should we be directing our research on the economic status of individuals? We can discuss substantive research possibilities and problems better if we agree on the purposes and goals of the research. Methods and procedures and specific areas of research then derive from judgments about possible paths to attaining these objectives. We now have two main public goals that are in partial conflict: We want to abolish poverty, so that no one lacks some basic minimum standard of living (and perhaps even so that everyone has a minimum of insecurity); we also want to reduce dependence so that more people can be independent and self-sustaining. Determining whether providing economic security and income floors discourages the search for economic independence has long been a prime research objective. In fact, the reverse may be true.

A broader approach to the problem should lead us to ask just how our economic system produces poverty and dependence, and what responses by individuals or by governments might change the situation. An economist's distinction between impact and incidence is appropriate here. Any change in individual behavior, in laws and regulations, or in government programs produces immediate impact, such as a flow of money. The whole system then reacts to that change and a new equilibrium is at least possible.

Hence, there are two broad classes of research, each of which requires both theoretical models and empirical research, and both of which have a symbiotic relationship requiring repeated interaction and cooperation. There is research on individual behavior and its responses to changes in environment, rules, and policies of government. Ultimately the functioning of any economic system depends on the way individuals respond, not only to changes in income but also to many other changes, so behavioral research is required.

We also need to know how a system responds or would respond to dif-

[James N. Morgan is research scientist at the Institute for Social Research and professor of economics at the University of Michigan.]

ferent kinds of changes. Various methods are used in such systems analysis or social research. Structural equation models can be estimated at many levels of disaggregation and richness of detail and their response characteristics estimated. As such systems become more complex, interpreting their characteristics in terms of overall response to specific changes cannot be done by simply taking derivatives of the functions but requires computer simulations of some kind.

The interdependence of the two types of research, which we can call behavioral research and social research on poverty, is crucial. Systems analysts can use models to tell us what overall responses to expect to changes that one might consider or forecast, but they soon discover that their forecasts of change are more sensitive to the size of some estimated response coefficients (behavioral assumptions) than they are to others. This focus on what matters most should set the agenda for behavioral research. Conversely, if behavioral research shows that some plausible responses (such as substitution effects that encourage more work at higher wage rates) are insignificant in size and are swamped by other factors, the models can be altered to reflect the reality.

Given this broad picture of two interacting types of research, and keeping in mind that one cannot have one without the other, I focus in this paper on needs in the area of behavioral research. I do this partly because I know more about that area, and partly because, perhaps myopically, I am convinced that we have exhausted most of what we can do with systems models until we have better behavioral information to put into them. We are more in need of new data of a richer sort than we are of additional sophisticated analyses of the limited existing data. Alternative statistical models applied to the same existing data sets are coming up with inconsistent answers. We need more robust inferences about behavior.

Robust behavioral findings will result when we get similar answers using a wide variety of both data and methods and models, and when we have data rich enough to show not only statistical relationships but also the mechanisms and paths by which things happen. Inferences about dynamic behavioral responses can best be made with data on changes in individual behaviors that are related to data about other changes, to individual information, insights, purposes, and expressed reasons. Making such inferences does not always require expensive panel studies that take years to produce results. I believe we have underestimated the possibilities of retrospective questions. Memories can be aided by various methods and supplemented by the use of recorded data. Emotional biases may be as likely to appear in simultaneous or immediately-afterward panel data as in the somewhat calmer retrospect of a few years later. In any case, cross-checks among expressed reasons and inferences from related facts are possible.

Actually, in addition to behavioral research and systems analysis, there is a third set of relevant factors: the policy makers who are responsible for seeing that laws and policies are both acceptable to the electorate and potentially effective. Ideally, interactions should take place among policy makers, systems analysts concerned with the aggregate dynamic implications of changed policies when individuals respond to them, and behavioral researchers trying to estimate what those individual responses are likely to be.

Behavioral Research

Behavioral research progresses naturally from description and measurement, to inferences about relationships and causes, to collection of data tailored to improve the ability to select the best behavioral model and estimate its parameters. This ideal process has been sidetracked in the case of poverty research because of costly administrative needs. Federal programs dealing with poverty and a number of other problems call for expenditure allocations—federal revenue sharing and others—that in turn require data on the characteristics of small local areas. It is extremely costly to measure anything in each of thousands of small areas, such as congressional districts or smaller administrative areas. And since local area data are so expensive, the content of the data and the range of alternative methodologies are severely limited. One cannot afford to experiment with alternative methods or definitions once a study is under way, since the goal is the best estimate of the required variables. Nor can one afford to include any of the rich body of questions about attitudes, information, insights, and related facts that would increase the understanding of the main factual variables. Such work may be very well done, but it does not improve the understanding of poverty or dependence or lead to improved public policies to eliminate one or reduce the other.

Examples of these large federal data programs are the Annual Housing Survey, the Consumer Expenditure Survey, the Survey of Income and Education, and the developing Survey of Income and Program Participation. The ongoing Current Population Survey is also limited in its range and flexibility by the need for maximally defensible current trend data on a few crucial variables.

There are, of course, some exceptions, notably the H.E.W.–Michigan Panel Study of Income Dynamics and the Labor Department–Ohio State Labor Force Panels. But they cover only a fraction of the issues and are restricted by the fact that they must collect comparable data in each wave.

The Michigan data dramatize the shortcoming of the massive national measurement efforts related to allocation formulas. Dramatic differences in the poverty population appear when one uses a longer time period than one year, includes nonmoney income, or takes account of the free time left after work to enjoy the income. Precise measurement of the wrong thing (short–run, narrowly defined poverty) can lead to misallocation of federal funds, particularly if those funds were intended to deal with long–run dependence.

Experiments with human populations, focused on the most obviously crucial behavioral response questions, have been widely applauded as introducing a new era and have indeed provided both findings and possibilities for additional analysis. But there have been relatively few of them because they are so expensive. Also, like any attempt to experiment in situ with human populations, the experiments have been confounded by uncontrolled events. The negative income tax experiments were restricted to small areas where the welfare laws were changed in midstream, the Boeing plant was shut down, and where other local events or publicity affected the outcomes. Such experiments are inevitably short–run and often bewilder their subjects. For these reasons and because of natural inertia, an expected outcome of such experiments should be no change in behavior. When such a finding had positive policy implications, as in the negative income tax experiments and the effect of income support on work effort, the results were acclaimed. When the expected experimental results were changes, as in the housing allowance experiment, the no-change results were less appealing. And the narrowness of the income maintenance experiments is now apparent in the findings that the treatments had more effect on family composition (divorce) than on work. Yet experimental manipulations and rules were never clearly designed to illuminate the effects of the alternative treatments on family cohesiveness. It is difficult to find in descriptions of the experiments a clear statement of the rules affecting payments in the case of divorce or other changes in family composition.

There is also a wide variety of studies assessing the impact of specific programs, an accountability justifiably demanded by Congress. But these studies are also expensive, difficult, and narrow. They are difficult because, thought of as experiments, they have no clear, easily located "control group." Potentially eligible people not in the program are not only difficult to locate, but they may also be quite different from those who did get into it—less well informed, located in the boondocks, less motivated, and even less competent or less experienced. Programs themselves may select participants, with an eye to their potential—a perfectly sensible procedure and an efficient use of funds.

Social scientists have oversold the notion of tightly controlled experiments that involve not only random allocation to treatment and control groups but also prior specification of the details and a separation of the measurement-assessment aspects from program administration. Given the complexity of human beings, and the possibilities of misunderstandings and of the occurrence of exogenous events, the enforced rigidity of an experiment is likely to doom it to failure because of its lack of adaptive flexibility. In the middle of an experiment one may discover that the subjects do not understand the rules they are supposed to respond to, or that unfounded rumors are rampant. Or unexpected problems may arise that, if not solved, would inhibit response for reasons totally independent of the experiment.

The likely outcome is a series of experiments, each showing what did not work and why, but never ending with a viable program. What needs to be developed and tested is not a rigid set of programs, policies, and rules, but a set of adaptive mechanisms that promise to make a program work in a wide variety of circumstances and to allow it to adapt to a wide variety of shocks and problems. A good theory for any successful institution or venture is that success depends on the capacity to solve various problems as they arise.

Designing experiments to test not programs, but metaprograms—that is, procedures for operating programs and adapting them—is a scientific endeavor in desperate need of development before we invest much more in expensive experimentation. Scientific method can still be applied, including careful measurement, random allocation, and so on. For those not convinced, I might note that in a number of experiments in inducing social change (family planning, new agricultural practices), there has been greater difference in results among the several experimental groups than between the experimental and the control groups. The implication is that the program managers in the experimental sites were doing different things. Without careful measurement of what they were doing differently, one does not end up with notions about what leads to successful programs.

What then is the future for flexible behavioral research not tied to immediate programs or revenue-sharing formula demands? If the action agencies cannot spare the resources or attention, who can? The National Science Foundation has been set up and funded in such a way as to restrict its focus to grants too small to support even a modest collection of new data. And its review procedures have made it difficult to compare the relative merits of secondary analysis proposals with new–data studies because the amounts of money involved are so disparate. The private foundations have funded little social or economic research on domestic poverty in recent years.

As a result, researchers have focused on ingenious uses of existing data to test deductive inferences from theory, usually, a theory that is unrealistic and lacks adequate data to test it. In such situations the results are likely to be sensitive to the particular statistical model and the methods employed. There is, in addition, a propensity to focus on testing particular popular theories rather than to ask broader questions about alternative explanations. There is justification in directing attention to estimating the effects of things that are potentially changeable through public policy, but alternatives exist even within that group. The few rich data sets, particularly the panel studies, have been underutilized in the sense that much of the secondary analysis has focused on a limited number of theories derived from human capital considerations or income and substitution effects in labor supply. If, as recent research (Morgan 1979) suggests, income goals dominate work-hour decisions rather than marginal substitutions between work and leisure, and if rising real wages lead to reductions in overtime and second jobs, and if rising prices (lower real wages) lead to demands for more overtime and extra jobs, then the policy implications for both inflation and unemployment would be quite different from the usual ones. Inflation can concentrate employment among those with rights to overtime and increase underemployment and unemployment for the remaining workers. And a work-reduction response to rising income at the bottom—reducing hours to merely full time—might be considered a social benefit rather than a cost.

An Agenda for Behavioral Research

The agenda for behavioral research should develop through interaction with a parallel research program using dynamic models of the whole system. We can make some shrewd guesses now as to the kinds of information about human motivation and behavior that are needed most. We must keep in mind that the data should be usable in simulation models of the whole system. We postpone concerns about whether laboratory experiments, field experiments, cross-section surveys relying on memory for change data, or panel studies are best for each topic. A great deal of behavior is habitual, since most of us continue to do what we have been doing except when the situation becomes sufficiently uncomfortable to demand attention and a choice about change. At that point, persons or families can be thought of as engaging in problem-solving or coping behavior, based on some goals or values, often multiple goals. While any set of goals can be converted into a single utility-function that could be maximized, real understanding of behavior requires knowledge of its components.

Human decision making, then, combines some basic motives (values, personality, goals) with current incentive levels for each of them as well as with beliefs, insights, and information about the possible outcomes of alternative decisions. These last subjective probabilities of the payoffs to alternative choices are called "expectancies" by psychologists, and motivation toward a particular choice is seen as a product of motive, incentive, and expectancy (Atkinson 1958, Atkinson et al. 1974, Morgan 1961).

Since basic personality characteristics determine motives, and since these characteristics are presumably not very changeable, they are of concern only as they affect reactions to policies, not as factors that policies can change. Even incentive levels, seen as a kind of marginal utility of satisfying that motive, are important in explaining and understanding behavior, not as tools of change. Information, insight, perceptions, and beliefs about the world may be the most crucial factors both affecting behavior and subject to change in themselves.

Facts and Insight

Facts and insight (or understanding) are not identical. Insight is the cognitive ability to know what facts one needs and what to do with them. We are bombarded with a plethora of facts, most of them irrelevant, at least in the form we receive them, and some are actually misleading. "The social security system is going broke" is an example. A vital element in poverty research should be to investigate methods of improving the information and insights that individuals have available to them as a basis for making their own choices. Particularly in household management, insight should come first (Simon 1978, p.13):

> In a world where attention is a major scarce resource, information may be an expensive luxury, for it may turn our attention from what is important to what is unimportant.

Occasionally, all one needs to know is where one can purchase some standard commodity most cheaply. Improvements in market information would of course be helpful, but research on how to educate people in the handling of their own economic affairs is more crucial. There is evidence that poor people are quite aware of price differences, but perhaps less capable of making substitutions that save money. We need both research on factors that block understanding of economic insights, and experiments on ways of improving such understanding.

Goals and Motives

The measurement of poverty represents one narrow aspect of a much larger program of goals and motivation. Instead of arguing deductively about better measures of well-being, we might call for some research about what people's goals are, and how they change. Do people ignore nonmoney income in evaluating their own circumstances? What about leisure time? In theory one could design a measure of well-being that is a kind of linear homogeneous utility function, with terms for net real income relative to needs and for the amount of free time to enjoy it; one could attempt to estimate the exponents of the two components—do people really value leisure at all? One could also, as the quality-of-life researchers are doing, attempt to assess the whole range of criteria that people apply to valuing their life and environment. Perhaps stability and security are as important to many people as their level of income. Certainly, we have already produced evidence from the Michigan Panel Study indicating that persistent poverty is distributed quite differently in the population from one-year poverty (based on one year's income). It seems premature, therefore, to engage in expensive measurements of the level and trend of one narrow definition of poverty.

Another piece of evidence of the need for better notions of peoples' goals is the persistent association of higher wages with less total work, at least at the lower levels of income, indicating that people may have a target income or basic standard of living that they attempt to maintain under low wage rates by working longer hours. Should public policy, then, be opposed to raising wages on the grounds that such a strategy induces or at least allows people to work less? Much of the discussion of the work-incentive effects of income maintenance programs seems focused on people who drop out of the labor market, rather than on people who give up a third or a second job or drop back to 2000 hours of work a year.

If income and career aspirations are subject to change, then it is important to know what can change them. Does aspiration really rise with accomplishment, and do unemployment or other economic trauma disrupt or reverse this process? A pioneering study indicates differences between countries in the levels and the elasticity of aspirations, but we need more detailed research on the process for individuals, particularly as it affects the poor (Katona et al. 1971). If failure leaves some people aspiring to little more than economic survival, is stability of income more important than its level in encouraging rising aspirations and effort?

I have suggested elsewhere (Morgan 1978a) that if people were to maximize a measure of well-being that took account of the leisure left to enjoy their money and nonmoney income, the use of such a measure as a base for income maintenance and taxation programs would distort choices about such things as work, family, and children less than would a measure of pure money income or money income relative to needs. But to achieve genuine neutrality in such programs so as not to distort people's choices requires knowing what people are trying to do (perhaps they are trying to maximize some function, but which one?).

Perceptions

It should be possible also to find out about what options people see open to them, what they think their own goals are, and how they explain their own choices. Do people at the lower end of the wage scale really know of a range of available jobs? Do they have a "reservation wage" to indicate which ones to turn down because they do not pay enough? Do they see any possibilities of job mobility? Do they know of insuperable obstacles to choices one assumes they have?

The main goals and motives of the poor may be relatively simple and obvious, but a great deal more research is needed on the way they cope with their environment both in the business of daily living and in dealing with crises and emergencies. While one could study coping mechanisms in general, six major decision and behavior areas are suggested by prior studies. These are:

1. Jobs, job mobility, and use of time;
2. Family, marriage, children, and cohesion;
3. Nutrition and health care;
4. Housing and home maintenance;
5. Transportation choices and maintenance and repair of cars;
6. Family finance—efficient use of money, savings, and insurance.

1. JOBS, JOB MOBILITY, AND USE OF TIME

Considerable work has already been done on people's behavior in getting jobs and on "labor supply," even though many of the poor have limited job opportunities or are not working at all. Both the Labor Department

National Longitudinal Studies (Ohio State–Parnes) and the Michigan Panel Study have provided analyses and data for secondary analysis, with increasingly sophisticated models and methods. The new Labor Department panels will provide additional information on the process of getting started in the job market. The results of these studies so far are inconclusive; various human capital and dual labor market theories have claimed partial victories, often with the same data but different models.

More important, some of these are theories of economic macro-dynamics, not of individual behavior, and whatever their implications for public policy, new policies could not be designed without much more information about individual motivation and behavior. We know very little, for instance, about how people get jobs, or how they decide about jobs if and when they have a choice. In spite of much work on job search as an information and investment process, almost nothing is known about the extent to which people are actually helped in their job search by friends and relatives. The evidence is accumulating that much of the sex difference in earnings comes from early sorting into good and bad jobs, those with and without on-the-job training and chances for advancement. So a crucial question is how that sorting takes place. The eleventh wave of the Michigan panel asks a few questions, retrospectively, but much more needs to be done.

Another limitation on both the data and the analysis of labor supply is that they generally ignore the possibility that a series of interrelated decisions are also being made about a spouse's job and job location. Particularly when the first, crucially important, job choices are made, an individual may very well be also making related decisions about getting married, spouse's job, whether to have children, and in what part of the country to live. This crucial decision process deserves systematic study in its entirety, not as a set of separate decisions.

The field of labor supply and human capital is desperately in need, not of more sophisticated application of models to inadequate data, but of better data on the actual behavior, motivation, information, insights, and perceptions of individuals. Do individuals even know about the things that are theorized to be influencing them? Would better information change their behavior and reduce otherwise unexplained disparities in wage rates, for example, between blacks and whites, between women and men, or just among different people?

We also need more studies of the use of time, including time not spent on the job but related to earning a living, such as time spent when unemployed, ill, or commuting. Time is also spent in taking care of children, in training, in learning, and in securing information both on and off the job. We need to know how people allocate their time.

There is a broad question of motivation, only a fragment of which was touched by the income maintenance experiments, namely whether there is an optimal middle level of economic security and certainty. Dysfunctional discouragement and narrowness of horizon might occur when there is too little security and certainty, while indolence and inertia might result from too much security. It is at least a plausible hypothesis, though difficult to test, that for many of the poor, increased security could lead to increased striving, willingness to try new possibilities, and ultimately more self-reliance.

2. FAMILY, MARRIAGE, CHILDREN, AND COHESION

Sweeping demographic changes can have substantial impacts on the nature and extent of poverty, but we cannot be sure without knowing more about possible behavioral responses. The generation now reaching retirement age had large families (the postwar baby boom), but succeeding generations will have fewer children.

The family remains the primary source of support for otherwise dependent people in our society. Change in family composition are a major source of change in the economic status of individuals, and are probably more under the discretionary control of individuals than their wage rates or hours of work. The focus on fertility and on marriage and divorce needs to be broadened to study the set of decisions about who lives with whom and who contributes how much time and money inside the family. The resulting intrafamily transfers are an important source of support for otherwise dependent individuals (see Morgan 1978b).

There is evidence that the amount of interfamily aid among those not living together is small, yet it is possible that emergency help and psychological security provided by the extended family are far more important than we think. We need more information about extended family relations, past, present, and potential. We also need to know a lot more about investments of time and money in child-rearing by persons inside and outside the family, since changes in market work by mothers must be creating massive changes in child care, some of which may have important future consequences, particularly among the poor.

3. NUTRITION AND HEALTH CARE

While there has been a good deal of data collection and research on health and on the utilization of medical care, and even some on nutrition, more is needed on this most important aspect of well-being, particularly for the poor and the aged. Further studies should focus on the behavioral aspects of preventive care, good health practices, and nutrition. Nutrition is a subject not easily simplified. Yet, particularly at low incomes, good health can be preserved by practicing good nutrition. The evidence is that people with lower incomes are increasingly eating out, perhaps because all the adults in a family are working and time is scarce, but we know little about what this situation is doing to the family's nutrition.

Economy in the use of health care facilities may call for better preventive care and more productive use of existing facilities and personnel. The poor have traditionally had their health care rationed by both cost barriers and endless delays and waiting times. There are more efficient ways of allocating scarce (and expensive) medical resources, but they involve teaching new behavior patterns to both the dispensers and receivers of these services. Once again, we are thrown back on a whole series of questions about current behavior and potential changes in behavior that are unlikely to be answered by analysis of existing data, however sophisticated the methods.

4. HOUSING AND HOME MAINTENANCE

Housing for the poor has always received a lot of attention, perhaps because it is the most offensively visible aspect of poverty. It is entirely possible that the poor are in general coerced or bribed into having more ample and expensive housing than they would want if they could allocate the subsidy money themselves. Before more programs invest in attempting to improve the housing of the poor, it might be useful to find out who benefits from these expenditures. There are theories that home ownership increases respectability, responsibility, and stability, and hence should be encouraged among the poor. Such asserted behavior and attitude changes can be measured. The premise is potentially researchable. At the same time the effects of ownership on mobility and of mobility on earnings, economic security, and economic advancement should be studied. There is some evidence that people who move to the cities are better off than those they leave behind but worse off than those who are already there with connections and good jobs. Better information about the experiences of movers (and nonmovers) might indicate whether encouraging mobility would do any good, and if so for whom. Another set of problems, particularly for the poor, has to do with maintenance and repair of housing, even rented housing. Studies of the possibility of more self-reliance in this area might be worthwhile. For the repairs that require difficult skills, the poor may need information about obtaining services.

Experiments in improving information and access to efficient repair services may substantially benefit the poor. Studies of the possibility of training some otherwise unemployable (and probably younger) members of the low-income population in the efficient repair of ordinary household items such as wiring, plumbing, windows, and roofing might also be considered.

5. TRANSPORTATION CHOICES AND MAINTENANCE AND REPAIR OF CARS

Transportation has rarely been suggested as something to be subsidized primarily to help the poor. Housing and food have been the preferred items. Yet transportation may well be crucial to the poor in opening up a wider range of housing and job opportunities as well as access to social services. Just how crucial is a researchable topic requiring not just secondary analysis but new data.

A clear conceptual and theoretical case can be made for free public transportation in large cities, but the distribution of potential benefits needs study because it depends on behavioral responses to the availability of transportation. Who actually would use it, and for what? The cost of medical care is in part a cost of getting to hospitals and doctors. Current concern with the cost of delivering medical care, rather than the cost of getting to it, is leading to hospital locations that increase the transportation problems of the poor. Whether the establishment of local clinics offsets this trend is also a testable question.

We need to know more about the current burden of transportation costs and about the potential of different, cheaper, more adequate transportation over short and long adjustment periods. Would cheap, fast transportation reduce the housing costs of the poor by opening up a wider range of alternatives?

As with housing, repair and maintenance of cars may be more of a problem for the poor than the basic capital involved in their purchase. Information may help, but training some low-income people themselves to repair cars might provide employment and income for some and cheaper transportation for others. Experimental studies would answer that question.

6. FAMILY FINANCE—EFFICIENCY IN USE OF MONEY, SAVINGS, AND INSURANCE

Poverty in its broadest sense means a low level of well-being, and even the most elaborate measures made up of broadly defined, net real income relative to family needs and leisure time to enjoy it do not encompass the variety of ways people satisfy their requirements with what they have available. Efficiency in the use of income is difficult to measure because we do not mean simply the nutritional results of a diet, but the resulting satisfaction or happiness—the ultimate outcome. Ever since Ben Franklin opined that "If your outgo exceeds your income,/Your upkeep will be your downfall," we have known that family financial management matters. But it is a complicated concept. Middle-class notions, like buying large-sized economy packages, wither before the devastating logic of one respondent who said, when asked whether she did that, "Hell no, you buy too much beer that way."

Starting at the descriptive level, we have no decent data on people's retirement provisions or plans, and no monitoring of changes in them. The rudimentary data we do have indicate a polarization: on one hand, the poor, who have not been able to accumulate pension rights and assets, hope never to retire, and do so unwillingly and often unexpectedly with inadequate resources; on the other hand, those with savings, multiple pension rights, and an unmortgaged house, who often retire early but purposefully and happily. Differences between successive generations in the balance between these two groups are likely to be substantial, depending on their historic experience (see Barfield and Morgan 1978a, 1978b).

Models of the labor force, social security, and so on, need better behavioral data to reduce the range of possible variation in parameters. Since people's retirement rights and savings are accumulated slowly over lifetimes, repeated measurements can provide not only updated forecasts but also information about changes in the behavior of different groups. The models, simulation or analytical, can then spell out the implications for such things as job opportunities for younger workers or welfare burdens among the aged.

Suggestions have been made that for some near-poor elderly, the right to convert their home into a combination of housing and a lifetime cash annuity by bequeathing it at death would ease their burdens. But conventional wisdom and one survey indicate emotional resistance to giving up the home, even at the death of the surviving spouse. We do not know if this stems from the desire for financial security against inflation and rent increases, or a belief that the children will want the house, or what. Additional research could clear up these uncertainties. For example, an inflation-adjusted annuity (based on the fact that the value of the house will rise with prices) might allay fears of inflation, and hence be more popular. In the same study one could ask people whose aged parents have homes how they would feel if their parents bequeathed their home to a government corporation in return for a lifetime inflation-adjusted annuity to help out with their living expenses.

In other areas consumer economists are convinced that people with low incomes could get more from their money. Are the insights into the economics of efficient resource allocation and efficient consumption too difficult to understand, or are poor people so beset with other problems that they cannot pay attention to managing their own economic affairs? Perhaps the efficient plans of consumer economists are designed and appropriate only for people with stable incomes and job security?

The economic status of some families depends on when retirement occurs, and in an increasing number of households two people now work and must decide when to retire. If wives tend to be several years younger-than their husbands, with life expectancies six or more years longer, with somewhat shorter work experiences and more potential promotions, who will retire when? If the result is that both work longer, a model to spell out the implications for jobs for new entrants and other marginal workers is called for. Substantial changes have been made in laws relating to private pensions and retirement age and consequently also in pension plans themselves. The Longitudinal Retirement History Survey indicates that few of the recently retired have any capacity or desire to return to work, but we need to know a great deal more about the present and expected mix of pension coverage, retirement equities, and rules.

This summary of important areas in need of research has clearly not covered everything. In particular I have ignored the evaluative studies of the impact of programs, which are going on and will continue, particularly with the aid of the proposed Survey of Income and Program Participation. There should, of course, be more research on why some programs like food stamps are underutilized, and studies are in order describing the wide variety of treatments afforded to poor people in roughly equal circumstances, sometimes even in the same state.

One cautionary note. It is not a particularly useful or salutary exercise to study popular opinions about complex policies that are not understood or whose implications are not understood. Studies of people's behavior, the explanations they give for that behavior, and inferences about the reasons from their attitudes and information and related facts are useful, but we should not base public policy in complex areas on the basis of public polls.

No attempt has been made here to summarize or evaluate the analysis of the two available bodies of panel data (Ohio and Michigan), but in view of my comments that our analytic capabilities have outrun the data base, it may be worth repeating that in the case of these two bodies of data, there is still much analysis to be done.

Methods

While this discussion may seem both biased and self-serving, it presents an underrepresented view about the allocation of research funds. In sum, there is a wide variety of questions important to public policy in the poverty area, that may well be answered more rapidly, efficiently, and at less cost by collecting new data rather than by the most sophisticated manipulating of existing data. Only when a variety of data and methods produces congruent results should we have confidence in them. There has been a great lack of imagination in answering the question whether experiments in or out of the laboratory, panels, or interviews could allow us to understand and predict people's behavior better. Current emphasis on sampling error and selection bias ignores the fact that the results are far more dependent on the details of the design and analysis than on sample size.

As an example of design problems, consider the set of interrelated decisions, which we mentioned earlier, made by young people when deciding about leaving school, getting a job, choosing a spouse, deciding when to start a family, finding the spouse's job, and choosing where to live. Even the new Ohio State–Labor Department panels will deal only with some of these decisions, and then largely by inferring interrelations from timing, sequences, and correlations, not from asking people about what affected what. The temporal order in which decisions are made does not reveal how they affect one another. An action taken later may have been decided on earlier. In the meantime, while waiting for the results of those panels to become manifest, we could learn a great deal by asking retrospective questions of a broader range of respondents. These are salient events, likely to be recalled, and the distortions can be dealt with.

A Program of Research

If it is true that a variety of methods and approaches, even replication of studies is necessary to provide dependable estimates of behavioral relations, and that an interaction between such research and analytic model building, fitting, and running is necessary to improve both behavioral research and policy analysis through modeling and simulation, more is needed than a lot of independent research, however fine. Yet we do not want to dictate research designs. A series of possibilities can be considered:

Those researchers who find some questions difficult to answer with existing data should be encouraged to give some thought to whether those problems might lend themselves to new research through surveys, experiments, or panel studies.

Those engaged in modeling, simulation, and forecasting should be encouraged to do sensitivity studies and to indicate which of the response parameters in a model are most crucial to its predictions and least reliable in its source estimates.

There should be a massive increase in research involving new data about human behavior and responses, using a variety of methods, but tied to analysis and modeling by focusing on the most crucial behaviors and the most likely changes in factors affecting those behaviors. Specialization is necessary and efficient, but each piece should justify itself at least in part by its relationship to a whole program of research.

Priorities

How can one decide on priorities? Some areas promise relatively rapid and certainly usable results, but they are largely those dealing with frequent decisions involving nutrition or transportation. Crucial areas such as decisions about marriage, living arrangements, and jobs are more difficult to study, but ultimately more important. And the most basic and most difficult of all to study is the level of initiative, striving, and the range of alternatives considered, particularly as they are affected by the level of security and stability in the environment. Perhaps we should start on all fronts at once, realizing that some are longer-term projects than others.

Evaluation

Finally, there needs to be a much more formal mechanism for evaluating not research proposals but the output of specific research projects. Ideally there should be replication—different teams tackling the same problem and each of them formally comparing their results with the others. If that is not feasible, there should be two or more funded evaluators for any research project too large to be replicated, with an iterative procedure by which the researchers can respond to criticisms in midstream if they wish. The current refereeing of journal articles and reviewing of books is a totally inadequate process unsuitable for large-scale or interdisciplinary research, because it is based on voluntary evaluators from a single discipline. Congress has mandated systematic evaluations of federal projects and programs, so it seems imperative that we also evaluate the research that is to be the basis of future designs for those programs.

References

Atkinson, J., ed. (1958) *Motives in Fantasy Action and Society.* New York: Van Nostrand.

Atkinson, J., Raynor, J. O., et al. (1974) *Motivation and Achievement.* Washington, D.C.: V. H. Winston and Sons (also New York: Wiley).

Barfield, R., and Morgan, J. (1978a) Trends in satisfaction with retirement. *The Gerontologist* 18(1):13–23.

Barfield, R., and Morgan J. (1978b) Trends in planned early retirement. *The Gerontologist* 18(1).

Katona, G., Strumpel, B., and Zahn, E. (1971) *Aspirations and Affluence.* New York: McGraw Hill.

Morgan, J. N. (1961) Household decision-making. In Nelson Foote, ed., *Household Decision-Making.* New York: New York University Press.

Morgan, J. N. (1978a) Individual Behavior, Economic Analysis and Public Policy. The W. S. Woytinsky Lecture. Department of Economics and Institute of Public Policy Studies, University of Michigan, Ann Arbor.

Morgan, J. N. (1978b) Intra-family transfers revisited: the support of dependents inside the family. In Greg Duncan and James Morgan, eds., *Five Thousand American Families: Patterns of Economic Progress.* Vol. 6. Ann Arbor, Mich.: Institute for Social Research.

Morgan, J. N. (1979) Hours of work by family heads: constraints, marginal choices, and income goals. In G. Duncan and J. Morgan, eds., *Five Thousand American Families: Patterns of Economic Progress.* Vol. 7. Ann Arbor, Mich.: Institute for Social Research.

Simon, H. A. (1978) Rationality as process and as product of thought. The Richard T. Ely lecture. *American Economic Review* 60:1–16.

Guy Orcutt, Alice Nakamura, and Masao Nakamura

Poverty Research on Family Determination of Labor Income

Introduction

Economic research on poverty has led to the identification of different types of poverty. This development in turn has facilitated both the formulation of goals in continuing the war on poverty and the design of programs aimed at ameliorating the social consequences of specific types of poverty. Much still is left to be learned, however, about the determinants of relative family income levels. In particular, a better understanding of the determinants of wage rates and family labor supply would allow economists to make more reliable estimates of the costs and benefits of alternative programs intended to benefit the poor. Such an understanding also might provide some insight into the question of what can be done to reduce the number of families in need of public financial assistance.

In this paper we first survey the findings of some of the more recent cross-sectional studies of the labor supply of married men and married women based on nonexperimental data and attempt to identify questions of interest that these studies leave unanswered. Next we indicate the need for a policy-response, or what we refer to as a treatment-response, approach to use of nonexperimental data. Then we mention advantages of planned experimentation and focus our remarks on implications of the limited randomization actually used in the negative income tax experiments. We believe that the analyses done do not reflect an adequate awareness of the type of randomization used and as a result do not benefit from its use. We conclude with a few general comments about a severe lack of balance in poverty research in general and the need for a less inhibited view of research problems, methods, and data needs than

[Guy Orcutt is a member of the Institution for Social and Policy Studies and professor of economics at Yale University. Alice Nakamura and Masao Nakamura are associate professors in the Faculty of Business Administration and Commerce at the University of Alberta.]

seems to be provided by the theoretical framework adopted by the current generation of neoclassical, human capital theorists. The appendix deals more concretely with the implications of limited randomization for estimation and testing.

A Survey of Nonexperimental Findings

In our survey of nonexperimental findings, observed aspects of the labor supply include labor force participation, work status, hours of work, and earned income. The particular aspect, or aspects, of labor supply analyzed vary from study to study. The findings of the studies surveyed, however, can be placed in a common framework by considering all of these aspects of labor supply to be outcomes of comparisons between the wage rate that an individual must receive to be willing to work an additional hour and the wage rate that employers are willing to pay for that hour of work. As Heckman (1974, 1976) does, we refer to the first of these wage rates as the asking wage, and the second as the offered wage. Factors that increase an individual's offered wage or decrease an individual's asking wage are believed by the authors surveyed to increase both the probability of labor force participation and the probability of working. Factors that decrease the asking wage are also believed to unambiguously increase both the expected hours of work and earned income. The impact of an increase in the offered wage on hours of work and earned income remains a point of dispute. Thus, findings about the impacts of various variables on labor force participation, work status, hours of work, and earned income are presented and interpreted in the following discussion in terms of the implied impacts of the variables on the asking and offered wage rates.

FACTORS THOUGHT TO AFFECT THE OFFERED WAGE

The factors thought to affect the offered wage that have received the most research attention are education, previous job experience, and labor market conditions. In addition, considerable attention has been devoted to the possible effects of discrimination on the offered wage rates of specific groups such as blacks, women, young people, and the elderly.

Years of formal education are found to be significantly positively related to the offered wage rate of both married men and married women.[1] The main unanswered questions about the impact of education on the offered wage concern the causal significance of this finding. As

Bowen and Finegan (1969, p. 61) point out: "Educational attainment is presumably related . . . to intelligence, ambition, and physical and mental health. . . ." However, the extent of this interrelationship may differ for different groups of people. Bowen and Finegan (p. 57) argue, for instance, that inclusion in the lower educational categories is clearly a much less selective process for blacks than for whites.

One other aspect of the impact of education on the offered wage, which existing cross-sectional studies do not come to terms with, is the relative nature of educational attainment. Variations over time or space in the general level of educational attainment must surely affect the market's evaluation of the educational attainment of individuals. Thus existing cross-sectional studies do not provide direct estimates of the extent to which the offered wage rates of the poor could be raised through the provision of more education.

Vocational training is another type of education that has been found to be significantly positively related to the offered wage (Rosen 1976). The problems involved in using this finding to predict the impact of additional vocational training on the offered wage rates of the poor are similar to those mentioned in our discussion of formal education. Moreover, these problems are accentuated by the fact that the material covered in different vocational training programs is much more diverse than the material covered in different formal education programs. Ashenfelter (1978) has made limited headway in confronting these problems, using data on individuals aged 16–64 in four trainee and comparison groups broken down by race and sex. The data used in his study were obtained by matching program records for all classroom trainees who started training under the Manpower Development and Training Act in the first three months of 1964 with social security records on earnings. Ashenfelter's results also suggest that further progress in this area probably awaits the development of data sets for which trainees and comparison individuals, or controls, are matched with respect to more of the variables affecting earnings, which also covary with participation in a training program.

Previous job experience is another variable found to be significantly positively related to the offered wage rate (Heckman 1976, Rosen 1976). Again, this variable is heterogeneous and undoubtedly can be correlated with a variety of other characteristics, such as intelligence, ambition, and physical and mental health as well as with job seniority and union membership. Thus inferences are at best tenuous as to the impact of previous job experience on the offered wage rates of those reentering the labor force after periods of absence due, for example, to the loss of a previous job, child rearing, or illness. Nor can much be inferred about the possible impact of planned, publicly funded programs designed to give participants limited job experience. More attention needs to be devoted, perhaps, to taking some account of the different types of job experience that individuals accumulate.

In the literature, relatively little attention has been paid to the incorporation of variables describing local labor market conditions into studies of wage rates or labor supply. In a study such as Heckman's (1976), which includes no market variables, the demand for the labor of married women, in any given class of education and experience (and hence the offered wage) is implicitly assumed to be infinitely elastic. An additional drawback of failing to include labor market variables in studies of the offered wage rate is that, as Garfinkel (1973, p. 238) notes, the predicted values of the wage rate variable in many studies are "little more than an education variable scaled in wage units." Limited research attention has been devoted, however, to two labor market variables.

Sex-specific local job opportunities have been found to be significantly positively related to the offered wage rates of married men and married women, respectively. Also, there is weak evidence that the unemployment rate is negatively related to the offered wage rate.[2] However, it is clear that efforts to unravel the impacts of different aspects of labor market conditions on wage rates and the supply of labor are in their infancy.

FACTORS THOUGHT TO AFFECT THE ASKING WAGE

Turning now to the asking wage, we will first survey findings as to the impacts of child status and other income on the asking wage rates of married women. Next we will look at the available evidence concerning the effects of the earnings of married women and nonlabor income on the asking wage rates of their husbands. We will then examine recent evidence suggesting that the offered wage rate itself also affects the asking wage rate.

Child status variables are by far the most powerful variables in studies of the labor force behavior of married women. Several researchers have found a large and significantly positive relationship between the numbers of preschool children in families and the asking wage rates of the married women. School-age children have been found to exert a significantly positive, though smaller, impact on the asking wage rates of their mothers.

Because child status is such an important determinant of asking wage rates and hence of labor supply for married women, the choice of variables used to account for child status is particularly important. There are at least four different dimensions of the child status of married women that may be of importance in examining their labor force behavior: (1) the presence of children of different age groups, (2) the numbers of children in different age groups, (3) interactive effects resulting from the presence of children in two or more different age groups, and (4) the total number of children cared for. Yet most researchers have taken a parsimonious approach to the incorporation of child status information. For instance, Hall (1973) included separate dummy variables for the presence of children younger than 7 only, the presence of children 7–13 years of age only, and the presence of children in both age groups. His omitted category is no children younger than 14. Heckman (1974, 1976) included a linear variable for the number of children younger than 6. And Rosen (1976) included separate dummy variables for one child younger than 6, two children younger than 6, and three or more children younger than 6. Rosen's omitted category is no children younger than 6. While limiting the amount of information about child status incorporated into their studies, researchers have also tended to include in their data samples older married women who normally exhibit a wide range of different child status configurations. For instance, Hall's (1973) study included married women 20–59 years of age, while the studies of Heckman (1974, 1976) and Rosen (1976) examined the labor force behavior of married women 30–44 years of age.

Nakamura et al. (1978) show that controlling for child status as proposed by Hall (1973), Heckman (1974, 1976), or Rosen (1976) still leaves a strong residual correlation for working married women between number of children ever born and the estimated offered wage rate, leading to biases in the estimation of the response of hours worked to changes in the offered wage rate. On the other hand, the indiscriminate incorporation of large numbers of child status variables does not necessarily yield desirable results, either. For instance, Gramm (1975) incorporated 6, 12, 15, and a phenomenal 29 child status dummy variables into labor supply regressions based on 55, 90, 54, and 414 observations, respectively. Of the 62 estimated coefficients for these child status dummies, only 13 are significantly different from zero with even a 90-percent level of confidence. Moreover, none of the constant terms in these regressions are significant at a 90-percent level. This finding suggests that, since most of the child status dummies take the value of zero most of the time, many of them may be highly collinear with the constant term. In Gramm's regressions for one-child, two-child, and three-child families, it is also interesting to note that the coefficient for the wage of married women changes from 0.097 to 0.080 to 0.059, respectively. This finding suggests that even after the incorporation of seemingly massive amounts of child status information, the effects of child status on the labor supply have not been fully removed.

New insights into how to effectively control for the effects of child status in studies of the labor supply of married women would make it easier to obtain unbiased estimates of the coefficients of other variables of interest, such as the wage rate of married women. However, the extent to which these child status variables are accounting for the costs of child rearing, as opposed to tastes and preferences for home versus market activities, will remain unknown. Moreover, to the extent that costs are being accounted for, it is far from clear exactly what those costs are and to what extent they can be reduced through the public provision of day care services, for example.

Income from other sources, such as a married man's earnings or nonlabor income, has been shown to be significantly positively related to the asking wage rates of their wives.[3] Again, what is not known is the extent to which these observed effects reflect differences in tastes, preferences, and social mores as opposed to income effects as defined in economic theory.

There is less consensus among researchers as to the effects of income from other sources on the asking wage rates of married men. Ashenfelter and Heckman (1974) found, for instance, that the uncompensated cross-substitution effect of an increase in the wage rate of a married woman on the labor supply of her husband is essentially zero. Boskin. (1973, p. 172) also concludes that the "effect of the spouse's wage on the husband's labor supply appears negligible." On the other hand, Kniesner (1976) found that the gross effect of a change in the wage of a married man differs depending on whether his wife works, and moreover that the labor supply of a married man is positively related to the wage rate of his wife, for married men with working wives.

In the case of nonlabor income, some researchers, including Kniesner (1976, p. 661), have actually found this variable to be positively related to the labor supply of married men, and hence negatively related to their asking wage rates. Other researchers have found the opposite effect, with the reported estimates ranging widely. A number of possible reasons have been put forward for the diversity of findings. Several researchers argue, for instance, that it is due to difficulties with the way the nonlabor income variable is defined. For instance, Greenberg and Kosters (1973, p. 25) argue that "The measure of nonemployment income that is conceptually appropriate . . . is the income flow that could be sustained over a family head's expected working life from the conversion of the family's assets and nonemployment-income payments into such an annuity." They also argue that attention should be paid to the possible differential impacts on the labor supply of a married man of imputed nonlabor income flows resulting from such sources as the ownership of durable goods, real estate, liquid assets, and businesses or farms as well as to the negative nonlabor income flows associated with consumer debt. Hill (1973, pp. 197–198) suggests that, in imputing nonlabor income flows, the choice of the annuity rate is important. Garfinkel (1973) suggests that both the exclusion of those with incomes above some arbitrary figure and the inclusion of married men receiving public assistance, unemployment insurance, veterans' and workmen's compensation, or pensions results in negatively biased estimates of the effects of nonlabor income on the labor supply of husbands. Finally, Greenberg and Kosters (1973) contend that even if the nonlabor income variable could be perfectly defined, biased estimates of the impact of nonlabor income on the labor supply of married men would still be obtained because of the disturbing influence of tastes and preferences for asset accumulation. Their solution to this problem is to introduce a proxy variable for these tastes and preferences, which they found to be significantly positively related to the labor supply of married men.

It is clear, however, that more work is required to clarify our understanding of the impacts of various types of other income on the labor force behavior of married men. Moreover, there must surely be other unexplored characteristics of married men that have important impacts on their asking wage rates, and hence on their labor supply.

Finally, recent research suggests that the offered wage rate itself has a positive impact on the asking (or reservation) wage rate for both married women and married men. Two sorts of arguments have been advanced for the inclusion of this variable in the asking wage function. Heckman (1978, p. 205) asserts that "if consumers work in other periods, higher current wages are associated with . . . higher values of the reservation wage." The reason is that, if the wage in a given period is correlated with the wage in other periods, then increases in the wage rate will result in increases in permanent or lifetime income. Thus, if leisure is a normal good, there will be negative income effects that will act to reduce labor supply in the present period. Nakamura et al. (1978) argue that, even in a one-period model, there will be a positive impact on the asking wage rate of increases in the offered wage because, as hours of work are increased, the household budget constraint will be relaxed more rapidly the higher the offered wage rate.

Omission of the offered wage rate from the asking wage function is theoretically equivalent to assuming that an increase in the offered wage will have positive substitution effects, but no negative income effects, on labor supply. Thus the relationships between the offered wage and measures of labor supply, such as hours worked, must be positive. Yet Hall (1973, pp. 149–156) and other researchers have found a negative relationship between hours worked and the offered wage for married men. And recent research by Nakamura et al. (1978) and Nakamura and Nakamura (1978) indicates that this relationship is negative for working married women as well. An understanding of the relationship between labor supply and offered wage rates is, of course, essential for predicting the effects of proposed government programs that are expected to affect offered wage rates, or offered wage rates net of income taxes.

IDENTIFICATION OF ASKING WAGE AND OFFERED WAGE FUNCTIONS

If an individual's asking wage depends in part on his or her offered wage, then the asking wage function clearly will not be uniquely identified (see Nakamura et al. 1978, Nakamura and Nakamura 1978, and Heckman 1978). Nor will the offered wage function necessarily be identified if the wage offers that employers make to prospective employees are conditional on the wage offers that the employers think each prospective employee would be willing to accept. Identification of the offered wage function can be achieved, however, under at least two possible sets of conditions. The first set of conditions is that, for reasons of anti-discrimination legislation, union agreements, and so forth, employers refrain from obtaining certain information they would otherwise like to have concerning factors such as marital and child status, income category of a spouse, outstanding debts, and so forth, which are likely to be important determinants of the asking wage rates of potential employees. The second set of conditions is that, for reasons of cost efficiency, most employers are not interested in tailoring wage offers to take account of differences in the asking wage rates of individual prospective employees. Rather, positions are advertised at set wage rates, or at wage rates subject to mechanical variation as a function of, for example, years of experience or certification or degrees held. Applicants for these jobs would then be accepted or rejected on the basis of their qualifications for the job in question. This situation does not mean, of course, that in setting the wage rates for different types of positions employers need be thought of as ignoring the conditions prevailing in the labor markets from which they intend to recruit; it simply implies that many of the personal factors leading to differences among prospective employees in their asking wage rates are assumed not to enter into the determination of their offered wage rates.

Whether either of these two sets of conditions occurs in reality is a topic that deserves further investigation.

CHOICE OF THE FORM IN WHICH TO ESTIMATE THE LABOR SUPPLY FUNCTION

As Hall (1973, p. 151) points out, the overall or unconditional labor supply function can always be written as the product of a function for the probability of working times a conditional labor supply function defined for those who do work. We agree with Hall that for many purposes estimates of the overall labor supply function are required. This does not necessarily mean, however, that it is desirable to directly estimate the overall supply function. In fact, there are at least three reasons why we feel that the component parts of the overall labor supply function should be estimated separately, with estimates of the overall supply function being obtained as the product of these components.[4]

The first reason is simply a matter of objectives. Although estimates of the overall labor supply function are often what is required, estimates of the functions for the probability of working and for the labor supply of those who do work are also of interest for both policy and research. Clearly, while the overall labor supply function can be reconstructed given estimates of its component parts, the same cannot be said for the parts given the estimated overall function.

Secondly, as Hausman and Wise (1976, p. 430) note in the case of another measure of labor force activity that can be expressed as the product of two component parts, the variance of the error term for the overall labor supply function should be larger than the variances for the error terms for either the function for the probability of working or the function for the conditional labor supply. Thus both the accuracy of the resulting parameter estimates and the power of the tests of significance for these parameters should be improved by estimating the component parts of the overall labor supply function.

Finally, there may be differences in the labor supply responses of individuals to changes in variables, such as the wage rate, depending on whether each individual works, or depending more generally on the initial number of hours worked by each individual. Presumably, the response of the probability of working to an increase in the offered wage rate must be positive, because some of those who are not working can be induced to work, while it seems unlikely that anyone who is working will respond to a wage hike by ceasing to work. However, those who are working may reduce their hours of work, though not generally to zero, because of an income effect. Moreover, the magnitude of this income effect would be expected to be larger the larger the initial number of hours of work. If these response differences are not explicitly accounted for in the estimation of an overall labor supply function, the resulting parameter estimates will be difficult to interpret, owing to their dependence on the labor force supply behavior of the particular sample of individuals from which the estimates were derived. Nakamura et al. (1978) and Nakamura and Nakamura (1978) provide empirical evidence of the importance of this point in estimating labor supply relationships for married women, while similar empirical evidence for married men can be found in the results presented by Garfinkel (1973, pp. 215–217) and by Da Vanzo et al. (1976).

On the Need for a Treatment-Response Approach

A central focus of econometric research using nonexperimental data has been on accounting for and predicting the variation of one or more variables given current and lagged values of other variables. The "explained" or predicted variables are referred to as dependent or endogenous variables, and the variables used in explaining or predicting the dependent variables are referred to as predetermined variables. Yet the ultimate goal of this research is not variance reduction. Rather, it is usually the identification of the effects of recognizable and possible human actions. In addressing similar sorts of problems in areas of science for which controlled experimentation is possible, relatively little attention is focused on variance reduction. Rather, experiments are designed so as to facilitate observation of the impacts of well-defined treatments. This sort of treatment-response approach to research could also be applied more widely in analyzing nonexperimental data. The key elements of this approach are the identification of well-defined treatments, and the collection of data that allow observation of the impacts of these treatments. We will consider these elements one at a time.

ACTIONS OF INTEREST NEED TO BE SPECIFIED
SO AS TO BE RECOGNIZABLE IN PRACTICE

Models are expressed in terms of relationships between variables, but policy makers need to know about consequences of the actions they might take. Policy makers are likely to have an operational understanding of actions they might or might not take, but do they know how such actions may be specified in terms of statements about the values of parameters and input variables of relevant models? And, for that matter, do model builders have a clear idea of how policy actions of interest should be expressed in terms of input variables of the models they build for use by policy makers?

Experimentalists frequently use the value of a variable as a measure of the level of application of some treatment, but this use does not prevent them from recognizing that actions are almost always complex and multidimensional physical phenomena. The value of a single variable such as weight, voltage, income, or price, for instance, may indeed serve to measure the level of application of an action, but clearly does not fully describe it. Indeed, a given variable such as income or income change could serve as a measure of many different actions, or even of many combinations of many actions.

Since the experimentalist is likely to have an operationally satisfactory idea of when an action of interest is taken and when it is not, the relating of outcomes to an action as measured by a single variable poses difficulty that is manageable. The experimentalist knows, and users of the experimentalist's results are expected to know, that claimed relationships between outcomes and the value of a variable indicating the treatment level are meant to apply only to changes in the level of the indicator variable in response to a particular action or set of actions. Nothing is asserted about movements of the indicator variable in association with other actions, or in association with any of a variety of other naturally occurring developments.

But what can we say about the nonexperimentally oriented econometrician or statistician, or about the statistician who limits attention to relationships between variables and never clearly relates the movements of variables used as inputs to the occurrence or nonoccurrence of actions of interest? For example, it seems reasonable to believe that a person's disposable income might change because he or she is fired. But it also might change because that person decides to go back to school. It also might change because of a temporary layoff. Still another possibility is that it might change because the person takes on a job or a second job in order to finance the purchase of a house, the education of a child, or the payment of medical expenses. All of these actions or events might be associated with an income change. But will it be satisfactory to predict that all of these actions will have the same implications for expenditures, savings, etc. just as long as they are associated with the same change in disposable income? Clearly this is a matter for investigation and the potential users of asserted relationships need to be told the range of physically recognizable actions for which they are expected to hold.

Unfortunately, movements of macro time series variables can seldom be clearly identified with specific actions, since they reflect the aggregated impacts of enormous numbers of varied and timewise overlapping actions occurring at less aggregative levels. At the level of the individual, family, or firm, it is possible to determine unambiguously when actions of interest are taken, by whom they are taken, where they are taken, and so on. Thus it is possible to distinguish an income change due to a firing from one due to a wage rate change from one due to temporary overtime employment. All of these treatments of persons, with their possibly different implications for the relationship of, for example, expenditures to income, could be differentiated from each other and from actions taken by individuals to modify their own incomes.

Econometricians accustomed to working with macro time series have learned to use every possible observation in estimating any relation, because they often have so few effective degrees of freedom relative to the number of parameters to be estimated. They also look with justifiable concern on the selection of sample points to be used in estimation by the elimination of apparently nonconforming sample points. They thus tend to try to use all sample points involving a set of variables hypothesized to be related in some way or other. But what researcher tries to pool data, even before estimation and testing, from quite different experiments? The fact that the same or an overlapping set of variables happens to be involved is not sufficient. Clearly, in trying to learn from naturally occurring treatments of persons, families, or firms, it is just as essential to recognize when treatments of interest were taken and when they were not as when trying to learn from planned experiments. Of course it is worth differentiating changes in the sales of a firm due to consumer actions from ones due to a teamsters' strike or due to a planned withdrawal from or entry into a given market.

In planned experimentation an attempt is made to apply an action of interest on at least three or more widely separated levels of application. If implications of two or more actions are being explored, then an attempt is made to avoid or minimize covariation between assigned treatment levels. In an effort to avoid mistakenly attributing outcomes to treatments, experimentalists make use of observations on carefully selected control groups, which are intended to be similar to the treatment groups both in their basic nature and with respect to their environment. However, the control groups do not receive the treatments of interest or receive different levels of the treatments of interest. It is hoped, of course, that skillful matching of entities experiencing different levels of treatment will counterbalance the disturbing effects of variables that are not even measured or, if they are measured, that might have nonlinear and interactive effects that would make interpretation of typical regression results difficult and hazardous.

The experimentalist is thus extremely selective with respect to sample points. He or she selects, not on the basis of outcomes, but in such a way as to ease the problems of interpreting and learning from the observed outcomes of selected treatments. The researcher who wishes to learn from naturally occurring applications of treatments of interest has every reason to be equally selective of sample points. If we knew enough about a social system, all data points might be of some value. But when very little is known, great selectivity is required in order to focus on situations and comparisons simple enough to be learned from.

Garfinkel (1973) gives evidence that serves to illustrate the importance of sample selection, using data from the 1967 Survey of Economic Opportunity for married men aged 25–61. Garfinkel shows, for instance, how sensitive the coefficients of a nonemployment-income variable are to the inclusion or exclusion of special groups of married men like pensioners. In his basic sample of 4,035 married men, only 39 nonpensioners reported more than $3,500 of nonemployment income, while 16 pensioners reported nonemployment income in excess of this figure. Moreover, of these 16 pensioners, all but 5 worked fulltime. Yet when the pensioners are included in regressions explaining the sum of weeks worked and weeks spent looking for work in the previous year, the sign of the nonemployment income variable changes from insignificantly positive to significantly negative. Thus, even very large sample sizes are seen to offer only limited protection against coefficient instability resulting from the inclusion or exclusion of small numbers of individuals responding to circumstances that are markedly different from the circumstances affecting the majority of individuals in the sample.

The Negative Income Tax Experiments

ADVANTAGES OF PLANNED EXPERIMENTATION

Studies based on nonexperimental data leave unanswered many questions concerning the extent to which observed effects of various variables on offered wage rates and labor supply are actually attributable to related differences in unmeasured tastes and preferences, or other characteristics such as intelligence and physical and mental health. Nor is it obvious that demand effects are adequately accounted for through the introduction into labor supply relationships of an imputed wage variable. There may be demand effects on hours worked that are not reflected in the offered wage. Depending on the local occupational-industrial mix, for instance, there may be scarcities of jobs in certain categories of hours of work. Or the offered wage itself may depend on hours of work as suggested by Lewis (1969) and Rosen (1976), and this dependence may not be adequately accounted for in the imputed wage rate variable. Also, as mentioned above, little effort has been devoted to the incorporation of variables reflecting general labor market conditions into the offered wage relationships from which the imputed offered wage rates used in most labor supply studies are calculated. Moreover, the percentages of the variation in the dependent variable explained by the offered wage relationships appearing in the literature are generally very low. Finally, some of the proposed public programs for aiding the poor involve the imposition of circumstances that would not otherwise exist. As Hausman and Wise (1976) point out, for instance, under existing tax laws, no observations of families with low incomes would be observed with high marginal tax rates of, for example, 50–70 percent. Thus, application of the results of cross-sectional studies based on nonexperimental data to predictions of the impact of a program such as a negative income tax on the labor supply and earned incomes of poor families would require extrapolating far beyond the limits of observed variation for the tax variable. Nor is there any way of knowing whether the labor force responses of the poor to, for instance, a new type of lump-sum transfer payment would be similar to the observed responses of generally more affluent families to other types of nonlabor income.

As Hausman and Wise (1976, p.421) note: "The oft-touted power of controlled experiments derives from their theoretical ability to isolate the effects of specific actions, treatments, or more general policies." First, this is because, in theory at least, treatment levels can be assigned such that they are independent of other characteristics that might cause differences between subjects that could be mistakenly interpreted as treatment effects. Second, by administering different levels of treatments, including no treatment, to groups of subjects who are otherwise similar, treatment effects can be distinguished from the effects of environmental or other general factors affecting the response levels for all subjects. Thus the powers of controlled experimentation rest on the two principles of careful randomization and the proper utilization of controls.

Of course, experimental data can be gathered only with respect to the effects of variables that can be experimentally manipulated. Social mores clearly forbid the direct experimental variation of factors such as child status or formal education. Nor is it considered ethical to assign to individuals or families treatments that leave them less well off than they would have been if they had not participated in the experiment. In an attempt to separate the effects on the offered wage rate of experience from other factors such as job seniority, for instance, it would not be reasonable to sever randomly selected workers with various amounts of experience from their jobs in order to observe the wage offers they would receive when searching for new jobs.

However, randomly selected individuals can be offered the chance to obtain specified amounts of training, education, child care, lump-sum transfer payments, medical benefits, and so forth beyond what would be available to them in a nonexperimental setting. The net offered wage rate can also be experimentally controlled through changes in tax rates, although, again, the tax packages experimented with must leave participating individuals better off than they would be in the absence of experimentation. Otherwise it would be impossible to obtain the requisite informed consent of those selected to participate in an experiment.

For suitable variables, therefore, different levels of treatment can be allocated to different subjects in such a way as to avoid correlations with the uncontrolled variables suspected of having similar types of effects on the dependent variable, or variables, of interest. Control groups can also be used to account for the effects of other disturbing factors, such as demand conditions. These are the ideas that have motivated the various social experiments undertaken in recent years.[5]

TESTING FOR EXPERIMENTAL EFFECTS
UNDER CONDITIONS OF LIMITED RAMDOMIZATION

In an effort to increase the amount of information obtained per dollar spent, the percentages of families assigned to different tax programs in the various negative income tax experiments were conditioned on the preexperimental incomes of these families. Table 1 shows the percentage distributions for each preexperimental income level of families by the tax plan to which they were assigned in the New Jersey income tax experiment.

One would expect the preexperimental income levels of families to be correlated with their attitudes about work and their abilities to work. One would also expect to observe differences in the labor supply responses of the groups of families eligible for these various tax plans due not only to differences between the tax plans themselves but also to systematic differences in the characteristics of the families eligible for each plan.[6] This is, of course, an invitation to biased estimation of treatment effects.

If the observations for the New Jersey income tax experiment on preexperimental income were distributed over K discrete values, with K a small number, then an obvious solution to this problem would be to carry out separate analyses for the families in each of the K preexperimental income groups. Such a strategy would provide a clear basis for tests of significance for the presence of experimental responses.

Unfortunately, the observed values of preexperimental income for families in the New Jersey income tax experiment are spread more or

Table 1
Percentage Distributions of Preexperimental Income Level
of Families by Assigned Tax Plan

Assigned Tax Plan (Percentage of Poverty Line Guaranteed Tax Rate)	Distribution of Families Within Pre-Experimental Income Level by Plan			Percentage Distribution of Families by Plan
	Low	Medium	High	
50–30	2.8	10.8	4.6	6.6
50–50	16.6	12.8	1.9	9.8
75–30	20.0	4.9	21.1	14.4
75–50	2.8	23.3	17.6	16.3
75–70	10.3	22.9	0.0	11.6
100–50	12.6	13.5	7.7	11.2
100–70	6.3	9.0	16.5	11.0
125–50	28.6	2.8	30.6	19.1

Source: Calculated from Table 1A, p. 264 in Dickinson and Watts (1975).

less continuously over the entire range of this variable. Intervals for preexperimental family income could, of course, be used in place of discrete values. Nevertheless, there is an obvious conflict between selecting enough such intervals to minimize the approximation involved in grouping, while keeping the number of intervals small enough to maintain reasonable sample sizes.

An alternative approach for taking advantage of the randomization that was actually attained in the New Jersey income tax experiment is to carry out separate analyses for each combination of α and β, with the relevant aspects of the labor force behavior of families expressed as functions of their preexperimental income levels and perhaps other variables included to reduce residual variation. The resulting estimated relationships would not be of interest considered separately for each combination of values for α and β. Rather, interest lies in the differences between the predicted values of the dependent variable, or variables, for different combinations of values for α and β at given values of preexperimental income. These differences, conditional on the level of preexperimental income, represent the treatment effects resulting from the application of the various tax plans. In effect, what is being proposed is to estimate the values of the dependent variable, or variables, of interest that the families in each tax plan group would have had if all of them had had the same preexperimental income level.

Concluding Statement

We began this paper with a brief, highly selective survey of recent nonexperimental studies of the wage rates and labor force behavior of married men and married women. For expositional convenience we framed our survey in terms of factors thought to affect the offered and asking wage rates, since the studies surveyed examine different aspects of observable labor force behavior, such as participation, hours of work, wage rates, and earned income. The asking wage rate was taken to be synonymous with labor supply and the offered wage rate was taken to be synonymous with labor demand.

Despite the many questions left unanswered by the nonexperimental studies we have surveyed, certain conclusions emerge. There seems to be a widespread consensus that both married men and married women with more years of formal education, more vocational training, or more previous job experience generally have higher probabilities of working and earning higher wage rates, and that married women who have fewer children or who live in families with less income from other sources also have higher probabilities of working and tend to work more hours per year.

In retrospect, however, it seems possible that we may have considered the literature surveyed from an unfair vantage point. We conclude that the literature surveyed has less to offer the policy maker concerned with understanding the bearing of actual or potential government policies on relative wage rates, employment, and unemployment than we had hoped; we may be grossly unfair to many fine researchers in assuming that the body of research surveyed was intended, or even should have been intended, to markedly increase our understanding of the bearing of actual or potential policy on these matters. At this point, however, we can only beg forbearance and proceed to set forth a few concluding thoughts to which our survey, reflection, and writing have led us.

First, we admit to considerable uneasiness over what we take to be an overdeveloped penchant for dependent variables that for all practical purposes may be unmeasurable. In our opinion, the asking wage is certainly close to being unmeasurable and whether even the offered wage should be thought of as unmeasurable is debatable. "Measurement without theory" may be a crime, but theory that cannot be related to measurement may be worse, at least for policy guidance.

Next we express a fear that, while a concern for structure is frequently to be applauded, the body of the research surveyed exposes a misplaced concern for structure. To obtain a structural understanding of a system is to obtain an understanding of how separable entities of a system would behave if they were not in fact bound together in a system. Clearly, such an understanding would be useful in trying to predict the implications of introducing new entities, in modifying the behavioral responses of old entities, or in considering implications of other structural changes. But what are the different entities supposedly represented by equations given as determining the offered wage and the asking wage?

At first sight, we might suppose that the offered wage equation is to represent the behavior of firms, and the asking wage equation is to represent the behavior of persons or perhaps families. But if the offered wage equation is to represent the demand behavior of firms, how is it that for all practical purposes the only nonperson or nonfamily input variable, if any is introduced, is something like unemployment? Clearly, some serious identification problems remain to be considered in sorting out person and family behavior from the behavior of corporations, firms, unions, and so forth in the determination of employment and wage rate response to government policies. Unfortunately, data are not currently available to study these interrelationships. Existing data on the behavior of firms and unions, for instance, do not usually include detailed information on who is employed by or belongs to these firms and unions. On the other hand, the cross-sectional microdata bases on which most of the existing studies of the labor force behavior of married men and married women are based contain little detailed information on the firms and labor unions, for example, to which these people belong. Thus the only nonperson or nonfamily variables introduced into most microstudies of labor force behavior are variables such as unemployment rates, which are usually added to the information supplied by the primary data source by utilizing the information on place of residence given for individuals or families. The result is that little can be learned from these studies about how, for instance, government policies can influence the amount and kind of labor actually demanded.

There are, of course, vast bodies of economic literature that focus on the relationships between average wage rates, hours of work, and earnings on one hand, and the behavior of corporations, unions, and various levels of government on the other. Numerous studies have also attempted to measure the impacts of various types of discrimination and locational factors on access to the education and job experience that many researchers, in turn, see as leading to higher probabilities of working and higher wage offers. However, collection of linked family and firm data as well as a more direct incorporation into micro labor force studies of factors that lie beyond the direct control of individuals and their families would provide a richer basis for policy formulation and analysis.

Perhaps we have already focused enough attention on the attractiveness of planned experimentation as a tool for achieving deeper understanding about implications of government policy than could be obtained by sole reliance on learning from natural experiments. Clearly, we believe that analysis of data already obtained from experiments like the negative income tax experiments could be improved to take advantage of the limited randomization done, and we have offered some suggestions for doing so. Moreover, it should be recognized that while experimental data hold the promise of allowing researchers to cut through the iden-tification tangle, it is unfortunately true that existing experimental data from negative income tax experiments contain relatively little informa-tion relating to the demand side of the picture. Perhaps new experiments can be designed to fill this gap, and improvements could be made in the analysis of existing experimental data. In any case, there is a need for more policy-oriented research in the related fields of labor force behavior and poverty research, accompanied by the development of both ex-perimental and nonexperimental data sources and by use of a treatment-response approach to use of nonexperimental as well as experimental data.

We have emphasized the need for policy-oriented research and a wider use and development of a treatment-response approach to use of nonex-perimental data. In closing, however, we cannot resist the plea that the victim should not always be considered the criminal. Of course no one would charge that those concerned with poverty believe that the poor, in some sense, deserve what they get. But looking over the entire body of poverty-oriented research gives us, at least, the uncomfortable feeling that we are too ready to assume that the poor bring on their misery by their inadequacies and misguided behavior. No doubt they sometimes do, but how has it happened that almost all poverty research focuses on the conditions, needs, and behavior of the poor? Isn't it at least possible that some of the causes of poverty and part of the remedy for poverty have something to do with the way our entire system functions and with the role and behavior of corporations, unions, even of government itself?

Notes

1. See Bowen and Finegan (1969), Hall (1973), Ashenfelter and Heckman (1973), Heckman (1974, 1976), Rosen (1976), Nakamura et al (1978), and Nakamura and Nakamura (1978).
2. See Bowen and Finegan (1969), Fleisher and Rhodes (1976), Nakamura et al. (1978), and Nakamura and Nakamura (1978). Apparently conflicting results are reported, however, in Ashenfelter and Heckman (1974).
3. See Bowen and Finegan (1969), Heckman (1974, 1976), Rosen (1976), Nakamura et al. (1978), and Nakamura and Nakamura (1978).

4. See Hall (1973) for a discussion of a possible statistical problem inherent in this proposal, and Heckman (1974) for a suggested solution to this problem.
5. See, for instance, Orcutt and Orcutt (1968) for a more complete discussion of the possible advantages of social experiments.
6. See Hall (1975) for further discussion of this point.

References

Ashenfelter, O. (1978) Estimating the effect of training programs on earnings. *Review of Economics and Statistics* 60 (1):47–57.

Ashenfelter, O., and Heckman J. (1973) Estimating labor-supply functions. In G. Cain and H. Watts, eds., *Income Maintenance and Labor Supply*. Chicago: Markham.

Ashenfelter, O., and Heckman, J. (1974) The estimation of income and substitution effects in a model of family labor supply. *Econometrica* 42:73–85.

Boskin M.J. (1973) The economics of labor supply. In G. Cain and H. Watts, eds., *Income Maintenance and Labor Supply*. Chicago: Markham.

Bowen, W.G., and Finegan, T.A. (1969) *The Economics of Labor Force Participation*. Princeton, N.J.: Princeton University Press.

Da Vanzo, J., De Tray, D.N., and Greenberg, D.H. (1976) The sensitivity of male labor supply estimates to choice of assumptions. *Review of Economics and Statistics* 58 (3):313–325.

Dickinson, K., and Watts, H. (1975) The experimental panel data resources at the poverty institute data center. *American Economic Review* 65 (2):263–269.

Fleisher, B.M., and Rhodes, G. (1976) Unemployment and the labor force participation of married men and women: A simultaneous model. *Review of Economics and Statistics* 58 (4):398–406.

Garfinkel, I. (1973) On estimating the labor supply effects of a negative income tax. In G. Cain and H. Watts, eds., *Income Maintenance and Labor Supply*. Chicago: Markham.

Gramm, W.L. (1975) Household utility maximization and the working wife. *American Economic Review* 65:90–100.

Greenberg, D.H., and Kosters, M. (1973) Income guarantees and the working poor: the effect of income-maintenance programs on the hours of work of male family heads. In G. Cain and H. Watts, eds., *Income Maintenance and Labor Supply*. Chicago: Markham.

Hall, R. (1973) Wage, income and hours of work in the U.S. labor force. In G. Cain and H. Watts, eds., *Income Maintenance and Labor Supply*. Chicago: Markham.

Hall, R. (1975) Effects of the experimental negative income tax on labor supply. In J.A. Peckman and P.M. Timpane, eds., *Work Incentives and Income Guarantees: The New Jersey Negative Income Tax Experiment*. Washington, D.C.: Brookings Institution.

Hausman, J.A., and Wise, D.A. (1976) The evaluation of results from truncated samples: The New Jersey income maintenance experiment. *Annals of Economic and Social Measurement* 5:421–445.

Heckman, J. (1974) Shadow prices, market wages and labor supply. *Econometrica* 42:679–694.

Heckman, J. (1976) The common structure of statistical models of truncation, sample selection and limited dependent variables and a simple estimator for such models. *Annals of Economic and Social Measurement* 5:475–492.

Heckman, J. (1978) A partial survey of recent research on tte labor supply of women. *American Economic Review* 68 (2):200–207.

Hill, C.R. (1973) The determinants of labor supply for the working urban poor. In G. Cain and H. Watts, eds., *Income Maintenance and labor Supply*. Chicago: Markham.

Kniesner, T.J. (1976) An indirect test of complimentarity in a family labor supply model. *Econometrica* 44:651–669.

Lewis, H.G. (1969) Interes del Empleador en las Horas de Tabajo del Empleado. *Cuadernos de Economia* 18:38–54.

Nakamura, M., and Nakamura A. (1978) A Comparison of the Labor Force Behavior of the Married Women in Canada and the United States, with Special Attention to the Impact of Income Taxes. Unpublished working paper. University of Alberta, Edmonton, Canada.

Nakamura, M., Nakamura, A., and Cullen, D. (1978) Job Opportunities, The Offered Wage and the Labor Supply of Married Women. Unpublished working paper. University of Alberta, Edmonton, Canada.

Orcutt, G.H., and Orcutt, A.G. (1968) Incentive and disincentive experimentation for income maintenance policy purposes. *American Economic Review* 58:754–772

Rosen, H.S. Taxes in a labor supply model with joint wage-hours determination. *Econometrica* 44:485–507.

Appendix

IMPLICATIONS OF LIMITED RANDOMIZATION
FOR ESTIMATION AND TESTING

Notation

Let us suppose that our data derive from a negative income tax experiment on N entities with data for the i th entity distinguished by the subscript i. Income of the i th entity for the period of observation before assignment of treatments to experimental entities will be designated by

PY_i. Income of the i th entity for the t th period of observation after the assignment of treatments to experimental entities will be designated by Y_i. The corresponding income after tax after application of the negative income tax appropriate to entity i will be dentoed by DY_i. The negative income tax law applied to entities contains the two parameters,α_i and β_i, specific to the entity, and has the following form:

$$DY_i = \max [\alpha_i + (1 - \beta_i) Y_i, Y_i]\qquad \text{Equation 1.}$$

Randomization of Assignment of Treatment Levels of α and β to Entities

Only randomization in assignment of selected treatment combinations to entities within groups specified according to PY was actually used. The proportions of different treatment combinations of α and β levels assigned was made to be conditional on PY in an effort to maximize the value of the information obtained per dollar of expenditure on the experimentation.

The Model Considered

$$Y_i = e^{F(\alpha_i, \beta_i, PY_i)} + E_i\qquad \text{Equation 2a.}$$

$$\text{or } ln\ Y_i = F(\alpha_i, \beta_i, PY_i) + E_i\qquad \text{Equation 2b.}$$

where the function, F, might of course be different for different values of t. It is hoped that F is reasonably smooth and interest centers on how its value depends on the values of α_i and β_i. α_i and β_i will be known without error since they are assigned. PY could also be regarded as known without error since the variable intended here is whatever measure of preexperimental treatment income was actually taken into account in determining the number of entities to be assigned each combination of α and β.

The randomization process of assigning entities to treatment combinations should result in the following covariance expectations of zero.

$$E [(\alpha_i - \bar{\alpha}) . E_i \mid PY_i] = 0\qquad \text{Equation 3.}$$

$$E [(\beta_i - \bar{\beta} . E_i \} PY_i] = 0$$

Clearly unconditional covariances of α_i with E_i and of β_i with E_i cannot be expected to be zero by virtue of the randomization process actually used. This desirable property can only be expected for these covariances conditional on PY.

Estimation

If every PY_i had been located at for example, K discrete values, with K a small number, then an obvious form for the analysis to take, to capitalize on randomization actually used, would be a covariance form of analysis in which a separate relationship is estimated for each of K groups of entities with grouping of entities according to their value of PY. Thus we might have observations of $ln\ Y_i$, α_i, and β_i for each of K levels of PY_i as follows:

PY Group I			$\cdots$	PY Group K		
$ln\ Y_i$	α_i	β_i		$ln\ Y_i$	α_i	β_i
x	x	x		x	x	x
.	.	.		.	.	.
:	:	:		:	:	:
x	x	x		x	x	x

$$ln\ Y_i = F_{PY_I}\ (\alpha_i,\ \beta_i) \quad \cdots \quad ln\ Y_i = F_{PY_K}\ (\alpha_i,\ \beta_i)$$

The functions of α_i and β_i to be estimated for each group are indicated below the indicated data for each group.

Only the observations within each group would be used for estimating the treatment response function for each group. The advantage would be that within each group all observations would relate to entities with the same value of PY_i and thus the zero expected covariances of Equation 3 above would hold

The K functions for time period t could then be used jointly to estimate a treatment response surface that was in fact conditional on the level of PY_i. An undesirable aspect of the above analysis of covariance approach to estimation and testing is that the PY_i values are spread more or less continuously over the entire range of PY. Thus there is some tension between selecting K to be large so as to minimize the approximation involved in grouping and selecting K to be small so as to increase the sample sizes of the K groups. Also, how one should proceed from K distinct relations for K groups to a smooth treatment response function conditional on PY_i remains to be dealt with.

A slightly modified approach for taking advantage of the randomization that was done follows. It does of course trade upon the presumption that certain functional forms can be satisfactorily approximated with analytically specified forms or at least with essentially free forms, assuming only some degree of local continuity. The procedure is as follows.

For each combination of α and β estimate

$$ln\ Y_i\ =\ F_{\alpha,\beta}\ (PY_i)$$

Equation 4.

The functional form for each $F_{\alpha,\beta}\ (PY_i)$ could be a rather flexible analytic form such as

$$ln\ Y_i\ =\ k_o\ +\ k_1\ ln\ PY_i\ +\ k_2\ (ln\ PY_i)^2\ +\ k_3\ (ln\ PY_i)^3$$

Equation 5.

where the estimated ks could be ordinary single equation least square estimates. The estimated ks would, of course, be specific to the α, β group for which they were estimated.

Interest in the estimated functions does not, in fact, lie in their forms considered individually but rather in the way in which predicted $ln\ Y_{it}$ or Y_{it} differ between themselves at specified levels of PY. It is only these differences, conditioned as they are on PY, that are to be attributed to treatment level influence. Each of the estimated equations, of the type shown in Equation 5, could be used to yield a predicted value of $ln\ Y$ corresponding to each of K selected values of PY. Since each equation is estimated using entities all exposed to a common assignment of α and β, we would then have as many triplets, $ln\ Y$, α_i, β_j, for each of K selected levels of PY, as there were experimental treatment combinations. These could be arrayed in an analysis of covariance set up as on page 77, and a function

$$ln\ Y_i\ =\ F_{PY_l}\ (\alpha,\beta)$$

Equation 6.

could be estimated for each of the K groups.

In effect what has been done is to use the estimated equations of the type shown in Equation 5 to estimate the values the $ln\ Y_i$ of each group would have had if each entity i of the group had had the same value of PY_i. In addition this procedure might have some advantages in balancing out all additive and systematic components of errors in predicting $ln\ Y$ with equations of the type shown in Equation 5, since for given values of PY such errors should add the same error to each predicted $ln\ Y_i$. If so, they should just displace estimated functions of α and β by a constant.

Also, if predictor variables subject to error measurement were included, as might well have been the case with the model used in the previous section, then this averaging procedure *before* estimating the effects of α and β might be valuable as a method of dealing with bias due to random and unbiased measurement error in predictor variables.

Presentation of Results

For purposes of presenting results, it would be useful to present them for α_i^* and β instead of for α and β where α^* is defined as indicated in Figure 1. Doing this would help users sort out what they might think of as a tax rate effect from an income effect.

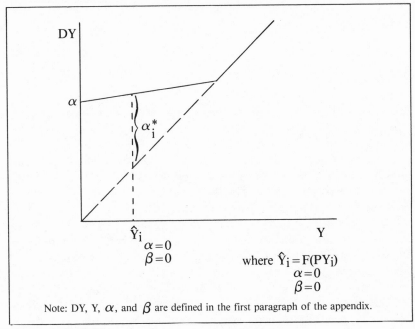

Figure 1. Definition of α_i^*

Ernst W. Stromsdorfer

Labor Market Behavior and Employment Strategies

Introduction

In a major operational sense, the basic domestic business of government, especially at the federal level, is income redistribution. Rules and regulations that define market behavior, such as those of the Occupational Safety and Health Administration, as well as the network of taxes and subsidies, while they may be intended to influence economic efficiency and the level of national output, most certainly always affect the size distribution and functional distribution of income.

Currently, with respect to the labor market, vast sums of the gross national product are transferred and taxed annually. Social security alone approached $85 billion in 1977. The 1975 recession resulted in unemployment insurance transfers of about $19 billion; it was the worst year of the recession. The Comprehensive Employment and Training Act (CETA) and related programs such as local public works hover in the $10-billion range as do federal, state, and local expenditures on Aid to Families with Dependent Children (AFDC) (Garfinkel and Skidmore 1978). And, depending on whose estimates one reads, the administration's Program for Better Jobs and Income would have cost in the neighborhood of $30 billion a year in 1978 prices had it been instituted, though this is not a net increase over the programs it would have replaced. Finally, total expenditures on major income transfers at the federal, state, and local levels amounted to more than $185 billion in fiscal 1977. Each of these programs affects the relative wage structure as well as the occupational and the industrial structures of employment, the rate of saving, the structurel and the level of national output, and the size distribution and functional distribution of income, to list a few major dimensions of the economy and the labor market. More specifically, each of these pro-

[Ernst W. Stromsdorfer is vice-president and director of employment studies at Abt Associates, Inc., Cambridge, Mass.]

grams affects labor force participation and hours worked both from the standpoint of the person taxed and from the standpoint of the person receiving the transfer. To complicate matters further, there are multiple taxation and transfer schemes whose interactive effects on behavior are unclear except in the most general conceptual sense via analysis of such things as "notches" and "cumulative marginal tax rates" (see Hausman 1971, 1975). Information on the ways in which tax and transfer programs affect the allocation of individual and family unit time among market work, home production, education, leisure, and other activities "can be obtained only by estimating labor supply functions." (Greenberg and Kosters 1973). However, as Cain and Watts discuss, determination of the impact of tax and transfer programs on labor supply behavior is not sufficient to predict the nature and quantity of the structural dimensions discussed above. One needs to relate the supply function, whose shape or position has been affected by a social policy, to a demand function, which also may have been affected by the policy (Cain and Watts 1973). In addition, there are behavioral interactions between demand and supply factors in the labor market such that the estimation of labor and supply functions (in response to, for example, a wage rate subsidy) can be seriously biased if labor demand considerations are ignored.

Plan of the Paper

This paper focuses mainly on two issues on the supply side. First, what has been the nature and quality of past work on labor supply and labor market behavior, much of which has been done at the Institute for Research on Poverty? I should make the point at the outset that the work of the institute reflects the general nature and relative scientific concentration of all work in this area. Thus, in general, gaps in institute analysis also reflect gaps in the relative treatment of the same issues in the literature on labor market supply and labor market behavior. Second, what is a desirable future course for such research on labor supply and labor market behavior? However, since the analysis of the demand for labor, especially low-skilled labor, has been relatively ignored, this issue is also discussed.

The plan of this paper has two parts: first is a discussion of the relative strengths and gaps in analyses of labor supply and labor market behavior done under the auspices of the institute. Next, the relative absence of labor demand analysis is criticized. A proposed program of research is then suggested to fill a few of the major gaps in this area.

For purposes of discussion, the accumulated studies and analyses of the institute have been broken into the following categories:

1. Supply Analysis:
   - Labor Market Behavior: Empirical Estimates,
   - Analysis of Effects of Tax and Transfer Policies on Labor Supply,
   - Income Maintenance Experimentation,
   - Analysis of Ongoing Social Programs, and
   - Methodology.
2. Demand Analysis.

The specific studies and analyses of the institute are listed in the appended bibliography.

This discussion will not deal with methodology except to note that the studies examined here in many cases represent the cutting edge of methodological development in the estimation of labor supply; the work of Greenberg and Kosters (1973), Ashenfelter and Heckman (1973), Hall (1973) and Dickinson (1975a, 1975b) are examples thereof. In particular, the recognition of differences in preferences and the influence of preferences on the estimated income effect are of note. Awareness of the bias created by using transfer payments that are directly related to employment behavior (e.g., unemployment insurance) as an explanatory variable in measuring labor supply is another improvement in technique, as is the separation of the decision to enter the labor market from the decision to supply a given number of hours of work. Finally, the concept of whole income, an innovation recommended by Gary Becker, has been incorporated into the more recent analyses of labor supply (Ghez and Becker 1975)[1].

Second, we should note again that this discussion will focus on the major gaps in the extant research and suggest the most policy relevant strategies to fill these gaps.

Labor Market Behavior: Empirical Estimates

About one-third of the studies on labor market behavior deals with the labor supply behavior of women. This emphasis is well placed, in view of the changing structure of female labor force participation and the heavy proportions of single-parent households on welfare that are headed by women.

However, a major problem in the past decade has been youth unemployment, especially the apparent structural nature of low labor force participation and high unemployment rates of black youth. In addition, the overwhelming majority of people on welfare are children;

since there remains considerable uncertainty as to the relationship between having been nurtured on welfare and future labor force behavior, this group of young people is also an important target group for analysis. While high quality labor market analysis of young people has been done under the auspices of the Institute for Research on Poverty, there has been a relative shortage of such work. A major review of the research on labor market behavior reveals the same general shortage of analysis on youth labor force participation and employment behavior across the discipline of economics as a whole (Keeley 1977). Most of the analysis of the Parnes National Longitudinal Survey, one of the best data sources on labor market behavior, has been rather descriptive in nature.

Only within the past few years has the application of such techniques as multinomial logit analysis been applied to tracing the "transition of youth from school to work" (compare Stephenson 1978). A major research emphasis has been placed on analysis of the youth unemployment problem by the National Bureau of Economic Research through the impetus of Feldstein, Freeman, and others. The major cross-sectional and longitudinal data sets that have information on the labor supply behavior of youth are being reanalyzed (by Freeman, Wise, and others at the National Bureau of Economic Research) in a consistent framework in order to attempt to clarify the facts concerning the behavior of youth in the labor force. Likewise, analysis on youth unemployment is now heavily under way in a variety of other settings, including the institute. The information to be discovered on this issue with existing data sets may soon be available in a more coherent and systematic fashion.

The same concentration of energy and talent that has been sharply focused on female labor market behavior for more than a decade deserves to be focused on youth labor market behavior. The necessary concentration is more than 10 years too late, for it was back in the early 1960s that the conundrum of "transition from school to work" was first set forth. The Vocational Education Act of 1963 was a response to that perceived problem; a response that apparently has been misplaced to a major degree, though understandably so given the vacuum in our knowledge of youth labor markets.

At the other end of the life cycle, analysis of the labor market behavior of the aged has also been given relatively short shrift (see, however, Garfinkel and Masters 1974a, 1974b). The major studies in this area can be counted on the fingers of one hand, and these studies have major shortcomings. For instance, the work of Boskin (1976)[2] was based on less than 200 observations from the Michigan Panel Study of Income Dynamics. Perhaps more so than with youth in view of the looming demographic shifts, analysis of the labor supply responses of older persons to social security benefits and other related transfer and tax schemes is critical for the maintenance of economic growth and intergenerational equity. Since changes in demographic characteristics of the population will begin to have their major impact in about 20 years, it is not too soon to begin concentrated and accelerated work in this area particularly if one looks back on the 10-year gestation of the negative income tax analysis. The Retirement History Survey of the Social Security Administration provides a start for a data base, but public use tapes for these data have been extremely slow to materialize. The Parnes National Longitudinal Survey data are the other major source of information and have not yet been fully exploited.

Analyses of Effects of Tax and Transfer Policies on Labor Supply

The Institute for Research on Poverty has led the conceptual discussion on the relative effects of negative income tax plans, wage subsidies, vouchers, and related schemes to increase the income of the poor with a minimal loss of efficiency, both administratively and in terms of reduced labor supply. A valuable contribution to the literature is Garfinkel's (1973) study, "A Skeptical Note on 'The Optimality' of Wage Subsidy Programs," which demonstrates that wage subsidies are not necessarily more efficient than a negative income tax. This conclusion is particularly significant from a theoretical standpoint, in view of the conflict between the two approaches that exist in the debate surrounding the administration's welfare reform strategies. Garfinkel's conclusion reduces the debate to an empirical level as to which strategy—a negative income tax, some combination of public service employment and earned income tax credits, or other form of employment subsidy—is least inflationary and has the largest net effect on improving the size distribution of income. The theoretical development that is now needed focuses on the net employment and inflationary impact of public service employment for the structurally unemployed, including youth and chronic welfare recipients. Haveman's theoretical work (1974) anticipates in an important way the work of Johnson (1977) and Tobin and Bailey (1977)—namely, that such programs may have serious implications for incentives to invest in human capital, for income redistribution from skilled to unskilled workers, and for possible short- and long-run declines in gross national product and increases in the price level, to list a few possibilities.[3]

Thus far the best analysis of ongoing public service employment is the work on the Dutch experience by Haveman (1977a, 1977b, 1977c), at the Institute for Research on Poverty, and the analysis of the Supported Work Experiment by Kemper and Moss (1977), working at Mathematica, Inc.[4] However, both of these studies largely ignore in an empirical sense the major macroeconomic implications of targeted public service employment. Nor do they consider well the issues of displacement and substitution, though both authors are well aware of the significance of these two major problems.

In this area of analysis, both the demand and the supply sides of the market must be considered. And there is now sufficient theoretical analysis to suggest the nature of the empirical work that must be performed. Indeed, in my judgment, this is the greatest priority of analysis at the current time, other than perhaps the effect of government programs on the private rate of saving, an issue highlighted by the work of Feldstein (1976), Munnell (1977), and others.

On the surface of things it appears that this set of micro- and macro-related problems would be well on its way to solution since the U.S. Department of Labor has recently funded 15 CETA prime sponsors with planning grants to develop demonstration models of targeted public service employment. However, 15 demonstrations may fail to resolve the major conceptual and empirical questions for several reasons.

Rather than being targeted on the most serious cases of the structurally unemployed, the CETA demonstrations are intended to focus mainly on two-parent welfare families and to focus on providing a job for the presumed male head, though other low-income and disadvantaged families can also avail themselves of the program.

About 31,000 jobs are intended to be "created," somewhat more than 2,000 jobs per site on the average. If the labor market is not saturated such that all the structurally unemployed who want jobs can get them, then the effects of the policy on wage and occupational structure in the local labor markets are not likely to be effectively tested.

The research design of the demonstrations is likely to be faulty on several counts.

1. Except in one site, there will not be a classical experimental design with random assignment among treatments or to treatment and non-treatment groups. Random assignment is no panacea, but it does allow one to draw cause-and-effect inferences. Even systematic variation of treatments among sites would be a help, rather than simply allowing the prime sponsors to follow their particularistic political inclinations. Such a technique will likely be used in one additional site.

2. The major focus appears to be on the "creation" of jobs and placement of people in them. There will be less focus on fiscal substitution

and labor market displacement, two major long-run social issues, although a separate major study of these issues is planned. Instead, the basic focus will likely be on the practical political problems of making the demonstration operational, an area of operation analysis that we already know is difficult to do, due to the involved politics at the local scene and the difficulties of estimating the demand for merit or public goods.

3. There may be an insufficient number of observations, by site, especially in light of the natural experimental setting, to allow unambiguous tests of the program's effects on the most relevant target groups, except perhaps for heads of single-parent families, mainly women. However, the number of observations planned overall appears to be sufficient.

4. The study will have a problem of bias in its statistical estimates due to missing variables. Analysis of the demand side in such an experiment is critical to its success. Detailed data will be needed on the structure of the demand for the labor of the target groups and their close substitutes, which are not now currently available and which are costly to acquire. Indeed, even the monthly unemployment rate for CETA sites, estimated by the so-called 70-step method, has been characterized as a random number by the late commissioner of the Bureau of Labor Statistics. Yet it is only one of a set of crucial variables needed for the analysis. In addition, time series data are needed on a sample of employers in the public and private sector concerning such elements as their sex-specific and wage-specific occupational structure, output, sales and profits, and their production functions. These demonstrations will have to commit considerable resources to such an analysis. It is not clear that collecting such detailed microdata on firm behavior is possible, since there is considerable political reticence in imposing such data collection costs on firms and government and private non-profit agencies.

In summary, while proper analysis of public service employment targeted to structurally unemployed persons is currently one of the most significant issues for social policy analysis, analysis of it will be successfully executed only if significant political and intellectual support for such analysis is generated beyond the few groups in the Congress and the Labor Department who currently have a direct interest in the program. At the time of this writing, it does appear that such support is forthcoming.

Income Maintenance Experimentation

The Institute for Research on Poverty and its staff, many of whom have migrated to other institutions to continue their work, have written the first as well as many of the continuing chapters in the book on the analysis of income maintenance programs. To the extent that there are inadequacies in this work, they are mainly due to inadequate funding of the required data bases and, therefore, insufficient observations. There has been a political penchant for overloading the experiments (especially the Rural Income Maintenance Experiment) with extra treatments, thus increasing the likelihood that sample sizes for certain subgroups will be too small for definitive analysis. Nevertheless, there is probably enough consistency of results between the New Jersey/Pennsylvania and the Seattle/Denver experiments to adequately inform public policy. The Gary experiment provides further corroboration of these general results (Burtless and Hausman 1978). The relative cost of these experiments was small. For a few million dollars of real social costs (net of transfers), information on the potential behavior of people who are clients of programs involving annual tax and transfer flows of several tens of billions of dollars has been gained. The basic dimensions of the real social cost of such a program are now generally defined. In addition, on a more scientific basis, the concept of a large-scale classical experimental design to test social programs has proven feasible. Thus, such methods can and should be generalized to the analysis of other social programs, such as the minimum wage, unemployment insurance, wage subsidies and vouchers, and public service employment, to name a few areas. These are programs for which insufficient analysis has been done at the institute, although it could be argued that other institutions and scholars were adequately carrying out this responsibility. Nevertheless, the next logical step for the Institute is to systematically devise experiments for these types of programs, under private auspices if governmental funding is not feasible.

Issues with Respect to the Analysis of the Demand for Labor

As noted in the introduction, the analysis of the effects of labor market policies on labor market behavior is seriously deficient if demand considerations are ignored. In short, such omission can create biases in the estimation of supply responses. Except for a few studies, the most notable of which is Cain's study (1976), "The Challenge of Segmented Labor Market Theories to Orthodox Theory: A Survey," the institute has focused relatively little of its efforts on the analysis of the demand for labor among different classes of labor at the level of the firm or enterprise.

Hamermesh (1976) has recently surveyed the most important studies of labor demand through 1974. His presentation and reanalysis of some of these data reveal that wage tax and wage subsidy programs can have a range of short-run economic effects on the demand for labor varying from "small" to "substantial." However, the evidence presented here is indirect, based on estimates of wage- and employment-output elasticities that are then related to changes in tax or subsidy rates. Fairly strong assumptions are also made about the "state of the labor market, the incidence of the policy, and changes in the supply of money." What is required is analysis that directly relates the impact of tax and subsidy policies on the demand for labor by firms at the firm or enterprise level. For instance, the work of Johnson (1978) and Bailey and Tobin (1978) makes strong predictions that low-skilled workers will displace high-skilled workers in the event that a public service employment program of significant size is initiated. This assertion has generated considerable heat in ensuing debates but little or no light. It should be possible to measure what actually happens if a well-targeted wage subsidy program (of whatever institutional variety) is instituted. Study of this kind should obviously be undertaken.

On the other hand, labor supply analyses of socially deserving groups should consider the role of job availability on labor supply. Tightness of the labor market will differ across sites and should be reflected in estimates of the elasticity of demand for different types of labor. The cross-substitution elasticities should also be influenced by firm behavior and more general demand conditions. Acquiring such knowledge could then provide policy makers with some indication of the overall likelihood of success of their policies and what the likely impacts will be on the functional and size distribution of labor incomes.

In short, analysis of how demand conditions at the firm or enterprise level interact with wage, tax, and subsidy programs is imperative at this time. Such analyses would provide the key to settling the issue of the extent and time dimension of labor market substitution.

A Suggested Research Agenda

It is poor strategy to suggest a laundry list of issues to be researched, though such is often the result after discussions such as the above. I think that there are a few very critical policy priorities that will continue to be significant three to five years from now. The above discussion has pinpointed a select set of high-priority research issues that are directly related to labor market analysis, labor supply and labor demand, and household behavior in general. The highest priority issue in the near term is that of analyzing the efficacy of public service employment in alleviating structural unemployment. Both demand and supply questions are involved in this issue. A second important issue is the analysis of labor supply behavior of youths and older persons. A third issue of importance is the institution of classical experimental analyses of major social programs such as the minimum wage and unemployment insurance.

But, the Institute for Research on Poverty and the federal government have long-run scientific goals that must also be pursued. These scientific objectives, however, must be forced to ultimately tie in with policy needs and objectives.

Basically, the institute and the federal government should organize and coherently systematize the knowledge on how individuals across income and social groups respond to different economic incentives and disincentives in different institutional settings over their life-cycles. These analyses should involve not only the poor but also lower income, working-class, and middle-income persons. These groups, after all, represent the overwhelming majority of people who are affected by tax and transfer programs such as that of the Social Security Administration, for instance. They are absolutely and relatively more important to study from a standpoint of economic policy. Surely, their behavior interacts with policies that are generated to help the poor. Analysis of this broad nature is both feasible and necessary.

Such analysis is feasible since the essential resources to collect the data exist at the national level. Indeed, there is considerable waste at present in collecting one-shot cross-sectional topical statistics instead of a coherent set of longitudinal data targeted on specific groups, policy issues, and social programs. The Survey on Income and Program Participation is an initial first step in the right direction. However, it does not go far enough. For instance, its sample sizes are likely to be too small to analyze certain groups and programs—again underfunding is the bane.

The sample frame should include persons from major sociodemographic groups. It should track the entry of young people into the labor market—how and when they enter and under what conditions. It should track the maintenance of attachment during years of prime working age with an emphasis on factors that cause a variation in attachment, such as disability. Finally, it should track exit from the labor market—how and when and under what conditions. For each of these cohorts there should be a detailed focus on the way people allocate their time among competing activities over the life-cycle. Also, the analysis should focus on major socioeconomic issues, such as the effect of income transfer programs on the savings and growth rate. Finally, the samples should key in on major social programs. The most unambiguous set of priorities is that of the relative funds spent on such programs. The obvious target programs are listed below (in rounded fiscal 1977 dollars):

Social Security	$85 billion
Unemployment Insurance	15 billion
Medicare	21 billion
Medicaid	17 billion
Aid to Families with Dependent Children	10 billion
Supplemental Security Income	6 billion
Workers' Compensation	7 billion
Comprehensive Employment and Training Act	12.7 billion

If funds are short, program inclusion should be cut off at some convenient number, like $10 billion. It is much better to establish how people behave with respect to a few highly significant programs than to gather a great deal of inconclusive data on many programs; yet the latter result has usually been the case in the past.

Such a data set and its analysis by research groups such as the Institute for Research on Poverty is necessary to avoid the ultimate political polarization of social classes in society. It may well be that the income and substitution elasticities with respect to labor supply may not vary much across social groups as these groups respond to various social policies. Social groups may respond similarly to different types and levels of incentives. For instance, unemployment insurance has been referred to as "welfare" for the blue-collar workers or working-class people. And, as we saw in the last recession and in recent court cases, the distinction between welfare and unemployment insurance is becoming blurred. Likewise, different social classes may be responding in similar fashion to the incentives built into the social security system both in terms of savings behavior and labor supply behavior. In short, a more consistent and more carefully organized body of knowledge on economic response to incentives and disincentives across social classes would both clarify important policy issues and dispel ignorance in this area. Depending on the outcomes, the analysis might even reduce (although it could also enhance) social tensions as society discovers that different social groups respond similarly (dissimilarly) to a given set of economic incentives.

Summary

This paper's judgments can be summed up succinctly.

1. The research on labor market behavior carried out by the Institute for Research on Poverty, has been of high quality and of considerable policy relevance, although there are gaps in research concentration, especially on the side of demand for labor on how labor demand interacts with labor supply.

2. The most important current policy issue involves the micro- and macro analysis of public service employment designed to reduce structural unemployment. The emphasis should shift from analyzing the politics and mechanics of implementing such programs to the long-run effects of such programs on basic economic dimensions.

3. The concept of the Survey of Income and Program Participation should be expanded. The sample sizes should be increased so that statements concerning economic and social behavior vis-a-vis the major social programs in the United States can be made with predetermined levels of statistical significance. Conscious choice as to which programs and social groups to be studied should be publicly debated. The analysis should cut across all the major social programs and include socio-economic groups at every level in society.

Notes

1. For a further discussion of many of these issues, see Borjas and Heckman (1979).
2. See also Fleisher et al. (1973).
3. See also Bailey and Solow (1978).
4. Both of these studies are included in slightly different form in Palmer (1978).
4. See also Ashenfelter and Ehrenberg (1975).

References

Ashenfelter, O. C., and Ehrenberg, R. G. (1975) The demand for labor in the public sector. In D. S. Hamermesh, ed., *Labor in the Public and Nonprofit Sectors.* Princeton, N. J.: Princeton University Press.

Ashenfelter O. C., and Heckman, J. J. (1973) Estimating labor-supply functions. In Glen G. Cain and Harold Watts, eds., *Income Maintenance and Labor Supply* New York: Academic Press.

Bailey, M.N., and Tobin, J. (1978) Inflation-unemployment consequences of job creation policies. In J.L. Palmer, ed., *Creating Jobs: Public Employment Programs and Wage Subsidies.* Washington, D.C.: Brookings Institution.

Boskin, M. J. (1976) Social Security and the Retirement Decision. Unpublished paper. Department of Economics, Stanford University.

Borjas, G., and Heckman, J. J. (1979) Labor supply estimates for public policy evaluation. *American Economics Association Proceedings.*

Burtless, G. and Hausman, J. (1978) The effect of taxes on labor supply: evaluating the Gary Negative Income Tax Experiment. *Journal of Political Economy* 86(6):1103–1130.

Cain, G. G. (1976) The challenge of segmented labor market theories to orthodox theory: a survey. *Journal of Economic Literature.* xiv(4):1215–1217.

Dickinson, J. (1975a) *Implicit and Explicit Preference Structures in Models of Labor Supply.* No. 311-75. Madison, Wis.: Institute for Research on Poverty.

Dickinson, J. (1975b) *Theoretical Labor Supply Models and Real World Complications.* No. 312-75. Madison, Wis.: Institute for Research on Poverty.

Feldstein, M. S. (1976) Social security and saving: the extended life cycle theory. *American Economic Review* 66(2):77–86.

Fleisher, B. M., Parsons, D. O., and Porter, R. D. (1973) Asset adjustments and labor supply of older workers. In G. G. Cain and H. W. Watts, eds., *Income Maintenance and Labor Supply.* New York: Academic Press.

Garfinkel, I. (1973) A skeptical note on the "optimality" of wage subsidy programs. *American Economic Review* 63(3):447–453.

Garfinkel, I., and Masters, S. (1974a) *The Effect of Income and Wage Rates on the Labor Supply of Prime Age Women.* No. 203-74. Madison, Wis.: Institute for Research on Poverty.

Garfinkel, I., and Masters, S. (1974b) *The Effect of Non-Employment Income and Wage Rates on the Labor Supply of Prime Age and Older Males.* No. 193-74. Madison, Wis.: Institute for Research on Poverty.

Garfinkel, I., and Skidmore, F. (1978) *Income Support Policy: Where We've Come From and Where We Should Be Going.* Discussion Paper 490-78. Madison, Wis.: Institute for Research on Poverty.

Ghez, G. R., and Becker, G. S. (1975) *The Allocation of Time and Goods Over the Life Cycle.* New York: Columbia University Press.

Greenberg, D. H., and Kosters, M. (1973) Income guarantees and the working poor: the effect of income-maintenance programs on hours of work of male family heads. In Glen G. Cain and Harold W. Watts, eds., *Income Maintenance and Labor Supply.* New York: Academic Press.

Hall, R. E. (1973) Wages, income, and hours of work in the U.S. labor force. In Glen G. Cain and Harold Watts, eds., *Income Maintenance and Labor Supply*. New York: Academic Press.

Hamermesh, D. S. (1976) Econometric studies of labor demand and their application to policy and analysis. *Journal of Human Resources* 11(4):507–525.

Hausman, L. J. (1971) Marginal tax rates on earnings in existing transfer programs for the poor. In Larry L. Orr et al., *Income Maintenance: Interdisciplinary Approaches to Research*. Chicago: Markham.

Hausman, L. J. (1975) Cumulative tax rates in alternative income maintenance systems. In Irene Lurie, ed., *Integrating Income Maintenance Programs*. New York: Academic Press.

Haveman, R. H. (1974) *Work-Conditioned Subsidies as an Income-Maintenance Strategy: Issues of Program Structure and Integration.* No. 112. Madison, Wis.: Institute for Research on Poverty.

Haveman, R. H. (1977a) *Determinants of Performance in Public Employment Projects—Evidence from the Dutch Employment Program.* No. 396–77. Madison, Wis.: Institute for Research on Poverty.

Haveman, R. H. (1977b) *Public Employment of Less Productive Workers—Lesson for the U.S. from the Dutch Experience.* No. 359–77. Madison, Wis.: Institute for Research on Poverty.

Haveman, R. H. (1977c) *Report Submitted to the Ministry of Social Affairs of the Netherlands.* No. SR-15. Madison, Wis.: Institute for Research on Poverty.

Johnson, G. (1978) Structural unemployment consequences of job creation policies. In J. L. Palmer, ed., *Creating Jobs: Public Employment Programs and Wage Subsidies*. Washington, D.C.: Brookings Institution.

Johnson, G., and Tomola, J. D. (1977) The fiscal substitution effect of alternative approaches to public service employment policy. *Journal of Human Resources* 12(1):3–26.

Keeley, M. C. (1977) *The Economics of Labor Supply: A Critical Review.* Menlo Park, Cal.: SRI International.

Kemper, P., and Moss, P. (1977) *The Efficiency of Targeted Job Creation: Conjectures Based on the Early Supported Work Experience.* No. 409–77. Madison, Wis.: Institute on Poverty.

Munnell, A. H. (1977) *The Future of Social Security.* Washington, D.C.: Brookings Institution.

Palmer, J., ed., (1978) *Creating Jobs: Public Employment Programs and Wage Subsidies.* Washington, D. C.: Brookings Institution.

Stephenson, S. (1978) Transition from School to Work of Male Youth. Prepared for the Assistant Secretary for Planning, Evaluation and Research, U. S. Department of Labor.

Tobin, J., and Bailey, M. N. (1977) Macro-economic effects of selective public employment and wage subsidies. *Brookings Papers on Economic Activity.* 2:511–544.

Appendix

PUBLICATIONS OF THE INSTITUTE FOR RESEARCH ON POVERTY: A BIB-
LIOGRAPHIC EXTRACT ON LABOR SUPPLY ANALYSIS AND RELATED BEHAVIOR
AND POLICY APPLICATIONS

Labor Market Behavior: Empirical Estimates

9 "Unemployment and the Labor-Force Participation of Secondary Workers"
Glen G. Cain, 1967

43 "Urban Poverty and Labor Force Participation," Joseph D. Mooney;
"Comment," Glen G. Cain, 1970

123 "Labor Force Reentry by Mothers of Young Children" James A. Sweet,
1974

149 "Work Behavior of Low-Income, Rural Nonfarm Wage Earners" D. Lee
Bawden, 1975

194 "Family and Work: The Social Life Cycle of Women" Karl E. Taeuber
and James A. Sweet, 1976

198 "Job Experience and Earnings Among Middle-Aged Men" Duane E.
Leigh, 1976

200 "Estimation of a Model of Labor Supply, Fertility, and Wages of Married
Women" Glen C. Cain and Martin D. Dooley, 1976

56-69 "Labor Force Participation in Rural Nonfarm Areas of North Carolina
in 1960" David R. Essig

59-69 "Industry Differences in Stability of the Rate of Negro Employment"
Seymour Spilerman

120-72 "The Employment of Wives and the Inequality of Family Income"
James A. Sweet

124-72 "The Employment of Rural Farm Wives" James A. Sweet

153-73 "An Appropriate Econometric Framework for Estimating a Labor
Supply Function from the SEO File" Dennis J. Aigner

192-74 "Simulating Labor Market Equilibrium" Donald A. Nichols

193-74 "The Effect of Non-Employment Income and Wage Rates on the
Labor Supply of Prime Age and Older Males" Irwin Garfinkel and
Stanley Masters

203-74 "Effect of Income and Wage Rates on the Labor Supply of Prime
Age Women" Irwin Garfinkel and Stanley Masters

220-74 "The Equilibrium Level of Unemployment: A Simulation: Donald A.
Nichols

226-74 "The Effect of Income and Wage Rates on the Labor Supply of
Younger Men and Women" Irwin Garfinkel and Stanley Masters

227-74 "The Effect of Income and Wage Rates on the Labor Supply of Older
Men and Women" Iwin Garfinkel and Stanley Masters

311-75 "Implicit and Explicit Preference Structures in Models of Labor
Supply" Jonathan Dickinson

312-75 "Theoretical Labor Supply Models and Real World Complications"
Jonathan Dickinson

Analyses of Effects of Tax and Transfer Policies on Labor Supply

202–74 "Income Maintenance and Welfare Reform: Papers and Comments" Robert J. Lampman, James Tobin, Alice M. Rivlin, and Alvin L. Schorr

233–74 "Tax Effects on Job Search, Training, and Work Effort" Jonathan R. Kesselman

256–75 "Efficiency and Equity Effects of Income Transfer Policy: A Simulation Analysis" Frederick Golladay and Robert Haveman with Kevin Hollenbeck

279–75 "Tax Credits for Employment Rather than Investment" Ernst R. Berndt, Jonathan R. Kesselman, and Samuel H. Williamson

382–76 "A Reappraisal of Negative Income Tax and Employment Subsidy Approaches to Reforming Welfare" Robert Lerman

386–77 "The General Equilibrium Impact of Alternative Antipoverty Strategies: Income Maintenance, Training, and Job Creation" John H. Bishop

SR–12 *Employment Subsidy Proposals Compared with the Negative Tax Approach to Reforming Welfare* Robert I. Lerman

SR–16a *The Administration of a Wage Rate Subsidy* John Bishop

Income Maintenance Experimentation

127 "The Labor-Supply Response of Husbands" Harold W. Watts et al., 1975

128 "The Labor-Supply Response of Married Women, Husband Present" Glen G. Cain, Walter Nicholson, Charles D. Mallar, and Judith Wooldridge, 1975

129 "The Labor-Supply Response of the Family" Robinson Hollister, 1975

130 "The Effects of Welfare Programs on Experimental Responses" Irwin Garfinkel, 1975

163 "An Overview of the Labor Supply Results" Albert Rees and Harold W. Watts, 1975

65–70 "The New Jersey-Pennsylvania Experiment: A Field Study in Negative Taxation" David Elesh, Jack Ladinsky, Myron J. Lefcowitz, and Seymour Spilerman

69–70 "Adjusted and Extended Preliminary Results from the Urban Graduate Work Incentive Experiment" Harold W. Watts

98–71 "Mid-Experiment Report on Basic Labor-Supply Response" Harold W. Watts

106–71 "After 15 Months: Preliminary Results from the Urban Negative Income Tax Experiment" David Elesh, Jack Ladinsky, Myron J. Lefcowitz, and Arnold Shore

147–72 "Labor Force Participation Among Male Heads cf Households in the New Jersey-Pennsylvania Negative Income Tax Experiment: Preliminary Results" David Elesh and Kevin McCarthy

196–74 "Basic Labor Supply Response Findings from the Urban Experiment (New Jersey-Pennsylvania)" Harold W. Watts and Glen G. Cain

SR-10 *The Rural Income Maintenance Experiment: HEW Summary Report*
Summary Report: The New Jersey Graduate Work Incentive Experi-
ment Conducted by the Institute for Research on Poverty, University of
Wisconsin, Madison, Wis., and by Mathematica, Inc., Princeton, N.J.,
for the Office of Economic Opportunity. December, 1973

Larry L. Orr, Robinson G. Hollister, and Myron J. Lefcowitz, editors, with
the assistance of Karen Hester: INCOME MAINTENANCE: INTER-
DISCIPLINARY APPROACHES TO RESEARCH, Chicago:
Markham Publishing Co., 1971
Glen G. Cain and Harold W. Watts, editors: INCOME
MAINTENANCE AND LABOR SUPPLY: ECONOMETRIC
STUDIES, New York: Academic Press, 1973

Harold W. Watts and Albert Rees, editors: THE NEW JERSEY INCOME-
MAINTENANCE EXPERIMENT, Volume 2: LABOR-SUPPLY
RESPONSES, New York: Academic Press, 1977

Analysis of On-Going Social Programs

Public Service Employment

SR-15 *Report Submitted to the Ministry of Social Affairs of the Netherlands*
Robert H. Haveman

395-77 "Public Employment of Less Productive Workers—Lessons for the
U.S.
from the Dutch Experience" Robert H. Haveman

396-77 "Determinants of Performance in Public Employment Projects—Evidence from the Dutch Employment Program" Robert H. Haveman

409-77 "The Efficiency of Targeted Job Creation: Conjectures Based on the
Early Supported Work Experience" Peter Kemper and Philip Moss

Unemployment Insurance

56 "Partial Benefit Schedules in Unemployment Insurance: Their Effect on
Work Incentive" Raymond Munts, 1970

378-76 "How Much Does Unemployment Insurance Increase the Unemployment Rate and Reduce Work, Earnings, and Efficiency?" Irwin Garfinkel and Robert Plotnick

400-77 "Unemployment Insurance Payments as a Search Subsidy: A Theoretical Analysis" Kenneth Burdett

Methodology

161 "The Challenge of Dual and Radical Theories of the Labor Market
to Orthodox Theory" Glen G. Cain, 1975

210 "The Challenge of Segmented Labor Market Theories to Orthodox Theory" Glen G. Cain, 1976
411–77 "The Ashenfelter-Heckman Model and Parallel Preference Structures"
Jonathan Dickinson

Bibliographies

"Hard-core Unemployment: a Selected, Annotated Bibliography"
(revised edition, 28 pages) Colin Cameron and Anila Bhatt Menon,
1969
SOURCE: Poverty Institute Publications by Subject Category, Institute for
Research on Poverty, University of Wisconsin, Madison, Wisconsin,
February 1978
NOTE: Arabic numbers are for reprints, e.g., 1, 124, etc. Hyphenated Arabic
numbers are for Discussion Papers, e.g., 98-71, 196-74, etc. Numbers
with the alphabetic prefix "SR" are for *Special Reports,* e.g., SR-15.
Books and large monographs are uncoded. There is duplication of titles
among reprints, discussion papers, and the general published books.

James M. McPartland and Robert L. Crain

Racial Discrimination, Segregation, and Processes of Social Mobility

An understanding of exactly how racial discrimination and segregation impede the progress of minority groups is necessary if successful practical reforms are to be developed. With few exceptions, however, theories and research on discrimination and segregation in the processes of social mobility have been general rather than specific, indirect rather than direct, and static rather than developmental. Much more attention has been given to estimating the total effect of discrimination or segregation on racial differences in attainment than to developing and testing theories of specific direct and indirect exclusionary processes that create special difficulties for minorities.

There are many ways that research could proceed to stimulate more specific theories of how discrimination and segregation may continue to damage the occupational opportunities of minority groups. Rather than attempt to cover all the possibilities, this paper concentrates on discrimination and segregation, particularly against blacks, in this country and provides selected examples of particular topics for study; it argues that future research on specific exclusionary processes should be given high priority. These examples are organized according to a general distinction between overt and systemic exclusionary processes.

In simplest terms, members of minority groups may be excluded from desirable opportunities and attainments in two general ways. Overt exclusionary processes occur at the point of selection among available applicants for jobs, educational opportunities, housing, capital, or other resources and opportunities. Overt discrimination includes the actions of selection officials who withhold jobs, student status, or other resources from qualified minority applicants. Overt discrimination appears on the demand side of labor market processes, when racial considera-

[James M. McPartland is codirector of the Center for Social Organization of Schools, Johns Hopkins University. Robert L. Crain is principal research scientist in the Center for Social Organization of Schools, Johns Hopkins University, and senior social scientist, the Rand Corporation.]

tions work against the recruitment and selection of minorities for desirable positions.

Systemic exclusionary processes are those that inhibit qualified members of minority groups from appearing in the first place as applicants for desirable openings and opportunities. These processes channel them in less promising directions, exclude them from important avenues of access used by other groups, and create burdens that foreclose their consideration of potential opportunities. These processes are likely to be imbedded in the organization of the major institutions of society, to be related to segregation, and to operate developmentally across stages of the life cycles of minority citizens. Systemic exclusionary processes show up on the supply side of labor market processes, when people fail to appear as qualified candidates for desirable positions due to their experiences in society as members of a racial or ethnic minority.

A Characterization of Past Research Emphases

Most past research on the effects of discrimination has not distinguished between different types of exclusionary processes. In fact, most studies estimating the extent to which discriminatory factors create major gaps in the attainments of blacks and whites have not used any direct measures of discrimination at all; discrimination has usually been indirectly measured as the residual gap between the occupational success of blacks and whites after individual differences in job credentials or competencies and labor market locations have been statistically controlled for. For example, the "discrimination" gap in income or employment has been estimated after one or more of the following variables have been taken into account: years of school completed, academic achievement test scores, on-the-job training, labor market experience, rates of unemployment, region or locality of residence and recency of migration to the region, and industrial composition and unionization in the area as well as age and sex. Studies in this tradition include Siegel (1965), Duncan (1969), Guthrie (1970), O'Neill (1970), Ashenfelter (1972), Griliches and Mason (1972), Jencks et al. (1972), Weiss and Williamson (1972), Wholsetter and Coleman (1972), Welch (1973), Porter (1974), Masters (1975), and Wright (1978).

Operationally, the observed difference between the average income of blacks and whites is compared with the expected black-white difference if one group's productivity resources are replaced by the average resources of the other group. Expected income is estimated by substituting the mean values of one group's resource variables in the functional equations for the other group that relate these resource variables to variations in income or occupational status.

Different researchers have used different combinations of the group resource means and functional equations to estimate the expected income to be used in determining the discrimination gap. Some substitute white resources into black equations; some substitute black resources into white equations; and others use combinations of both estimates and the observed black-white income differences. For example, Masters (1975) defines labor market discrimination as the difference between the observed average income of blacks and the expected income estimated by substituting average black resources in the functional equation for whites; and he defines the gap due to productivity disadvantages as the difference between the observed average income of blacks and the expected income estimated by substituting average white resources in the functional equation for blacks; and he uses both of these estimates to define the interaction between discriminatory and productivity factors. In most cases of this kind of research, a significant residual black-white income gap has been found, although it appears less in the North than in the South, less for young highly educated workers than for others, and less for women than for men. Studies showing a recent convergence of black and white processes of social mobility for particular classes of workers include Slotzenberg and D'Amico (1972). Featherman and Hauser (1976), Hogan and Featherman (1977), Smith (1978), and Smith and Welch (1978).

Even though these investigations have been conducted at a high level of technical sophistication and with increasingly thorough data, the problems inherent in this kind of research are the same as for any studies that identify causal factors residually. First, there is always the chance that important variables have been omitted that could account for the residual gap without resorting to a theory of discrimination. Second, the importance of discrimination and segregation will be underestimated to the extent that they contribute to racial differences in productivity resources through unspecified developmental processes. For example, the discrimination gap in income would be underestimated in an analysis that statistically controls for the entire racial differences in educational attainment or residential location if these differences should more correctly be seen as partially due to earlier discriminatory processes and segregation. Third, there is a question whether estimates of expected income based on substituting one group's average resources into functional equations for the other group make good sense: that is, whether the function relationships would be the same at a very different level of resources and whether different correlations among predictor variables in the separate groups give prediction equations that can be used inter-changeably. Fourth, nothing has been learned about the specific character and mechanisms of discrimination, because discrimination is not directly conceptualized or measured; thus remedial actions cannot be clearly identified.

Clearer ideas are needed about the specific definitions, forms, and processes that discrimination can take, with direct assessments of their impact on different age, race, and sex groups. Perhaps these ideas can be drawn from economic definitions of discrimination based on the notion of a taste for discrimination and its costs (Becker 1957, Flanagan 1973, Marshall 1974). But we believe that it will be more fruitful (1) to directly study selection and promotion processes that work against minorities, in order to learn about overt discrimination and how it might be minimized in practice, and (2) to investigate the specific developmental processes that channel minorities to poorer opportunities because of the organiza-tion or segregation of major institutions, in order to learn about systemic exclusionary processes and how they may be counteracted.

The case can best be made by presenting examples of specific processes that seem to reduce the chances of minorities', particularly blacks', get-ting ahead, not only because of their social class origins but also because of their race. The examples are drawn more from sociological than economic frameworks, and are currently in early stages of investigation. They are offered not in an attempt to provide a complete list of specific exclusionary processes that now need careful study but to make the general point that future research should shift from indirect estimates of the effects of discrimination to studies of particular forms of dis-crimination and specific developmental models of how minorities may be excluded from important opportunities.

Overt Discrimination in Selection Processes

Whether qualified minorities are excluded by overt discrimination from good schools and good jobs boils down to a question of the fairness of the recruitment processes and selection criteria in use. In many cases, the subtleties of recruitment and selection decisions make it difficult for an applicant or an outsider to know whether a selection process is fair and objective. Three kinds of research might reveal how selection processes may work against the interests of minorities: detailed audits of employer selection processes, experiments with alternative selection criteria, and studies of the relationship between segregation in employment or higher education and the proportion of minority members in a locality.

AUDITS OF EMPLOYER RECRUITMENT AND SELECTION PROCESSES

Most of the research on job placement processes has been from the perspective of the job seeker rather than the employer (Becker 1977). Yet the racial composition of work forces at each occupational level varies widely among places of employment (Becker 1978). Only one study has attempted to explain these variations in terms of recruitment and selection processes. This study is more than 10 years old and based its findings on cross-sectional comparisons of interview data from firms' personnel managers (Rossi et al. 1968, 1974). As demonstrated by the recent study of housing discrimination from the Department of Housing and Urban Development (1978), careful study of actual behaviors and records over time is needed to learn about the important ways in which black and white applicants may be treated differently. It will not be easy or inexpensive to audit the detailed selection processes of firms that have had different rates of employment of minority workers, but better data on present practices are essential to learn why some employers have racially mixed work groups and others do not. Detailed studies are also needed of practices of promotion or seniority and policies for layoffs or discharges, which are decisions that can discriminate against minority workers after they have been hired (Feagin and Feagin 1978).

EXPERIMENTS WITH ALTERNATIVE SELECTION PROCESSES

Research on variations in current employment practices may reveal that differences in the hiring of minorities and others are best explained by the attitudes and predispositions of employment officers or other subtle factors that are difficult to monitor or reform in everyday practice. To evaluate potential new practices, it may be necessary to devise experiments with new structural alternatives for employment recruitment and selection processes.

Ideas for selection experiments may be developed by considering the probability of error using specific admissions criteria. In any selection procedure, there are two kinds of possible errors: selection of candidates who fail to perform up to standards, and rejection of applicants who would have successfully filled a position. An employer desires to avoid the first mistake but ordinarily will have little concern about the second. As a consequence, selection criteria that produce overqualified employees are often quite acceptable, since there is little risk of obtaining a worker who cannot adequately do the job, even though many potentially successful candidates will lose out because they fall below others on measures of overqualifications. To be sure, there are many other worker difficulties, besides the inability to perform a job, that an employer wants to avoid, for example, absenteeism, turnover, and disciplinary problems; such difficulties may be perceived by employers as strong incentives to select applicants who score highest on generalized measures of achievement.

Much attention has been paid to the relevance of selection tests for the actual requirements of a job (Educational Testing Service 1976). Firms have been required by the courts to use only tests that select candidates on job-relevant indicators *(Griggs vs. Duke Power* 1971). While serious research to develop better tests of applicants for particular work is certainly in order, the problem remains that most conceivable efficient screening devices will be poor predictors of actual job performance. No amount of test wizardry will allow an employer to judge applicants as well as observing actual performance on the job over a reasonable amount of time.

The task then becomes to find selection alternatives that give all applicants who could actually do the work an equal chance to fill a position, while allowing an employer to make and revise choices on evidence as close as possible to on-the-job performance without unfair risk of legal or political troubles. The ideal procedure might involve using initial screening devices to establish sensible thresholds of adequate job potential (perhaps with some variation in the probability of selection depending upon a candidate's initial screening scores); providing individual opportunities to demonstrate on-the-job performance by a random or probability lottery of the remaining candidates; and permitting employers to reject unsuccessful candidates at the end of the provisional training and performance period. The degree to which experiments of alternative selection procedures may be successful rather than visionary probably depends on their capacity in execution to reduce added employer risks and to legitimate effective provisional procedures.[1]

To address problems of discrimination that appear at the point of employee selection, more may be needed than efforts to improve tests or to reduce individual prejudice. In particular, improvements in the organizational structure of selection procedures may reduce the errors of unfairly rejecting applicants who could prove their qualifications by actual job performance. Good ideas as well as adequate incentives and guarantees would be needed to get employers to participate in experiments with selection alternatives, but such experiments may produce politically acceptable, practical methods of fair competition that will open new opportunities to minorities. Without question, the current differences between racial groups in the distribution of job competencies will remain a major source of unequal attainments in employment. The goal of selection experiments is to find better ways to bring observed inequities of occupational attainment closer to the actual individual differences in potential to perform a job adequately.

STUDIES OF SEGREGATION IN EMPLOYMENT AND HIGHER EDUCATION

Until recently, tabulations of national and regional trends in racial segregation have been available only for public elementary and secondary schools and residential location. However, data from the federal government on racial and ethnic distribution in most places of work and from all colleges and universities have been used recently to calculate comparable segregation indices in these institutions by level and location (Becker 1978, Michael 1978, Thomas et al. 1978). Besides showing that overall segregation is lower nationwide in employment firms than in institutions for higher education, and both are lower than segregation in public elementary and secondary schools and residences (McPartland 1978), some interesting relationships have been found across levels and localities that may have implications for research and policies on selection processes and desegregation.

Recent comparisons of racial differences among localities and among levels of higher education or employment have shown a relationship between minority access and segregation. Racial segregation is greatest across places of work or across institutions of higher education when the proportion of blacks in the labor market or enrollment population is high, or conversely, black representation in work forces or in higher education enrollment is highest where there is the largest proportion of segregated firms or schools (Becker 1978, Thomas et al. 1978). The index of segregation used in these studies measures the actual distribution of racial groups across units of employment or higher education standardized for the expected distribution if the available blacks and whites were randomly distributed (Becker et al. 1978). This result suggests the danger in measuring progress on desegregation at a given level or location without giving attention to equity of access to employment and education, or in assessing improvements in the access of minorities without considering desegregation, because progress on one goal may be obtained at the expense of the other.

Policy makers concerned with higher education at the federal level and in some states are attempting to devise regulations and practices to positively influence both minority enrollment access and desegregation

(Haynes 1978), and these resulting experiences should be instructive for other settings in which standards of selection and admissions are involved. Moreover, the recent descriptive findings of aggregate relationships between minority representation and racial segregation in employment and higher education now need to be probed to investigate the underlying processes at work. To what extent are the causes to be found in structural factors, such as differences in selection standards; demographic factors, such as the racial composition of immediate recruitment areas; or social-psychological factors, such as white reluctance to be in a substantially black setting, black preference for programs with an ethnic identification, or community evaluations of minority and white institutions? In other words, basic research is called for to increase our understanding of which selection and sorting processes are operating to produce aggregate conditions of either relatively low minority access and low minority segregation or relatively high minority access and high minority segregation.

Developmental Exclusionary Processes

Besides research on selection and allocation processes used by employment and education officials, studies are needed of the processes that occur well before this point to eliminate minorities as applicants or candidates for promising positions.

Three examples are outlined of developmental exclusionary processes that affect minority chances for adult success. First, we shall discuss the processes of occupational socialization that result in large differences in the broad types of occupations chosen by blacks and whites and in the types of careers and labor markets entered by these groups. Second, we shall discuss the processes of job search used by blacks and whites, especially in the availability of informal networks of job information and employment contacts. Third, we shall discuss attitudinal processes concerning employment opportunities that may produce racial differences in individual planning strategies or in the sequence and patterns of major life events regarding education, family formation, and employment.

These examples were chosen for three reasons: (1) there is evidence that there are major black-white differences in these processes; (2) there is evidence that these processes are important for achieving adult occupational or educational success; and (3) an argument can be made that these processes are linked to past and continuing racial discrimination or to segregation in schools and residences.

1. PROCESSES OF OCCUPATIONAL SOCIALIZATION

The problem of large racial gaps in income may begin at the point at which blacks develop expectations of the broad types of occupational careers they will enter: blacks are much more likely than whites to develop expectations for and to eventually enter those types of occupations that will return the smallest payoff for additional years of education. There are three parts to this argument. First, differences exist in the major fields of study in school and in the resulting types of occupational careers that blacks and whites follow. Second, there are multiple labor market processes and multiple social mobility processes that correspond to broad occupational types, and these processes differ in the importance and value for economic success that they give to education. Third, because of past and continuing discrimination and segregation, blacks tend to be channelled by occupational socialization processes into those specific occupations with the least potential for closing racial income gaps. There is growing evidence from recent research on the first two points, but little research on the factors that create different occupational socialization processes.

Black-White Differences in Occupational Type

Although there has been much research on racial differences in occupational level (in terms of prestige and income), black-white differences in occupational type have been examined only recently. Classifications of occupational types, developed by psychologists, group jobs according to the kinds of activities involved and the kinds of competencies that are required and rewarded. For example, some occupations emphasize work with data, others emphasize work with people, and others emphasize work with physical objects. Occupational type (or occupational "situs" as it has been termed in some studies) is a separate dimension of the occupational stratification system that is different from income or prestige, because many of the broad classes of occupational types include jobs that provide the complete range of income and prestige levels. In a sense, occupational type is a horizontal dimension, whereas income and prestige are the vertical dimensions of the occupational stratification system.

The different ways used to classify occupational types have a great deal in common, but the most theoretically based and thoroughly researched typology has been developed by John Holland (1973) and defines six broad classes of occupations, with multiple categories within each broad class. This classification scheme has been used in most studies of black-white differences in occupational type. These studies show that black workers are much more concentrated than whites in "social" occupations, such as education and social service jobs: for the most highly educated workers in 1970, 47 percent of black men were in "social" occupations, compared with 19 percent of white men of similar age and education. And black workers are greatly underrepresented in "enterprising" occupations, such as business management or sales, and in "investigative" occupations, such as scientific work: for highly educated workers in 1970, 12 percent of black men compared with 39 percent of white men were in enterprising occupations, and 12 percent of black men compared with 21 percent of white men were in investigative occupations (Gottfredson 1977, 1978a).

A recent study by the Congressional Budget Office (1977) also showed significant racial differences among major occupational groups defined by the U.S. Bureau of the Census and among subcategories of the major occupational categories. For example, among male professional and technical workers of similar age who had graduated from college, blacks were strongly underrepresented as engineers (6–7 percent of blacks compared with 16–21 percent of all workers in this category) and strongly overrepresented in teaching jobs (nearly 50 percent of blacks compared with 20–30 percent of all workers). Also, blacks were somewhat underrepresented as accountants and physicians and somewhat overrepresented as social and recreational workers. Among male managers and administrators of similar age and education, blacks were strongly underrepresented as salaried managers in manufacturing and commercial industry and overrepresented in school and public administration.

Among male sales workers with similar schooling and years in the labor force, blacks were seriously underrepresented as sales representatives in manufacturing and wholesale trade (12 percent in manufacturing and 29 percent in wholesale trade for blacks compared with 36 and 39 percent for all workers in this category) and overrepresented as retail sales clerks and insurance agents, brokers, and underwriters. The largest racial differences among male service workers of similar education were the overrepresentation of blacks as cleaning service workers and the underrepresentation of blacks as firemen and policemen. The racial differences in occupational subcategories among women were generally smaller than for men. The main differences were a somewhat higher percentage of black women as teachers and a slightly lower percentage of black women as nurses among professional and technical workers, and a much higher percentage of black women as household workers among service workers.

Studies of the black-white differences in the major fields of college study and in the occupational aspirations of elementary and secondary students show the same tendencies. Tabulations of 1974 enrollment statistics for four-year undergraduates (Thomas 1978) show as much as 38 percent of black males majoring in education, social sciences, or social work compared with 24 percent of white males, and only 16 percent of black males majoring in natural or technical sciences compared with 25 percent of white males. The differences between the races were smaller for females but showed the same patterns. The differences in major field distributions are more dramatic at the graduate levels, even though blacks have not gained the same overall enrollment access at this level relative to whites as they have in undergraduate programs (Thomas 1978; Institute for the Study of Educational Policy 1976). Of male graduate majors in education, social science, or social work 44 percent were black and 27 percent were white; of female graduate majors in the same fields, 58 percent were black and 44 percent were white. Of graduate majors in natural and technical sciences or professions, 11 percent were black males, 29 percent were white males, 6 percent were black females and 13 percent were white females.

A recent study of elementary and secondary school student aspirations for different occupational types indicates that racial differences occur well before enrollment in college. Specifically, the 1976 National Assessment of Career and Occupational Development study showed that black and white students have similar occupational expectations and values at elementary school age, but diverge toward the end of high school to match traditional race and sex stereotypes and continue to diverge after initial employment (Gottfredson 1978b).

Although research findings show definite black-white differences in occupational types, continued study is needed to address some differences of opinion on recent trends. Some optimistic observers of recent trends of blacks toward natural sciences, medicine, and other fields traditionally dominated by white males believe that racial differences in occupational type are rapidly disappearing (Freeman 1973), but these studies may largely overlook some of the major continuing occupational differences between blacks and whites, for example, in sales and management.

Occupational Type and Processes of Social Mobility

The second step in presenting the argument that occupational socialization is an important exclusionary process that inhibits minorities is to show that black-white differences in occupational type are linked to different labor market and social mobility processes.

The most prominent sociological research on social mobility has adopted a model to explain occupational success in this country. This model, first developed by Blau and Duncan (1967) and elaborated by others, links an individual's social class to his or her educational attainment and subsequent job prestige and income. It has been assumed that this model operates for all occupational types and can be used to analyze the processes of occupational attainment for both blacks and whites. In contrast to this view of a uniform process of social mobility are multiple-labor-market theories of occupational attainment. These theories maintain that several processes of social mobility are in operation, and these theories differ in their assessment of the importance of social class and educational attainment for occupational success. There is growing evidence that separate mobility or labor market processes operate for broad classes of occupational types, and that these processes match the major differences in black and white distributions in occupational aspirations or destinations.

The analysis that has received the most attention uses the notion of a dual labor market to distinguish the sector of lower level, unstable jobs from the sector of career ladder jobs available in the economy. According to this view, blacks and other minority workers are more often channeled into the lower level sector of jobs, which neither offers high pay and sustained employment nor leads to dependable career lines (see, for example, Marshall 1974, Piore 1977, Wilson 1978, Wright 1978). Dual labor market analysts are mostly concerned with the difficulties of minorities at the lowest level of education and job opportunities, but other theories of multiple labor markets describe the possible segmentation of employment opportunities across a wider variation in education and job preparation.

Recent studies of multiple labor markets using the Holland classification of major occupational types have found major differences in the payoff from additional years of education for different occupations. The three broad types of occupations that show the largest differences in racial distribution also appear to involve different labor market processes of occupational attainment (Gottfredson 1977). An additional year of education is associated with an additional income of $200 to $300 per year in social occupations; $400 to $600 in investigative occupations; and about $1,000 in enterprising occupations. Moreover, the mixture of occupational prestige and income associated with additional years of education varies significantly according to occupational type. Studies of the returns from additional years of education show that social occupations yield relatively large payoffs in occupational prestige but small returns in added income; enterprising occupations provide much higher income payoffs but lower prestige returns; and investigative occupations offer high returns in both income and prestige. Thus, the result of racial differences in occupational aspirations and destinations is that blacks are greatly overrepresented in occupational types with the smallest returns from additional years of education in terms of income, and they are greatly underrepresented in occupational types with the largest returns in income. Other research has also shown racial differences in social mobility processes that result in higher job prestige at the expense of lower income for blacks (Coleman et al. 1972).

Focusing specifically on the significant proportion of all current jobs that constitute entrepreneurial occupations, the disadvantages that both poorly educated and well-educated blacks suffer by their underrepresentation in managerial and administrative jobs become clear. Entrepreneurial occupations require a smaller investment in education than other fields of work: the percentage of high-level managers and administrators without advanced education is much greater than for high-level technical and social workers. And incomes are much higher on the average for all levels of education in entrepreneurial occupations than in social service and education occupations for the same amount of education (Gottfredson 1978b).

The Congressional Budget Office study (1977) of income disparities between black and white Americans also demonstrates the importance of occupational classifications in accounting for racial income gaps after differences in years of education are taken into account. This study did not use an occupational classification developed to specifically reflect kinds of activities and competencies required and rewarded, but instead used the familiar Census Bureau major categories of occupations and subgroups within these categories. Finding major black-white differences across occupational categories and subcategories net of region, sex, and educational level, the study concluded: "Before the large part of the overall (racial) income disparities is removed, the occupational distributions, and particularly the distributions within the subcategories of the major occupational groups, must be equalized." (See also Kluegel 1978).

Although strong evidence shows that blacks are underrepresented in those types of work that either require modest levels of education for high income, or that have the highest payoff in income for each additional year of education, more research is needed on the topics of multiple labor markets and social mobility processes. Economists and sociologists have resisted the study of multiple-labor-market theories linked to psychological classifications of occupational types, perhaps because of a preference for theories that confront classical (Marxist) notions of stratification and economic development. Multiple-labor-market theories tied to occupational types derived from psychology offer rich theoretical explanations for racial diffences in attainment, and need to be developed and tested by more researchers and disciplines.

*Segregation, Discrimination and the Process
of Occupational Socialization*

After establishing that major black-white differences in occupational type have consequences for social mobility and occupational success, we must then understand how and why these racial differences develop in occupational expectations and destinations. However, there is currently little research on the occupational socialization processes of blacks and whites and the role of discrimination and segregation in these processes.

It seems reasonable that past or continuing job discrimination and segregation contribute to the narrow range of occupational types that characterize black expectations and destinations (Spilerman 1977), because present racial differences correspond to the historical stereotypes and locations of black workers before segregation and discrimination were declared unconstitutional. Historically, most black professionals and high-level social service workers worked in the segregated black schools and institutions or worked in government jobs where racial exclusion was somewhat less intense. Blacks continue to be overrepresented in education and social service occupations and in government employment, perhaps because they avoid other fields in which they expect discrimination or because segregation of schools and neighborhoods continues to present black students with professional role models who have been restricted to the traditional occupational types.

Research is needed to directly examine the effects of segregation and anticipated discrimination on the occupational aspirations of blacks and whites from different social classes. This research would include studies of the type of occupational expectations of youngsters in segregated schools and neighborhoods; studies of the effects of special minority educational orientation and recruitment experiments to address students' anticipation of exclusion in fields in which blacks have been traditionally underrepresented, such as engineering and business; and studies of the underlying values and attitudes of blacks and whites about working in certain fields and relating to members of the other race in supervisory or subordinate positions.

In the end, major black-white differences in income will remain even after existing disadvantages in social class and educational attainment are removed unless there is a change in the occupational socialization processes that differentially channel blacks into those traditional occupational types whose labor markets return less income for each level of education. Further research is needed to explain why separate social mobility processes exist for broad occupational types, and what processes result in the unequal distribution of blacks and whites across occupational types.

2. NETWORKS OF OPPORTUNITY: INFORMATION, CONTACTS,
AND PROXIMITY IN THE JOB SEARCH PROCESS

There is a growing recognition of the need for research on how the lack of useful social networks for obtaining good jobs may contribute to racial income gaps. Again the argument has three parts: major race and sex differences exist in the way that people hear about, are recruited to, and obtain good jobs; informal mechanisms of job finding tend to produce the most successful employment opportunities for minorities; and segregation and discrimination exclude minorities from the best channels of information, recruitment, and job contacts. We do not currently have adequate studies on any of these elements, but there is some evidence to suggest that further research on these topics would reveal an important minority exclusionary process.

Racial Differences in Job Search Methods and Their Importance for Occupational Success

Labor economists have been interested for some time in job search methods and have developed theoretical models of factors to predict strategies of rational job seekers (Lippman and McCall 1976). However, these models have not been tested extensively with data. The major empirical sources of descriptive information on job search behaviors are the January 1973 supplement to the Current Population Survey (CPS), covering about two-thirds of the 16 million persons who spent time looking for jobs and who actually found work in 1972 (U.S. Department of Labor 1975), and the Department of Labor's National Longitudinal Survey (NLS), covering a nine-year period since 1966 for a sample of 5,225 young men. These surveys used a series of questions about job search methods that include direct application to an employer, formal methods, such as using employment services or newspaper ads, and informal methods, such as asking friends or relatives.

Although the CPS and NLS surveys disagree on the relative importance of the informal methods over other approaches for finding work, both surveys indicate that minority workers use information or referrals by friends and relatives somewhat more often than whites to obtain work. The CPS tabulations report that 31.6 percent of minority workers compared with 25.7 percent of whites used informal methods to get their current jobs (U.S. Department of Labor 1975), and the NLS found that 52 percent of black employed males 14–24 years old used friends or relatives to find their current jobs, compared with 47 percent of comparable whites (U.S. Department of Labor 1970).

More important than general racial contrasts in job search methods is whether racial differences in obtaining the better paying and more satisfying careers derive from the networks available to each group for informal job information and contacts. Granovetter's (1974) thorough study of a small sample of professional, technical, and managerial workers indicates that the informal, interpersonal sources of information about job vacancies often produce better quality employment. The CPS tabulations suggest that blacks and other minorities depend more than whites on information or sponsorship from friends or relatives to obtain higher level jobs in both white-collar and blue-collar occupations. On the other hand, whites find jobs more often than blacks at these levels by applying directly to the employer. The racial differences in the proportion who used informal means to obtain jobs were greater for higher level, white-collar jobs (31 percent of blacks compared with 19 percent of whites at the professional and technical level) than for lower level, white-collar jobs (26 percent of blacks compared with 22 percent of whites at the clerical level). Similarly, among blue-collar occupations, racial differences in the percentage who used informal networks to obtain employment were higher for higher-level positions (42 percent of blacks compared with 27 percent of whites at the craftsmen level) than for lower level positions (26 percent of blacks compared with 29 percent of whites at the operative level and 35 percent of blacks compared with 36 percent of whites among laborers). Among all service workers except those in private households, blacks also relied somewhat more than whites on informal networks to obtain work—35 percent compared with 28 percent (retabulations from U.S. Department of Labor 1975, Table C-3). The NLS survey of young men out-of-school and obtaining early jobs in 1966 shows the same pattern of racial differences for white-collar occupations: informal methods were used by 52 percent of blacks and 24 percent of whites for professional and technical jobs, and by 32 percent of blacks compared with 44 percent of whites for clerical jobs. In these data, blacks also report using informal means more than whites to obtain service jobs (55 percent compared with 33 percent). But among blue-collar occupations, NLS reports only slightly greater use by blacks of informal methods to obtain jobs, with no noticeable trend across the levels of blue-collar occupations. (Parnes et al. 1970, Table 4.15.)

If the suggestions from these findings are correct that minorities rely more on informal methods to obtain higher level positions, we need further information to understand the processes at work. Do the formal methods not work as well for minorities? Is it because employers require additional sponsorship before they hire minorities? Because minority workers look for informal reassurance about the working conditions before seeking employment in firms at higher levels? Or because of other factors in the use of formal and informal networks or job opportunities? Moreover, the inconsistencies and serious limitations of existing data sources need to be addressed first to obtain more reliable estimates of the actual differences between racial groups in the use and value of different methods of job search behavior (Becker 1977). Consequently, it remains a largely untested hypothesis that, for reasons other than overt employer discrimination and differences in job training, blacks are under-represented in the best jobs because they are not tied into important networks of opportunity.

Segregation, Discrimination, and Networks of Opportunity

Some research has examined how segregation and discrimination may withhold important networks of opportunity from minorities, but the evidence is either weak or indirect because of inadequate data. This research includes a number of studies on the importance of residential segregation for proximity to job opportunities, some studies on the segregation of unions affecting minority chances, and a very limited set of studies that either directly or indirectly address segregation and the use of informal social networks of job information and access.

Although research on residential segregation and union segregation may be related to issues of the availability of informal social networks of opportunity, it has not been conceptualized in these terms. Residential segregation is viewed mainly as posing a transportation problem for minorities who live in the inner city but need to reach the growing job openings in the suburbs. Union segregation is also viewed as a problem of labor market dislocation, to the extent that good jobs are tied to union memberships, in which minority access is restricted. Thus, residential segregation and union segregation are studied to assess the formal barriers to minority job success rather than the segregation from informal social networks of information and contact. In any case, research by economists on residential or union segregation has not demonstrated strong effects on black-white income gaps net of educational and job qualifications.

The Institute for Research on Poverty monograph by Masters (1975) reviews research on residential location and unionization and presents additional empirical analyses on housing segregation, concluding that these factors do not account for major racial income differentials. Reviewing Ashenfelter's (1972) analyses of trade unions and racial discrimination, Masters concludes "it appears that, on the average, unions have had little effect on labor-market discrimination. In fact, they may have reduced it slightly" (Masters 1975, p. 30; see also Andrisani and Kohen 1975, Bielby et al. 1978). In terms of housing segregation, criticisms are made of the methodologies of previous research, and new empirical studies are offered to discount the view that the black-white male income ratio is lower in cities with the most housing segregation (Masters 1975; see also Meyer et al. 1965, James 1974, and Orr 1975).

There is very little evidence on the effects of segregation in limiting access to important informal networks of opportunity. Although the idea was offered several years ago (Crain 1970, McCall 1972) that school or residential segregation and discrimination may cut blacks off from valuable job information and contacts, there are no direct studies of the effects of segregation on job search behaviors. Some indirect evidence, however, suggests that this is a promising area for future research.

Most of this evidence comes from a study of 434 personnel managers of the largest employers in 15 major cities conducted in 1967 by Rossi et al. (1968, 1974) for the National Advisory Commission on Civil Disorders. In this study, each personnel manager reported the number of blacks among the last 20 individuals who applied for work and among those who were hired at 3 broad skill levels (professional and white collar, skilled workers, and unskilled workers). This information was related to other data about each firm and about each city's labor supply, including the firm's personnel recruitment practices, the racial composition and size of the work force in the firm and the city, city differences in industrial composition, and the degree of concurrent school segregation and racial educational differences in the city.

The authors reasoned that the past employment practices of a firm (as measured by the percentage of blacks in the current work force) could be used as a variable to indirectly assess the importance of social networks of opportunity in the job recruitment process and the willingness of that firm to admit blacks in the hiring process. According to the authors, if the current racial composition of a firm is the best predictor of the rate of recent black application, we would have indirect evidence that the social networks through current black employees provide an important recruitment channel to reach potential new black applicants. If a firm's current racial composition is the best predictor of the rate at which black applicants have been recently hired, it could be inferred that a firm's evaluation of blacks as potential employees is more positive after it has had some experience with blacks in its work force. If current racial composition is the best predictor of both the rate at which blacks had recently applied and the rate at which black applicants were recently hired, it could be argued that both disadvantages of informal networks for blacks and racial preferences of firms for their employees can account for employment outcomes that discriminate against blacks. This study finds that the proportion of blacks in a firm's current work force is an important predictor both of the likelihood that blacks had recently applied for work and of the fact that black applicants were recently hired, even after all other measured characteristics of the firm and the city (including racial composition of the city) were taken into account. The result was particularly strong for professional and white-collar applicants and hiring; in those occupations, the current percentage of blacks in the work force accounted for more variance than any other measured characteristic of the firm or city. Yet without time series data on rates of black employment, applications, and hiring in different firms, it is difficult to view the reported correlations as good evidence that social network mechanisms are actually operating to affect the employment access of minorities.

An analogous result has been obtained by Becker (1978) in his recent study of racial segregation in places of work. Becker used the Equal Employment Opportunity Commission survey of the racial composition of firms to calculate an index of the segregation of employment across firms for nine occupational levels. He found that the racial composition of an establishment's work force in one occupation is strongly related to its racial composition in other occupations, particularly for occupations within the blue-collar and white-collar subgroups.

Although the Rossi et al. data (1968, 1974) from personnel managers include direct measures on the recruitment channels used by firms and on the concurrent level of school segregation in each city, results using these measures were not consistent and strong in explaining differences of black application and hiring rates at each occupational level. The reported use of specific recruitment channels did not relate to minority rates of application or employment, but the authors point out the available data do not indicate which channel was actually used by the black applicants or employees. The degree of school segregation in each city also fails to be significantly related to the rates of application or hiring of blacks by firms at any occupational level. However, this is not a test of the long-term effects of school segregation on occupational opportunities for blacks, because the measure was not of the school desegregation experiences of those blacks presently in the work force but of the segregation of students still in school who resided in the same city as the firms whose employment practices were being studied. The only research that links the school desegregation of blacks to their own later life employment success is the retrospective study conducted in 1967 for the U.S. Commission on Civil Rights (1968, Crain 1970). Although the sample size was small in this study and covered an earlier historical period, the study shows a positive effect of earlier school desegregation on present black income and job status. This study also suggests that black adults who had attended desegregated schools had developed a more useful social network for job referrals and had a better knowledge of specific job opportunities (Crain and Weisman 1973).

We can look for important research on these topics in the next few years. For example, the ongoing Panel Study of Income Dynamics of the University of Michigan's Institute for Social Research plans to place more emphasis in the near future on race and sex differences in how people hear about and get jobs (ISR Newsletter, Summer 1978; also, the Social Science Research Council 1978, Peterson 1978). In addition, surveys in single local labor markets are being used to incorporate measures of social networks in social mobility models, although these studies have not specifically addressed racial differences (Lin et al. 1978, Vaughn and Lin 1976).

The research requirements for advancing knowledge about networks of opportunity are probably different from those of other topics we are discussing. Many other underresearched topics in discrimination and income inequalities can be studied with existing data using more thoughtful models and methods. In this case, however, attention to the shortcomings in available data appears to be a first-order requirement.

3. DEVELOPMENTAL PROCESSES AFFECTING CAREER STRATEGIES

There are a number of social-psychological and attitudinal variables by which racial differences have been observed, which are likely to be related to behaviors affecting adult success, and which may be explained by the discrimination or segregation experienced by minorities. The classes of social-psychological variables we choose as examples are individual attitudes about opportunities and planning (such as measures of personal efficacy, internal control, and inclination to postpone immediate rewards) and selected social-psychological requirements of certain job and adult situations (such as coping skills in interracial situations). These variables can affect minority adult success because they may be related to whether an individual follows a long-run or short-run strategy for achievement and to how an individual responds to alternative opportunities.

Racial Differences in Planning Attitudes or Behavior and their Importance for Adult Success

Adult achievement is in part the consequence of the order and pattern of the major events in life—getting an education, joining the labor force, and assuming responsibilities for family dependents. Different sequences and combinations of these major events can change the probability of achieving success in any one of the major events. For example, after an individual has assumed responsibilities for supporting a family, he or she is less able to continue schooling or to quit a job to look for better work because of the demands of family obligation. In fact, the organization of major institutions in society establishes a conventional or normative pattern for major life events in this country: ordinarily, education is completed through full-time attendance, and is followed by full-time attachment to the labor force and family formation (Hogan 1978). To depart from this pattern requires that a person has special resources or motivation to endure the strains of either combining part-time education and part-time work, or completing education in a sequence of interrupted attendance while still finding ways of saving, borrowing, or sharing to meet personal and family obligations. In other words, the planning or timing of major events in early adult life can foreclose or make more difficult later adult success.

Research on social mobility processes has just begun to consider the pattern and sequence of major career events (Featherman and Carter 1976, Karweit 1977, Hogan 1978). Until recently, social mobility models have measured educational attainment by the number of years of schooling completed without differentiating full-time versus part-time attendance or continuous versus interrupted education. Also, there have been no careful research assessments of the importance of the ordering of education, employment, and family events. So, empirical evidence is not strong on either racial differences in career patterns or their effects on adult success. However, there has been a good deal of research on social-psychological variables concerned with the planning attitudes and perceived opportunities of blacks and whites, and these may be related to different behaviors in the sequence and pattern of major events in life.

In terms of behavior, there is some indication that black men do not use continuing or part-time education to the same extent as whites, being more likely to stop their schooling without later resumption, either part-time or full-time. For black men who do resume their education after entering the labor market, the average length of time between stopping and continuing education exceeds that for white men by several years. Overall, black men are more likely to stop their education at an earlier age with less attainment, to use continuing or part-time education less frequently, and to more often follow a linear progression from full-time education to full-time work than are white men (Karweit 1977). The evidence on family responsibilities of young women also indicates behavioral differences between black and white populations, most dramatically in the incidence of pregnancies and births before first marriage (U.S. Bureau of the Census 1978). But much more thorough and current data are needed to describe the behavioral differences between blacks and whites in the sequence and pattern of major life events at particular ages in the life cycle for particular socioeconomic class categories.

There is better evidence of significant social-psychological differences between blacks and whites in their sense of opportunity and the associated belief that planning for the future will pay off. Not surprisingly, blacks are often found to be more discouraged about their chances for getting ahead in life, and to feel they cannot successfully control their own destinies. Studies using different measures of personal efficacy, locus of control, or anxiety about the future are not always consistent about the existence or the size of racial differences, but the empirical evidence of significant black-white differences is much stronger for these measures than for other social-psychological dimensions, such as global measures of self-esteem, values, or aspirations (see, for example, Coleman et al. 1966, Epps 1975, Dreger 1973, Crain and Weisman 1973, Rossi et al. 1974, Epps 1975).

The research task is to move to more explicit theories and studies of the developmental processes that tie discrimination, segregation, and limited opportunity structures to those attitudes and behaviors concerning career strategies that have important consequences for adult success. Existing research on social-psychological variables is useful for this endeavor because some preliminary work has been done on the effects of segregation and limited opportunities.

Segregation, Discrimination and Individual Career Strategies

Some research suggests that discrimination and segregation are part of the processes that diminish black chances for adult success by contributing to those career strategies and behaviors in early adulthood that foreclose opportunities in the future. First, there is general evidence that a lower sense of personal efficacy is a consequence of real experiences, such as personal experiences of discrimination. Second, there are findings that school desegregation may have an effect on the sense of opportunity of blacks, net of their own social class and the school's social class composition. Third, there is evidence that segregation is perpetuated across stages of the life cycle, suggesting that the ability to cope successfully with the demands of desegregated settings later in life depends on earlier experiences with desegregation.

The correlation is well established between individuals' sense of personal efficacy and their achievement in various dimensions of life, but the direction of causality is not. Assumptions about the direction of causality produce different theories and implications. On one hand, a low sense of personal efficacy has been viewed as a psychological weakness suffered by individuals from particular cultures, which produces low achievement. On the other hand, a contrasting theory is that individuals who experience discrimination and restricted achievement opportunities will develop a low sense of efficacy as a realistic assessment of their own experiences. Although there are not many empirical studies to test the causal direction of these correlations, there is at least some evidence to show that a low sense of efficacy follows real experiences of being unfairly treated as an inferior or an outsider. The evidence includes studies of sense of personal efficacy among experienced workers who had been fired or permanently laid off and who felt age discrimination (Parnes and King 1977), comparisons of the sense of personal efficacy of blacks who were born in the North and in the South before the court decisions that declared segregation illegal (Crain and Weisman 1973), and comparisons of the sense of personal efficacy of the average black population in 15 cities that differed in the fair delivery of city services (Rossi et al. 1974).

The research on the effects of school segregation on students' social-psychological outcomes is a mixture of positive and negative findings (St. John 1975), but the work on measures of sense of personal efficacy differs in an important way. In contrast to other student outcome variables, where positive effects can be largely accounted for by differences in the social class composition of the school rather than the racial composition, school desegregation has been found to be positively related to black students' sense of efficacy due to the racial mixture of the environment per se (Coleman et al. 1966, McPartland 1968). This finding suggests that desegregation, in itself, delivers a positive message to minority students about their future opportunities to control their own fate: if the white majority has not withheld desegregated schooling to a black student, that fact may be taken by the student as a positive indication that later opportunities will also not be withheld. In addition to this evidence, Crain and Weisman (1972) found, in a 1966 retrospective study of black adults, that those who had attended desegregated schools earlier in life were more likely to be currently living and working in desegregated environments and to express a positive sense of personal efficacy. Preliminary findings from the National Longitudinal Study of the High School Class of 1972 also indicate that blacks in both the North and the South from desegregated elementary and secondary schools who go on to college are more likely to enroll in desegregated institutions than those with equal qualifications whose educational environment was segregated before high school graduation (Braddock and McPartland 1979).

Although it is a plausible hypothesis that discrimination and segregation can produce additional burdens on minorities by discouraging a positive sense of personal efficacy and coping skills that are often needed to lead to success in the future, the available evidence can be taken as only suggestive of such connections. Future work with existing and improved data sources is needed to clarify and empirically demonstrate the linkages between segregation or discrimination at one stage of the life cycle to an individual's sense of opportunity and career-related behavior at later stages of the life cycle.

Summary

There are two general lines of research on discrimination in social mobility processes: one that seeks to estimate the total effect of discrimination as the racial gap in occupational attainment after other factors are taken into account, and one that seeks to incorporate direct measures of discriminatory or exclusionary processes into theories and models of occupational attainment. We argue that greater emphasis needs to be placed on the latter direction to increase our practical understanding of how minorities may lose out in social mobility processes because of factors linked to race.

We provide examples of studies of overt discrimination against blacks by employers or other selection agents. Other examples illustrate systemic exclusionary processes that channel blacks in less promising directions, exclude them from important avenues of access that others find useful, or create special burdens that foreclose consideration of potential opportunities. We invite others to disagree with these examples and propose better agendas for research. Our general point is that in order to obtain more useful knowledge, we now need many more ideas and studies that focus on the specific ways in which discrimination and racial exclusion may continue to operate in social mobility processes.

Notes

1. Ideas for practical ways of reducing the risks for employers may be found from studies of training programs for poor minority workers (Bray 1974), of large-scale industrial programs of increasing minority employment (Wallace 1977), or from industrial psychologists' suggestions for modifications in selection procedures for equal employment opportunity purposes (Dunnett 1976).

References

Andrisani, P., and Kohen, A. I. (1975) *Career Thresholds*. Vol. 5. Columbus, Ohio: Center for Human Resource Research, Ohio State University.

Ashenfelter, O. (1972) Racial discrimination and trade unionism. *Journal of Political Economy* 80:435–464.

Becker, G. S. (1957) *The Economics of Discrimination.* Chicago: University of Chicago Press.

Becker, H. J. (1977) *How Young People Find Career-Entry Jobs: A Review of the Literature.* Report No. 241. Baltimore: Center for Social Organization of Schools, Johns Hopkins University.

Becker, H. J. (1978) *Racial Segregation among Places of Employment.* Report No. 262. Baltimore: Center for Social Organization of Schools, Johns Hopkins University.

Becker, H. J., McPartland, J. M., and Thomas, G. E. (1978) The measurement of segregation: the dissimilarity index and Coleman's segregation index compared. *Proceedings of Social Statistics Section, American Statistical Association.* 1978:349–353.

Bielby, W. T., Hawley, C. B., and Bills, D. (1978) *Research Uses of the National Longitudinal Surveys.* Washington, D.C.: Social Science Research Council.

Blau, P. M., and Duncan, O. D. (1967) *The American Occupational Structure.* New York: Wiley.

Braddock, J. H., and McPartland, J. M. (1979) *The Perpetuation of Segregation Across Educational Levels.* Baltimore: Center for Social Organization of Schools, Johns Hopkins University.

Bray, T. J. (1974) Leon Sullivan pushes job training as key to blacks' success. *Wall Street Journal* May 17.

Coleman, J. S., Berry, C. C., and Blum, Z. D. (1972) White and black careers during the first decade of labor force experience. Part III: Occupational status and income together. *Social Science Research* 1:293–304.

Coleman, J. S., Campbell, E. Q., Hobson, C. J., McPartland, J., Mood, A. M., Weinfeld, F. D., and York, R. L. (1966) *Equality of Educational Opportunities.* Washington, D.C.: U.S. Government Printing Office.

Congressional Budget Office (1977) *Income Disparities Between Black and White Americans.* Washington, D.C.: U.S. Government Printing Office.

Crain, R. L. (1970) School integration and occupational achievement of Negroes. *American Journal of Sociology* 75:593–606.

Crain, R. L., and Weisman, C. S. (1972) *Discrimination, Personality, and Achievement.* New York: Seminar Press.

Dreger, R. M. (1973) Temperament. Pp. 231–248 in K. S. Miller and R. M. Dreger, eds., *Comparative Studies of Blacks and Whites in the United States.* New York: Seminar Press.

Duncan, O. D. (1969) Inheritance of poverty or inheritance of race?. Daniel P. Moynahan, ed., *Understanding Poverty.* New York: Basic Books.

Dunnett, M. D. (1976) *Handbook of Industrial and Organizational Psychology.* Chicago: Rand McNally.

Educational Testing Service (1976) *Proceedings of Annual Conference.* Princeton, N.J.: Educational Testing Service.

Epps, E. G. (1975) Impact of school desegregation on aspirations, self-concepts, and other aspects of personality. *Law and Contemporary Problems* 39(Spring):330–313.

Feagin, J. R., and Feagin, C. B. (1978) *Discrimination American Style.* Englewood Cliffs, N.J.: Prentice Hall.

Featherman, D. L., and Carter, T. M. (1976) Discontinuities in schooling and the socioeconomic life cycle. Pages 133–160 in W. H. Sewell, R. M. Hauser, and D. L. Featherman, eds., *Schooling and Achievement in American Society.* New York: Academic Press.

Featherman, D. L., and Hauser, R. M. (1976) Change in the socioeconomic stratification of the races, 1962-73. *American Journal of Sociology* 82:621–651.

Flanagan, R. J. (1973) Racial wage discrimination and employment segregation. *Journal of Human Resources* 8:456–471.

Freeman, R. B. (1973) Decline of labor market discrimination and economic analysis. *The American Economic Review* 63:280–86.

Gottfredson, L. S. (1977) *A Multiple-Labor Market Model of Occupational Achievement.* Baltimore: Center for Social Organization of Schools, Johns Hopkins University.

Gottfredson, L. S. (1978a) An analytical description of employment according to race, sex, prestige and Holland type of work. *Journal of Vocational Behavior.* 13:210–221.

Gottfredson, L. S. (1978b) *Race and Sex Differences in Occupational Aspirations: Their Development and Consequences for Occupational Segregation.* Report 254. Baltimore: Center for Social Organization of Schools, Johns Hopkins University.

Granovetter, M. S. (1974) *Getting a Job: A Study of Contacts and Careers.* Cambridge, Mass.: Harvard University Press.

Griggs v. *Duke Power* 401 U.S. 424 (1971).

Griliches, Z., and Mason, W. (1972) Education, income and ability. *Journal of Political Economy* 80:Supplement.

Guthrie, H. (1970) The prospect of equality of incomes between white and black families under varying rates of unemployment. *Journal of Human Resources* 5 (Fall):431–436.

Haynes, L. L., III (1978) *A Critical Examination of the Adams Case: A Source Book.* Washington, D.C.: Institute for Services to Education.

Hogan, D. P. (1978) The variable order of events in the life course. *American Sociological Review* 43:573–586.

Hogan, D. P., and Featherman, D. L. (1977) Racial stratification and socioeconomic change in the American North and South. *American Journal of Sociology* 83:100–126.

Holland, J. L. (1973) *Making Vocational Choices: A Theory of Careers.* Englewood Cliffs, N.J.: Prentice Hall.

Institute for the Study of Educational Policy (1976) *Equal Educational Opportunity for Blacks in U.S. Higher Education: An Assessment.* Washington, D.C.: Howard University Press.

James, F. J. (1974) *Models of Employment and Residence Location.* New Brunswick, N.J.: Center for Urban Policy Research, Rutgers Unirsity.

Jencks, C. et al. (1972) *Inequality: A Reassessment of the Effect of Family and Schooling in America.* New York: Basic Books.

Karweit, N. (1977) *Patterns of Educational Activities: Discontinuities and Sequences.* Report No. 222. Baltimore: Center for Social Organization of Schools, Johns Hopkins University.

Kluegel, J. R. (1978) The causes and cost of racial exclusion from job authority. *American Sociological Review* 43:285–301.

Lin, N., Vaughn, J. C., and Ensel, W. M. (1978) *Social Ties and Occupational Achievement.* Albany, N.Y.: International Center for Social Research, State University of New York at Albany.

Lippman, S., and McCall, J. (1976) The economics of job search: a survey. *Economic Inquiry* 14:155–189.

McCall, J. J. (1972) The simple mathematics of information, job search and prejudice. Pp. 205–224 in A. H. Pascal, ed., *Racial Discrimination in Economic Life.* Lexington, Mass.: D.C. Heath.

McPartland, J. M. (1978) Desegregation and equity in higher education and employment: is progress related to the desegregation of elementary and secondary schools? *Law and Contemporary Problems* 42(3):108–132.

McPartland, J. M. (1968) *The Segregated Student in Desegregated Schools.* Baltimore: Center for Social Organization of Schools, Johns Hopkins University.

Marshall, R. (1974) The economics of racial discrimination: a survey. *Journal of Economic Literature* 12:849–871.

Masters, S. H. (1975) *Black-White Income Differentials: Empirical Studies and Policy Implications.* New York: Academic Press.

Meyer, J. R., Kain, J. F., and Wohl, M. (1965) *The Urban Transportation Problem.* Cambridge, Mass.: Harvard University Press.

Michael, J. A. (1978) *Geographic Aspects of Black Enrollment in Higher Education in 1976.* Washington, D.C.: National Center for Education Statistics.

O'Neill, D. M. (1970) The Effect of Discrimination on Earnings: Evidence from Military Test Score Results. *Journal of Human Resources* 5:479–481.

Orr, L. L. (1975) *Income, Employment and Urban Residential Location.* New York: Academic Press.

Parnes, H. S., and King, R. (1977) Middle-aged job-losers. *Industrial Gerontology* 4:77–95.

Parnes, H. S., Miljus, R. C., Spitz, R. S. and Associates (1970) *Career Thresholds.* Volume 1. Monograph No. 16. Washington, D.C.: U.S. Department of Labor Manpower Research.

Peterson, J. L. (1978) Research on the socioeconomic life cycle. *Social Science Research Council Items* 32(2):27–31.

Piore, M. J. (1977) The dual labor market. Pp. 93–97 in D. Gordon, ed., *Problems in Political Economy.* 2d ed. Lexington, Mass.: D.C. Heath.

Porter, J. N. (1974) Race, socialization and mobility in educational and early occupational attainment. *American Sociological Review* 39:303–316.

Rossi, P. H., Berk, R. A., and Eidson, B. K. (1974) *The Roots of Urban Discontent: Public Policy, Municipal Institutions, and the Ghetto.* New York: Wiley.

Rossi, P. H., Berk, R. A., Boesel, D. P., Eidson, B. K., and Groves, W. E. (1968) Between white and black: the faces of American institutions in the ghetto. In *Supplemental Studies for the National Advisory Commission on Civil Disorders.* Washington, D. C.: U.S. Government Printing Office.

St. John, N. H. (1975) *School Desegregation: Outcomes for Children.* New York: Wiley.

Siegel, P. (1965) On the costs of being a negro. *Sociological Inquiry* 35 (Winter):41–57.

Smith, J. P. (1978) *The Convergence to Racial Equality in Women's Wages.* Santa Monica, Cal.: Rand Corporation.

Smith, J. P., and Welch, F. (1978) *Race Differences in Earnings: A Survey and New Evidence.* Santa Monica, Cal.: Rand Corporation.

Social Science Research Council (1978) *A Research Agenda for the National Longitudinal Surveys of Labor Market Experience.* Washington, D.C.: Center for Coordination of Research on Social Indicators, Social Science Research Council.

Spilerman, S. (1977) Careers, labor market structure, and socioeconomic achievement. *American Journal of Sociology* 83:551–593.

Stolzenberg, R. M., and D'Amico, R. J. (1977) City differences and nondifferences in the effect of race and sex on occupational distribution. *American Sociological Review* 42:937–950.

Thomas, G. E. (1978) *Equality of Representation of Race and Sex Groups in Higher Education: Institutional and Program Enrollment Statuses.* Report No. 263. Baltimore: Center for Social Organization of Schools, Johns Hopkins University.

Thomas, G. E., Daiger, D. C., and McPartland, J. M. (1978) Desegregation and Enrollment Access in Higher Eduction. Paper presented at 1978 meetings of American Sociological Association.

U.S. Bureau of the Census (1978) Fertility of American women. June 1977 *Current Population Reports,* Series P-20. No. 325. Washington, D.C.: U.S. Department of Commerce.

U.S. Commission on Civil Rights (1968) *Racial Isolation in the Public Schools.* Washington, D.C.: U.S. Government Printing Office.

U.S. Department of Housing and Urban Development (1978) Background Information and Initial Findings of the Housing Market Practices Survey. Paper presented at 1978 National Fair Housing Conference. National Committee Against Discrimination in Housing, Washington, D.C.

U.S. Department of Labor (1970) *Career Thresholds.* Vol. 1. Research Monograph no. 16. Washington, D.C. U.S. Department of Labor.

U.S. Department of Labor (1975) *Jobseeking Methods Used by American Workers.* Bureau of Labor Statistics. Bulletin 1886.

Vaughn, J. C. and Lin, N. (1976) Social Resources and Occupational Mobility. Paper presented at annual meeting of American Sociological Association.

Wallace, P. A. (1977) A decade of policy developments in equal opportunities in employment and housing. Pp. 329–359 in H. Haveman, ed., *A Decade of Federal Antipoverty Programs: Achievements, Failures and Lessons*. New York: Academic Press.

Weiss, L., and Williamson, J. G. (1972) Black education, earnings and interregional migration, some recent evidence. *American Economic Review* 62:372–383.

Welch, F. (1973) Black-white differences in returns to schooling. *American Economic Review* 63:893–907.

Wilson, W. J. (1978) *The Declining Significance of Race*. Chicago: University of Chicago Press.

Wohlstetter, A., and Coleman, S. (1972) Race differences in income. In A. H. Pascal, ed., *Racial Discrimination in Economic Life*. Lexington, Mass.: D.C. Heath.

Wright, E. O. (1978) Race, class and income inequality. *American Journal of Sociology* 83(6):1368–1397.

Robert W. Hodge and Barbara Laslett

Poverty and Status Attainment

The effort to eliminate poverty has been accompanied since the 1960s by a continuing research endeavor to understand the causes of poverty and to devise new strategies for coping with it. During roughly the same period there has also been a virtual explosion of research dealing with the process of status attainment. Research on poverty has been conducted by a large and diverse group, while research on status attainment has primarily been the work of a few: Blau, Duncan, Sewell, and their students and associates, especially Haller, Hauser, and Featherman.

Although poverty can be seen as one possible outcome of processes of status attainment, it has been largely ignored in the research on this topic. Similarly, although processes of status attainment would seem to be especially relevant to poverty, much of the literature dealing directly with poverty proceeds without benefit of an acquaintance with the literature on status attainment. There are several reasons why research on poverty and research on status attainment have developed more independently than one might expect. Not the least of these reasons is that much of the research on poverty has been designed and executed by economists, whereas the research on status attainment has been in large measure the province of sociologists. But this explanation alone does not suffice to explain the disparity between these research traditions in the published literature, for many of the signal contributors to both topics are well acquainted with each other's work. One must look, instead, to intellectual considerations, rather than to institutionalized divisions between academic disciplines, to account for the failure of the two research traditions to inform each other in any but a casual manner.

In this paper, we seek to analyze some of the reasons why the research on poverty and the research on status attainment have not converged. By so doing, we will attempt to indicate why poverty, as a variable, has been

[Robert W. Hodge is professor of Sociology in the Department of Sociology at the University of Southern California. Barbara Laslett is associate professor of Sociology at the University of Southern California.]

largely ignored in the research on status attainment and to evaluate the research on status attainment with specific reference to poverty.

Undertaking these tasks necessarily involves an assessment of the assumptions underlying the research on status attainment. In many ways, the most crucial of these assumptions is that research on status attainment explores the attainment process by converting information about individual occupations to a continuous index of socioeconomic status in a single occupational hierarchy. Consequently, part of this paper is devoted to analyzing the properties of Duncan's Socioeconomic Index for All Occupations (Duncan 1961b)—the main vehicle in the status attainment literature for indexing an individual's socioeconomic status. In addition, it is necessary to consider whether the individual is the appropriate unit of analysis for an understanding of poverty and whether the assumption of a single occupational hierarchy adequately describes the occupational system within which the attainment process occurs. It is also necessary to ask whether a model that focuses on individual attributes alone can provide an adequate causal model for understanding the differential achievement of individuals. We would suggest that any analysis of poverty, like analyses of other social phenomenona, requires that attention be paid to relationships that describe the social organization as a whole; the whole cannot be understood simply in terms of its individual parts. Thus, although this paper is limited to a review of the relationship between poverty and processes of status attainment, it may be useful to place this topic in perspective by sketching in broad outline how the competition of people for posts relates to the larger, macrosociological forces that determine who gets what, when, and why.

Some Elements in the Analysis of Poverty

The fundamental fact about poverty as it is conceived in the literature is that it is defined for families rather than for individuals, the only exception being isolated, single-person familial units. Thus, an individual's poverty status depends not only on individual income, resources, and productivity but also on the joint attainments and resources of the family unit of which he or she is a member. Furthermore, since in poverty statistics the family is defined primarily as a group that resides together, the kinship unit that makes up the definition of poverty is typically the nuclear family rather than the extended family. While an individual's earnings may suffice to elevate him or her as an individual *qua* individual above the poverty level, he or she may be a member of a nuclear family whose pooled resources drop them below that level. Even when nuclear families and their members are also part of an extended kinship group that has aggregate resources well above the poverty level, it cannot automatically be assumed that the extended kinship group can or should distribute its resources among its constituent nuclear units.

The first problem, then, in the analysis of poverty is straightforward: poverty is a family affair, but the process by which the individual members of families acquire resources that may ultimately be pooled to determine the poverty status of those families is largely an individual matter. Family farms and businesses are perhaps exceptions to this generalization, but they have become historically less important as self-employment in this country has waned. Even these cases can be analyzed within an individual framework so long as earnings can be attributed to the individual members of joint family enterprises.

The second problem in the analysis of poverty is largely a consequence of the first: although individual family members compete for jobs in the marketplace, joint contingencies govern whether and which specific family members enter the competition. Although the success of any particular family member in this competition can be conceived as a function of individual characteristics, whether he or she competes at all is intertwined with the labor market opportunities and skills of cofamily members. Wives and children may be more likely to enter the labor market if their husbands and fathers cannot find work or have few marketable skills. Conversely, the incentive to work among men is doubtless affected by the employability of their wives and children. Once an individual gets into the labor market, individual characteristics—including ascriptive ones such as race and family background—may govern his or her success, but the decision to enter the labor market at all may reside partially in the competitive labor market potential of other members in the immediate family.

The implications of the analysis of poverty to this point are straightforward. First, an equation for the economic attainment of every individual would not suffice to determine his or her poverty status, since poverty depends on family rather than individual earnings. Thus, in determining poverty, one must consider not only the earnings function for an individual, but also the earnings functions for all members of the relevant family unit. Second, the labor force status of an individual is obviously related to his or her earnings, but an individual's labor force status is also determined, at least in part, by the labor force potential of cofamily members. In addition, an individual's market behavior may also be affected by the labor market characteristics of other family members. These intrafamilial contingencies in labor market behavior mean that the family, rather than the individual alone, is involved in the supply of labor to the market.[1]

A third problem in the analysis of poverty is rooted in two observations about income: (1) most income is job-related and (2) employers, not employees, determine the number and type of jobs as well as the rewards attached to them.[2] Workers compete in the labor market for jobs, not for earnings: the employment opportunity columns of a newspaper's classified section do not carry advertisements for wages, but for jobs to which wages and salaries are already attached. To be sure, some jobs, while similar in the demands placed upon those who hold them, differ in the earnings, fringe benefits, and other perquisites that accrue to those who hold them. However, with rare exceptions, individual employees do not set the level and kind of rewards attached to their jobs. These are fixed instead by employers; from the point of view of an individual employee—whose income is largely derived from employment—rewards are simply predetermined features of the job held.[3]

This problem is of considerable importance, for it means, among other things, that poverty among those who do work is in some measure a structural problem that cannot be understood by reference to processes of status attainment alone. Studying status attainment can provide insight into who finds work in jobs that pay poverty-level wages, and why they get them. However, such insights provide no clue as to why there are poverty-level jobs in the first place. Minimum wage laws, child labor legislation, the job vacancy rate, the substitutability of capital (technology) for labor, unions, other employee associations, and business associations are some of the factors that may explain the differences in wage return for labor and the incidence of jobs whose potential offers scant hope of escaping poverty.

Eliminating jobs with poverty-level wages is a task that must be addressed at the macrosociological level; microsociological investigations of processes of status attainment cannot tell us very much about how wages get attached to jobs; they can tell us only about the sorting mechanisms that govern the access of individuals to jobs differentiated according to their wage levels. Knowing who is in poverty does not tell us why there is poverty; the answers to these questions seem to require attention to different levels of analysis. The former question requires analysis of the fates of individuals; the latter demands analysis of the social organization of production as a whole.

The difference between these two levels of analysis is illustrated by the results of the Blau-Duncan study of "Occupational Changes in a Generation" (Blau and Duncan 1967) and its replication in 1973 by Featherman and Hauser (1975). At the time this paper was drafted, a comprehensive analysis of the 1973 replication of the Blau-Duncan study was yet to be published. The best available estimates, however, suggest that minimal change took place in the basic processes of stratification between 1962 and 1973 or, for that matter, during the longer period that can be traced with less comprehensive surveys (see, e.g., Hauser and Featherman 1974, Hauser et al. 1975). Yet between 1962 and 1973 there was substantial change in the gross level of poverty. In 1962, the percentage of all persons falling below the government-defined poverty level stood at 21.0 percent; by 1973, the percentage was nearly halved to 11.1 percent (U.S. Bureau of the Census 1977, Table 1, p. 15). Evidently, this change reflects changes in American society other than the way in which individuals are matched to jobs.[4] Observations such as these support the rather obvious but occasionally overlooked generalization that a comprehensive understanding of poverty must necessarily go beyond the analysis of individual processes of status attainment. There are problems in the analysis of poverty other than those noted here, one of the most important being that voluntaristic elements—such as fertility and marital dissolution—enter into the calculation of poverty. The points we have reviewed, however, are sufficient to reveal that the analysis of poverty involves complexities that can be ignored in the investigation of individual status attainment. We now turn to a discussion of the characteristics of poverty as a variable in status attainment.

Poverty as a Variable in Status Attainment

The government indicator of poverty is a complex variable defined for families and for individuals living alone. The income level that defines poverty varies for farm and nonfarm families, for families with male and with female heads, for families of different size, and for families of equal size but with differing age compositions of household members. In single-person and two-person households, the poverty threshold also varies according to the age of the head. Despite these complications in the definition of poverty, it is convenient to think of poverty as simply being determined by the ratio of resources to persons, that is, the ratio of family income to family size. This continuous variable is then arbitrarily divided at a level deemed adequate to meet the family's needs for housing, clothing, food, medical care, and so forth. Families above this threshold are considered out of poverty and those below are considered in poverty.

Table 1 shows the relationship of poverty to family income and family size in 1970. As the upper panel of the table shows, virtually all of the families in the lower left hand corner of the upper panel—in which family income is small relative to family size—are in poverty, while only a handful of those in the upper right hand corner—in which family income is large relative to family size—are in poverty. If only family income and family size were involved in the definition of poverty, then the relationship between these variables and poverty would be perfect. There would be only three types of cells in Table 1—those in which no families were in poverty, those in which all families were in poverty, and a diagonal set of cells dividing these two extreme types, in which only some families were in poverty. The third type of cell, in which some are in and others are out of poverty, would occur only because the poverty threshold is included in the income intervals used to tabulate the data, rather than falling exactly at an endpoint of the relevant intervals.

Inspection of Table 1 reveals that while the relationship of poverty status to family income and family size is not perfect, it is nearly perfect. In most of the cells, virtually everyone or virtually no one is in poverty and the drop-off around the diagonal dividing these two types of cells is precipitous. The full extent to which poverty is determined by family income and family size is shown in Table 2, which gives the relationship between actual and predicted poverty. In order to generate the results given in Table 2 from those in Table 1, all of the families in each cell of Table 1 were classified as being in poverty if 50 percent or more of them were actually in poverty. Similarly, all of the families in each cell of Table 1 were classified as being out of poverty if less than 50 percent of them were actually in poverty. In this way, predicted poverty was derived and related in Table 2 to actual poverty.

The results displayed in Table 2 leave no doubt that the poverty status of families is largely a function of their income and their size. One can compute from the table that the assignment of poverty levels to families on the basis of their income and size alone results in a misclassification of a scant 1.8 percent of all families. (In addition, one can compute from Table 2 that the value of Yule's Q between actual and predicted poverty is an astronomical 0.998. The value of ϕ is not quite so large, but still an impressive 0.902.)

In view of these results, we feel that little information is lost by simply regarding poverty as the ratio of family income to family size. Since the poverty threshold is necessarily somewhat arbitrary and reflects prevailing, if minimal, standards of an adequate level of living, we can also treat this variable continuously across its full range rather than dichotomizing it around a poverty level. A variable of this kind has never, to the best of our knowledge, been considered in the context of models of status attainment.

There are several reasons why research on status attainment has neglected poverty as a variable in its models. First, models of status attainment refer to the achievements of individuals, but poverty is a variable defined for families, all of whose members share a similar poverty status. Writing an equation for the poverty status of a family is

Table 1
Percentage of Families Below Poverty Level by Family Size and Family Income, 1970

Family Size	Total, All Families	Family Income					
		Less than $2,000	$2,000-$2,999	$3,000-$3,999	$4,000-$4,999	$5,000-$5,999	$6,000 or more
		Percent Below Poverty Level					
Total, all families	10.68	99.81	57.66	24.98	13.71	6.01	0.04
Without related children < 18	9.16	99.62	34.73	0.90	0.12	0.03	0.00
With related children < 18	11.79	100.00	92.49	54.68	27.83	11.01	0.07
1	8.65	100.00	80.74	8.91	1.57	0.17	0.00
2	8.77	100.00	98.49	54.85	6.52	0.81	0.02
3	11.81	100.00	100.00	93.31	39.10	3.56	0.09
4	16.82	100.00	100.00	99.94	81.54	14.66	0.31
5	26.04	100.00	100.00	100.00	96.62	85.14	0.28
6 or more	34.99	100.00	100.00	100.00	99.80	92.70	0.00

	Number (in thousands)					
Total, all families	51,143	3,003	2,244	2,486	2,598	2,929	37,883
Without related children < 18	21,657	1,506	1,353	1,373	1,324	1,334	14,767
With related children < 18	29,486	1,497	891	1,113	1,274	1,595	23,116
1	9,698	529	328	405	468	570	7,398
2	8,997	388	227	274	331	449	7,328
3	5,510	251	142	177	203	265	4,472
4	2,888	152	86	116	125	154	2,255
5	1,396	90	52	72	76	86	1,020
6 or more	997	87	56	69	71	71	643

Source: U.S. Bureau of the Census (1973) Tables 32 and 33, pp. 328–348.

Table 2
Relationship between Actual Poverty and Poverty Predicted
on the Basis of Family Income and Family Size, 1970

Predicted Poverty	Total All Families	Actual Poverty Level		Number of Families (Thousands)
		Out of Poverty	In Poverty	
	Percentage Distribution			
Total, All Families	100.0	89.3	10.7	51,143
Out of Poverty	100.0	98.5	1.5	46,112
In Poverty	100.0	5.0	95.0	5,031

Source: Computed from Table 1

necessarily more complicated than specifying an equation for the earnings of individuals. The achieved and ascribed characteristics of husbands, wives, and other adult family members are clearly involved in the former, while one might assume, for analytic purposes, that only the relevant achieved and ascribed characteristics of the individual are involved in the latter. In addition, a fertility function complicates any model of the poverty status of families, although it is typically ignored in models of individual earnings. Poverty is quite simply a more complicated empirical phenomenon than the matters typically handled in the literature on status attainment.

A second reason why poverty, as we have conceived it, has been ignored in the research on status attainment is rooted in its very definition as the ratio of family income to family size. Among other things, fertility is a significant determinant of family size, especially since newlyweds typically maintain separate residences from their parents. Consequently, one can conceive of poverty as being roughly determined by two factors: (1) the sum of the individual earnings functions for family members (since most income is derivative from current jobs) and (2) the outcomes of family formation and dissolution processes, which clearly involve the fertility schedule of procreating family members.[5] There is good reason to believe that these two factors are themselves causally intertwined.

The evidence for the foregoing conclusion is piecemeal. The single most relevant study is reported by Duncan et al. (1972, pp. 236–244) who observe, among other things, a positive linkage between fertility and current income. They conjecture (p. 243):

> Perhaps the most plausible ground for this interpretation is
> that a man with many children, if he proposes to support

them, is highly motivated to seek and retain such employment
as will yield the greatest total income among the alternatives
that may be open to him. He is not in a favorable position to
trade off some decrement to his earnings for a job with higher
prestige or better working conditions, for example. Indeed, he
may find it expedient to hold more than one job
simultaneously in view of the need for the additional income
afforded by the second job.

Although the implicit theory of motivation that lies behind this explanation can be questioned, one surely cannot ignore the possibility that past
behaviors—including procreative ones—are determinants of current income. Insofar as this is the case, the study of poverty invites analytical
confusion, because the measure of poverty essentially combines causes
and effects into a single variable. In our view, poverty is best regarded as
an outcome of plural processes that must be modeled independently; it
cannot be adequately understood by focusing on individual achievement
alone and it also does not conveniently fit in the model of individual
competition that informs the literature on status attainment.

The Measurement of Occupational Attainment

Occupation, rather than poverty or even earnings, has been the main
focus of research on processes of status attainment. Some attention, in
any appreciation of research on these processes, must therefore be given
to the measurement of occupational attainment. The measurement of occupational status typically begins with the classification of a person's job
according to the detailed occupational code of the U.S. Bureau of the
Census. Three pieces of information are needed to assign a person a code
in this classification scheme: (1) a job description, specifying the kind of
work the person actually does, (2) the industry or type of business in
which the work is performed, and (3) the class of worker, that is, private
wage and salary worker, self-employed worker, government employee,
or unpaid family worker.

Most labor force surveys are of insufficient size to sustain tabulations by detailed occupational categories, and information on detailed
occupations is available only from the decennial censuses. Consequently,
for purposes of analysis, detailed occupational information is typically
reduced to manageable proportions by one of two alternative strategies.
First, detailed occupational information can be collapsed into broader
clusters of occupations that are qualitatively similar in certain features of
the type of work involved, the amount of training required to perform

the work, the level of rewards associated with the occupation, the context in which the work is executed, and so forth. Many researchers do not code occupational information in detail for the simple reason that the sample size in their research would require them to collapse it for analytic purposes into the major occupational categories of the U.S. Bureau of the Census or according to the even cruder distinction between white-collar, blue-collar, and farm workers. Many sociological inquiries rely upon such gross classifications of jobs, including a number that evaluate quite sophisticated probability and other mathematical models of occupational mobility (see e.g., Matras 1960, Spilerman 1972, Sørensen 1975, 1976).

For the most part, however, the research on processes of status attainment of concern in this paper has utilized the alternative strategy of reducing detailed information on occupations to manageable proportions by scoring them with an index of their status or prestige. By far the most widely used measure for this purpose is Duncan's Socioeconomic Index for All Occupations (Duncan 1961a, 1961b). This index combines the age-standardized proportions of the male experienced civilian labor force with at least a high school education and with an income of at least $3,500 in 1949 into a single continuous indicator of an occupation's hierarchical location in this classification system.

At the time Duncan constructed his index, prestige scores based on the ratings of a national sample were not available for all occupations. However, 45 of the titles included in the 1947 North-Hatt prestige inquiry (National Opinion Research Center, 1947) were judged to have good matches to detailed occupations identified in the census code. For these 45 titles, Duncan considered the regression of the percentage of "excellent" plus "good" ratings received by each occupation on his measures of income and education. The weights received by these indicators in the regression were roughly equal and they were used to combine the income and education variables, which were available for all detailed occupations, into a composite measure of an occupation's socioeconomic status.

The proper interpretation of Duncan's index is not entirely clear. For example, because prestige ratings were used as the exogenous criteria for selecting the weights of the income and education indicators, one possible interpretation of the index is simply as an estimate of the percentage of "excellent" plus "good" ratings that an occupation would have received had it been included in the North-Hatt study. Duncan (1961b, p. 129) explicitly rejected this interpretation of his index, preferring to regard the index as a measure of an occupation's socioeconomic level.

In the interim since Duncan constructed his scale, prestige scores have become available for all occupations (Siegel 1971). When the detailed occupations of fathers and their sons have been alternately coded with Duncan's socioeconomic index and with pure prestige scores, analyses of intergenerational occupational mobility reveal that the association between the occupational prestige of fathers and sons is entirely accounted for by the association between the socioeconomic status of their occupations (Duncan et al. 1972; Featherman and Hauser 1976b). The connection between the occupations of fathers and sons appears, therefore, to be rooted more nearly in their socioeconomic level than in the prestige accorded to them by the general public.

The differential performance of socioeconomic and prestige scales in the analysis of occupational mobility makes it clear that one way of converting detailed occupational information to a continuous scale is not as good as another. In the light of this observation, one can plausibly wonder whether even a socioeconomic index of occupations captures all that is relevant about occupations with respect to not only the intergenerational transmission of them but also the levels of poverty associated with careers in them.

There are over 400 codes in the detailed occupational classification of the U.S. Bureau of the Census; scoring them according to their socioeconomic status reduces the degrees of freedom lodged in occupations from the number of distinct codes minus one to a single degree of freedom.[6] If all that is relevant about occupations in the study of poverty and status attainment can, in fact, be captured in this way, then the socioeconomic status of occupations is a sociological workhorse of considerable proportions. In fact, however, there has been but limited experimentation with alternative ways of summarizing detailed occupational information.

At this writing, little more can be said than what we have already noted, to wit, that socioeconomic scales appear to be superior to prestige scores as a way of summarizing detailed occupational information for purposes of studying intergenerational occupational mobility. In view of the known differences in the performances of prestige and socioeconomic indicators of occupational status, specifying the precise nature of the differences between these measures—occupation by occupation—is of considerable interest because, as shall be presently shown, it suggests features of occupations, other than their location in a continuous status hierarchy, that may well be involved in the way occupation affects earnings and poverty level.

An examination of the differences between the prestige and socioeconomic levels of detailed occupations goes beyond the scope of this paper. We can, however, report the results of a preliminary investigation by examining the residuals from a two-equation model of the determinants of the prestige and income levels of the 61 occupations included in the North-Hatt study (National Opinion Research Center 1947) and its replication (Hodge et al. 1964), which have approximate matches to detailed titles in the occupational classification of the U.S. Bureau of the Census.[7]

In this model, the median income of males in an occupation (I) is regarded as a function of the percentage of high school graduates (E), the percentage of self-employed (S), and the percentage of those working 50–52 weeks (W), among the male experienced civilian labor force of an occupation. The prestige level of an occupation, as measured by the percentage of "excellent" plus "good" ratings it received in the North-Hatt inquiry and its replication (P), is taken to be a function of the income and educational levels of its incumbents, as defined above. The prestige ratings were obtained from Hodge et al. (1964); the remaining variables (I, E, S, W) were calculated from census tabulations (U.S. Bureau of the Census 1963).

Estimates of this model are contained in Figure 1 in the form of a path diagram, which also shows the correlations one must postulate between the residuals and the predetermined variables in order to reproduce the known associations among all of the variables. Two sets of estimates are provided: one set refers to 1950 census data with the prestige indicator being taken from the 1947 North-Hatt study; the other set, given in parentheses, pertains to 1960 census data with the prestige variable coming from the 1963 replication of the North-Hatt study. The values of the residuals from the two structural equations that underlie this model are shown in Appendix Table A; they are summarized by broad occupational categories in Table 3, in which the results for the two years are pooled. (Even a casual inspection of Table A reveals that the results for the two years are quite similar; consequently, when the results are pooled, the observations are not, strictly speaking, independent of each other. For this reason, no tests of significance are provided in the discussion that-follows.)

The most relevant feature of Table 3 in the present context is the column that deals with the prestige residuals. The prestige equation contains measures of the income and education levels of occupations as predictors; consequently, the residuals from this equation effectively summarize the difference between a prestige score and a socioeconomic indicator of occupational status. Table 3 reveals that these differences are organized according to broad occupational categories involving somewhat different types of work. Relative to a socioeconomic index composed of the median income and the percentage of high school graduates in an occupation, prestige scores assign relatively higher positions in the occupational hierarchy to managerial and craft occupations and relatively lower ones to clerical, sales, and service occupations. The

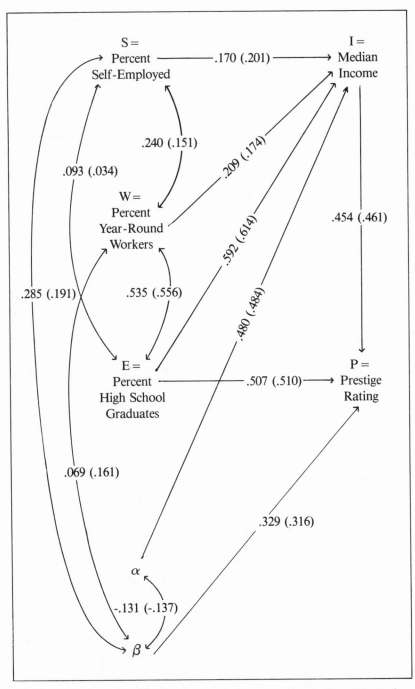

Figure 1. A Model of Prestige and Income Determination for Occupations

Table 3
Summary of Residuals from Regressions for Prestige and Income,
by Broad Occupational Category, Pooled Results, 1950 and 1960

| | Number of | Residuals From | |
Total	Cases	Income Equation	Prestige Equation
		Percentage Positive	
Total, All Cases	122	42.6	48.4
Managerial	14	64.3	85.7
Professional	42	38.1	47.6
Clerical and Sales	10	0.0	0.0
Craftsmen	12	100.0	100.0
Operatives and Laborers	22	54.5	31.8
Service	18	16.7	22.2
Farm	4	0.0	100.0

Source: Computed from Appendix Table A.

pattern of results in Table 3 also indicates that the broad occupational categories whose constituent occupations are likely to receive a prestige surplus or deficit relative to their socioeconomic status are also those whose constituent detailed occupations are also more likely to receive an income surplus or deficit relative to that expected on the basis of the relative numbers of year-round employees, self-employed workers, and high school graduates in them.

Another striking feature of Table 3 is the movement of the residuals within the blue-collar and white-collar sectors. In both groups, the fraction of occupations with positive residuals declines with the skill or authority level of the work done within them. These results suggest the possibility of at least a dual hierarchy of labor in which a "surplus" of rewards is governed by those occupations at the "top" of the hierarchies of manual and nonmanual labor. This result is obtained in the white-collar sector only by transposing the usual order of managers and professionals. Such a transposition, however, is consistent with the authority positions of members of these two groups in core industries. Also, one needs to remember that the category "professional" is extremely diverse, spanning even in this data set the spectrum from college professors to playground directors. (See Appendix Table A.)

The numerical values of the residuals from the prestige and income equations of the model depicted in Figure 1 will be uncorrelated over the

61 detailed occupations to which the results pertain if the model is correctly specified.[8] The modest association observed in Figure 1 between the two sets of residuals comes about only because the self-employment (S) and weeks worked (W) variables enter the equation for income, but not the equation for prestige. The results in Table 3, of course, do not refer to the numerical values of the residuals, but to their classification according to sign. Nonetheless, there is but a scant relationship between them. The value of Yule's Q between occupations with a prestige increment or deficit and those with an income increment or deficit is a modest 0.124.

A somewhat different picture emerges, however, when the 61 occupations are classified into broad occupational categories as shown in Table 4. (The reader should remember that the number of cases is 122 rather than 61 since the results from the two periods have been pooled.) Among professional and managerial occupations, there is an inverse relationship between the prestige and income residuals—that is, occupations with a

Table 4

Relationships between Residuals from Prestige and Income Equations Within Broad Occupational Categories, 1950 and 1960

Broad Occupational Category	Total	Prestige Residuals		Number Of Cases	Yule's Q
		Positive	Negative		
		Percent Distribution			
Total, All Occupations	100.0	48.4	51.6	122	
Income Residual Positive	100.0	51.9	48.1	52	.124
Income Residual Negative	100.0	45.7	54.3	70	
Professional and Managerial	100.0	57.6	42.4	58	
Income Residual Positive	100.0	48.0	52.0	25	−.368
Income Residual Negative	100.0	66.7	33.3	33	
Clerical, Sales, and Crafts	100.0	54.5	45.5	22	
Income Residual Positive	100.0	100.0	0.0	12	1.000
Income Residual Negative	100.0	0.0	100.0	10	
Operatives, Service, and Laborers	100.0	31.0	69.0	42	
Income Residual Positive	100.0	20.0	80.0	15	−.404
Income Residual Negative	100.0	37.0	63.0	27	

N.B. "Farmers, owners, and tenants" are included in the "professional and mangerial" category, while "farm laborers, wage workers" are placed among "operatives, service, and laborers."

Source: Computed from Appendix Table A.

prestige increment tend to have an income deficit and vice versa. The same holds true among the lower level blue-collar occupations: operatives, service workers, and laborers. This result is reasonably consistent with the functional theory of stratification, wherein prestige and income are seen as alternative types of rewards that can be substituted or exchanged for each other so long as the total reward package of an occupation remains unchanged. Given a fixed reward level for an occupation, those with relatively more income than expected on the basis of the determinants of income ought on the average to receive relatively less prestige than expected on the basis of the determinants of occupational prestige and vice versa. What is gained in prestige is lost in income and vice versa: socially respected occupations, *ceteris paribus*, need not be remunerated to the same extent as socially disreputable ones. Although the relationship is far from perfect, this situation appears to characterize the occupations falling at the extrema of the occupational hierarchy.

At the center of the occupational hierarchy, around the division between manual and blue-collar workers, a quite different relationship appears between the prestige and income increments and deficits of occupations. Here the relationship for the limited set of occupations available for analysis is perfectly positive: those in skilled craft occupations receive both more income and more prestige than expected from their determinants, while those in lower level white-collar occupations are shortchanged in both these commodities. Relative to the presumed causes of occupational income and prestige levels, the lower tier of white-collar occupations is deprived, while the upper tier of blue-collar occupations are distinctly advantaged by these same criteria. This is, we believe, impressive and novel evidence of the dual processes of "embourgeoisment" among manual occupations and proletarianization among white-collar positions. Interestingly enough, Wright's effort (n.d.) to chart the class distribution of the labor force by major occupation group reveals a parallel observation. His classification (n.d., Tables 3 and pp. 26–29) of work positions into a system of class arrangements based on Marxist considerations reveals that less than a third of those classified as craftsmen, foremen, and kindred workers are "workers" in the traditional sense, while more than half of clerical and sales workers can be designated in this way.

In view of the limited number of occupations available for this analysis, it would be misleading to regard the present results as anything but suggestive of possible ways in which the reward structures of detailed occupations differing in the general character of the work they involve can diverge. How, if in any way, these features of occupations are involved in the mobility between occupations, in the levels of poverty characteristic of occupations, in their attractiveness to workers, in the supply of workers for occupations, and the demand for their services are largely unexplored issues.

One would think issues such as these might hold center stage in the analysis of patterns of inter- and intragenerational occupational mobility, but they have not. For the most part, investigators have been content to summarize detailed occupational information either by resorting to their gross classification into very heterogeneous groups only roughly similar in the type of work characteristic of them or by reducing them to a continuous hierarchical variable and assigning socioeconomic or prestige scores to them. The end result is that we know a great deal about how occupational status is involved in processes of mobility within and between generations, very little about how work is involved in those same processes, and virtually nothing about how the occupational histories of families and individuals are conducive to either chronic poverty or the escape from it.

Missing Variables in the Study of Poverty and Status Attainment

We have already indicated in the preceding section that there are at least ambiguities of interpretation and conception in the way occupational information has been converted for purposes of analysis in the literature on status attainment. This literature is also deficient in other important ways, largely owing to the exclusion of potentially significant variables from the basic specification that informs it. These missing variables are of two kinds: first, there are alternative ways of summarizing occupational information that have not been explored and, second, there are some variables whose role in the process of status attainment remains largely unexamined. In both cases, the missing pieces of information seem of considerable potential importance in understanding the way in which status attainment, and especially occupational attainment, is related to poverty.

Before spelling out in some detail avenues of inquiry, largely unexplored in the status attainment literature but nonetheless relevant to the analysis of poverty, due credit must be given for the analyses that have been carried out in the tradition of status attainment research launched by Blau and Duncan (1967). Given that one chooses to summarize occupational information with a socioeconomic index and given the variables that have been available for investigation, research on status attainment has, in our judgment, been carried out with an unparalleled degree of technical sophistication and expertise. Researchers have been careful to spell out their procedures in precise detail and they have been attentive to errors of measurement (see especially, Bielby et al. 1977a). One can, in fact, be relatively precise about what else might be done only because extant research on status attainment has been executed with the attention to detail and the careful specification of assumptions characteristic of inquiries of the first rank in quality. The literature on status attainment may be less relevant to the analysis of poverty than it might have been, but one needs to remember that researchers studying status attainment did not set out to understand poverty but to chart the processes governing the intergenerational transmission of occupational status. Owing to their work, we now understand that process very well; the complaints offered here are not criticisms of what real progress has been made. Instead, these comments should be interpreted only as suggestions about how one might proceed if one set forth to understand the relationship between poverty and status attainment—a matter removed from center stage in the status attainment literature.

The characteristics of occupations that contribute to the poverty of their incumbents are not necessarily well summarized by their socioeconomic levels, at least as characteristics of occupations are measured by Duncan's socioeconomic index for all occupations. To be sure, Duncan's index includes an income indicator as one of its components, but it reflects the fraction of individuals—occupation by occupation—falling in roughly the upper third of the income distribution. By comparison, poverty refers to the bottom line of the same distribution; the characteristics that put an occupation toward the upper end of earnings and earnings potential are not necessarily the same as the characteristics that put an occupation toward the lower extreme of the same continuum. Among the characteristics of occupations potentially implemented in the present and/or prospective poverty of their incumbents are the following: (1) the seasonality of the work, (2) the growth stability and potential of the industries in which they are located, (3) the extent of unionization, (4) the security of employment, (5) the opportunity for advancement, (6) illness and medical leave policies and benefits, and (7) health and personal injury hazards encountered on the job. How these characteristics of occupations give rise to occupation-specific rates of poverty is largely unknown, as is their connection with the socioeconomic levels of occupations. Exploring these relationships would appear to be first-order business in any program of research designed to understand how and in what way occupational pursuit is linked to poverty.

Not only is the way in which detailed information is typically coded in the status attainment literature inadequate for understanding the relationship between occupation and poverty, but also a variety of job- and status-related characteristics of potential relevance to poverty have received insufficient attention. Recently, Wright (1976, n.d.) has launched a significant effort to classify the labor force of industrial societies into categories that reflect their location in the economic structure of advanced capitalism. While others have attempted this task in the past, they have tended to base their analyses upon extant statistics rather than upon a thoughtful consideration of the relevant underlying dimensions, which, as Wright indicates, have often gone unmeasured and thus unanalyzed. Among the variables that enter into a classification of the labor force into Marxist class categories are the following: (1) self-employment, (2) number of persons employed, (3) number of employees supervised, (4) type of control over subordinates, (5) type of control by superiors, (6) extent of control over new investments, and (7) control over the organization of work and production. Wright (n.d., pp. 32ff.) provides a set of questions more detailed than these.

As we have noted before, the main focus of research on status attainment has been understanding the intergenerational transmission of occupational status and, especially, specifying the intervening individual-level variables that account for the association between the occupational status of fathers and sons. Beyond that, detailed information about the nature of work that is required to define one's relationship to the means of production is unlikely to be known by an individual's family or associates. Reports by sons about the job autonomy, number of employees, etc. of their fathers are not likely to be reliable; the analysis of intergenerational class mobility almost surely would require interviews with both fathers and sons. Any such inquiry could never refer to the labor force as a whole, owing to the simple demographic fact that there is no single point in time at which all fathers of the persons currently in the labor force are alive.

Nonetheless, there is good reason to suspect that the variables identified by Wright as necessary for defining Marxist class categories are involved in the determination of poverty and perhaps more powerfully implicated in that process than is occupational status. Using a rather crude trichotomous version of class arrangements, Wright and Perrone (1977, p. 43) report for one national sample that "when class is added to the equation containing [occupational] status, the R^2 increases by 7.6 percent, whereas when status is added to the equation containing class, the increase is only 2.3 percent. Status and class alone each explain just over 14 percent of the variance in income. These results are highly suggestive that an extremely simple version of the Marxian class typology is at least as potent a variable in predicting income as the full Duncan socioeconomic scale."

These findings suggest that there is good reason to believe that our understanding of processes of poverty and income determination will remain incomplete so long as the variables that enter into the formation of a classification based on Marxian theory remain uninvestigated. Even if one rejects some aspects of a Marxist-paradigm, such a rejection does not deny that variables included in that paradigm—like self-employment, number of workers employed or supervised, job autonomy, etc.—may be implicated in income determination.

Quite apart from the general neglect of variables central to the determination of one's class position, the literature on status attainment is flawed in several other significant ways. Occupation and industry, for example, are analytically distinct bases of the division of labor, occupations being collections of jobs whose tasks are similar and industries being collections of jobs (or work organizations) whose products are similar. Yet, simple as this distinction may be, it is severely confounded in the literature on status attainment. Except for some unpublished work by Lane and an important contribution by Hauser and Featherman (1977), little attention has been paid in the status attainment literature to inter- and intragenerational interindustry mobility. Indeed, Duncan's socioeconomic index for all occupations in fact confounds these two variables, since it is based on a scheme of occupational classification that subdivides gross occupational groups such as managers, sales workers, operatives, and unskilled laborers according to their industrial affiliations. Consequently, there is no certain way of knowing to what extent the father-to-son and other correlations reported in the status attainment literature are the product of purely occupational inheritance and stability or the product of industrial inheritance and stability.

Hodge (1962) has shown that the socioeconomic levels of managers, operatives, and laborers are differentiated across industries; furthermore, he shows that those industries in which one of these occupational groups is relatively advantaged are also the industries in which the others are similarly advantaged. In view of this evidence, there seems to be little question that industry is a potentially important dimension of social stratification. There are several reasons for this. First, the demography of the labor force dictates that most fathers cannot, in any literal sense, endow their sons with their own jobs for the simple reason that they are still working when their sons enter the labor force. Thus, a likely mechanism whereby fathers can advance the occupational careers of their offspring is through their organizational or industrial connections. Second, many of the features of occupations that drive their incumbents to poverty are derivative from their industrial location, for injury rates, health benefits, employment security, seasonality, etc. are more nearly characteristics of certain industries than of occupations per se. Disentangling the industrial component of occupational mobility and establishing the contributions of both industry and occupation to permanent income levels would appear to be the first order of business in a program of research designed to illuminate the causes of poverty in contemporary industrial societies.

Although the individual-level determinants of income have long been of concern in research on status attainment, rather less attention has been paid to intra- and intergenerational income mobility. In part this situation has resulted from the presumed inability of respondents to report their parent's or father's earnings reliably or to recall their own wage histories. There are, of course, bodies of data relevant to this topic, but they have not been as exploited as they might be for what light they could shed on income mobility—especially the linkage between occupational and earnings shifts over the career cycle. The National Longitudinal Surveys and the Panel Study of Income Dynamics would seem especially valuable in this regard.

A significant exception to the general neglect of income mobility in research on status attainment is found in the work of Treiman and Hauser (1977), who are able to put meaningful limits on the likely impact of parental income on son's income. Carefully pointing out the limitations of their exercise, they conclude (1977, pp. 301–302),

> The extent of income mobility is no less than that of occupational or educational mobility, father's income accounts for no more than 15% to 25% of the variance in son's income, which is comparable to the proportion of variance in son's occupational status explained by father's occupational status and the proportion of variance in son's educational attainment explained by father's education. Whatever the exigencies of life which make successes or failures of men, it is clear that their social origins are of modest importance, at least in comparison with the host of factors which do not vary systematically with social origins.

This conclusion and the estimates upon which it is based strike us, when taken together with the models elaborated by Bielby et al. (1977a, 1977b), as ample grounds for rejecting the significance attributed to parental income by some writers (see, e.g., Bowles 1972, Bowles and Gintis 1976, also, Heyns 1978 for a review of the issues at stake). Knowing that individual background variables do not account for much of the variance in income still leaves considerable room for further research on what does explain individual differences in wealth and income as well as the variance in earnings.

In closing this section, one additional point is worthy of mention. While educational and occupational attainment have received rather more attention in the literature on socioeconomic attainment than has either income or poverty status, it is important to remember, as noted above, that most current income is derived from one's occupational pursuit. Thus, the literature dealing with occupational attainment has an obvious bearing upon questions of poverty. Indeed, it is even possible that occupation, rather than current income, is, in fact, the better indicator of one's potential for drifting into or remaining securely removed from poverty. The reason for this is that occupation may be an excellent indicator of permanent income, while current income figures can conceal a transitory component of considerable magnitude.

Poverty Programs and Status Attainment: Some Connections

A major theme of this essay has been that research on status attainment, as it has been developed in the United States by Blau, Duncan, Hauser, Featherman, and others, has little direct bearing upon poverty. As we have already explained, this stems both from the peculiar characteristics of poverty as a socioeconomic variable and from the interest of students of status attainment in understanding the intergenerational transmission of occupational status rather than economic resources. Nonetheless, there is a very important connection between research on status attainment and the national effort to combat poverty in the United States. This relationship derives in large measure from the very nature of programs designed to attack poverty.

Many programs designed to eliminate poverty or to alleviate its effects on subsequent generations essentially seek cures at the family level for what can be regarded as structural problems. Rather than, for example, reforming the allocation of wages to jobs, they redress the problem by allocating welfare to families with insufficient income, retraining workers for jobs they don't have but might get, and by providing special programs for youth from disadvantaged backgrounds. They do not attack the socioeconomic system that produces poverty, but the capacity of those whose fortunes have put them in it.

Regardless of what one thinks of such major efforts to alleviate poverty as welfare programs, job retraining efforts, and educational innovations like Head Start, it is evident that among the primary effects they are presumed to have are those that operate on the process of status attainment. Sewell and Hauser (1975) have shown, for example, that parental income influences postsecondary schooling among a cohort of nonfarm Wisconsin high school graduates. On the basis of this evidence, it is not unreasonable to assume that parental income in general influences the educational attainment of their offspring. If this is so, then welfare payments may not only enable families to maintain a current standard of living above their means, but also may raise the probabilities that their children will complete high school and possibly college in the future.

Programs like Head Start and those concerned with job training are involved in the educational and occupational attainment of those participating in them; no one would support these programs if their effects in these regards were not presumed to be salutary. Any effort to evaluate these programs, then, involves a model of status attainment, for the comparison of the socioeconomic outcomes of participants in these programs relative to a matched (or statistically controlled) sample of non-beneficiaries enables one to assess the impact of social interventions of this kind. Much of this evaluative work remains to be done and little of it has been undertaken by students of status attainment; however, it is also the case that it is premature to evaluate many of the programs initiated to attack poverty, since the cohorts affected by them are still establishing their careers. Nonetheless, we believe that any student of poverty should have a permanent interest in processes of status attainment, even if the literature on that subject has not yet regarded poverty as an outcome variable, because the success of efforts to reduce poverty will be registered in processes of status attainment. Through the study of these processes the impact of such programs is most likely to be detected and potential ways of improving them may be uncovered.

We may close this section by noting that at least one major thesis concerning the generation of poverty is largely undercut by the status attainment literature. We refer, of course, to the so-called culture of poverty. Although the concept of culture has various meanings, we believe that most definitions make reference, explicitly or implicitly, to a core of values that are widely shared by the members of a culture and are transmitted without major change from generation to generation. The literature on status attainment leaves no doubt whatsoever that a culture of poverty in the foregoing sense cannot possibly characterize the vast majority of persons who are in poverty in the contemporary United States.[9]

Although they do not address the question save in passing, the evidence for the above conclusion is contained in a series of unrelated papers by Hodge (1966), Duncan (1968), and Featherman and Hauser (1976a), among others. The basic argument, not elaborated here, rests on the substantial volume of both inter- and intragenerational occupational mobility that has been documented in the United States. In this context, it is important to remember that we are talking about a world in which no more than 15–25 percent of the variance in any socioeconomic characteristic is shared between fathers and sons. Consequently, one can only conclude that, as between generations, there must be considerable mobility both into and out of any hypothetical culture of poverty. This is plainly inconsistent with the idea that a culture perpetuates itself via the intergenerational transmission of values. The values associated with any culture of poverty in the United States must necessarily be fluid enough to allow many to escape from it and others to sink into it. But, if that is so, one can seriously wonder whether there is any such culture at all, given what is commonly meant by that concept.

The available data on intragenerational occupational mobility and the sparse information on intragenerational income mobility lead one to the same conclusion: people must be moving in and out of poverty all the time, not just between, but within generations. Life-cycle variation in poverty and related features of the socioeconomic position of families and their members remain important subjects for further research. Analyses of such longitudinal data sets as the Sewell study of Wisconsin high school graduates, the National Longitudinal Surveys, and the Panel Study of Income Dynamics can shed light on this topic, but none of these data sets is comprehensive.[10]

Summary and Discussion

In this paper we have examined some of the relationships between poverty and status attainment, with special attention to the implications of research on the latter topic for our understanding of the former. The main themes around which the paper has been organized are as follows:

1. As a status attainment variable, poverty has some very unusual properties, essentially combining in its numerator and denominator variables—income and children ever born—that can be thought to be causally related to each other. This characteristic helps to explain why poverty has been largely ignored in the study of status attainment.
2. There are features of occupation, other than their socioeconomic status as measured by educational and income levels, that are relevant to the actual and potential poverty levels of their incumbents.
3. A number of variables seemingly implicated in the generation of poverty have been largely ignored in the analysis of status attainment. These include, for example, industrial affiliation, job security, and occupational hazards.

4. Finally, even though the literature on status attainment does not bear directly upon poverty, it remains relevant to the analysis of poverty programs insofar as these are designed to affect socioeconomic outcomes.

In sum, the literature on status attainment has surely enlightened our understanding of the processes governing the intergenerational transmission and intragenerational maintenance of socioeconomic status. However, viewed as a program of research designed to illuminate the causes of poverty, the research on status attainment has made a contribution that is, in our view, at best marginal. This judgment should not detract from the real achievements in the research on status attainment.

The issues addressed in the present review of the relationship between poverty and status attainment implicitly harbor some much more fundamental questions about the bases of social and economic inequality in societies such as our own. In particular, one of the enduring sources of conflict in our society is the interface between the family, on one hand, and the economy, on the other. Families are, for the most part, the primary suppliers of labor. However, the labor they supply competes primarily at the individual level in the marketplace, where the outcome of the competition for jobs is a major factor in determining the distribution of rewards. Consumption, however, for most people is not an individual but a family matter. There is inevitable tension—and poverty is but one result of that tension—in a system that distributes rewards to individuals who are the major source of sustenance for collectivities, to wit, families.

Students of status attainment, as well as those of human capital, have simplified the intellectual problems they address by assuming that families do not exist, a complication that, as has been shown, must enter into any effort to understand the causes of poverty. While this research strategy needs to be abandoned if the socioeconomic locations of families, rather than individuals, is to become the centerpiece of research on social and economic inequality, an analysis of its intellectual justifications provides an additional insight into why the literatures on poverty and on status attainment have not converged. Consideration of this matter requires a brief review of the structural changes associated with the development of industrial capitalism in the western historical experience.

In precapitalist societies, production was organized primarily for consumption; it took place within a local context and the major unit of production was the family. The division of labor occurred within the family, although for certain purposes and at certain seasons of the year, such as at harvest time, it might extend to the local community. With the development of capitalism, material goods came to be produced in a more highly differentiated and specialized system of social organization; the division of labor occurs on a societal or world level rather than a local or familial one.

As a consequence of these changes, the family is no longer the appropriate unit for understanding the immediate process of production. Instead, the individual wage worker, operating within a competitive market system, is the producing unit. An argument can therefore reasonably be made that knowledge of the process by which individual producers are distributed within the system of production is important for understanding the operation of that system. Thus, the status attainment model and its focus on the placement of individuals within varying occupational or socioeconomic positions can be seen as reflecting one aspect of the system of production itself.

Poverty, however, cannot be understood in terms of a system of production based on individual wage labor alone. Questions need to be asked not only about the production of individual income but also about its distribution and aggregation in families as well as factors related to fertility, family formation and dissolution. Given their potential interdependence, as has already been suggested, these factors need to be modeled independently.[11] While the status attainment model accurately reflects one dimension of the social organization of production—that it is based on individual wage labor—the explicit variables included in it account for only a modest fraction of the variation in the distribution of income or family size.

Researchers in the field of status attainment, and those investigating the human capital perspective as well, rest their analyses of income and fertility on the impact of individual attributes. The economic value of these attributes ought, so it seems to us, to be conditioned by the characteristics of the labor market in which they are sold. There is, however, an accumulating body of empirical evidence that suggests that the distribution of income cannot be adequately explained by individual characteristics alone. A recent analysis by Beck et al. (1978), for instance, suggests that the income return to the individual for varying levels of educational attainment, as well as the probability of being in poverty, differs depending on the sector of the economy in which those achievements are sold. Thus, the nature, degree, and causes of labor market segmentation need to be included in any analysis of the status attainment process.

The literature on labor market segmentation, which has been developed primarily by economists (see, for instance, Edwards et al.1975), cannot be reviewed here. Findings from it suggest, however, that the distribution of individual attributes is inadequate to account for the distribution of income. Not only is it necessary to independently model processes of family formation and income distribution within a potentially segmented labor market, but it is also necessary to model the process of labor market segmentation itself. Without considering these questions, an adequate causal explanation of status attainment or poverty will not be achieved.

Appendix

Table A
Residuals From Regressions Over 61 Detailed Census Occupational Groups Matching NORC Occupational Titles

Census Detailed Occupational Group (NORC Title)	Income Residuals[a]		Prestige Residuals[b]	
	1950	1960	1950	1960
Professional, technical, and kindred workers (mean residual)	- 65	- 51	0.1	-0.2
Accountants and auditors (Accountant for a large business)	- 518	-1,028	2.2	1.6
Airline pilots and navigators (Airline pilot)	944	3,059	- 1.1	- 2.7
Architects (Architect)	736	428	- 0.8	2.5
Artists and art teachers (Artist who paints pictures that are exhibited in galleries)[c]	- 591	- 808	8.2	1.5
Authors (Author of novels)	- 540	-1,074	1.0	- 1.7
Chemists (Chemist)	- 370	- 451	6.1	7.7
Clergymen (Minister)	-1,950	-3,428	17.2	15.0
College presidents, professors, and instructors, n.e.c. (College professor)	243	391	6.6	6.9
Dentists (Dentist)	1,235	3,570	- 6.8	- 7.6
Editors and reporters (Reporter on a daily newspaper)	125	- 521	-11.1	- 9.0
Engineers, civil (Civil engineer)	232	297	2.8	4.6
Farm and home management advisors (County agricultural agent)[c]	- 543	-1,727	- 3.6	- 3.2
Funeral directors and embalmers (Undertaker)	-1,289	-1,891	0.2	- 0.8
Lawyers and judges (Lawyer)	1,115	2,238	- 5.7	- 3.7

Musicians and music teachers (Musician in a symphony orchestra, Singer in a night club)c	– 610	–1,200	– 1.9	– 4.8
Natural scientists, n.e.c. (Scientists, Government scientist, Nuclear physicist, Biologist)c,d	– 209	– 87	5.5	6.8
Physicians and surgeons (Physician)	3,149	6,127	– 8.5	– 9.4
Recreation and group workers (Playground director)c	–1,069	–2,268	– 8.4	– 9.1
Social and welfare workers, except group (Welfare worker for a city government)	–1,012	–1,743	– 1.3	– 1.7
Social scientists (Psychologist, Sociologist, Economist)c	0	77	1.0	– 0.1
Teachers (Instructor in the public schools)d	– 433	–1,039	1.4	3.9
Managers, officials, and proprietors, except farm (mean residual)	*460*	*496*	*3.8*	*2.8*
Conductors, railroad (Railroad conductor)	1,768	3,008	1.5	– 1.0
Managers, officials, and proprietors, n.e.c., self-employed:				
—Construction (Building contractor)	48	– 246	11.6	10.9
—Eating and drinking places (Owner of a lunch stand)c	– 659	–1,515	0.4	0.9
—Manufacturing (Owner of a factory that employs about 100 people)	286	526	8.3	5.9
Managers, officials, and proprietors, n.e.c., self-employed and salaried, combined:				
—Banking and other finance (Banker)c	1,319	986	3.0	2.5
—Retail trade (Manager of a small store in a city)c	– 434	–1,208	3.2	0.2
Officials, lodge, society, and union (Official of an international union, Official of a local union)c	891	1,920	– 1.5	0.3

Table A continued

Census Detailed Occupational Group (NORC Title)	Income Residuals[a]		Prestige Residuals[b]	
	1950	1960	1950	1960
Clerical and kindred workers and sales workers (mean residual)	- 492	-1,041	- 4.0	- 4.7
Bookkeepers (Bookkeeper)	-1,146	-2,041	- 2.4	- 0.6
Insurance agents and brokers (Insurance agent)	- 288	- 778	- 5.9	- 6.2
Mail carriers (Mail carrier)	- 108	- 757	- 2.7	- 3.6
Salesmen and sales clerks, n.e.c., Retail trade (Clerk in a store)	- 816	-1,412	- 5.1	- 6.7
Salesmen and sales clerks, n.e.c., Wholesale trade (Traveling salesman for a wholesale concern)[c]	- 103	- 215	- 4.0	- 6.5
Craftsmen, foremen, and kindred workers (mean residual)	793	1,476	7.9	8.0
Carpenters (Carpenter)	506	1,062	9.5	10.6
Electricians (Electrician)	508	1,161	8.0	9.0
Locomotive engineers (Railroad engineer)	2,308	3,674	11.3	8.6
Machinists (Trained machinist)	525	1,107	11.1	11.6
Mechanics and repairmen, automobile (Automobile repairman)	33	187	5.3	5.9
Plumbers and pipefitters (Plumber)	880	1,663	2.2	2.6
Operatives and kindred workers (mean residual)	166	272	- 2.9	- 2.9
Attendants, auto service and parking (Filling-station attendant)	- 586	-1,063	- 3.2	- 2.4
Laundry and dry-cleaning operatives (Clothes-presser in a laundry)[c]	- 422	- 838	- 8.8	- 8.8

Mine operatives and laborers, n.e.c., coal mining (Coal miner)	1,019	518	– 2.5	– 8.0
Motormen, street, subway and elevated railway (Streetcar motorman)	634	1,445	– 3.1	– 4.2
Taxicab-drivers and chauffers (Taxi-driver)	– 117	– 105	– 5.3	– 5.2
Truck and tractor-drivers (Truck-driver)	175	896	– 1.0	3.0
Operatives and kindred workers, n.e.c., manufacturing (Machine-operator in a factory)	457	1,049	3.3	5.0
Service workers, except private household (mean residual)	– 362	– 585	– 5.4	– 3.6
Barbers, beauticians, and manicurists (Barber)	– 571	– 868	3.9	6.5
Bartenders (Bartender)	– 111	– 592	–13.7	– 9.8
Bootblacks (Shoe-shiner)	–1,102	–1,259	–10.5	– 8.5
Cooks, except private household (Restaurant cook)	24	– 126	– 0.4	– 0.2
Counter and fountain workers (Soda fountain clerk)	– 689	–1,455	– 7.9	– 7.9
Janitors and sextons (Janitor)	– 220	– 106	– 7.2	– 3.9
Guards, watchmen, and doorkeepers (Night watchman)	174	503	– 8.2	– 6.7
Policemen and detectives, govt. (Policeman)	– 151	– 52	1.2	3.8
Waiters and waitresses (Restaurant waiter)	– 609	–1,308	– 6.2	– 5.9
Laborers, except farm and mine (mean residual)	*134*	*434*	*– 0.7*	*+ 0.0*
Fishermen and oystermen (Fisherman who owns his own boat)[c]	– 293	– 613	8.8	7.7
Longshoremen and stevedores (Dock worker)[c]	964	2,448	– 6.2	– 5.9
Lumbermen, raftsmen, and woodchoppers (Lumberjack)[c]	– 198	– 346	6.6	7.7
Laborers, n.e.c., non-manufacturing industries, including industry not reported (Railroad section hand, Garbage collector, Street-sweeper)[c]	64	248	–11.9	– 9.3

Farm owners, managers, laborers, and foremen (mean residual)	-1,300	-2,210	7.8	5.8
Farmers, owners and tenants (Farm-owner and operator, Tenant farmer, Sharecropper)c	-1,783	-3,501	11.5	9.6
Farm laborers, wage workers (Farm hand)c	- 818	- 919	4.1	2.1

aResiduals from regression of median income on per cent high school graduates, per cent self-employed, and per cent working 50–52 weeks of the male experienced civilian labor force for 61 census detailed occupational groups matching NORC occupational titles.

bResiduals from regression of prestige on per cent high school graduates and median income of the male experienced civilian labor force for 61 census detailed occupational groups matching NORC occupational titles.

cNORC title judged a poor or partial match with census detailed occupational group, according to matchings effected by O.D. Duncan, "A Socioeconomic Index For All Occupations," in A.J. Reiss, Jr., *Occupations and Social Status* (New York: The Free Press of Glencoe, 1961). Tables VI-1 and VI-2, pp. 122–126.

dDetailed titles identified in 1960 census adjusted to match categories employed in 1950 census. (Census titles in table are 1950 titles.)

Notes

1. For an elaboration of this point in the context of nineteenth-century England, see Humphries (1977).
2. Although the number of jobs is primarily determined by employers, unions are also parties to the determination of the supply of jobs in some industries. Unions are actors in many situations discussed in this paper, but we have largely ignored their role because (1) the evidence about their impact is less than complete or satisfactory, and (2) we are ourselves divided over the question of their significance. See, for example, Lewis (1963), Lipset and Gordon (1953), and Hicks et al. (1978) for a sampling of research examining the effects of unions in different situations.
3. There are, or course, cases in which there is some flexibility in earnings, depending upon the qualifications of a prospective employee or the performance of an existing one, but in most occupational pursuits the range over which income is negotiable is quite narrow. Among the exceptions are salespeople whose earnings are tied to commissions, executives whose bonuses are pegged to profits, piece rate workers whose pay is linked directly to their productivity, and, possibly, workers in highly unionized industries. However, even in these cases, the employer, not the employee, establishes the relevant percentage shares and piece rates.
4. Alternative ways of measuring poverty may reveal different amounts of change. Also, it should be noted that there has been little change but quite possibly some increase in the level of poverty since 1973. For the movement of alternative indicators see Plotnick and Skidmore (1977).
5. Other factors also enter into the determination of poverty. For example, family income obviously has sources other than the earnings of family members. These include, for instance, income from property, investments and transfer payments. This makes the analysis even more problematical in the context of status attainment. The reason is that one presumably needs different equations for the various types of family income. Students of status attainment have been concerned primarily with the analysis of individual earnings. Other factors than fertility are involved in the determination of family size as well. These include divorce, separation, mortality, marriages of children, and the doubling-up of nuclear family units.
6. Formally, one can represent membership in a detailed occupational category by a series of dummy variables, each taking on the value of 1 if the person is in a particular detailed occupation and the value of 0 otherwise. Since there are over 400 detailed occupations, one would need over 400 such dummy variables to describe detailed occupational pursuit. To be precise, one less dummy variable than the number of detailed occupational categories would be needed since if an individual

who holds an occupation is not a member of the first $m-1$ of m detailed occupations, he or she is necessarily a member of the mth category. Scoring detailed occupations with a continuous index like Duncan's SE1 scale reduces the 400-odd dummy variables needed to describe a person's detailed occupation to a single variable.

7. Of the 61 detailed census occupations with matching titles in the North-Hatt inquiry, 45 have good matches. These were used by Duncan in constructing his index. An additional 16 detailed occupations have more approximate matching prestige scores. Duncan (1961b) shows, however, that their scatter about the regression of prestige on his education and income indicators is about the same as that observed for the 45 titles with good matches. Consequently, we have used all 61 occupations in this analysis.

8. It might be argued that the model in hand is misspecified because allowance has been made neither for the racial nor sex composition of occupations—factors known to affect income at the individual level and surely likely to affect evaluations of occupations that are sexually and racially coded. Neglect of these factors is potentially important because they could explain the pattern of residuals discussed below. In defense of the specification in hand, we may note, however, that in a cross-sectional analysis of more detailed occupations, Siegel (1971) found that an increase in the fraction female among the experienced civilian labor force of an occupation by one percent yielded an increase (!) of less than one-fiftieth of a prestige point—the range of the prestige scale being about 70. He also found a decrement of about seven one-hundreths of a point associated with a similar rise in the relative numbers of blacks in an occupation. Meyer (1978) found a relationship between prestige ratings and an occupation's sex composition only among male raters; the effect is in the expected direction, but it is quite small. Furthermore, Hodge and Hodge (1965) found only negligible consequences of racial and sexual composition for occupational income levels and even the small effects they reported were seriously questioned by Taeuber et al. (1966).

9. This critique of the culture of poverty thesis does not rule out the possibility that there are small and possibly isolated segments of the society that are caught up in a cultural milieu conducive to persistent poverty. The critique does imply, however, that, if such groups exist, and doubtless they do, they are numerically insignificant.

10. Cross-sectional data can also shed light on this subject. See Dubnoff (1978) for an analysis of the adequacy of individual incomes between 1860 and 1974.

11. When we speak of modeling these factors independently, we do not mean that they cannot appear in the same system of equations or that they are not potential causes of each other. We mean only that it is an analytical error to prejudge the outcome of these possibilities by a priori combining income and family size into an index of poverty.

References

Beck, E.M., Horan, P.M., and Tolbert, C.M., II. (1978) Stratification in a dual economy: a sectorial model of earnings determination. *American Sociological Review* 43:704–720.

Bielby, W.T., Hauser, R.M., and Featherman, D.L. (1977a) Response errors of black and nonblack males in models of the intergenerational transmission of socioeconomic status. *American Journal of Sociology* 82:1242–1288.

Bielby, W.T., Hauser, R.M., and Featherman, D.L. (1977b) Response errors of nonblack males in models of the stratification process. Pp. 227–252 in D.J. Aigner and A.S. Goldberger, eds., *Latent Variables in Socioeconomic Models*. Amsterdam: North Holland.

Blau, P.M., and Duncan, O.D. (1967) *The American Occupational Structure*. New York: John Wiley.

Bowles, S. (1972) Schooling and inequality from generation to generation. *Journal of Political Economy* 80:S219–S251.

Bowles, S., and Gintis, H. (1976) *Schooling in Capitalist America: Educational Reform and the Contradictions of Economic Life*. New York: Basic Books.

Dubnoff, S. (1978) Long Term Trends in the Adequacy of Individual Incomes in the United States: 1860–1974. Paper delivered at the Annual Meetings of the Social Science History Association, Columbus, Ohio.

Duncan, O.D. (1961a) Properties and characteristics of the socioeconomic index. Pp. 139–161 in A.J. Reiss, Jr., et al., *Occupations and Social Status*. New York: The Free Press of Glencoe.

Duncan, O.D. (1961b) A socioeconomic index for all occupations. Pp. 109–138 in A.J. Reiss, Jr., et al., *Occupations and Social Status*. New York: The Free Press of Glencoe.

Duncan, O.D. (1968) Inheritance of poverty or inheritance of race? Pp. 85–110 in Daniel P. Moynihan, ed., *On Understanding Poverty: Perspectives from the Social Sciences*. New York: Basic Books.

Duncan, O.D., Featherman, D.L., and Duncan, B. (1972) *Socioeconomic Background and Achievement*. New York: Seminar.

Edwards, R.C., Reich, M., and Gordon, D.M., eds. (1975) *Labor Market Segmentation*. Lexington, Mass.: D.C. Heath and Co.

Featherman, D.L., and Hauser, R.M. (1975) Design for a replicate study of social mobility in the United States. Pp. 219–251 in Kenneth C. Land and Seymour Spilerman, eds., *Social Indicator Models*. New York: Russell Sage Foundation.

Featherman, D.L., and Hauser, R.M. (1976a) Changes in the socioeconomic stratification of the races, 1962–1973. *American Journal of Sociology* 82:621–651.

Featherman, D.L., and Hauser, R.M. (1976b) Prestige or socioeconomic scales in the study of occupational achievement? *Sociological Methods and Research* 4:403–422.

Hauser, R.M., and Featherman, D.L. (1974) Socioeconomic achievements of U.S. men, 1962-1972. *Science* 185:325-331.

Hauser, R.M., and Featherman, D.L. (1977) *The Process of Stratification: Trends and Analyses.* New York: Academic.

Hauser, R.M., Koffel, J.N., Travis, H.P., and Dickinson, P.J. (1975) Temporal change in occupational mobility: evidence for men in the United States. *American Sociological Review* 40:279-297.

Heyns, B.L. (1978) Review essay on Bowles and Gintis' *Schooling in Capitalist America. American Journal of Sociology.* 83:999-1006.

Hicks, A.M., Friedland, R., and Johnson, E.D. (1978) Class power and state policy: the case of large business corporations, labor unions and governmental redistribution in the American states. *American Sociological Review* 43:302-315.

Hodge, R.W. (1962) The status consistency of occupational groups. *American Sociological Review* 27:336-343.

Hodge, R.W. (1966) Occupational mobility as a probability process. *Demography* 3(1):19-34.

Hodge, Robert W., and Hodge, Patricia (1965) Occupational assimilation as a competitive process, *American Journal of Sociology* 71:249-264.

Hodge, R.W., Siegel, P.M., and Rossi, P.H. (1964) Occupational prestige in the United States, 1925-1963. *American Journal of Sociology* 70:286-302.

Humphries, J. (1977) Class struggle and the persistence of the working class family. *Cambridge Journal of Economics* 1:241-258.

Lewis H.G. (1963) *Unionism and Relative Wages in the United States: An Empirical Inquiry.* Chicago: University of Chicago Press.

Lipset, S.M., and Gordon, J. (1953) Mobility and trade union membership. Pp. 491-500 in R. Bendix and S.M. Lipset, eds., *Class, Status, and Power.* Glencoe, Ill.: The Free Press.

Matras, J. (1960) Comparison of intergenerational occupational mobility patterns: an application of the formal theory of social mobility. *Population Studies* 15:163-169.

Meyer, Garry S. (1978) Sex and marriage of raters in the evaluation of occupations. *Social Science Research* 7:366-388.

National Opinion Research Center (1947) Jobs and occupations: a popular evaluation. *Opinion News* 9:3-13.

Plotnick, R.D., and Skidmore, F. (1977) Progress against poverty: 1964-1974. In M. Zeitlin, ed., *American Society, Inc.* second edition. Chicago: Rand McNally.

Seigel, P.M. (1971) Prestige in the American Occupational Structure. Unpublished Ph.D. dissertation. University of Chicago Library.

Sewell, W.H., and Hauser, R.M. (1975) *Education, Occupation and Earnings: Achievement in the Early Career.* New York: Academic.

Sørensen, A.B. (1975) Models of social mobility. *Social Science Research* 4:65-92.

Sørensen, A.B. (1976) Models and strategies in research on attainment and opportunity. *Social Science Information sur les Sciences Sociales* 15:71–91.

Spilerman, S. (1972) Extensions of the mover-stayer model. *American Journal of Sociology* 78:599–626.

Taeuber, Alma F., Taeuber, Karl E. and Cain, Glen G. (1966) Occupational assimilation and the competitive process: a reanalysis, *American Journal of Sociology* 72:273–285.

Treiman, D.J., and Hauser, R.M. (1977) Intergenerational transmission of income: an exercise in theory construction. Pp. 271–302 in R.M. Hauser and D.L. Featherman, *The Process of Stratification: Trends and Analyses.* New York: Academic.

U.S. Bureau of the Census (1963) *U.S. Census of Population: 1960. Subject Reports. Occupational Characteristics.* Final Report PC(2)-7A. U.S. Government Printing Office, Washington, D.C.

U.S. Bureau of the Census (1973) *Census of Population: 1970: Subject Reports,* Final Report PC(2)-9A, *Low Income Population.* Washington, D.C.: U.S. Department of Commerce.

U.S. Bureau of the Census. (1977) Characteristics of the population below the poverty level: 1975. *Current Population Reports,* Consumer Income, Series P-60, No. 106.

Wright, E.O. (1976) Class boundaries in advanced capitalist societies. *New Left Review* 98:3–41.

Wright, E.O. (n.d.) Class Structure and Occupation: A Research Note. Unpublished Discussion Paper No. 415-77. University of Wisconsin, Institute for Research on Poverty, Madison, Wisconsin.

Wright, E.O., and Peronne, L. (1977) Marxist class categories and income inequality. *American Sociological Review* 42:32–55.

Michael Lipsky

Poverty and Administration: Perspectives on Research

Administration is both an expression of power and the exercise of power. It is an expression of power in the sense that, broadly speaking, administration is the medium through which authorities seek to realize articulated policies. It is an exercise of power in the sense that administrators are themselves endowed with authority (to realize articulated policy), and they exercise authority to realize separate although often related objectives.

Correspondingly, we can identify, at least schematically, two interests that are articulated and manifest in the administrative process. The first is summarized in the initial articulation of policy. The second is identified with the administrative process itself. Out of the practice of administration emerge interests that have a stake in maintaining and enhancing the power of administrators. This is the case not only in the usual sense that administrators have an interest in maintaining their jobs, building the reputation of their agencies, or expanding the scope of their jurisdiction or duties; it is also the case in the sense that administrators have a vital and separate interest in work-related aspects of implementation, such as accomplishing their job expeditiously, maintaining a congenial environment, gaining recognition for individual competence, and receiving material and psychological rewards for tasks associated with their jobs.

The relationship between poverty and administration is political, not only because administration involves the exercise of power, but also because administration involves the systematic allocation of goods and services, utilizing positions of public authority. To say that administration is political is to assert that some people are aided, some harmed, by the structure and behavior of administrative units.[1]

Of particular concern in the study of poverty and administration is the fact that poor people tend to have nonreciprocal relationships with

[Michael Lipsky is professor of political science at the Massachusetts Institute of Technology and director of policy studies of the Legal Services Institute in Boston.]

public agencies and their staffs. Of course the relationship of most citizens to the state and its administrative apparatus tends to be one of dominance and subordination, in theory checked by the diffuse guidance of representative government, the claims of citizens for prompt, fair, and civil treatment, and the ideology of public service. However, poor people and other stigmatized groups more than most tend to be denied the dubious protection of citizen status. They tend to lack alternative opportunities for service, and therefore must utilize government programs or suffer serious deprivation. They are generally excluded from the groups that comprise the reference publics of public officials. And they tend to be ignored by politicians whose interest in appointing administrators responsive to the poor is less than their interest in other sectors of the population.

Programs for the poor tend to be essentially redistributive. During periods of economic growth and expansion the conflict intrinsic in distributive policies may be masked. However, in a period of fiscal scarcity, the conflict between support for programs for the poor and the interests of the middle-class majority becomes distinctly manifest whereas in periods of growth it may have been latent and less acutely felt. For these and other reasons the relationship of poor people to state administrative structures tends to be even less reciprocal than that of more affluent citizens.

The imbalance of the relationship between poor people and administrative structures is perhaps obvious in the case of coercive public institutions such as courts, police departments, or some schools. In these settings the power of the state and its monopoly on the legitimate use of force or the threat of force explicitly reinforces administrative actions. But it is also true of more utilitarian institutions, such as hospitals, welfare offices, and certain aspects of schools, in which poor people obtain goods and services from programs but realistically are not free to reject them.[2] This is the coercive dimension of utilitarian institutions, which raises what one may call the sleeping-under-bridges false paradox. Rich and poor alike may be free to sleep under bridges. Likewise, rich and poor alike may clip coupons or purchase the most expensive legal and medical advice. But if by chance they lack money, their alternatives for service and income are restricted to the social welfare structure of the state.

What criteria allow us thoughtfully to identify issues as appropriate to a research agendum focusing on the relationship between poverty and administration? The answer is implicit in recognizing that the study of administration and poverty is a political study, requiring attention to issues of dominance and subordination among parties in the relationship as well as attention to issues of distributional consequences. We should seek to discover the contributions of administrative structures to the relative subordination or autonomy of poor people and the possible contributions of alternatives or variations in structures to enhancing the political capacity of poor people and their ability to mobilize for collective action. We should seek to discover what difference administrative structures make to the relative well-being of poor people as citizens, clients, and claimants.

To be sure, this approach is not the one taken by those primarily interested in administration as such. But it is surely an appropriate approach for those who are mostly concerned with the poverty side of the poverty-administration nexus. Likewise, it is not the approach of those who would focus on categorical programs nominally directed toward helping poor people, such as public welfare or compensatory education. There are several reasons why focusing on the administration of categorical programs is to be avoided, although there is certainly considerable interest in it.

First, discussing administration by policy area diverts attention from the generic issues involving poor people and administrative systems. For example, we may discover intriguing aspects of welfare administration while failing to direct attention to broader problems of subordination that are inherent in program administration.[3]

Second, intuitively there are few reasons to assume that programs nominally focused on poor people have unique administrative properties in comparison to programs that are not so targeted. Only in the stigma attached to clients does there seem on first examination to be an important difference in the administration of programs targeted toward poverty populations and those that are not. And this difference may affect only an agency's external relations, so that internally the agency resembles those that do not deal with poverty populations (see Cloward and Epstein 1965, Steiner 1971).

Third, it would be a major (if all too common) mistake to focus attention on programs nominally charged with helping poor people when so many agencies vitally affecting poor people ignore or harm their interests. The administration of urban renewal or the draft, for example, had, speaking broadly, substantial negative impacts on poor people, yet they were programs that were publicly dedicated to aiding the poor or honoring norms of administrative neutrality.[4]

In short, administration can substantially contribute to problems of poverty, not simply fail or succeed in alleviating the poverty symptoms they are supposed to address. Indeed, one of the greatest contributions to the study of poverty and administration might simply be to insist that the impact on poor people be calculated and assessed in any major administrative undertaking. At the local level, relocating a neighborhood police station or welfare office, for example, or increasing the reporting requirements of victims for burglaries or clients for welfare eligibility may have potentially significant implications for the distributional consequences of administration. At the national level, one could say the same for changing the educational requirements for admission to the armed services or for subsidizing research on mechanization in agriculture.

The Carter administration's urban policy recognizes that tax, highway, and energy policies have major implications for urban areas and therefore has called for urban impact statements to provide an assessment of the impact of policy proposals on cities. In the same way public policies with no apparent targeting of poverty populations can have significant implications for exacerbating poverty conditions. Public agencies cannot be neatly divided into those that are related to poverty and those that are not. Rather, public agencies are problematically related to poverty, and often they perversely affect poverty in ways to which we could be much more sensitive.

The Individual and Poverty Program Administration

If, as I have argued, the study of the relationship between administration and poverty properly focuses on the political relationship between program administration and citizens, then we should devote attention to those agencies that most apparently impact directly on poor people as individuals. Admittedly public agencies such as the Federal Reserve Board have considerable impact on the lives of poor people by virtue of their impact on inflation and employment. Still, limited funds might best be directed toward research on programs that directly engage the lives of the poor, dispensing benefits and sanctions, and structuring life chances. Such programs are administered by public service agencies whose workers interact directly with poor people in the course of their jobs and who exercise substantial discretion in making decisions about them.

Public service agencies whose workers exercise considerable discretion in the course of their jobs and have extensive interaction with poor people include social welfare agencies, such as public welfare departments and employment security offices; schools and other training and therapeutic institutions, such as drug rehabilitation programs and public hospitals, where transformation or maintenance of the individual is the agency's ostensible purpose; and agencies of judgment and punishment, such as the police and the courts. In these agencies, individual line workers operate at the boundary between administrative structures and citizens,[5] "delivering" policy to citizens either by providing direct services or determining the fit between citizens' characteristics and behavior and the requirements of agency categorization (as in determinations of eligibility for public housing or of probable guilt by police officers).

The relationship between line workers and clients is a dynamic one. Workers' discretion gives them considerable flexibility in policy determinations. And the reactions of clients to workers' judgments and actions are themselves a part of the policy process. The responses of children to teachers' efforts to maintain order and the willingness of citizens to cooperate with police are both the objects of policy as well as a condition of policy.

Elsewhere I have discussed in detail the dynamics of the worker-client relationship in the public agencies I have called street-level bureaucracies (see Lipsky 1979). The important point is that the policy to be delivered consists of the action of line workers. Line workers are relatively free to act with discretion in critical policy areas. Indeed, in important respects it may be observed that line workers essentially "make" policy.

For example, the policy of a police department consists of the aggregrated responses of individual officers to the problems of selective enforcement and appropriate responses to diverse and problematic encounters. The policy of a welfare agency in many ways consists of the responses of individual case workers to large case loads. The "policy" of line workers consists of the aggregation of their responses to the familiar dilemma that they must cope on the job with inadequate resources, overwhelming demands on their time and capabilities, and apparently endless demands for their considered attention. At the same time, other aspects of their jobs, such as lack of clarity in goals, the difficulty of devising measures of job performance, and the relative unimportance of clients in influencing role definitions, contribute to workers' relative freedom from conventional work disciplines.

Thus the clients of street-level bureaucracies are subject to latent agency policies that in many respects are never articulated as the dominant pattern of agency behavior. This tendency in part accounts for the fact that research on policy implementation regularly discovers discrepancies between "official" policy and actual practice. For example, the official policy of a police department may be to respond to citizens fairly and evenhandedly. Yet police officers, confronted on the street with a tense situation in which they must respond quickly and with limited information, may very well stereotype members of minority groups when confronted with what they perceive as questionable behavior. Likewise, teachers may informally place pupils in putative ability "tracks" despite administrative guidelines discouraging formal tracking. Judges may accord importance to the appearance and demeanor of defendants despite public expectations that they will consider only the facts surrounding a crime. (see Rist 1975). Again and again we discover that lower-level line workers effectively distribute the benefits or sanctions of their offices in ways that differ distinctly from officially articulated policy.

Do bureau chiefs of the Federal Bureau of Investigation, acting zealously, engage in questionably legal behavior? Do building inspectors regularly take bribes to speed construction certification? Do life insurance industry mortgage and repair funds, allocated to assist ghetto development, flow primarily to relatively prosperous people and enterprises? Do special education personnel, newly charged with making assessments of childrens' needs on an individualized basis, persist in programming for them in large part on the basis of their own capabilities, needs, and their schools' financial resources? Do legal services lawyers respond to clients in a highly routinized fashion, despite their professional pledge to serve as advocates and to respond fully to their clients' legal needs? They all do indeed.[6] To many administrators it is apparently incredible that accumulated systematic agency biases can be so much at variance with official agency expectations. In a traditional study of administration we would expect to look for the origins of these discrepancies in failures of command and control, and recommend "tighter" organizational procedures, perhaps at the expense of flexibility and innovation. However, in the case of street-level bureaucracies, we should expect instead to understand these discrepancies by examining the consequences of line workers' extensive discretion and relative autonomy in important spheres from the control of superiors.

Distribution, Rationing, and Administration

The first task of research on poverty and administration is to inquire into the nature of street-level policy toward the poor. We are just beginning to recognize that street-level interactions are significant and to recognize that we ought to know much more about the ways in which these interactions are structured. Valuable inquiry into the attitudes of poor people toward agents of government should continue and be encouraged (see Katz et al. 1975, Jacob 1972), but we know very little about actual practices, in terms of which, presumably, citizens' reactions at least in part are formulated. Systematic research on the ways in which housing inspectors, school teachers, and legal services attorneys structure their tasks is most welcome because such work reveals the systematically constructed underlife of public service workers in interactions with clients.

These and other studies enhance our appreciation of the structured nature of street-level policy. They are particularly significant because they seek explanations for discrepancies between official policy and actual practice that do not depend upon sloth or lack of incentives for better performance (compare Nordlinger 1972, Savas and Ginsburg 1973), lack of experience or training, or racial bias (Westley 1970). These explanations may have some validity but they conspicuously detract from examination of the structure of the jobs street-level bureaucrats are asked to perform, and thus deflect attention from what I would regard as a critical area for potential reform and reconstruction.

In seeking systematic information on the nature of street-level practice it is particularly important to recognize the limitations of official statistics and other indicators that tend to be generated by public agencies themselves. Agency data on performance outcomes and rates provide only the most superficial indicators of agency policy, reflecting, as has been observed before, more about the structure and internal dynamics of the agency than about the phenomena they purport to measure (Kitsuse and Circourel 1963). Stated simply, the primary problems with agency-generated data are that they often do not reflect agency performance (e.g., crime rates that say more about the community than about the police); or they are highly responsive to the incentive structures of the agency. Thus, agency personnel may contrive to score well on the indicators while neglecting other features of the job, or to comply spuriously with the measure, as in the case of city marshalls who, instead of delivering summonses, provide "sewer-service," dumping notices while reporting high delivery rates. Most important, perhaps, agencies report data in such a way as to hide the implications of their reports for individual clients, thus making very difficult the assessment of the implications of service for classes of client claimants.

In order to assess the relationship between administration and people in poverty, as I have outlined the problem, one auspicious approach requires observation of the interaction between clients and the administrative agents with whom they come in contact as well as the specific results of these interactions for the clients. These observations should focus on the critical characteristics of the way clients present themselves, combined with observations of client background characteristics and the work environment of the administrative agent. These specific observations should be combined with studied exposure to and mastery of the work problems that line administrators normally have to solve. These data should permit analysis of the contribution of the kind of clients, the actions of clients, and the circumstances experienced by workers to explanations of differential outcomes for clients (if any).

It is important to study the work context of the street-level agent because differential responses to clients may very well be situationally conditioned. For example, in a study of emergency room personnel responses to patrons at Cook County Hospital, Barry Schwartz (1975) discovered that blacks and whites tended to be treated equally if activity was slow or if patients had serious injuries or complaints. However, he observed a significant difference in responses to blacks with nonemergency complaints when the emergency room was crowded.

"Poverty" not only summarizes a relative command of resources. It also signals a social condition and evokes a series of social reactions. Moreover, poverty is closely associated with a great many conditions that also evoke social responses, including such labels as "mentally ill," "criminal," or "handicapped." The process of becoming a client is at the same time the process of receiving a label that may have important social consequences. Administrators not only respond to these labels but also deliver and attach them.

We are perhaps most familiar with this process in the area of education, where early informal labeling of students as capable or incapable of rapid learning affects childrens' subsequent educational careers (see Kirp 1973). It is less obvious how previous criminal records affect sentencing, or previous welfare status affects the quality of service and responsiveness in later encounters with welfare personnel. Of equal interest is the significance of one label, for example, "delinquent," or "welfare recipient," for encounters in other administrative settings. The distribution of these labels is a significant product of the street-level administrative process and needs to be much better understood if we are to account fully for the consequences of the interaction of poor people with administration.

An important current contradiction in American social welfare policy is that government increasingly takes responsibility for providing for the needs of poor people while at the same time political and fiscal constraints limit the amount of resources and services that are provided. Managing the tension between promising to provide for people while limiting the resources spent on them is a critical governmental problem in the largest sense, since it bears on the legitimacy of the regime. In understanding the relationship between administration and poverty, a primary task is to understand how this tension is managed. In one sense it is managed at the point of policy development, where levels and quality of welfare programs are first shaped. But in another sense it takes place at the point of street-level administration, where social welfare is actually experienced by citizens. How can services be limited and yet remain theoretically open? How can some people receive resources or services when not everyone can, yet the belief prevail that everyone is entitled to equal treatment?

One subject worthy of considerable scrutiny in this connection is the limiting of public service provision through low-level administrative practice. Here I raise a problem that is generic to problems of free goods. Theoretically, if goods have no cost then demand for them will be insatiable; therefore some kind of cost must be attached to them even if actual prices are not imposed (see Downs 1967). Agencies that provide theoretically free public goods must and will devise ways to ration them. To ration goods or services is to establish the level or proportion of their distribution. This may be done by fixing the amount or level of goods and services in relation to other goods and services. Or it may be done by allocating a fixed level or amount of goods or services among different classes of recipients. In other words, services may be rationed by varying the total amount available or by varying the distribution of a fixed amount. While real prices are sometimes imposed, as in the case of increasing recipients' share of food stamp costs, in many other instances inconvenience, cash outlays for transportation or baby sitting, or time become the coin by which the theoretically free goods are made costly.

Another way in which rationing occurs is in the choice among classes of clients. There has long been an interest, of course, in identifying the biases that lower-level workers introduce into administrative agencies. The importance of recognizing biases in service provision as rationing is that we then can analyze discriminatory behavior as functional for lower-level workers forced to limit services to some people and not others. If rationing has its origin in the need of public agencies to serve some and not others when all cannot be served, then we have discovered an institutional basis for these invidious distinctions. The terms on which these distinctions are made and the populations that are harmed thereby may provide an important commentary on poverty as an element in discrimination, and may lead to a better understanding of the influence of stigmatized characteristics on unequal treatment.

Rationing in field administration may be a neglected dimension of administrative studies because to a significant degree it is a part of the underlife of the agencies that practice it. While some rationing of course takes place at higher administrative levels, as in the establishment of eligibility requirements, important rationing also takes place in the routines, simplifications, and other mechanisms that street-level bureaucrats develop in order to cope with jobs in which they chronically have inadequate resources relative to the tasks at hand. Large case loads, inadequate information about clients, and the need to make decisions rapidly and expeditiously lead street-level bureaucrats to develop coping mechanisms. These routines are likely to be structured so as to obscure the limitations placed on the service or place the blame for service limitations on the client ("application denied: late filing"). The more obscure the limitations or the more clients are held responsible for their treatment, the more the belief can be maintained that services are freely and readily available.

Recognition of the ubiquity of rationing in government programs also draws attention to the problem of assessing service demand. If it is recognized that organizations normally ration services by manipulating the nature and quantity of the information made available about them, then it is easily seen that demand levels are themselves a function of public policy. Client rolls and client expressions of interest will be seen as a function of clients' perceptions of service availability and the cost of seeking services. Client demands will be manifest, in this view, only to the extent that clients themselves are aware that they have a social condition that can, should, and will be ministered to by public agencies. Research on the "demand" for social welfare policy should consider the contributions of the following to the structuring of demand and the perceived availability of services.

To what extent does an agency's apparent receptivity to clients affect their willingness to persist in seeking service or seek assistance a second time? In legal services offices, according to one study, 40 percent of the eligible applicants for assistance failed to show up for an initial appointment when they were asked to wait before seeing an attorney. Did the problems of these dropouts disappear, or were they initially discouraged from returning by the nature of their original reception (Hosticka 1976)?

To what extent does the quality and the character of information provision affect demand? Public housing authorities often suggest that their waiting lists indicate the demand for public housing. But what accounts for the differences among authorities in the size of the waiting list? On one hand, public housing authorities can fail to purge old names from the list, thereby inflating apparent demand for public housing in that district. On the other hand, they may fail to publicize the availability of public housing, thereby diminishing the size of the apparent need. Or potential applicants may despair over long waiting lists and never apply.

What costs, hidden and unhidden, do clients have to pay in seeking service? For example, how difficult is it to obtain access to administrative personnel? What are the problems of transportation with respect to getting to the center where eligibility must be determined? For example, when the lower courts in Manhattan were consolidated so that Harlem and other Upper Manhattan residents had to travel long distances to obtain a hearing, what was the impact on tenants *vis a vis* landlords, or on debtors *vis a vis* creditors, that resulted from this move?

Controlling the Client

Any social order depends upon the general consent of its members. Even the most coercive of institutions, such as prisons, function only so long as those affected by the institution can be made to cooperate in its activities (even if the cooperation ultimately is secured by force) (see, for example, Sykes 1958). At some level, clients must be made to comply with the requirements of administration. Teachers must secure pupils' cooperation before they can begin to teach. Social workers must obtain the cooperation of welfare recipients in case determinations or confront huge case backlogs and time-consuming appeals.

Typically, cooperation is best understood as neither actively coerced nor freely given but rather as emerging from the structure of alternatives provided by the institution. The structure of choices available to clients limits the range of alternative behaviors that clients consider available. Admittedly, we can only infer that it is a managed consensus because clients cooperate in their own management. The suppression of overt dissenting behavior is rarely exhibited. Except in the more coercive bureaucracies, line workers rarely offer direct "commands" to clients. Rather, clients control themselves because they require the services of poverty bureaucracies and lack alternatives.

Controlling the client has double significance for this discussion. On one hand, managing the clientele and gaining clients' consent directly affects the outcomes of the transactions between administrative representatives and clients. On the other hand, managing the clientele affects the extent to which administration is responsive to clients collectively. The lack of reciprocity between clients and workers in poverty administration deprives these administrative systems of one of the few ways in which they might be induced to change. Clearly, public bureaucracies are not responsive to clients in the way that profit-maximizing firms are responsive to consumers (see Etzioni 1955). Instead, at best we expect government agencies to be accountable through political rather than market messages. Yet these messages are not transmitted when client compliance is structured and their involvement essentially nonvoluntary.

Research on the interaction of poverty and administration thus should be dedicated to discovering the ways in which the consent of poor people to administrative operations is secured. At one extreme, perhaps, prisoners, disruptive pupils, and others who challenge organizational climate are drugged (Divosky and Schrag 1975). At the other extreme, poor clients of professional services providing health and legal benefits are manipulated by claims of expertise and behaviors that exclude clients from involvement in decisions about themselves.[7] Poor people generally are encouraged in the belief that their problems are of their own making and that assistance in overcoming them will be limited at best. Meticulous and exhaustive observations of the behavior of clients and policy providers in the past have afforded considerable insight into the micropolitical relations between the dispensers and receivers of public policy in prisons, court rooms, legal services settings, and aspects of school administration. Similar research may shed light on other aspects of the control behavior of administrative personnel affecting poor people.

Directions for Research on Reform Associated with Poverty and Administration.

Thus far I have emphasized research on poverty and administration that would yield a greater understanding of the impact of administrative systems on poor people, primarily at the point of contact between government and citizens. In this section I consider research that would contribute to a better understanding of the efficacy of reform proposals designed to improve the performance of administrative systems toward poor people.

These proposals are offered in the light of two important reservations. First, we must be aware that the structure of administration in public service bureaucracies is deeply rooted in the ideology and manifest preferences of the society, reinforced by the work structures and resulting coping behaviors of public employees who have to carry out public policies. Thus, while we may search for opportunities to change administrative structures in desired directions, we should have no illusions of the difficulties that exist or the extent to which these administrative systems are likely to be responsive to piecemeal reform efforts. This is particularly the case in the current period of public concerns over governmental fiscal capabilities, when most reform proposals would appear to have the direct result of making the condition of the poor and near-poor more difficult to sustain.

Second, proposals to encourage research on reform opportunities ought not even faintly to be presumed to have a positive bias. We should be prepared, indeed in many cases we should expect, to discover that proposals for change are likely to prove ultimately ineffective, and for the same reason: the structure of administration is deeply rooted. However, as research this should not be dispiriting, so long as negative findings contribute to the ongoing process of developing an analysis of the political economy of poverty and social welfare.

In focusing attention on these matters I recognize that my comments may bear to some degree on current concerns with the "taxpayers' revolt." But one should be skeptical about the relationship of this discussion and solutions to the current climate of fiscal alarm. Taxpayers' criticism is not primarily focused on how to improve the effectiveness of services devoted to ameliorating poverty. However, to the extent that it involves a critique of the quality of government services my suggestions may be responsive to issues raised by the campaign for Proposition 13 and its progeny (see *Boston Globe* 1978).

Three major lines of research would contribute to the widely varying efforts to improve public service bureaucracies that impact on poor people. First, research should be encouraged to discover ways in which clients may be accorded greater autonomy in resolving their own problems and responding to their own needs. Second, we should seek to discover ways in which public service employees can be made more responsive to clients, and ways in which client-worker interactions can be improved. These necessarily marginal adjustments to bureaucratic functioning will not resolve the major structural tensions between agents of government and low-income citizens. Nonetheless, it does seem desirable to minimize the extent to which citizen interactions with government are unfair, damaging, or needlessly restrictive. Third, we should seek opportunities to help public service employees become more effective advocates for the rights of the poor, and for changing the relationship between poor people and government agencies.

Research on Directions for Greater Client Autonomy

There is some reason to think that efforts to provide poor people with greater autonomy in receiving government benefits and services and to respond more effectively to their needs are a contradiction in terms. Some might argue that the nature of public bureaucracies is such that meaningful changes toward greater client autonomy cannot be forthcoming. However, there are contradictory impulses in American society that encourage greater citizen self-direction and militate toward reduced dependence. In addition, the critical public bureaucracies are not held in such high esteem that support for a reduction in their influence could not be mustered. Moreover, increases in autonomy may lead to expressed demands for still greater self-direction. Thus, however much the structure of public bureaucracies appears fixed and unyielding, there remains room and support for innovations seeking the disestablishment of the bureaucratic network in which poor people are enmeshed. For these and other reasons, it seems important to monitor closely experiments that seek to extract poor people from the web of government and encourage greater collective self-direction. In this connection, the following developments seem worth close scrutiny and impact assessment.

One general approach to change in the relationship between poor people and administration is to eliminate public workers as buffers between government and citizens. A class of proposals utilizing such an approach is represented by plans to issue service "vouchers" to citizens. Voucher proposals, by providing clients with claims on public or private services (represented by the vouchers) would in theory make agencies more responsive to client preferences by introducing a measure of competition between and among service providers.[8]

On their face, voucher proposals are attractive because they evoke a model of a competitive market in which products are developed in response to consumer demand. Unfortunately, market models in service provision will not prove to be effective in practice so long as service providers monopolize the scarcely supplied skills for which vouchers are provided, dictate the conditions under which services will be supplied, or limit information available to service consumers. Moreover, even in theory, market models operate effectively only so long as clients can be expected to have an opinion about service quality. In addition, voucher proposals raise important problems associated with the possibility that vouchers will simply bid up the price of services without causing more services to be introduced or improving service quality.

Notwithstanding these and other difficulties, continued experimentation and associated research on voucher systems are consistent with attempts to discover ways to make clients more independent of public bureaucracies. In particular, research should be focused on the ways in which service-providing agents monopolize information, cue voucher recipients concerning their preferences (rather than respond to them), and otherwise are able to convert potentially competitive situations into regulated ones (see Edelman 1977, especially Chapter 3).

Continued experimentation and associated research should also be focused on eliminating mediating public workers from service contexts that, if properly supported, might be handled by citizens with little or minimum assistance. Community systems of dispute resolution, for example, promise to free citizens from the institutional nexus of the courts.[9] Home care services for the indigent chronically ill, for example, promise to liberate the poor and aged from the detrimental, nonessential requirements of hospitalization, at the same time promising some reduction in health care costs. These innovations spur the development of their own bureaucracies and public institutions, to be sure, but because they might be new, community based, and less dominated by professional trappings, they might well be an improvement over the alternatives.

Even more likely to eliminate mediating bureaucracies are experiments to make it possible for citizens to use legal systems without lawyers or secure their health requirements with only minimal assistance from physicians or trained health workers. Reforms directed toward these objectives do not entirely meet people's service needs. In a future society of greater client autonomy, there would still be a need for lawyers and doctors, particularly for the poor who were unable to buy their services. Nonetheless, we should support innovations that promise to reduce, however modestly, the bureaucratic burden on citizens.

Research should be supported to monitor and assess efforts to demystify bureaucratic practices and procedures. Of interest, for example, is a New York State law requiring consumer contracts to be written in language accessible to ordinary citizens. Of similar interest are patient rights statements, particularly with respect to their effectiveness in public hospitals that minister primarily to the poor.

Considerable attention should also be paid to current attempts to develop countervailing advocacy agencies to assist poor people in negotiating their claims with other public bureaucracies. Of great interest should be the extent to which legal services lawyers are able to play advocacy functions in assisting clients in dealing with other bureaucracies and the degree to which they are also disarmed in this purpose by the same forces that impact on other street-level bureaucrats and lead to the routinization of practice I have previously described.[10]

Opportunities should also be sought to investigate the effect of citizen advocates in other bureaucratic settings in which the role of advocacy is less well established. Experiments with ombudsmen, for example, deserve continued attention, as do other bureaucracies seeking to provide advocacy specialists. This research may ultimately prove quite critical of these practices. It is likely that ombudsman and advocacy offices, if located in the agencies they are supposed to monitor, will ultimately function to coopt and channel citizen demands rather than zealously pursue clients' interests. Nonetheless, research oriented toward finding more effective ways to help clients negotiate bureaucratic institutions ought not to ignore this class of innovations.

Also consistent with this orientation is research on the struggle of clients to organize and obtain some control over service provision. We should be particularly interested in opportunities that clients have to define the role characteristics of public employees, so that the interests of clients may be taken into greater account. Of course, over the last 15 years, considerable attention has been devoted to understanding the efficacy of citizen participation and decentralization experiments. Much of this research was discouraging, albeit instructive. However, it is inappropriate to conclude on the basis of recent history that research on increased citizen participation is not worth pursuing. There is a significant difference between evaluating experiments in citizen participation across the board and focusing research on the components of effective citizen participation. For example, the finding that citizen participation was relatively low, *vis a vis* expectations, in the poverty program and model cities is not instructive with respect to the effect of citizen participation on programs for which participation was relatively high. The researcher interested primarily in client autonomy rather than the degree of participation evoked would be sensitive to the ways professionals responded to client involvement, and the circumstances under which clients were able to display relatively high levels of involvement.[11]

The 1960s era of citizen participation in my view was more a comment on the deeply rooted relationship between poverty and participation than it was on the efficacy of participation by a distressed class. We should be wary of facile assumptions that relatively powerless groups can achieve significant influence over the character of government programs when government determines that their participation in administration will increase.[12] From the political perspective I suggested earlier, it does not make sense to expect administration to change as a result of increased citizen participation if no other aspects of the political relations between clients and administrators are altered. Still, opportunities to involve clients in helping to define the character of programs may be instructive in supporting efforts to define new relations between clients and professionals. In any event, continued focused research on citizen participation opportunities is not contradicted by the disappointments of previous epochs. In this connection we should support research that seeks to focus on institutions in which clients normally have control over their government through elected representatives. Specifically, consumer and producer cooperatives, which in some areas compete with government in providing services, deserve attention with respect to their relative responsiveness to low-income clients and constituents.

Research on Current Service Delivery

Increasingly, public agencies providing social welfare services are under pressure to streamline procedures and routinize formerly discretionary aspects of their work. These "reforms" are undertaken in the name of efficiency, (sometimes) fairness, and above all reducing the costs of service provision. Undeniably, there is a sense in which it would be desirable to remove discretion from bureaucratic procedures when that discretion is exercised as discrimination or when no clear purpose is served by maintaining discretionary options. Researchers sensitive to issues of poverty and administration will be interested in the reduction of street-level discretion in two contrasting respects. On one hand, opportunities should be sought to decouple people from public service workers if their forced relationship cannot be justified on grounds that nurturing or effective services are performed, or on grounds that human judgment is required to determine clients' status. On the other hand, officially routinizing formerly discretionary areas of judgment is likely to have major and unrecognized consequences for clients subject to the now greater indifference and impersonalism of government agencies. For example, placing mentally ill patients in community rather than institutional settings may bring smaller scale, more human and sensitive care, but it may also lead to greater neglect. In the same way, separating welfare recipients from the discretionary intervention of social workers may liberate some from unnecessary involvement with bureaucrats, but also may deprive others of the opportunity to appeal for assistance. These examples suggest the desirability of continuing research on the reduction of discretion in public service bureaucracies.[13]

What kind of research is most appropriate regarding reforms in the operation of current client-serving bureaucracies? This is too broad a question to answer specifically here, but it is possible to identify some guidelines that are all too often ignored in research on the efficacy of administrative reform.

First, problems of discretion and control in street-level program operations result from a variety of factors, including: pressures of the job and shortages of appropriate resources; lack of clarity in goals and inability to identify adequate performance measures; intrinsic difficulties with the technology and methodology of the individual public services; class discrepencies between workers and clients; and training that focuses more on theory and ideal performance than on practical problem-solving skills. Behavioral reform is therefore unlikely to be responsive to changes in any single aspect of administrative structure. Revised training procedures are not likely to be effective unless they are reinforced by changes in the work situation. Increased resources are unlikely to be effective if training practices remain unchanged. Just as change in one portion of a person's life may not be sufficient to change other deeply rooted life patterns, street-level administration is a syndrome from which change in one part of the syndrome does not lead to escape from the whole. The significance of this lies in the conclusions that are sometimes drawn concerning the efficacy of administrative reforms. Ideas that may have merit are sometimes inappropriately discredited because they are not implemented in the context of a strategy of comprehensive change.

Second, we should be sensitive to the likely occurrence of threshold effects in assessing reform proposals. This is particularly obvious in studies of the impact of varying case load size. The effectiveness of case load reduction may not be continuous but only apparent when case loads are reduced beyond a certain point. Clients may not be better off if caseloads are reduced from 100 to 50, but they may be substantially better off if case loads drop below a hypothetical threshold of perhaps 20, at which point it might be possible to provide people with significant individual attention. Some studies of the significance of reducing classroom size reinforce this perspective. Likewise, increasing patrols by a small fraction of available officers may have no community effect, but significant saturation of communities with policy officers may yield distinct results.

Third, by now most social researchers are aware that an increase in expenditures is not equivalent to an increase in services, and that budget allocations are not indicators of service provisions. However, not as obvious is where increases go, or where reductions are taken. What happens to money when it enters the service sector? Does it go primarily to supplementing the salaries of public employees? Does it go to hiring specialists who do not impact on the workloads of primary bureaucratic agents? Does it go to increasing the quantity of people serviced by agencies or programs without affecting the quality of the services already provided? In government programs, increases in the supply of service may lead to an increase in demand, in contrast to the classic direction of this relationship in a market context. Answers to these questions, which will vary from place to place but perhaps in patterned ways, would contribute to the current debate on what, precisely, the public receives in exchange for its commitment of resources.

Fourth, the most effective proposals for improving bureaucratic practice in the short run are likely to be those that are specifically related to coping with work dilemmas, that is, helpful in solving specific problems experienced by workers. For example, on-the-job training is likely to be more effective than classroom learning experiences because the training is provided in the context of problem-solving situations. Instruction relating to experiences that bureaucrats are likely to encounter is retained; instruction unrelated to direct problem solving is subject to erosion because of its irrelevance to workers' needs.[14] This suggests priorities for research on short-term practice improvement. For example, among studies of police practice, a most interesting experiment was the New York City attempt to build a team of crisis intervention specialists, notable because it concentrated almost exclusively on field skills.

Fifth, a final observation that might well guide research on current practice is the manipulation of the standards and measures by which administrators are judged and in terms of which they are rewarded. This is clearly a powerful method of inducing bureaucratic behavior. The diverse research findings in this area seem quite unambiguous.[15]

Manipulation of performance measures, even if those measures are spurious or problematic, may lead to significant changes in bureaucratic behavior. Deliberate experimental research in this area would appear warranted in light of the difficulties we otherwise have in identifying critical factors that may be reliably related to administrative performance.

Research on Training and Education

With regard to research on poverty and administration, a word should be said concerning the training of the professionals and semiprofessionals who populate public bureaucracies that affect the poor. Thus far, the burden of the discussion has been on structural conditions of the work setting. I have argued that much public policy bearing on the poor is made in the aggregation of routines and other coping devices that low-level workers develop in response to job pressures. This orientation leads to proposals to restructure work settings in some way. However, while it may be possible to clarify, simplify, or otherwise restructure poverty administration, there is an irreducible extent to which the society will not accept elimination of discretionary judgment of line workers. On the street police will still have to make quick decisions about ambiguous situations. In the classroom teachers will still be expected to respond to the needs of individual children. Doctors will still be expected to approach each diagnosis considering the possibility that unusual circumstances may present themselves. In short, there are limitations to restructuring job conditions. At some point we have to turn to the possibility of influencing public policy by changing the preparation of people who fill those roles. If this is the case, two observations may help to guide future research efforts.

First, we should be skeptical about research that proposes to inform us about the efficacy of professional training with respect to effective poverty administration. There is good reason to think that the social and technical structure of the work itself is much more salient to future work attitudes and performance than is social background and various approaches to conventional job training.[16]

Second, we should be alert to radical departures from conventional recruitment and training practices that deserve attention because they seek to develop substantially different bases for the work process. For example, experiments on training physicians to become family practitioners that begin by placing first-year medical students in poor, rural community health settings hold promise of contradicting socialization to the hierarchy of medical status that usually is experienced by medical students. Similarly, training toward a career in proverty law that is based on a poverty law practice rather than on three years of law school ought to provide significantly different socialization patterns for young attorneys.

Conclusion

A final word is in order concerning the conceptual framework within which research on the relationship of administration and poverty is structured. Most research on poverty and administration takes for granted that policy is directed toward stated objectives. This research tends to focus on the extent to which segments of the population are provided advantages by administration, or the extent to which the objectives of the program are achieved. This research rarely inquires whether demand for public services is discouraged or suppressed by administrative developments, or whether the degree of goal achievement in turn "feeds back" to affect poor people's engagement with government programs. In other words, research on poverty and administration usually does not take as problematic the effect of administration on the poor, but instead often assumes that the government objective is to ameliorate poverty, not to manage the consequences of deprivation, manipulate poverty populations, or otherwise achieve equally plausible outcomes. Concepts and methods in this research tend to involve the question of what people get from administration, rather than to entertain questions concerning the broader consequences of delivering governmental services.

The study of public policy and implementation has advanced considerably from the days in which issues of distributional consequences were hardly raised. But it would be useful to go beyond the insights of the last generation of policy studies to an expanded view in which "poverty policy" plays many roles in managing the consequences of persistent income inequalities.

Notes

1. On the use of the term "political," see, for example, Easton (1965) and Lasswell (1936).
2. On the distinctions between utilitarian and coercive organizations, see Etzioni (1961).
3. Studies of administration of specific policy areas affecting poor people include: Frieden and Kaplan (1975), Moynihan (1969), Rogers (1968), Murphy (1971), Lipsky (1970), and Piven and Cloward (1971).

4. See, for example, selected articles in Pynoos et al. (1973) and Davis and Dolbeare (1968).

5. For another perspective on "boundary workers," see Thompson (1962).

6. On building inspectors, see, for example, *New York Times* (1975); on the life insurance industry, see Orren (1971); on special education, see Weatherley and Lipsky (1977); on legal services attorneys, see Hosticka (1976).

7. See Edelman (1977). Of course, poor people are not the only clients to experience a degree of control on the part of administrators.

8. On voucher proposals in education, see Bridges (1977) and Cohen and Farrar (1977).

9. For a review, see Cratsley (1978).

10. For a recent discussion of the provision of legal services, see Handler et al. (1978).

11. Two instructive reviews of the experience with citizen participation are Yates (1973) and Peterson and Greenstone (1978).

12. Hypotheses concerning the effectiveness of participation when the initiative comes from public agencies are sketched in Lipsky and Lounds (1976).

13. James Q. Wilson (1968) offers one model for such research in his comparative study of police departments that adopt legalistic (rule-enforcing) styles and departments that condone more discretionary behavior.

14. For one study that attempted to assess the relationship of training to self-assessment in performance, see McNamara (1967).

15. An early statement of this relationship is found in Blau (1963); see also Ridgway (1976).

16. For a discussion of the evidence in the medical field on this point, see Freidson (1974).

References

Blau, P. (1963) *The Dynamics of Bureaucracy*. Rev. ed. Chicago: University of Chicago Press.

Boston Globe (1978) It isn't the tab, it's the services. October 6, p. 2.

Bridges, G. (1977) Citizen choice in public services: voucher systems. Pp. 51-109 in E.S. Savas, ed., *Alternatives for Delivering Public Services* Boulder, Colo.: Westview Press.

Cloward, R., and Epstein, I. (1965) Private social welfare's disengagement from the poor: the case of family adjustment agencies. In Meyer Zald, ed., *Social Welfare Institutions: A Sociological Reader*. New York: John Wiley.

Cohen, D.K., and Farrar, E. (1977) Power to the parents? the story of education vouchers. *Public Interest* 48:72-97.

Cratsley, J. (1978) Community courts: offering alternative dispute resolution within the judicial system. *Vermont Law Review* 3:1-69.

Davis, J.W., Jr., and Dolbeare, K. (1968) *Little Groups of Neighbors.* Chicago: Markham.

Divosky, D., and Schrag, P. (1975) *The Myth of the Hyperactive Child.* New York: Pantheon.

Downs, A. (1967) *Inside Bureaucracy.* Boston: Little, Brown.

Easton, D. (1965) *A Framework for Political Analysis.* Englewood Cliffs, N.J.: Prentice Hall.

Edelman, M. (1977) *Political Language: Words that Succeed and Policies that Fail.* Chicago: Academic Press.

Etzioni, A. (1955) Administration and the consumer. *American Sociological Quarterly* 3:257-264.

Etzioni, A. (1961) *A Comparative Analysis of Complex Organizations.* Glencoe, Ill.: Free Press.

Freidson, E. (1974) *Profession of Medicine.* New York: Dodd, Mead.

Frieden, B., and Kaplan, M. (1975) *The Politics of Neglect.* Cambridge, Mass.: MIT Press.

Handler, J.F., Hollingsworth, E.J., and Erlanger, H.S. (1978) *Lawyers and the Pursuit of Legal Rights.* Chicago: Academic Press.

Hosticka, C. (1976) Legal Services Lawyers Encounter Clients: A Study in Street Level Bureaucracy. Unpublished Ph.D. dissertation, Massachusetts Institute of Technology.

Jacob, H. (1972) Contact with government agencies: a preliminary analysis of the distribution of government services. *Midwest Journal of Political Science* 16:123-146.

Katz, D., Gutek, B., Kahn, R., and Barton, E. (1975) *Bureaucratic Encounters: A Pilot Study in the Evaluation of Government Services.* Ann Arbor, Mich.: Survey Research Center.

Kirp, D. (1973) Schools as sorters. *University of Pennsylvania Law Review* 121:705-797.

Kitsuse, J., and Circourel, A. (1963) A note on the use of official statistics. *Social Problems* 11:131-139.

Lasswell, H. (1936) *Who Gets What, When, How?.* New York: McGraw Hill.

Lipsky, M. (1970) *Protest in City Politics.* Chicago: Rand McNally.

Lipsky, M. (1979) Street-Level Bureaucracy: Dilemmas of the Individual in Public Services. New York: Russell Sage.

Lipsky, M., and Lounds, M. (1976) Citizen participation and health care: problems of government induced participation. *Journal of Health Politics, Policy and Law* 1:85-111.

McNamara, J.H. (1967) Uncertainties in police work: the relevance of police recruits' backgrounds and training. Pp. 163-252 in David Bordua, ed., *The Police.* New York: John Wiley.

Moynihan, D.P. (1969) *Maximum Feasible Misunderstanding.* New York: Free Press.

Murphy, J. (1971) Title I of ESEA: the politics of implementing federal education reform. *Harvard Educational Review* 41(1):35-63.

New York Times June 19, 1975, p. 1.

Nordlinger, E. (1972) *Decentralizing the City*. Cambridge, Mass.: MIT Press.

Orren, K. (1971) *Corporate Power and Social Change*. Baltimore: Johns Hopkins University Press.

Peterson, P. and Greenstone, J.D. (1978) Racial change and citizen participation: the mobilization of low-income communities through community action. In Robert Haveman, ed., *A Decade of Antipoverty Programs*. Chicago: Academic Press.

Piven, F., and Cloward, R. (1971) *Regulating the Poor*. New York: Pantheon.

Pynoos, J., Schafer, R., and Hartman, C., eds. (1973) *Housing Urban America*. Chicago: Aldine.

Ridgway, V.F. (1976) Dysfunctional consequences of performance measurements. Pp. 505–514 in Robert T. Golembiewski, ed., *Public Administration*. Chicago: Rand McNally.

Rist, R.C. (1975) Student social class and teacher expectations: the self-fulfilling prophecy in ghetto education. Pp. 517–539 in Yeheskel Hasenfeld and Richard English, eds., *Human Service Organizations*. Ann Arbor: University of Michigan Press.

Rogers, D. (1968) *100 Livingston Street*. New York: Random House.

Savas, E.S., and Ginsburg, S. (1973) The Civil Service—a meritless system?. *The Public Interest* 32:70–85.

Schwartz, B. (1975) *Queuing and Waiting*. Chicago: University of Chicago Press.

Steiner, G. (1971) *The State of Welfare*. Washington, D.C.: Brookings Institution.

Sykes, G. (1958) *The Society of Captives*. Princeton, N.J.: Princeton University Press.

Thompson, J.D. (1962) Organizations and output transactions. *American Journal of Sociology* 68:309–324.

Weatherley, R., and Lipsky, M. (1977) Street-level bureaucrats and institutional innovation: implementing special education reform. *Harvard Educational Review* 47(2):171–197.

Westley, W. (1970) *Violence and the Police*. Cambridge, Mass.: MIT Press.

Wilson, J.Q. (1968) *Varieties of Policy Behavior*. Cambridge, Mass.: Harvard University Press.

Yates, D. (1973) *Neighborhood Democracy: The Politics and Impacts of Decentralization*. Lexington, Mass.: D.C. Heath.

Part II: Theoretical and Comparative Perspectives

Thomas F. Pettigrew

Social Psychology's Potential Contributions to an Understanding of Poverty

Introduction

Social psychology as a discipline has not directed its attention to an understanding of poverty. There is considerable work relevant to the problem, and this paper reviews much of it. But focused social psychological theory and research, with rare exceptions, have not been brought to bear on poverty.

Since there is too little past research to provide guidance, I shall address the question of high priority areas for future research with a set of suggested ideas that might be usefully applied to poverty research. These ideas are drawn from various branches of the field; they range from a broad perspective on the problem to specific details of welfare administration. An illustration of how these ideas have been applied to other social problems is provided so as to give an idea of the types of applied research that typically flow from them. However, it is first necessary to establish just what the young discipline of social psychology is and how it is structured in order to evaluate its potential for contributing to an understanding of poverty.

The Discipline of Social Psychology

Social psychology is an interstitial field. Like physical chemistry and biochemistry, it has emerged from two parent disciplines with a distinctive focus. The mission of social psychologists is to study and understand the mediation processes between the psychological and the sociological levels of analysis. That social psychology is still evolving from its two parent disciplines is made clear by the awkwardness of its present-day

[Thomas F. Pettigrew is professor of social psychology and sociology in the Department of Psychology and Social Relations and the Department of Sociology at Harvard University.]

structure in higher education. Social psychologists are found in both psychology and sociology departments, often with little or no communication between them. Moreover, the discipline is rent by three diverse subgroups that have limited intercommunication: experimental social psychology, symbolic interactionism, and integrative social psychology. All three of these subgroups concentrate on the central mission of uncovering mediation processes, but in sharply different ways. A brief review of each of these subgroups follows.

EXPERIMENTAL SOCIAL PSYCHOLOGY

The largest, most mobilized, and perhaps the most prestigious of the three subgroups is experimental social psychology. Based almost entirely in psychology departments, this subgroup stresses controlled laboratory experimentation on individual psychological processes as the mediator of social and situational effects. Like its parent discipline, psychology, experimental social psychology relies heavily upon internal states as explanations (e.g., attitudes, attributions, comparisons, dissonance, expectations) and typically reduces the social world to the level of the individual. Experimental social psychology now emphasizes perceptual and cognitive factors over motivational and learning considerations. This emphasis derives from an insight that the subgroup shares with the other subgroups of social psychology: people's responses to social situations depend on their perceptions of the situation.

The mobilization of experimental social psychology stems from its organization as Division 8 of the American Psychological Association and its concentration in a few journals—the *Journal of Personality and Social Psychology* and the *Journal of Experimental Social Psychology* (and to a lesser extent, the *Journal of Personality* and the *Journal of Applied Social Psychology*). Inspection of these journals reveals the trade-offs that typify research in this area. Not only is it characterized primarily by laboratory experimentation, but college students predominate as subjects (Helmreich 1975). Sampling procedures for subject selection are rarely employed. And, surprisingly, individual differences are now generally ignored and considered only as "error." Experiments in this tradition often employ experimental confererates, programmed scripts, and contrived roles and situations. In short, the ability to make tight, causal inferences about a specific situation (internal validity) is maximized at the expense of the ability to generalize the results safely (external validity).

Kurt Lewin, the brilliant German transplant, is the modern father of this branch of social psychology. Today's trends, however, are marked by the work primarily of third-generation Lewinians who are the students of such Lewinians as Leon Festinger and Stanley Schacter. Missing, unfortunately, from the original tradition are Lewin's interests in natural groups, situational measurement, "action research," and close coordination between applied field work and laboratory studies.

Consequently, this subgroup has borne the brunt of harsh criticism, not the least of which has emanated from experimental social psychologists themselves. Charges of faddism, triviality, narrowness, and limited generalizability have been hurled repeatedly over the past decade. Tartly commenting on recent theories from this subgroup, Ivan Steiner (1974, p. 103), for example, writes: "On reading these models the . . . man from Mars might conclude that earthlings never converse with one another, never listen to another's judgments, and never accept the prefabricated verdict of social reality."

How well do the principles generated by experimental social psychologists apply in fact to the "real world," to such important applications as a better understanding of poverty in America? This paper argues that many of these principles do usefully generalize far better than one might suspect. Indeed, many of the more recent advances of experimental social psychology converge neatly with the conclusions of the other two subgroups of the discipline. To the extent that this is true, experimental social psychology provides a reasonably rigorous experimental base for the entire discipline's primary contentions and potential applications.

SYMBOLIC INTERACTIONISM

Smaller in number but equally mobilized, the subgroup of symbolic interactionists is based almost completely in sociology departments. They reject with equal vigor both Watson's behavioralist reductionism and Durkheim's sociologism. Instead, they trace their theory back to William James, John Dewey, Charles Cooley, and especially to George Herbert Meade and the Chicago School of the 1920s and 1930s. Herbert Blumer (1969), a Meade student and central leader of this subgroup, and his Berkeley students named and helped to maintain the symbolic interactionism tradition. As the label implies, this tradition emphasizes face-to-face interaction and symbolism; hence, its principal concerns include communication, roles, the self, identity, collective behavior, and deviance (e.g., Lindesmith et al. 1977). Like other social psychologists, symbolic interactionists stress cognitive factors in taking seriously W. I. Thomas's dictum that things defined as real are real in their consequences. Symbolic interactionists believe that process is the appropriate focus rather than static relationships between individual or structural

variables. Hence, they typically utilize field observation, open-ended in-
terviewing, and unobstrusive methods; and they are suspicious of both
experimental and survey methods for doing violence to the subtle, reflexive processes of human interaction. The trade-off for symbolic interactionism, then, is a surrendering of research rigor in order to get close to
the action and concerns of the real world.

House (1977) and others criticize symbolic interactionists for throwing
out the baby with the bath water. In rightly rejecting the extremes of
Watson and Durkheim, this subgroup is accused of having unduly
spurned quantitative methods, causal analysis, and macrosociology.
Ironically, the chief contentions of symbolic interactionism have increasingly been supported by the very methods of other social psychologists
that it rejected. With greater communication among subgroups within
social psychology in the future, there is no reason why symbolic interactionist theory (as opposed to methodological dogma) would not become
central to a united discipline. For the purposes of this paper, this tradition contributes two important items for looking at poverty: the labeling
of deviance perspective and a rich literature of direct field data.

INTEGRATIVE SOCIAL PSYCHOLOGY

The third subgroup of the discipline, integrative social psychology, is the
least mobilized and the least recognized. But its consistent attention to
individual factors in the context of macro-structural factors clearly
distinguishes it from the other subgroups. Its proponents are found in
both sociology and psychology departments as well as in interdisciplinary
programs. Thus, they have more communication with the other types of
social psychologists. Various labels have been applied to this group over
the years ("social structure and personality," "psychological sociology,"
etc.), but its necessarily interdisciplinary focus has made it hard to
define. Actually, those social psychologists who can most easily be identified with this subgroup have either studied or taught in (or both) such
interdisciplinary programs as the former interdepartmental social psychology program at the University of Michigan and the former Department of Social Relations at Harvard University.

Integrative social psychology shares with the other subgroups an emphasis on cognitive factors at the individual level of analysis. In addition,
it shares with experimental social psychology a concern for quantitative
methods and with symbolic interactionism a concern for real-world data
and applied problems. However, it is more interested in general personality and social structural considerations; and it more explicitly seeks
to integrate the discipline by specifying the mediators between these

levels. This combination of concerns usually dictates the use of quasi-experimental or nonexperimental methods, especially surveys using probability samples.

House (1977) points out that this subgroup's focus constituted central concerns for such leading social theorists as Max Weber (the Protestant ethic), Emile Durkheim (anomie), and Karl Marx (alienation). Its modern-day sociologist adherents include Merton, Stouffer, Lazarsfeld, Inkeles, Bales, Lenski, Kohn, Sewell, Gamson, Schuman, Rainwater, Runciman, and James Davis. Its psychologist adherents include Cantril, Sherif, Newcomb, Rokeach, Riecken, Kelman, Donald Campbell, Angus Campbell, Back, Kahn, Kenneth B. Clark, Harding, David Sears, and Pettigrew. Much of the work of these social psychologists stems from applications of the field to such realms as evaluation research (Stouffer, Lazarsfeld, Kohn, Davis, D. Campbell, Kahn, and Riecken), electoral politics (Lazarsfeld, A. Campbell, Gamson, and Sears), international relations (Cantril and Kelman), birth control and family relations (Kohn and Back), and intergroup relations (Lenski, Gamson, Schuman, Sherif, Cantril, A. Campbell, D. Campbell, Back, Clark, Sears, Harding, and Pettigrew).

The Applicability of Social Psychology

Integrative social psychology is the subgroup of social psychology most concerned with applying social psychology. Indeed, it is more precise to say that this subgroup of the discipline is itself the product of applied research. In particular, the applications of social science during World War II shaped its character and led directly to the founding of the interdisciplinary programs at Michigan and Harvard. And the subgroup's emphasis linking the individual and societal levels of analysis makes its theory and findings readily applicable to a wide range of social issues, since almost by definition such issues simultaneously involve critical individual, interactional, and structural components.

All three subgroups, however, can and have been usefully applied to social issues. Typically, these applications involve the causal specification of the mediation of structural and/or situational factors upon individuals and their interaction. Rarely have social psychological applications gone in the equally important and opposite direction of how individual and interactional factors affect social structure. Yet these one-way applications of social psychology have been extensive. In addition to the areas cited above as particular targets of integrative social psychologists, the area of health has recently benefited from applications of experimental social psychology (Taylor 1979), and issues of social deviance have benefited from the applications of symbolic interactionist analysis. Examples of these successful applications appear later in this paper, by way of suggesting analogous applications to the issue of poverty.

Nonetheless, the social psychological imagination has, not been exploited in attempts of social science to understand and ameliorate poverty. To be sure, there have been occasional contributions, especially during the Great Depression (e.g., Zawadski and Lazarsfeld 1935, Stouffer and Lazarsfeld 1937) and during the war on poverty of the 1960s (e.g., Guttentag 1970a, 1970b). But these reconnaissance probes into poverty issues have never had the sustained and widespread attention of social psychologists as have such issues as race relations and crime.

It is not clear why this neglect should be the case. The discipline's ready applicability to a range of comparable social problems has been demonstrated repeatedly over the past four decades. And the political biases of the field should have made poverty of special interest to social psychologists. One possibility is that a straightforward paradigm for making social psychological analysis relevant to poverty was not available. This paper introduces such a paradigm in terms of viewing American poverty as a type of labeled diviance. Another possibility is that social psychologists have found their skills and insights most immediately applicable to those social issues for which the "victims" (e.g., blacks, women) are more mobilized than the poor in America.[2] Yet another explanation is that social psychological contributions may have been viewed as relevant to such abstract questions as welfare ideology rather than to solving practical problems of welfare policy (as will later be discussed).[3] Perhaps, too, poverty, more than other social problems, has been seen in purely economic terms, with the social psychological dynamics involved simply assumed in macro-economic models. Finally, the potential usefulness of social psychological contributions may not have been recognized by funding agencies; and, consequently, social psychologists applied their ideas and methods to other areas for which research resources were more readily forthcoming.

At any rate, a series of content analyses conducted for this paper reveals the magnitude of the discipline's neglect of the issue of poverty. Consider first, the contents of 32 leading introductory texts in social psychology representing all three subgroups of social psychology over recent decades. While 94 percent of those volumes discuss racial issues, 88 percent of them do not even mention poverty. More specifically, 26 of these texts (82 percent) have lengthy discussions of racial prejudice but not a single reference to poverty. Interestingly, a number of these books claim in their titles to be relating the field to modern life and social relevance. Only one of the 32 texts has an extended discussion of poverty as an issue itself, and it cites largely anthropological and sociological work (Weissberg 1976). Similarly, both editions of the authoritative *Handbook of Social Psychology* devote whole chapters to prejudice but do not contain even an index reference to poverty (Lindzey 1954; Lindzey and Aronson 1969).

Consistent with these results are those from another content analysis of two social psychological journals dedicated to applied research. The official publication of the Society for the Psychological Study of Social Issues, the *Journal of Social Issues*, has focused on poverty in only three of its more than 120 issues since its inception in 1945. And one of these, issued in January 1965 at the height of the war on poverty, did not include a single social psychologist among its 13 contributors (Kaplan 1965). Likewise, the *Journal of Applied Social Psychology*, in its first 7 volumes (1971–1977), contains only 2 articles on American poverty out of its 219 papers. And these studies are of only indirect relevance; for example, one found that subject jurors in a simulated trial for armed robbery rated defendants with low socioeconomic status as more blameworthy but not more guilty than defendants with high socioeconomic status (Gleason and Harris 1976).

The principal exceptions to this trend of neglect involve a few books, such as Feagin's *Subordinating the Poor* (1975), and articles by social psychologists in *Social Problems*, the official publication of the Society for the Study of Social Problems. Henslin and Roesti (1976) made a content analysis of the first 23 volumes of this journal from 1953 to 1975, and found 30 articles on poverty. This number constitutes 3.5 percent of the total number of articles and represents less than half of the articles that were published over these same years for each of such topics as race and ethnic relations, juvenile delinquency, and the professions. Moreover, many of the 30 articles are not social psychological, though some are written in the symbolic interactionist tradition (e.g., Beck 1967)—the subgroup that has most consistently identified with society's outsiders.

Despite this demonstrated paucity of work, this paper contends that social psychology has many potential contributions to make to the study of poverty.

Possible Applications of Social Psychology to an Understanding of Poverty

APPROPRIATE POINTS OF ENTRY FOR SOCIAL PSYCHOLOGICAL ANALYSIS

Five distinct causal explanations for poverty have been advanced: genetic, the culture of poverty, situational, maldistribution, and restricted resources (Thomas 1977). Each of these deserves brief discussion, for taken together they outline the appropriate points of entry for social psychological analysis.

1. Genetic

From this perspective, poverty is a predictable outcome of a range of defects that have been transmitted genetically across generations. Poverty, in short, is a result of inferior genes. Harsh as this view may seem to many, Chase (1977), in his recent volume *The Legacy of Malthus,* traces how this explanation for poverty has maintained its popularity over the past two centuries. Indeed, it may be having a rebirth in some intellectual quarters. But social psychology obviously has no means to make direct tests at this level. The discipline can contribute only indirectly by uncovering new environmental evidence that cannot easily be accounted for by genetic explanations and by furthering the explanatory power of rival explanations.

2. The Culture of Poverty

Like the genetic explanation, the culture-of-poverty argument concurs with the Biblical assertion that "ye have the poor always with you." Poverty, in this view, is caused, maintained, and perpetuated by a life-style and particular attributes that are common to most of the poor and transmitted culturally. The term derives from Oscar Lewis's anthropological work among poor families in Mexico City and San Juan (Lewis 1959, 1961, 1965, 1966). But the idea has been widely generalized and is a venerable component of conservative thought (Chase 1977). Variants of it arise regularly, as in Banfield's (1970) attempt to explain poverty as a result of the poor being insufficiently future-oriented.

To the extent that the culture-of-poverty thesis centers on personal attributes, social psychological work becomes relevant—and this work has been generally critical of the culture-of-poverty thesis. Rodman (1964), for example, advances the rival concept of value stretch. He argues that the poor in America share basically the same values and orientations as their more fortunate fellow citizens, but that they must contort these values in order to cope with the special problems that engulf them.

Rodman's position has repeatedly received empirical support from studies of the attitudes and values of the poor. Goodwin (1971), for instance, has shown that the work orientations of both men and women receiving welfare do not differ from those of the non-poor. Indeed, no correlation was found between the degree of commitment to the work ethic and attitudes toward welfare assistance. Likewise, Kriesberg (1970) noted among single mothers no significant association between a variety of attitudes and whether welfare payments or earned income were utilized to support their families. The primary predictors of the use of public assistance by these single mothers were situational: the number and age of children as well as the amount received from such income as social security and alimony payments. The greater importance of external constraints over transmitted culture has also been demonstrated by Kaplan and Tausky (1972). They found 275 chronically unemployed persons to possess the same work ethic desires for a job as samples of blue-collar and white-collar employed workers. The unemployed respondents naturally cited money as their chief job incentive, but they also indicated that the social respect that went with holding a job was also an important incentive. Similar conclusions indicating value stretch have been arrived at by other social scientists, most notably anthropologists (e.g., Liebow 1967, Valentine 1968).

3. Situational

The situational perspective regards poverty as the end result of the array of social policies and practices exercised by the prosperous majority to exclude various stigmatized groups. Injustice, discrimination, the lack of opportunity, and situational constraints are said to be the basic ingredients that underlie poverty. Hence, any unique cultural or personal attributes found among the poor are simply the products of their unique situation. And the interpersonal dynamics involved in this process are revealed in how the non-poor and the poor view themselves and each other and in how they interact. Not only is this social psychology's favored explanation of poverty, but it directly involves the level of analysis most suited to social psychological theory and methods. Consequently, the major sections of this paper that dwell on possible applications of the discipline focus almost exclusively at this situational-interactional level.

4. Maldistribution

From this vantage point, poverty is caused by the maldistribution of the nation's ample resources. Inequities of socioeconomic resources by geographic area, social class, race, and ethnicity are especially marked. To the extent that this explanation remains at the macrolevel, without concern for the microprocessses that generate maldistribution, social psychological analysis is not relevant. Nor can social psychological analysis aid directly in the economic debate over whether there are in fact ample resources for all or whether there is a genuine scarcity of resources in the United States. The discipline can, however, contribute to an understanding of the subjective evaluations of the terms ample, scarcity, and maldistribution.

5. Restricted Resources

There are two versions of the explanation of restricted resources, only one of which can be dealt with by social psychology. The macrolevel, Malthusian version is that poverty derives from the fact that the nation's productivity simply cannot keep up with the expansion of the population and its increasing needs. The microlevel, subjective version holds that poverty results from the rising expectations of those Americans with the least money. This version related directly to a central concept of the integrative subgroup of social psychology—relative deprivation. The idea of relative deprivation is hardly new, of course. DeTocqueville and Marx, to name two, utilized it; and economists are familiar with it under the label of "interdependence" (Duesenberry 1949). But it has attracted by far the most attention from social psychologists. Named and demonstrated by Stouffer et al. (1949) in their famous book *The American Soldier,* relative deprivation has been conceptually refined, empirically tested, and widely applied over the past generation (e.g., Spector 1956, Merton and Rossi 1957, Davis 1959, Runciman 1966, Pettigrew 1967, 1971, Crosby 1976).

To sum up, the most appropriate points of entry for the social psychological analysis of poverty involve situational influences and microprocesses. Only indirectly will such analysis relate to the genetic and maldistribution explanations. It is also relevant to the testing of the subjective portions of the culture-of-poverty and restricted-resources explanations. And social psychological work lies at the heart of the situational explanation of poverty. To illustrate how the field can contribute at the situational level, we will first establish a perspective that invites social psychological analysis.

AMERICAN POVERTY AS PERCEIVED SOCIAL DEVIANCE[4]

Many ideas from all three subgroups of social psychology can be brought to bear on the subject of American poverty if we conceive of it as being generally perceived as a special case of social deviance. To be more percise, three propositions can be specified to set up the discussion:

1. Being poor in the United States in many significant ways constitutes social deviance in the eyes of many Americans, poor and non-poor alike.

2. Like other forms of deviance, poverty has its own unique
   characteristics. But the poor tend to suffer more from social
   stigma (as do the mentally ill and criminals) rather than
   physical stigma (as do the deaf and the blind) or tribal stigma
   (as do members of racial and ethnic groups).
3. Social stigmatization as outsiders is greatest for the visible
   poor who are held responsible for their condition.

Let's briefly consider each of these propositions.

1. Deviance can be defined in a variety of ways, but poverty in
America appears to meet each of them. The statistical view of deviants as
people who fall on the extremes of the distributions of salient attributes
has been employed in social psychological research (e.g., Freedman and
Doob 1968). But it suffers from an inattention to what attributes become
salient in different cultures and different eras, and it does not directly attend to the violation of rules or expectations implicit in the concept of deviance. Poverty in an affluent nation clearly meets this statistical definition. True, in particular locations, such as rural Mississippi or the Ozark
Mountains, poverty is the norm, but generally these areas come to be
regarded by others as backward and deviant.

Deviance as pathology is a traditional conception. In the extreme form
of this model, deviance is seen as an immutable dispositional property of
individuals, as in the prevalent 19th century notion of genetically determined criminality. In the more benign form of the model, deviance is
seen as a mutable quality of individuals, with mental illness serving as the
key example. Poverty, I have noted already, has long been believed by
conservatives to be immutably determined genetically (Chase 1977). The
more benign form of the model is exemplified by the culture-of-poverty
thesis. The pathology model of deviance has obvious limitations.
Because the model ignores the question of who determines what is
pathological and does not consider the full social context of deviance,
both sociologists and social psychologists have turned to more dynamic
perspectives that emphasize both situations and the society.

One of the most useful of the wider approaches is labeling theory, advanced by symbolic interactionists. Deviance is regarded as a behavior or
a condition that has been labeled as such by powerful social groups
(Becker 1963, p.9). A complete paradigm shift is involved: instead of
focusing on the presumed deviants and their attributes, labeling advocates focus on the process of labeling and the labelers themselves. This
view is interactive par excellence; it directs attention to such overlooked
aspects of the phenomenon as secondary deviance and the power
manipulations of the non-deviants. Labeling ideas help us to understand

the problems and the perceptions of the poor. But the labeling perspective is limited, too, and requires melding with other conceptions of deviance that focus on the labeled deviants and their acts as well.

I shall consider five characteristics as determinative of deviance, each of which fits with the social psychological portrayal of American poverty being advanced in this paper. Deviance denotes (1) perceived differences, (2) which are negatively evaluated by powerful others, (3) because these differences involve a violation of *their* expectations or norms. Deviance also usually (4) invokes some degree of threat to others, and (5) implies to others the need for correction, either through isolation or remediation.

Since the 1930s, poverty has become perceptibly unusual in the United States. As Potter (1954) notes, Americans have long thought of themselves as a people of plenty. Adding to this, much poverty is hidden from the view of the non-poor; this situation serves to make the visible poor seem all the more salient and outside the mainstream. There has been virtually no progress toward more equitable income in America since the 1940s, and this lack of progress during a period of vast and rising prosperity has increasingly isolated the poor as different.

Affluent Americans judge poverty as bad, for in this land of opportunity all citizens are thought to be able to make it if they try hard enough. To be sure, there is a category of poor unfortunates, sectors of the poor that are not held fully responsible for their plight. But, I shall shortly note, such exemptions from liability are the exceptions to the dominant ideology's general response to the poor.

Poverty, then, violates the expectations of the powerful and prosperous. And phenomena that challenge deeply held expectations about people and society not only create cognitive dissonance but often threaten the perceiver as well. This is especially true in modern society, in which achievement increasingly replaces ascription as a value and a norm. Being an insider requires getting ahead; thus, those who fail to achieve threaten the striving labeler and stigmatizer.

Finally, the existence of poverty, like other forms of labeled deviance, generally leads people to attempts at correction. For centuries, this impulse led to isolation through either poorhouses or even debtors' jails. "All crimes are safe but hated poverty; this, only this, the rigid law pursues," wrote Samuel Johnson ruefully in *London*. In more recent times, remediation efforts through various welfare programs, even the declared war on poverty, are more common. Yet American assistance to the poor, like remedial efforts for other perceived social deviants, comes at the price of indignity and degradation—a forceful reminder of their socially stigmatized status. I shall return to this critical topic when I consider aspects of welfare administration.

2. The second proposition contends that the special stigma affixed to the poor is social rather than physical or tribal. Consequently, the stigmatization of the poor is more like that of other socially stigmatized groups such as the mentally ill and criminals than it is like that of the handicapped and racial groups. This is an important observation, for we shall learn that responses to these various deviant classifications contrast in significant ways. Goffman (1963), in his classic *Stigma,* held stigma to be a unitary phenomenon with similar interactional dynamics across diverse stigmata. But in this instance, a position held by one subgroup of social psychology (symbolic interactionism) is not confirmed by another subgroup (experimental social psychology).

The proposition rests largely on the fact that poverty is causally intertwined with broken families, illness, limited education, and crime. The overlap with other social stigmata is widely known and frequently exaggerated by the non-poor. Thus, the social stigma of poverty derives in part from its perceived association with other socially stigmatized conditions. Yet it also derives from simply being poor in its own right, a condition seen as less ascriptive or accidental than those that typify tribal and physical stigmata. Admittedly, poverty spills over to these other dimensions, too. The poor are more likely to be physically handicapped and are overrepresented among many stigmatized racial and ethnic groups; and this accentuates the poverty stigma further. But our second proposition holds that these overlaps are less salient to the non-poor than those of illness, ignorance, and crime.

3. The poor are not seen as equally deviant. The third proposition specifies those among the poor for whom social stigmatization is likely to be the most severe—the visible poor who are held responsible for their condition. Social stigmata in general are lessened when the deviant is not perceived as culpable. And like other social deviants, the poor can often "pass." Those who can appear to belong to the people of plenty escape the direct force of the stigma. Yet there are costs in passing, from disproportionate spending on clothes and not taking advantage of needed public assistance to the strain of hiding one's situation from view.

Concerning this proposition, current contentions can be distinguished from those advanced by Matza (1971) and Beck (1967). We claim that poverty itself is perceived as a degraded condition and that a social stigma applies in varying degrees to all of those labeled poor by the non-poor. By contrast, Matza singles out those in hard-core poverty—the labeled dregs, skidders, and persons receiving assistance from the Aid to Families with Dependent Children Program (AFDC). He regards them as being perceived as the disreputable poor and as the targets of a stigma not directed at others who are poor. In short, Matza proposes a discontinuity hypothesis: the poor in general are not stigmatized, but the extreme poor are. By comparison, the position advanced in this paper is continuous: all of the labeled poor are stigmatized in varying degrees, with the visible poor held to be responsible (conditions usually associated with extreme poverty) and suffering from the most severe stigma.

Similarly, Beck (1967) uses labeling theory to view welfare as a moral category. He argues that residual members of society, such as welfare recipients, challenge the dominant theory of how society should work and, consequently, are held responsible for their situation. Beck writes (p. 261):

> They . . . have to be placed into some category created
> especially for them in order to bring them back within the
> system and to allow the system to deal with them. What is
> paradoxical is that the role to which they are assigned is that
> of the roleless. In a sense, being outside the Structure is a
> structural position.

But again the formulation of this paper is broader than Beck's in its expansion to the entire labeled poor. I agree that those on welfare will be regarded as among the most deviant; but I believe that the social stigma of poverty in affluent America extends beyond the potent label of "welfare."

Armed with this paradigm, let us turn to the realm in which social psychological analyses are most likely to contribute to an understanding of American poverty: the reactions of the non-poor and the poor both to poverty and to each other.

REACTIONS OF THE NON-POOR

The applicable social psychological literature on this question falls into two quite diverse categories. The first type of research emanates from integrative social psychology. It employs surveys to uncover in the aggregate both the content and the structure of the attitudes of the non-poor toward the poor, especially the visible poor receiving public assistance. The second type derives from both symbolic interactionism and experimental social psychology. It uses field observation and controlled experimentation to record the responses of the labeling non-deviants to the labeled deviants.

Feagin (1975) provides a useful overview of how a national probability sample of 1,017 adult Americans in 1969 looked at poverty. First, the respondents evaluated the importance of 11 reasons for poverty. The four most popular explanations involve personal dispositional attributions: the poor were widely thought to lack thrift, effort, and ability and to suffer from loose morals and drunkenness. (Note the infusion of the Protestant ethic in these beliefs.)

The next most prevalent reason for poverty involves sickness and physical handicaps, a response that combines both dispositional and situational attributions. Only in the last six ranks of importance come situational and societal reasons. And only small numbers of respondents regarded as very important: low wages, failure of society to provide good schools, prejudice and discrimination against Negroes, failure of private industry to provide enough jobs, being taken advantage of by rich people, and just bad luck. This strong preference to blame the victim was found to hold across a range of demographic groups, though it was strongest among white Southerners and the elderly and weakest among black and Jewish respondents. Even those with annual family incomes below $4,000 did not differ sharply from other Americans in holding those beliefs.

Not surprisingly, this individualistic perspective on poverty relates directly to negative attitudes toward welfare programs. Large majorities of Feagin's representative national sample agreed that: ". . . too many people receiving welfare money . . . should be working"; many on "welfare are not honest about their need"; and many welfare women "are having illegitimate babies to increase the money they get." Less than half thought that "we are spending too little money on welfare programs" and that ". . . welfare doesn't give people enough to get along on." These antiwelfare sentiments were least common among the young, blacks, and the poor themselves.

Two other national surveys corroborate these results. One found that two-thirds of its probability sample of respondents agree that the relief rolls are "loaded with chiselers" (Free and Cantril 1967). Another, conducted by Gallup in 1969, asked a probability sample, "How many people on welfare today do you think could earn their own way if they really wanted to?" Only 2 percent thought "hardly anybody," while 18 percent answered "some," 41 percent "about half," and 38 percent "most of them" (Lemon 1971).

Community surveys done in greater depth further confirm Feagin's findings. Williamson (1974a) asked a sample of 300 white women in Boston about their beliefs concerning welfare. On two points, his respondents were quite accurate. Both their mean estimates of the percentage of illegitimate children in AFDC families and the average monthly AFDC payments were essentially correct. But his respondents grossly overestimated the percentage of welfare recipients who were able-bodied unemployed males (a mean estimate of 37 percent instead of approximately 1 percent), and who "lie about their financial situation" (41 percent instead of HEW estimates of 7 percent and less). And they possessed an exaggerated notion of how many children under 18 years of age are in the average AFDC family (4.8 instead of 2.6). Interestingly, these beliefs concerned with idleness, dishonesty, and fertility bore only a small relationship in Williamson's sample to attitudes toward increasing welfare benefits. Instead, such policy attitudes related far more strongly to beliefs about the motivation of the poor, self-reported liberalism, and adherence to the Protestant work ethic.

In another study, employing a special sample of 354 adults in Muskegon, Michigan, Huber and Form (1973) bluntly asked, "Why are rich people rich? Why are poor people poor? . . . Back in the years of the Great Depression in the 1930s, what do you suppose was the main reason that most people were on relief? . . . What do you suppose is the main reason that most people have gone on relief in the last six years?" They found that only 4 percent named personal attributions as the cause of being on relief in the 1930s, but 54 percent did for recent recipients of relief. In accounting for why the poor are poor, 36 percent named negative personal traits of the poor in general (e.g., "don't work as hard," "don't want to get ahead"). Note that these results are consistent with the continuous conception of the poverty stigma proposed here, for the unspecified poor elicit two-thirds as many stigmatizing dispositional attributions as those who have gone on relief in the past six years.

Two additional findings of Huber and Form are of particular interest. In accounting for why the rich are rich, the Muskegon respondents remained true to the Protestant ethic perspective by utilizing favorable personal traits. Huber and Form term this the dominant ideology: wealth results from hard work, ability, and motivation; poverty from laziness, stupidity, and the lack of ambition. But this dominant ideology is not subscribed to throughout the social structure. Unlike Feagin's representative sample, these investigators oversampled among the very poor and the very rich. And, more than Feagin, they note that this ideology of personal responsibility is strongest among the wealthy and weakest among the indigent. Like Feagin, they also noted that white respondents believe in the dominant ideology somewhat more than blacks (though the difference is large only among the poorest sector, for whom genuine controls for income across race are most difficult to secure).

Rainwater (1974) plumbed deeper into the dominant ideology with another sample survey administered in Boston. He discovered that, while the ideology holds sway firmly, there are subtle tensions and qualifications operating within it. When Rainwater (pp. 178–184) focused his respondents' attention on those families in the lowest fifth of income (with roughly less than half the median family income), two widely held principles came into conflict: No one should have to exist on such meager funds, yet everyone should have to work for what he or she gets. The conflict is sharpened by the belief that there are some extremely lazy people who do not wish to work, and, thus, do not deserve a decent living. The dilemma tends to be resolved in this Boston sample differently by working-class and middle-class people. Working-class people argue for more traditional, union-like solutions for aiding the bottom fifth—more jobs and higher minimum wages. Middle-class people more willingly accept educational and welfare solutions, with the higher costs regarded as simply "the price one pays to reduce 'social pollution' " (Rainwater 1974, p.184).

A conflicting conclusion is reached by Smith and Kluegel (1978) from their random-sample survey of Riverside, California. They show that middle-class respondents oppose welfare spending more than working-class respondents, but that the working-class respondents have the more negative images of the poor. This latter finding conflicts in turn with Huber and Form's (1973, pp. 101, 106) Muskegon data that showed the attribution of unfavorable traits to the poor by whites related positively with social class. These conflicting results may reflect genuine differences among the three communities in such matters as union ideology as well as methodological differences among the three studies.

In any event, the more important consideration for our purposes is that Kluegel and Smith (1978) also found the dominant ideology as pervasive in Riverside as elsewhere. And they uncovered a number of reasons why this ideology is so resistant to change. Their 175 adult respondents reveal a low degree of consistency in their relevant beliefs; especially striking are the contradictions between what they think is true for themselves versus what they think is true for society as a whole. Nor are their evaluations of various aspects of inequality closely linked. Hence, their assessments of income inequality in society, their own position in society, inequality of opportunity, and welfare policies and recipients are loosely coordinated at best. This situation is not as irrational as it might appear. (I may think that society is in general fair but that I am not doing well in it; or that society is unfair but that I am fortunate enough to be doing well myself.) In any event, Kluegel and Smith concur with Lane's (1962) conclusion that, without the existence of a forceful counterideology, the challenge of even experiential facts is not translated into political terms and an attack on the dominant ideology.

These survey data from throughout the nation establish the context within which to ask how the non-poor respond to the poor in face-to-face interaction. The non-poor, we have seen, enter such interaction with a set of Protestant ethic beliefs that comprise a dominant ideology. The pervasive ideology is highly resistant to change and causes the non-poor to attribute a variety of negative stereotypes to the poor in general and those on public assistance in particular. This stereotype—lazy, stupid, dishonest, ambitionless—brands the poor with a social stigma that should make interaction between haves and have-nots strained at best. Later we will argue that these interaction strains have broad policy implications for welfare administration.

Research in experimental social psychology fills in the outlines of typical interactions between "straights" and various types of "deviants."[5] The physically handicapped tend to elicit an initially ambivalent pattern from others: on one hand, unusually positive evaluations combine with greater compliance to the handicapped person's requests, while, on the other hand, there are avoidance reactions, greater distance, discomfort, and even galvanic skin responses that indicate emotional arousal (Kleck 1966, 1968, 1969, Kleck et. al. 1966). Both of these tendencies seem to subside over time (Kleck 1969), but on first meeting, they are dramatically demonstrated. In a field study conducted on 121 housewives in Palo Alto, California, Doob and Ecker (1970) sought cooperation under four contrasting conditions: a person requesting a favor either did or did not wear an eye patch and further interchange with that person either would or would not be necessary. A strong statistical interaction resulted. When no further interchange was anticipated, compliance was much greater in the eye patch condition (69 percent versus 40 percent); but there was no difference when further interchange was anticipated. These researchers explain their results in terms of two conflicting motives: a desire to help a handicapped person and embarrassment in having to deal with a stigmatized person.

Langer et al. (1976) expand this view by emphasizing the attraction of a novel stimulus. We are taught as children not to stare at handicapped people, but the fascination of freak shows at circuses reveals the strong desire to view such novel human stimuli. First, these investigators demonstrated in a natural setting that subjects stared longer at photographs of people in leg braces than at photographs of unhandicapped people when the staring was unobserved; but the opposite effect applied when an observer was present. Second, they had subjects interact in a laboratory setting with either a "handicapped" or a physically normal partner. Half of the subjects were allowed to observe their partner in advance through a one-way mirror. And, as predicted, the subjects who had satiated their interest in the novel stimulus showed sharply less avoidance behavior during later interaction. Langer et al. conclude that typical avoidance reactions to the physically handicapped are mediated not so much by dislike or threat, as had been earlier suggested, but rather by "conflict over a desire to stare at novel stimuli and a desire to adhere to a norm against staring when the novel stimulus is another person" (p. 451).

To the extent that the poor present novel stimuli, either through distinctive dress or an increased number of physical handicaps, this analysis may well apply. But poverty has more in common with stigmatized conditions such as mental illness and criminality, for which the stigma is based on soiled reputations imputed to dispositional defects. Penned the playwright, George Farquhar, almost two centuries ago: "There is no scandal like rags, nor any crime as shameful as poverty."

Reactions to the socially stigmatized are typically less benign than reactions to the physically handicapped. These reactions are generally unambiguously unfavorable from the start of the interaction. In both laboratory and field settings, those thought to have been mentally ill are derogated in a variety of ways—general avoidance, negative evaluations, disregard for their opinions, and unjustifiably low ratings of their performance (Jones et al. 1959, Cohen and Struening 1964, Farina and Ring 1965, Farina et al. 1966). In one study, college student subjects even administered longer and more intense electric shocks to partners in a learning situation after their partners had admitted previous mental hospitalization (Farina et al. 1966).

There are some significant differences between mental illness and poverty that make any direct analogies tentative. An important feature of the perception of the mentally ill (and also, perhaps, of criminals) is the threat implied by the perceived unpredictability of their behavior (Gergen and Jones 1963). Such perceptions of unpredictability probably do not operate so strongly in responses to the poor, though there are stereotypes of those on welfare as "chiseling" and untrustworthy (Free and Cantril 1967). Another difference, however, acts to enhance the stigmatization of the poor: former occupants of mental and penal institutions are usually not as visible as such as the poor.

But there are strong similarities, too, between the domains. The mentally ill labor under a strongly negative, pervasive stereotype that, like the dominant ideology's stereotype of the poor, holds the victims to be defective and personally responsible for their condition (Cohen and Struening 1962, Nunnally 1961). And like the image of the poor, the image of the mentally ill contains such components as authoritarianism, benevolent paternalism, and the need for "social restrictiveness" (Cohen and Struening 1962).

Many of the explanations for these negative responses to the socially stigmatized open up interesting possibilities for future social psychological research on poverty. For example, Rokeach (1960) argues that those who are perceived and labeled as different are also believed to possess different values, and it is this perceived value dissimilarity that is critical in avoidance and other negative behaviors. Consistent with this position, I have noted survey evidence that indicates that many of the non-poor regard the poor as harboring deviant values—loose morals, lack of thrift, don't want to get ahead, etc. Fueled further by the projection of unacceptable id impulses, this perception of countervalues among the poor not only affects face-to-face interaction but policy preferences as well.

Another set of interesting explanations involves the attribution of responsibility. Stigmatized groups of all types bear the burden of having their distinctive behavior attributed by others to their condition. Thus, for example, one's sudden anger is not a result of the anger-inducing situation, but the result of one's blindness, or one's history of mental illness, or one's blackness—or one's poverty. This greater attribution of personal responsibility to the socially stigmatized has been held to be a function of defensive attribution—the enhancement of ego and the defense of self-esteem in causal attributions. The possibility of such negative consequences as poverty resulting from sheer chance threatens self-esteem. One must be dispositionally different from me; for if extreme poverty were due to chance, or to conditions beyond any individual's control, it could also befall me.

A similar explanation is Lerner's (1970) just-world hypothesis. Directly related to the dominant ideology, this view holds that human beings need to believe that the world is basically just. Consequently, people deserve what they get and get what they deserve. Thus, victims tend to be derogated by non-victims. Just-world assumptions may be, then, the basis for the common tendency to blame the victim, as with the third of a national survey sample who reported that their strongest reaction to hearing of the assassination of Dr. Martin Luther King, Jr. was to think that he brought it on himself (Rokeach 1970).

Both of these motivational explanations have attracted numerous experimental tests that specify the conditions under which they operate. Defensive attribution is enhanced when there is greater ego involvement in the situation (Miller 1975). Just-world predictions work best when the victim is significantly dissimilar from the perceiver; a similar victim in a role the perceiver will later assume is not derogated (Chaiken and Darley 1973). And victims with whom future interaction is anticipated are derogated less than those with whom no future contact is expected (Stokels and Schopler 1973). Nor is everyone a true believer in a just world. Rubin and Peplau (1973) successfully scaled the dimension, and their questionnaire offers a convenient technique for investigating individual differences in reactions to the poor.

More generally, the tendency of the non-poor to account for poverty in terms of the negative traits of poor individuals is a pointed case of a larger cognitive principle. In determining the causes of the implications of our actions and the actions of others, we often commit the fundamental attribution error (see Ross 1977): we generally underestimate the force of situational and societal pressures and overestimate the force of people's dispositions on their behavior. The fundamental attribution error is easily demonstrated in the laboratory. One study (Ross et al. 1977) had subjects play a quiz game with the assigned roles of questioner and contestant. Though the game allowed the questioners the enormous advantage of generating all of the questions from their own personal store of knowledge, later ratings of general knowledge were higher for the questioner. This dispositional attribution was made not only by uninvolved observers but especially by the disadvantaged contestants themselves.

A rough analogy to poverty comes readily to mind. The poor, like the contestants, have their behavior severely restricted by the conditions under which they must live. The non-poor, like the observers, are not unaware of these situational and societal constraints. Yet the fundamental attribution error still operates: the non-poor devalue the importance of the social constraints and exaggerate the importance of individual traits in their causal attributions about poverty. In addition, the poor themselves, like the contestants, will often commit the same attribution error and accept much of society's negative view of them.

Should the non-poor perceiver and the poor victim be of a different race or ethnicity, the fundamental attribution error is likely to be enhanced. Pettigrew (1978) argues that systematic misattributions often occur across groups, such that one does not grant outgroup members the same benefit of the doubt routinely granted to ingroup members. Thus, the ultimate attribution error results in attributing antisocial outgroup behavior more frequently to personal, dispositional causes, often seen as innate characteristics (e.g., "The black poor have a high crime rate, because they are born thieves."). But when acts are perceived as prosocial, outgroup behavior is more often explained in one or more of four ways. One can attribute positive outgroup behavior to situational requirements ("They saw the police watching them"), to motivational rather than innate dispositional qualities ("They just wanted us to like them"), to the special case ("She seems bright and hard-working—not at all like other poor Chicanas"), or to dumb luck. To the degree that blacks and other minorities are perceived to comprise a large proportion of those on welfare, this ultimate attribution error is likely to operate in a perception of the poor by the non-poor in general and the perception of those on welfare in particular. Glazer (1969) points out, for example, that the stigma among whites associated with AFDC has increased as the proportion of white widows in the client population has decreased.

Personal attributions are made still more likely, points out Walter Swapp in an unpublished article, by the type of information that is typically provided to both the labeler and the labeled. The behavior and the situation of the poor are likely to meet Kelley's (1967, 1972) conditions for maximizing internal causality attributions: low distinctiveness (the poor act similarly in other situations), high consistency (the poor act similarly in this situation on other occasions), and low consensus (the non-poor act differently in this situation). Ironically, though these conditions hold largely because of the situational constraints placed upon the poor, they make it more likely that poverty will be attributed to dispositional deficiencies in the poor. That this applies to the perceptions of the poor as well as those of the non-poor introduces the next central concern to which social psychology can contribute.

REACTIONS OF THE POOR

The process of deviance, especially the concept of secondary deviance suggested by Lemert (1967), provides a useful structure for reviewing what social psychologists have to say on the reactions of labeled deviants to their defined status. It consists of: (1) the primary deviant act; (2) pressure to conform; (3) failure to conform; (4) the labeling process; (5) secondary deviance and counter-labeling; and (6) confirmation of the label for the labelers. Most of our discussion will center on the fifth stage of secondary deviance.

(1) The primary deviant act that initiates the process is the focus of the traditional pathology model but is almost ignored by the labeling model. For the American poor, the condition of poverty itself is deviant. But there is also a range of specific acts in which segments of the poor may necessarily have to engage, which in the eyes of the non-poor constitute deviance—from the conspicuous wearing of old, ill-fitting clothes, not repaying debts, and even searching in waste cans to such subtle acts as avoiding the disclosure of one's slum address. Moreover, as Simmel (1908), Coser (1965), Beck (1967), and Matza (1971) emphasize, the very acts of seeking and receiving public assistance are seen as deviant.

(2) Conforming pressures to bring the deviant around often mark the next step in the process. Though neglected by symbolic interactionists, research (Schacter 1951; Festinger et al. 1950) in both the laboratory and the field emphasizes this stage. Deviants were typically recipients from other group members of increased communication to return to the fold. (3) But if they did not heed these messages and conform to expectations, rejection by the group was likely to occur.

(4) Now the labeling process is initiated. Refusing to conform is the final "evidence" needed that the labeled are in fact outsiders who do not belong. A common example of this phenomenon occurs when poor black urban youth are offered, with considerable political fanfare, dead-end

jobs at the minimum wage. When ghetto youth refuse such work, the labeling process is initiated. Their refusal "proves" that they really do not want to work, that they are "worthless dead-beats" at best and "juvenile delinquents" at worst. Becker (1963) stresses the negotiated nature that the labeling process can assume, as in plea bargaining with such high-status defendants as former Vice-President Agnew. But for those of low status, such stigmatizing labels as welfare recipient must often be accepted in exchange for the public aid legally due them.

(5) Now we arrive at the stage at which social psychology has the most to say, the stage of secondary deviance and counter-labeling. Here the defined outsiders react to their assigned label and their treatment as deviants. Often this reaction includes counter-labels; the poor can and do label their well-off fellow citizens in emotionally toned terms.

Evidence of the stigmatizing effect of being on welfare is abundant. And this evidence suggests that these effects derive not only from the external structure of the welfare system but from the client's own internalization of society's values as well. "A man guilty of poverty," wrote Samuel Johnson in *The Rambler*, "believes himself suspected." Handler and Hollingsworth (1969) note that more than half of their sample of Wisconsin welfare mothers reported that they "sometimes" or "often" feel embarrassed in the company of mothers who are not on welfare. Podell (1969) finds that more than half of his sample of New York City welfare mothers agree that "getting money from welfare makes a person feel ashamed."[6] "Life on welfare is so demeaning and depressing," writes a product of the system who grew up on welfare, "that anyone would avoid it if he could" (Atherton 1969).

Social psychology has a number of complementary means of accounting for these reports of shame and depression by welfare clients. This focus on the client must, however, always be nested within the social structure in which those on public assistance find themselves, a structure with the power to induce shame and depression among many types of people.

Reference group theory stresses that welfare recipients identify in varying degrees with the larger society and its dominant ideology. The socialization of values that uphold the sanctity of work in a society in which income and occupation determine in large measure both social status and self-esteem can by itself reduce feelings of self-worth. Add to this the fact that the welfare system is now carefully structured to reflect the dominant ideology, and the process is exacerbated.

Role theory is also relevant. A vast body of social psychological research convincingly demonstrates the power of role playing to change deeply held attitudes, values, and self-conceptions. These remarkable changes have been rendered experimentally by temporary role adoptions that are, compared with the long-term role of poor person, exceedingly trivial in nature. Imagine, then, the depth of the effects of having to play a role that has such vast personal and social significance that it effects virtually all aspects of daily living. Just as there are racial roles (Pettigrew 1971), there are also imposed social class roles, which are for the poor, perhaps, the most clearly delineated. The dominant ideology regards the proper role for the poor to be one involving humble, subservient behavior that reflects both gratitude for assistance and a strong desire for employment and escape from impoverishment.

Interactions with imperious workers of a welfare agency, sharpened by the fact that these workers represent the larger society (Jones et al. 1959), enforce such a role directly. Many welfare clients, for example, learn to trim their sails, to keep their requests modest for fear of complete rejection. But the role's debilitating force can also be triggered in more subtle ways. Recent experimental studies demonstrate this reflexive process along lines consistent with traditional symbolic interactionist theory.

One study demonstrated how naive white interviewers provide less intimacy, more speech errors, and less interview time to black compared with white job applicants (Word et al. 1974). A second experiment trained whites to interview naive white applicants. Half of this second round of interviews was conducted in the manner in which blacks had been interviewed in the initial experiment—that is, with less intimacy and less time. Whites so interviewed were later judged, like the blacks in the first study, to have been more nervous and to have performed less effectively than comparable whites "treated as whites." In addition, the whites interviewed "as blacks" reciprocated with greater distance from the interviewer and ratings of the interviewer as less friendly and adequate.

This self-fulfilling reciprocity is also shown in another experiment involving dyadic interaction between male and female undergraduate subjects (Synder et al. 1977). The males were induced prior to the interaction to believe that the female was either physically attractive or unattractive. And through apparent differences in the subsequent male behavior, those women "perceived to be physically attractive came to behave in a friendly, likeable, and sociable manner in comparison with [those] whose perceivers regarded them as unattractive" (Snyder et al. 1977, p. 656).

A third study with a similar experimental design had male undergraduates interact with male partners whom they expected to be either hostile or not hostile (Snyder and Swann 1978). As in the other research, the target partners from whom hostility was anticipated detected the non-verbal cues and did in fact display greater behavioral hostility than that of control subjects. Next the study placed these same target subjects in a second round of interactions with new subjects who had not been provided with any prior expectations about them. The results reveal that those target subjects, who had been induced to believe that their previous hostility reflected the type of person they were, continued their hostile behavior in the second encounter. In short, situationally induced behavior may be carried over into a new situation when we misattribute our behavior to dispositional causes.

A fourth investigation pushes this reflexive interaction phenomenon one step further (Farina et al. 1968). Undergraduate subjects thought that their partner had received incorrect information about them indicating previous hospitalization as a mental patient. Actually, the partner received a record describing him as a typical college student. Yet even thinking that he is being perceived as a stigmatized person greatly affected the conversation and task performance in later interaction. The experimenters noted that the self-perceived stigmatized subjects strove to dispel any unfavorable impressions about them, and in so doing generally led their partners to reject them.

The results of these important studies all illustrate the phenomenon of secondary deviance. Being treated as a stigmatized person, reacted to as physically unattractive or hostile, or even believing that one is stigmatized leads in turn to retarded performance and negative, self-defeating behavior. Consider the applications to poverty. Once the labels of poor person and welfare recipient are assigned, we can expect secondary deviance to emerge in the form of behavior that may well make escaping from poverty more difficult. Oliver Goldsmith understood this process as a participant observer: "To be poor, and to seem poor, is a certain method never to rise" (On Concealing Our Wants).

Goodban (1977) extracted support for these contentions in an ingenious secondary analysis of the Panel Study of Income Dynamics conducted by the Institute for Social Research of the University of Michigan. Annually since 1968, the household heads of about 5,000 American families are interviewed extensively by this study. Goodban isolated the data on 96 of these respondents, all of whom met the following criteria: they had answered the same 16 attitude questions every year from 1968 through 1972 and had been on welfare at least 2 consecutive years and off at least 1 year during this period. While simultaneously checking on a variety of other potential predictors, Goodban sought to determine if welfare status itself was related to attitude change within this group.

Her results are as suggestive as they are disturbing. Six of the items provide significant differences in respondents' attitudes depending on whether they were on or off welfare. With a variety of statistical procedures, Goodban shows that welfare status is related among these respondents to self-reports of: less certainty that "life would work out the way you want it to"; less ability to "finish things once you start them"; getting angry more easily; more concern over "what other people think about you"; and less trust of other prople. Typical of survey work, this evidence does not establish causal direction; and some of the results involve confounding between welfare status and such other predictors as a change of family composition. Nonetheless, these results fit closely with predictions about the effects of the welfare system derived from experimental research.

Not all of the impecunious react to being labeled poor in the same way, of course. Here we can draw on a recent social psychological analysis of the hospital patient by Taylor (1979). She emphasizes how patients forfeit control over much of their environment and respond to the consequent depersonalization by assuming either "bad patient" or "good patient" behavior. Bad patients become angry and distrustful, and they fight back at the hospital staff to regain some control over their environment—a response pattern social psychologists have studied and labeled reactance (Brehm 1966, Wortman and Brehm 1975). Good patients passively follow staff instructions but are actually in depressed or anxious states of helplessness. Taylor cites evidence for the pernicious effects of this depersonalization-reactance-helplessness cycle on both the treatment and recovery of patients. She argues for changes in hospital procedures and structure that would expand preoperative preparation and self-care in order to thwart the cycle through increased patient control.

The analogy between Taylor's convincing analysis and the plight of the poor in the welfare system is close enough to warrant discussion. The principal reactions of anger, distrust, helplessness, and concern over personal control parallel Goodban's results and the personal descriptions of what it is like to be a welfare recipient (e.g., Atherton 1969). The trade-off made by large, bureaucratic institutions in modern society, whether hospitals or welfare agencies, routinely maximizes staff efficiency and convenience at the expense of client options and control. There is good evidence, too, that the depersonalization-reactance-helplessness cycle has equally self-defeating, pernicious effects in the welfare domain. Hence, Taylor's remedial proposals for the hospital suggest possibilities for revamping the system for public assistance to the poor as well. To follow out this possibility, we need to look more carefully at the two types of secondary deviance suggested by this analogy: the angry poor and the helpless poor.

Like angry patients, angry welfare clients demand their rights and are resentful and distrustful of welfare staff personnel. They seek greater personal control over their situation. These reactions are evident in the demands and activities of the National Welfare Rights Organization (NWRO). This protest group, dominated by those involved with the AFDC program, has stressed public assistance as a right rather than a privilege and has attacked the degradation and depersonalization that it charges characterize the treatment received by its members. It has utilized direct public protest and regular political mechanisms in its attempts to alter the present welfare system. All of its direction, then, constitutes a rare mobilization of the poor to expand their control over their environment.

Such direct acting out while having a dependent status is, of course, risky. Lorber (1975) shows that medical staffs often react to "bad" surgical patients with greater use of tranquilizers and occasionally premature discharges. Similarly, overburdened welfare staffs may be unusually strict with unruly clients, and even unfairly remove them from the rolls. Taylor (1979) suggests that those who have lived active, controlling lives—often young, well-educated people—are most likely to take this risk and rebel against the sudden loss of personal control. She draws a connection between this acting-out type of individual and the Type A personality syndrome uncovered in coronary research. Type A individuals are characterized by strong needs to control, compete, and succeed. They work rapidly and hard, have a sense of time urgency, frequently become impatient and hostile when thwarted, and are twice as likely as others to develop heart disease (Friedman 1969, Jenkins 1971, Glass 1977). Type A people are especially aroused by slow-moving situations marked by frustrations and delay over which they have no control—common situations in both medical and welfare institutional settings (Glass et al. 1974).

Enviromental control is also central to the passive, helpless role: the Type B personality. Feeling powerless to alter the situation, Type B people simply do what they are told. The good patient role is rewarded by medical personnel and is the more commonly adopted role in hospitals (Taylor, 1979). Likewise, most welfare clients obey the rules and win approval by meeting the expectations of the agency staff. Many who initially resist the system's restrictions of their freedom may in time adapt to being on welfare, for there is often a temporal sequence from anger and reactance to later compliance and helplessness (Wortman and Brehm 1975). Beyond the welfare system, many of America's poor do not receive public assistance, either because of structural barriers or because of such personal barriers as pride, ignorance, or a sense of helplessness. Irwin Garfinkel (personal communication) estimates that about 60 percent of the working poor who are eligible for food stamps do not claim them and about half of the eligible recipients of the Supplementary Security Income (SSI) Program do not claim benefits.

The helpless role has its own dangers for both the poor directly and for society generally. The poor learn all too well that they cannot control most of the highly adverse events in their lives. In fact, they may learn this lesson so well that they incorrectly generalize this lack of control to situations that they could actually influence. Learned helplessness, a phenomenon of great interest to social psychologists, has, then, two major behavioral symptoms in new settings: one motivational (lessened response initiation), the other cognitive (lessened awareness that responding produces reinforcement). The symptoms could result from the typical life situations of the poor and current welfare programs. One study of young black males who reside in high-density public housing lends support to this possibility (Rodin 1976). And the poor reveal greater external locus of control (Phares 1976).

Learned helplessness has been demonstrated in fish, rats, cats, dogs, monkeys, and humans (Seligman 1975). A typical experimental demonstration of the phenomenon in humans begins by exposing subjects to either soluble or insoluble problems. When next they attempt to solve a series of anagrams, those who had been exposed previously to the insoluble problems perform less well on the anagrams (Hiroto and Seligman 1975). And the more previous experience with uncontrollable negative results, the worse the later performance becomes (Roth and Kubal 1975). This effect is limited to the control of negative events, for it does not emerge when subjects are unable to control only positive events (Benson and Kennelly, 1976). And the phenomenon appears to be mediated by attributions of personal incompetence; those who can attribute the uncontrollable adverse events to the situation rather than to personal inadequacies may well escape the phenomenon.

Learned helplessness is a potent process, for it generalizes broadly across situations and across the cognitive, affective, and conative domains. There is evidence, for example, that learned helplessness underlies feelings of hopelessness and depression—feelings often associated with poverty (Seligman 1975, Klein et al. 1976). And there is wider research support for the idea that personal control of the environment is a crucial psychological variable for a vast range of additional outcomes. Much of this work has been in the medical area, but it merits discussion here because of its direct implications for how systems of support for the nation's poor might be better designed in the future.

Two studies that dramatically reveal the force of personal control have been conducted with elderly patients in nursing homes. One study presented its experimental subjects with a communication that emphasized their responsibility for themselves and its control subjects with a communication that emphasized the nursing home staff's responsibility for them (Langer and Rodin 1976). Bolstering the communication, the experimental subjects were also given the responsibility of caring for a plant of their choice and asked to make such decisions as which night they wished to attend a movie. The control subjects were granted equal amounts of attention, assigned a plant that was cared for by the staff, and asked to make virtually no decisions. Both questionnaire ratings and behavioral measures reveal sharp differences between the groups after only three weeks. The experimental patients were markedly more alert, active, happy, and willing to participate in activities than control patients. Moreover, another follow-up revealed that these beneficial effects were sustained 18 months later (Rodin and Langer 1977).

A comparable study conducted independently obtained equally striking results (Schulz 1976). In this study there were four randomized groups of patients, and the independent variable concerned the amount of control the patients exerted over visits they received from college students. One group received no visits. A second received random visits beyond their control. A third group was informed when and how long they would be visited. The fourth could determine both the frequency and duration of the visits for themselves. There were in fact no differences between the latter three groups in the frequency and average duration of visits. Yet the results show that both the third and fourth groups two months later, relative to the first two groups, had improved self-reported psychological status, increased activity levels, and improved health status.[7]

Laboratory experiments bear out the results of these impressive field studies. One found that subjects report more physical symptoms than controls when they are exposed to adverse noise stimulation over which they have no control (Pennebaker et al. 1977). Another found that by inducing the perception of control over stress in hospital patients with a message that emphasized potential cognitive control, subjects requested fewer sedatives and pain relievers and were rated by nurses as less anxious (Langer et at. 1975). A third investigation, conducted in the test setting rather than a medical setting, also notes less anxiety among those allowed to choose the order in which they would take the tests (Stotland and Blumenthal 1964). Even the illusion of personal control can reduce the aversiveness of an event (Bowers 1968, Glass and Singer 1972, Kanfer and Seidner 1973) and increase confidence and risk-taking (Langer 1975).

Even more relevant to the poor is recent work on self-induced dependence, a process whereby an individual erroneously infers incompetence from situational factors. Langer and Benevento (1978) ingeniously studied this phenomenon by studying the effects of being (1) assigned an inferior label to another person ("assistant"), (2) engaging in a demeaning task, (3) being replaced by another person in performing a task, or (4) allowing someone to do something for you. To some degree, each of these situations tended to render the subjects helpless, even when the label was assigned randomly and there had been prior success on the task.

Lefcourt (1976 p. 424) cannot, then, be accused of hyperbole when he concludes that "the sense of control, the illusion that one can exercise personal choice, has a definite and a positive role in sustaining life."

(6) The final stage in the deviance process occurs when labelers consider the evidence of secondary deviance. Not surprisingly, the labelers are likely to view any type of secondary deviance as further proof for the original label rather than as a reaction of the "deviants" against the label and its consequences. A broad variety of secondary deviance forms can serve this legitimating function. If welfare recipients act out against their situation, mobilize in the National Welfare Rights Organization, for example, and demand their rights in Type-A fashion, the non-poor can easily regard this behavior as additional evidence that their stereotype of the chiseling, ungrateful welfare recipient who does not want to work is essentially valid. If the poor passively accept their lowly status in helpless, Type-B fashion, the non-poor can just as easily regard this behavior as confirmatory, too, of their stereotype of the lazy, ambitionless poor who do not really want to get ahead. The symbolic interactionist argument here is a strong one, for even logically opposite patterns of response are likely to confirm the original label for the labelers. And the labelers have the power to act on their interpretation of the secondary deviance.

Given this no-win situation, many of the poor understandably opt for a third possibility that has been mentioned throughout this paper. They simply attempt to pass as part of the mainstream of prosperous America; they hide their true status as poor from others and sometimes even from themselves; they spurn public assistance programs even when they are legally entitled to them and desperately in need of them; they spend a disproportionately large share of their meager funds for expensive-looking clothing; and they often appear proud and distant to middle-class acquaintances. If the social psychological analysis of poverty outlined in this paper is basically correct, this behavior is far more rational than it might at first appear. Though psychologically costly, such efforts are made to avoid the full social stigma of poverty, a stigma whose psychological costs are even greater. Such a strategy follows the perhaps wise advice of an old proverb: 'Tis true that poverty is not a sin, but all the same 'tis best to keep it in.

Summary and Suggestions

This paper has presented an array of social psychological concepts, ideas, and findings that appear to be applicable to an analysis of American poverty: value stretch; relative deprivation; deviance; social stigma; labeling; dispositional attributions; the dominant ideology; the stereotype of the poor perceived as lazy, stupid, dishonest, and ambitionless; value dissimilarity; defensive attribution; the just-world hypothesis; the fundamental attribution error; the ultimate attribution error; secondary deviance; reference group theory; role theory; self-fulfilling reciprocity in interaction; personal control over the environment; reactance; the depersonalization-reactance-helplessness cycle; and learned helplessness. And this list is not exhaustive. For example, social psychology has extensively analyzed altruism and pro-social behavior (Krebs 1970, Macaulay and Berkowitz 1970), applications of which can suggest the optimal conditions under which the powerful non-poor would more willingly accept a true war on poverty instead of the mere skirmishes of the 1960s.[8] Indeed, many social psychological ideas could be usefully and directly applied to the understanding of poverty were the discipline's resources sufficiently focused upon the issue.

We have contended that social psychological contributions are most likely to be made at the situational level of explanation. But, save for a few survey studies and symbolic interactionist discussions of the status of those on welfare, surprisingly little work in the discipline has been devoted directly to an examination of poverty. One reason for this neglect may be the lack of a broad paradigm that links the poverty domain with general social psychological thought. To overcome this barrier, the perspective of American poverty as stigmatized social deviance has been presented and some of its implications discussed.

Firm research priorities for social psychology in this area are difficult to set at this point. But three general foci have emerged from our discussion:

1. STUDIES OF THE NON-POOR

Poverty research has concentrated on the poor. But obviously the problem of poverty in America is importantly intertwined with the non-poor's dominant ideology and consequent response to the issue. Our review has uncovered a number of research leads:

a. National survey studies are needed to probe deeper into the dominant ideology in the manner pioneered by Rainwater (1974) and Kluegel and Smith (1978) in their community studies. National surveys to date have provided interesting data on attitudes, but they have not penetrated the surface of these attitudes. Of particular interest would be a more extensive model of various ways in which people resolve the many contradictions and strains in their attitudes toward poverty and relevant policy. Such a model could be the basis for generating social indicators of the poverty issue from the perspective of the non-poor.

b. Studies of the interactional responses of the non-poor to the poor are also needed to complement the survey work. This research should include both the field and laboratory approaches of the experimental social psychologists and the street observations of the symbolic interactionists. Some of it could test out ideas advanced here that American poverty is a social stigma, with the findings and research designs on interactions with the mentally ill serving as initial models (e.g., Farina et al. 1966). Additional work could test out in the poverty domain social psychology's many promising attempts to explain stigmatization effects, e.g., perceived value dissimilarity, defensive attribution.

2. STUDIES OF THE POOR

We have noted that social psychological attention has focused primarily on secondary deviance, on the reactions of the stigmatized to their situation. Building on this work suggests:

a. Research in non-verbal communications and in the self-fulfilling, reflexive nature of the interactions of the poor with the larger society. Research models for these investigations are provided by the cited work at Princeton (Word et al. 1974) and at the University of Minnesota (Snyder et al. 1977, Snyder and Swann 1978).

b. Primary and secondary survey analyses of the effects of poverty in general and being on public assistance in particular. Enormously expensive, well-conducted economic surveys are regularly sponsored by the federal government and shed light on the economic dimensions of poverty. But rarely do these surveys include social psychological questions. The 1968–72 Income Dynamics surveys of the Institute For Social Research at the University of Michigan were exceptions; and they made possible Goodban's (1977) secondary analysis on the attitude effects of being on welfare. Her interesting results suggest the need for more extensive, over-time survey data especially designed to address this question. Such data could be inexpensively generated if relevant questions were added to regularly funded economic surveys. And integrative social psychologists at the University of Michigan who have experience in cooperating with economists on these projects are the obvious people to conduct such research.

c. Field research on the problems of the poor dealing with welfare agencies. Similar questions concerning the social psychological effects of current public assistance programs need also to be addressed by detailed field research. While probability-sample surveys develop the broad perspective on the problem, field research is required to achieve a more sensitive fine-tuning of the causal relationships involved. Again, both experimental and observational methods are called for; and Taylor's hospital patient role analysis presents a useful model.

d. Experimental applications of the learned helplessness paradigm to poverty. One example in the research literature suggests what might be looked for in such investigations. Rodin (1976) performed her study with young black boys who lived in public housing. The classic Seligman model of learned helplessness did not apply to all of her sample but was concentrated among those children who were living in extremely crowded apartments. Unfortunately, there is some confounding of key variables that make the interpretation of these findings tentative. But the point is that such research, systematically conducted, could perhaps isolate those specific conditions that lead to learned helplessness among certain sectors of the poor. The policy implications and the potential benefits of such specification give this research high priority.

3. RESEARCH DIRECTLY AIMED AT AIDING THE REDESIGNING
OF PUBLIC ASSISTANCE PROGRAMS

Repeatedly we have noted the degradation of the poor involved with many of our public assistance programs. Like Taylor's suggested hospital reforms to benefit patients, social psychological analyses could aid in the generation of reforms of our welfare programs to benefit recipients.

a. Studies of the poor and non-poor interacting in situations that involve public assistance. Some might argue that interactional studies have no practical value for guiding public policy. This skepticism appears unwarranted, however, when we consider the recent history of the food stamp program. Why has this particular program been the target of so much criticism? One might have thought such a governmental effort would appeal to popular sentiment as an unusually humane means of bringing food and milk to hungry Americans. Moreover, in comparison to many other welfare programs, food stamps constitute a relatively modest endeavor. So why all the controversy?

One answer lies at the interactional level, for the food stamp program is one of the few programs for the poor that unfolds before the eyes of large segments of the non-poor. And considerable social psychological research has demonstrated the far greater cognitive potency of the vivid, concrete case than the pallid abstractions of base-line data (Borgida and Nisbett 1977). The use of food stamps in grocery stores in which both the poor and the not-so-poor shop is made vivid and conspicuous by the program's arrangements. Bright, large stamps are handed over the check-out counter while the non-poor in line eye the shopper's food cart for suspicious items. An incident that took place before me recently makes this point clear.

"Look," exclaimed one woman in a loud voice, pointing at a six-pack of beer in the food-stamp shopper's cart in front of us in line, "and paid for by *my* taxes!" That the beer in question was properly paid for with cash rather than stamps, that the rest of the cart contained relatively nutritious items, and that the irate shopper herself had three six-packs of the same beer in her cart did not deter her anger over detecting "another welfare chiseler." Some markets make the program even more salient by having specially marked check-out lines for those with food stamps. Thus, even the grocery line one stands in is determined by one's income level! Little wonder that some users of food stamps report that each week's trip to the market is a tense, traumatic occasion.

This situation is ripe for a symbolic interactionist analysis. And it highlights why studies of how the non-poor and poor interact have eminently practical implications.

b. Comparative studies of the social psychological dynamics involved in a variety of "welfare" programs for the poor and non-poor alike. Though detailing microprocesses, social psychological analyses frequently suggest direct structural reforms. Taylor's analysis of microprocesses in hospitals illustrates this potentiality. Similarly, in the domain of public assistance, the many considerations emphasized in this paper bear unmistakable structural implications. As opposed to current arrangements of such programs as AFDC, food stamps, and public housing, future programs would ideally not isolate the poor as a labeled, stigmatized, separate category of citizens to be administratively dealt with by a code not employed for other Americans.

Contrast the dignity-damaging arrangements of AFDC, for instance, with those that provide public aid for middle-income and upper-income citizens. No label is forthcoming when the non-poor write off from their taxes annually the interest paid on home mortgages. This massive federal welfare program for American homeowners is never called welfare; such a write-off is perceived as a right rather than a privilege; it is obtained in the privacy of one's personal office by filling out tax forms rather than in a welfare office by standing in long lines with other claimants; and, while the Internal Revenue Service may review the tax form, no social worker will set up constant surveillance of one's activities and intrude on one's privacy. Research on how the nation successfully administers with dignity and efficiency much larger programs of welfare for the prosperous will suggest the structural means by which nonstigmatized welfare programs for the indigent could be designed.

One survey study has attempted to compare the degree of stigma attached to 13 different types of existing or proposed programs (Williamson 1974b). A probability sample of 230 white women in the Boston area were handed cards in randomized order with short descriptions of each program. Employing ratio scaling, Williamson assigned unemployment compensation a rating of 100 and requested his respondents to rate the amount of stigma they attached to the other 12 programs relative to unemployment compensation.

Williamson's results are shown in Table 1. Not surprisingly, general relief and AFDC are accorded the greatest stigma; and, after four decades of universal application, social security is accorded virtually no stigma. More interesting are the intermediate ratings. Programs that involve low-income people improving their occupational or educational status (JOBS, New Careers, and Head Start) are minimally stigmatized, with lower ratings than even Old Age Assistance. Proposed programs guaranteeing employment or income, however, are about midway between the highly stigmatized and the minimally stigmatized programs. Williamson also found that more liberal and higher status women gave higher stigma ratings than others.

Crude and limited as this initial investigation is, it nonetheless demonstrates the potential of survey methods to ascertain at least the general order of magnitude of the problem across different forms of welfare programs. More detailed work using observational, quasi-experimental, and experimental methods are also needed to investigate the issue of differential stigmatization across programs and forms of administration. Beyond blocking out the problem's larger dimensions in surveys, these more detailed methods are needed to understand the over-time microprocesses involved. The nursing home studies (Langer and Rodin 1976, Rodin and Langer 1977, Schulz 1976), described earlier, offer one model for this type of study. Such research, for example, could examine both the personal and program effects of various procedures for granting more responsibility and choice to welfare clients. And organizational social psychologists (Katz and Kahn 1966, Weick 1969) could study how best to reorganize welfare administration in order to rationalize these new procedures within the total structural framework of these programs.

Table 1
Rated Stigma of Public Aid Programs and Proposals

Program	Median	Mean	Standard Error of the Mean
General Relief	125	137	7.8
AFDC	100	127	7.2
Unemployment Compensation (arbitrarily set as comparison standard)	100	100	
Public Housing	80	86	4.8
Government as Employer of Last Resort	75	88	6.4
Guaranteed Annual Income	75	82	4.4
Aid to the Permanently and Totally Disabled	75	72	4.5
Old Age Assistance	50	75	5.4
WIN	50	64	5.1
JOBS	25	47	3.4
Head Start	20	44	4.1
New Careers	20	37	3.2
Social Security	0	27	2.8

Source: Adapted from Williamson (1974b:220); see text for methodological description.

A FINAL WORD

In closing, two related caveats must be stated concerning the employment of social psychologists in the study of poverty. First, though it searches for the mediators between the individual and social levels, social psychology is still basically a microlevel social science. As such, its analyses run a constant danger of appearing to blame the victim, of making it appear as though the problem largely resided in the personal inadequacies of the poor (Caplan and Nelson 1973). Such valuable concepts as relative deprivation, learned helplessness, the role of the poor person, et cetera, can all be easily misused in this manner. Hence, unless these concepts and ideas are carefully embedded in a larger structural context and attention is paid to the prosperous as well as the poor, social psychological analyses can provide a dangerously one-sided view of this multi-level problem.

Related to this point is another problem. Two of the discipline's subgroups, experimental social psychology and symbolic interactionism, have not benefited from intensive interdisciplinary exposure for some years. Accordingly, their analyses are often incomplete when placed in a broader social context. Consequently, it would seem wise in the future to involve social psychologists in the study of American poverty as part of larger interdisciplinary research efforts. Such a broader perspective would enhance the scope and applicability of the social psychological contributions as well as benefit the emerging discipline itself.

Much the same argument can be made concerning the benefits of interdisciplinary research on American poverty for economics. Nobel prize winner Herbert Simon and Andrew Stedry (1969) have detailed how social psychology could help reformulate the too-simple model of economic man. Similarly, the combination of the disciplines in the study of poverty could broaden the applied perspectives of economics as well.

One example of the form this broadening might take arose during a discussion of an earlier draft of this paper at the University of Wisconsin's Institute for Research on Poverty. A clear implication of this paper, the potentially serious stigmatization consequences of the means test, drew particular attention from an audience that was comprised largely of economists. The costing out of eliminating the means test in various welfare programs seemed a trivial problem to many of the economists present, though the assumptions freely made about human dishonesty escaped my understanding. Absolute dollar estimates were even bantered about. But the difficult question posed concerned the costing out of the damage of having a means test. Soiled identities, lowered self-esteem, and increased crime and mental illness are hard to estimate. Consequently, these more hidden costs are likely to be ignored, and policy decisions unduly influenced by considerations that can more easily be costed out. Social psychology has no easy answers to this problem, of course; but it can at least raise these issues for economists and the poverty field generally. Thus, the theory and findings of social psychology become directly relevant to such critical practical issues as whether income maintenance programs should be income-tested or universal.[9] There is hope that the joining of this emerging discipline in the effort to understand and ameliorate American poverty will take place in the near future.

Notes

1. The term "integrative social psychology" is introduced here, but the general idea of three subgroups of the discipline has been noted previously by other writers (e.g., House 1977).

2. This possibility was suggested by Nancy Goodban. She notes that other groups, such as Asian Americans, who have not mobilized to protest discrimination, have been similarly neglected in the research literature of social psychology.

3. This possibility was suggested in a private communication from Hugh Heclo.

4. In response to those who rightfully complain that social problem analyses overstress abnormality, it should be noted that this perspective differs significantly from social science tradition. Poverty is not being viewed as deviant as such; rather, it is the perceptions of poverty as deviant by the poor and the non-poor alike that are under scrutiny.

5. The author is particularly indebted to Shelley Taylor for her ideas and help with this research literature.

6. Note that both of these investigations of the reactions of welfare mothers uncovered sizable minorities who did not report shame or embarrassment. These contrasting responses are the subject of an analysis to follow between reactance and helplessness.

7. The similarity between Schulz's (1976) third and fourth groups indicates that this phenomenon includes more factors than just personal control. Perhaps the ability to plan one's day and prepare for the visits, both of which were enhanced in the third and fourth groups, is also critical. And these factors may also be critical for the poor, as suggested by Goodban's (1977) findings described earlier.

8. A vast and interesting research literature has now developed on prosocial behavior, a literature too vast to discuss adequately in this paper. This area may be as important for an understanding of poverty as the stigma literature, though its conclusions do not conflict with those from the stigma area advanced here. Work on altruism challenges in significant ways many of the assumptions made about human nature in both economic models and popular conceptions of poverty. By way of illustration, this research suggests that altruism is more a function of the situation and of the affective state of the benefactor than of the benefactor's personality traits. In particular, interpersonally attractive recipients who are seen as dependent for external reasons most often elicit pro-social behavior. This is especially true if the recipient is perceived as similar to the benefactor—a factor that often does not hold in the poverty domain (Krebs 1970).

9. A 1979 Conference on Universal Versus Income-Tested Transfer Programs, convened by the Institute for Research on Poverty, was set up explicitly to bring together an interdisciplinary focus upon this issue, with invitations to historians, political scientists, sociologists, and social psychologists as well as economists.

References

Atherton, C. R. (1969) Growing up obscene: the byproduct of life on AFDC. *Public Welfare,* 27(Oct.):371-375.

Banfield, E.C. (1970) *The Unheavenly City: The Nature and Future of Our Urban Crisis.* Boston: Little, Brown.

Beck, B. (1967) Welfare as a moral category. *Social Problems* 14: 258-277.

Becker, H. S. (1963) *Outsiders.* New York: Free Press.

Benson, J. S., and Kennelly, K. J. (1976) Learned helplessness: the result of uncontrollable reinforcements or uncontrollable aversive stimuli? *Journal of Personality and Social Psychology* 34: 138-145.

Blumer, H. (1969) *Symbolic Interactionism.* Englewood Cliffs, N.J.: Prentice-Hall.

Borgida, E., and Nisbett, R. E. (1977) The differential impact of abstract vs. concrete information on decisions. *Journal of Applied Social Psychology* 7:258-271.

Bowers, K. (1968) Pain, anxiety, and perceived control. *Journal of Consulting and Clinical Psychology* 32:596-602.

Brehm, J. W. (1966) *A Theory of Psychological Reactance.* New York: Academic Press.

Caplan, N., and Nelson, S. D. (1973) On being useful: the nature and consequences of psychological research on social problems. *American Psychologist* 28:199-211.

Chaikin, A. L., and Darley, J. M. (1973) Victim or perpetrator?: defensive attribution of responsibility and the need for order and justice. *Journal of Personality and Social Psychology* 25: 268-275.

Chase, A. (1977) *The Legacy of Malthus: The Social Costs of the New Scientific Racism.* New York: Knopf.

Cohen, J., and Struening, E. L. (1962) Opinions about mental health in the personnel of two large mental hospitals. *Journal of Abnormal and Social Psychology* 64:349-360.

Cohen, J., and Struening, E. L. (1964) Opinions about mental health: hospital social atmosphere profiles and their relevance to effectiveness. *Journal of Consulting Psychology* 28:291-298.

Coser, L. (1965) Sociology of poverty. *Social Problems* 13:140-148.

Crosby, F. (1976) A model of egoistical relative deprivation. *Psychological Review* 83:85-113.

Davis, J. A. (1959) A formal interpretation of relative deprivation. *Sociometry* 22:280-296.

Doob, A. N., and Ecker, B. P. (1970) Stigma and compliance. *Journal of Personality and Social Psychology* 14:302-304.

Duesenberry, J. S. (1949) *Income, Saving and the Theory of Consumer Behavior.* Cambridge, Mass.: Harvard University Press.

Farina, A., Allen, J. G., and Saul, B. B. (1968) The role of the stigmatized person in affecting social relationships. *Journal of Personality* 36:169-182.

Farina, A., Holland, C. H., and Ring, K. (1966) Role of stigma and set in interpersonal interaction. *Journal of Abnormal Psychology* 71:421–428.

Farina, A., and Ring, K. (1965) The influence of perceived mental illness on interpersonal relations. *Journal of Abnormal Psychology* 70:47–51.

Feagin, J. R. (1975) *Subordinating the Poor.* Englewood Cliffs, N.J.: Prentice-Hall.

Festinger, L., Schachter, S., and Back, K. (1950) *Social Pressures in Informal Groups: A Study of Human Factors in Housing.* New York: Harper.

Free, L. A., and Cantril, H. (1967) *The Political Beliefs of Americans: A Study of Public Opinion.* New Brunswick, N.J.: Rutgers University Press.

Friedman, M. (1969) *Pathogenesis of Coronary Artery Disease.* New York: McGraw-Hill.

Freeman, J., and Doob, A. (1968) *Deviancy.* New York: Academic Press.

Gergen, K. J., and Jones, E. E. (1963) Mental illness, predictability, and affective consequences as stimulus factors in person perception. *Journal of Abnormal and Social Psychology* 67:95–104.

Glass, D. C. (1977) *Behavior Patterns, Stress, and Coronary Disease.* Hillsdale, N.J.: Erlbaum.

Glass, D. C., and Singer, J. E. (1972) *Urban Stress.* New York: Academic Press.

Glass, D. C., Snyder, M. L., and Hollis, J. F. (1974) Time urgency and the Type A coronary-prone behavior pattern. *Journal of Applied Social Psychology* 4:125–140.

Glazer, N. (1969) Beyond income maintenance—a note on welfare in New York City. *The Public Interest* 16(Summer):102–120.

Gleason, J. M., and Harris, V. A. (1976) Group discussion and defendant's socioeconomic status as determinants of judgments by simulated jurors. *Journal of Applied Social Psychology* 6:186–191.

Goffman, E. (1963) *Stigma: Notes on the Management of Soiled Identity.* Englewood Cliffs, N.J.: Prentice-Hall.

Goodban, N. (1977) Historical and Contemporary Aspects of the Welfare System and the Effects on Clients. Unpublished paper, Department of Psychology and Social Relations, Harvard University.

Goodwin, L. (1971) A Study of the Work Orientations of Welfare Recipients Participating in the Work Incentive Program. Unpublished report submitted to the Office of Research and Development, Manpower Administration, U.S. Department of Labor, Washington, D.C.

Guttentag, M., ed. (1970a) The poor: impact on research and theory. *Journal of Social Issues* 26: entire issue.

Guttentag, M., ed. (1970b) Professionals and the poor. *Journal of Social Issues* 26: entire issue.

Handler, J. F., and Hollingsworth, E. J. (1969) Stigma, privacy, and other attitudes of welfare recipients. *Stanford Law Review* 22:1–19.

Helmreich, R. (1975) Applied social psychology: the unfulfilled promise. *Personality and Social Psychology Bulletin* 1:548–560.

Henslin, J. M., and Roesti, P. M. (1976) Trends and topics in *Social Problems* 1953–1975: A content analysis and critique. *Social Problems* 24:54–68.

Hiroto, D. S., and Seligman, M. E. P. (1975) Generality of learned helplessness in man. *Journal of Personality and Social Psychology* 31:311–327.

House, J. S. (1977) The three faces of social psychology. *Sociometry* 40:161–177.

Huber, J., and Form, W. H. (1973) *Income and Ideology*. New York: Free Press.

Jenkins, C. D. (1971) Psychological and social precursors of coronary disease. *New England Journal of Medicine* 284:244–255, 307–316.

Jones, E. E., Hester, S. L., Farina, A., and Davis, K. E. (1959) Reactions to unfavorable personal evaluations as a function of the evaluator's perceived adjustment. *Journal of Abnormal and Social Psychology* 59:363–370.

Kanfer, F. H., and Seidner, M. L. (1973) Self-control: factors enhancing tolerance of noxious stimulation. *Journal of Personality and Social Psychology* 25:381–389.

Kaplan, B. H., ed. (1965) Poverty dynamics and interventions. *Journal of Social Issues* 21: entire issue.

Kaplan, H. R., and Tausky, C. (1972) Work and the welfare Cadillac: the function of the commitment to work among the hard-core unemployed. *Social Problems* 19:469–483.

Katz, D., and Kahn, R. L. (1966) *The Social Psychology of Organizations*. New York: Wiley.

Kelley, H. H. (1967) Attribution theory in social psychology. In D. Levine, ed., *Nebraska Symposium on Motivation, 1967*. Lincoln: University of Nebraska Press.

Kelley, H. H. (1972) Attribution in social interaction. In E. Jones, D. Kanouse, H. Kelley, R. Nisbett, S. Valins, and B. Weiner, *Attribution: Perceiving the Causes of Behavior*. Morristown, N.J.: General Learning Press.

Kleck, R. (1966) Emotional arousal in interactions with stigmatized persons. *Psychological Reports* 19:1226.

Kleck, R. (1966) Physical stigma and nonverbal cues emitted in face-to-face interaction. *Human Relations* 21:19–28.

Kleck, R. (1969) Physical stigma and task oriented interactions. *Human Relations* 22:53–60.

Kleck, R., Ono, H., and Hastorf, A. H. (1966) The effects of physical deviance upon face-to-face interaction. *Human Relations* 19:425–436.

Klein, D. C., Fencil-Morse, E., and Seligman, M. E. P. (1976) Learned helplessness, depression, and the attribution of failure. *Journal of Personality and Social Psychology* 33:508–516.

Kluegel, J. R., and Smith, E. R. (1978) The organization of stratification beliefs. Unpublished paper, Department of Sociology, University of California, Riverside.

Krebs, D. L. (1970) Altruism—an examination of the concept and a review of the literature. *Psychological Bulletin* 73:258–302.

Kriesberg, L. (1970) *Mothers in Poverty: A Study of Fatherless Families.* Chicago: Aldine.

Lane, R. E. (1962) *Political Ideology.* New York: Free Press.

Langer, E. (1975) The illusion of control. *Journal of Personality and Social Psychology* 32:311–328.

Langer, E., and Benevento, A. (1978) Self-induced dependence. *Journal of Personality and Social Psychology* 36:886–893.

Langer, E., and Rodin, J. (1976) The effects of choice and enhanced personal responsibility for the aged: a field experiment in an institutional setting. *Journal of Personality and Social Psychology* 34:191–198.

Langer, E., Janis, I. L., and Wolfer, J. A. (1975) Reduction of psychological stress in surgical patients. *Journal of Experimental Social Psychology* 11:155–165.

Langer, E., Taylor, S. E., Fiske, S., and Chanowitz, B. (1976) Stigma, staring, and discomfort: a novel-stimulus hypothesis. *Journal of Experimental Social Psychology* 12:451–463.

Lefcourt, H. (1976) *Locus of Control: Current Trends in Theory and Research.* Hillsdale, N.J.: Erlbaum.

Lemert, E. M. (1967) *Human Deviance, Social Problems, and Social Control.* Englewood Cliffs, N.J.: Prentice-Hall.

Lemon, R. (1971) *The Troubled American.* New York: Simon and Schuster.

Lerner, M. J. (1970) The desire for justice and reactions to victims. In J. Macaulay and L. Berkowitz, eds., *Altruism and Helping Behavior.* New York: Academic Press.

Lewis, O. (1959) *Five Families: Mexican Case Studies in the Culture of Poverty.* New York: Basic Books.

Lewis, O. (1961) *The Children of Sanchez.* New York: Random House.

Lewis, O. (1965) *La Vida.* New York: Random House.

Lewis, O. (1966) The culture of poverty. *Scientific American* 215(4):19–25.

Liebow, E. (1967) *Tally's Corner.* Boston: Little, Brown.

Lindesmith, A. R., Strauss, A. L., and Denzin, N. K. (1977) *Social Psychology.* Fifth ed. New York: Holt, Rinehart and Winston.

Lindzey, G., ed. (1954) *Handbook of Social Psychology.* Vols. I and II. Reading, Mass.: Addison-Wesley.

Lindzey, G., and Aronson, E., eds. (1969) *Handbook of Social Psychology.* 2nd Ed. Volumes I–V. Reading, Mass.: Addison-Wesley.

Lorber, J. (1975) Good patients and problem patients: conformity and deviance in a general hospital. *Journal of Health and Social Behavior.* 16:213–225.

Macaulay, J., and Berkowitz, L., eds. (1970) *Altruism and Helping Behavior.* New York: Academic Press.

Matza, D. (1971) Poverty and disrepute. In R. K. Merton and R. Nisbet, eds., *Contemporary Social Problems.* 3rd Ed. New York: Harcourt Brace Jovanovich.

Merton, R. K., and Rossi, A. S. (1957) Contributions to the theory of reference group behavior. In R. K. Merton, ed., *Social Theory and Social Structure.* New York: Free Press.

Miller, A. G. (1975) Actor and observer perceptions of the learning of a task. *Journal of Experimental Social Psychology* 11:95–111.

Nunnally, J. C. (1961) *Popular Conceptions of Mental Health.* New York: Holt, Rinehart and Winston.

Pennebaker, J. W., Burnam, M. A., Schaeffer, M. A., and Harper, D. C. (1977) Lack of control as a determinant of perceived physical symptoms. *Journal of Personality and Social Psychology* 35:167–174.

Pettigrew, T. F. (1967) Social evaluation theory: convergences and applications. In D. Levine, ed., *Nebraska Symposium on Motivation, 1967.* Lincoln: University of Nebraska Press.

Pettigrew, T. F. (1971) *Racially Separate or Together?* New York: McGraw-Hill.

Pettigrew, T. F. (1978) Three issues in ethnicity: boundaries, deprivations, and perceptions. In J. M. Yinger and S. J. Cutler, eds., *Major Social Issues: A Multidisciplinary View.* New York: Basic Books.

Phares, E. J. (1976) *Locus of Control in Personality.* Morristown, N.J.: General Learning Press.

Podell, L. (1969) *Families on Welfare in New York City.* Report of the Center for Social Research. New York: City University of New York.

Potter, D. M. (1954) *People of Plenty: Economic Abundance and the American Character.* Chicago: University of Chicago Press.

Rainwater, L. (1974) *What Money Buys: Inequality and the Social Meanings of Money.* New York: Basic Books.

Rodin, J. (1976) Density, perceived choice, and response to controllable and uncontrollable outcomes. *Journal of Experimental Social Psychology* 12:564–578.

Rodin, J., and Langer, E. (1977) Long-term effects of a control-relevant intervention with the institutionalized aged. *Journal of Personality and Social Psychology* 35:897–902.

Rodman, H. (1964) Middle-class misconceptions about lower-class families. In A. B. Shostak and W. Gomberg, eds., *Blue-Collar World: Studies of the American Worker.* Englewood Cliffs, N.J.: Prentice-Hall.

Rokeach, M. (1960) *The Open and Closed Mind.* New York: Basic Books.

Rokeach, M. (1970) Faith, hope, bigotry. *Psychology Today* 3(11):33–37.

Ross, L. (1977) The intuitive psychologist and his shortcomings: distortions in the attribution process. In L. Berkowitz, ed., *Advances in Experimental Social Psychology.* Vol. 10. New York: Academic Press.

Ross, L., Amabile, T. M., and Steinmetz, J. L. (1977) Social roles, social control, and biases in social-perception processes. *Journal of Personality and Social Psychology.* 35:485–494.

Roth, S., and Kubal, L. (1975) Effects of noncontingent reinforcement on tasks of differing importance: facilitation and learned helplessness. *Journal of Personality and Social Psychology* 32:680–691.

Rubin, Z., and Peplau, A. (1973) Belief in a just world and reactions to another's lot: a study of participants in the national draft lottery. *Journal of Social Issues* 4:73–93.

Runciman, W. G. (1966) *Relative Deprivation and Social Justice*. London: Routledge and Kegan Paul.

Schachter, S. (1951) Deviation, rejection, and communication. *Journal of Abnormal and Social Psychology* 46:190–207.

Schultz, R. (1976) Effects of control and predictability on the physical and psychological well-being of the institutionalized aged. *Journal of Personality and Social Psychology* 33:563–573.

Seligman, M. E. P. (1975) *Helplessness*. San Francisco: Freeman.

Simmel, G. (1908) *Soziologie*. Leipzig: Dunker and Humblot.

Simon, H. A., and Stedry, A. C. (1969) Psychology and economics. In G. Lindzey and E. Aronson, eds., *Handbook of Social Psychology*. 2nd Ed. Vol. V. Reading, Mass.: Addison-Wesley.

Smith, E. R., and Kluegel, J. R. (1978) Social Class and Attitudes Toward Welfare: Defensive Attribution Outside the Laboratory. Unpublished paper, Department of Sociology, University of California, Riverside.

Snyder, M., and Swann, W. B. Jr. (1978) Behavioral confirmation in social interaction: from social perception to social reality. *Journal of Experimental Social Psychology* 14:148–162.

Snyder, M., Tanke, E. D., and Berscheid, E. (1977) Social perception and interpersonal behavior: on the self-fulfilling nature of social stereotypes. *Journal of Personality and Social Psychology* 35:656–666.

Spector, A. J. (1956) Expectations, fulfillment, and morale. *Journal of Abnormal and Social Psychology* 52:51–56.

Steiner, I. D. (1974) Whatever happened to the group in social psychology. *Journal of Experimental Social Psychology* 10:94–108.

Stokels, D., and Schopler, J. (1973) Reactions to victims under conditions of situational detachment: the effects of responsibility, severity, and expected future interaction. *Journal of Personality and Social Psychology* 25:199–209.

Stotland, E., and Blumenthal, A. (1964) The reduction of anxiety as a result of the expectation of making a choice. *Canadian Review of Psychology* 18:139–145.

Stouffer, S. A., and Lazarsfeld, P. F. (1937) *Research Memorandum on the Family in the Depression*. Bulletin 29. New York: Social Science Research Council.

Stouffer, S. A., Suchman, E. A., DeVinney, L. C., Star, S. A., and Williams, R. M., Jr. (1949) *The American Soldier*. Vol. 1. *Adjustment During Army Life*. Princeton, N.J.: Princeton University Press.

Taylor, S. E. (1979) Hospital patient behavior: reactance, helplessness, or control? *Journal of Social Issues* 35:156–184.

Thomas, G. (1977) *Poverty in the Nonmetropolitan South*. Research monograph of the Regional Institute for Social Welfare Research. Athens, Ga.: University of Georgia.

Valentine, C. A. (1968) *Culture and Poverty*. Chicago: University of Chicago Press.

Weick, K. E. (1969) *The Social Psychology of Organizing*. Reading, Mass.: Addison-Wesley.

Weissberg, N. C. (1976) Applied social psychology. In B. Seidenberg and
    A. Snadowsky, eds., *Social Psychology: An Introduction.* New York:
    Free Press.
Williamson, J. B. (1974a) Beliefs about the welfare poor. *Sociology and Social
    Research* 58:163–175.
Williamson, J. B. (1974b) The stigma of public dependency: a comparison of
    alternative forms of public aid to the poor. *Social Problems*
    22:213–228.
Word, C. O., Zanna, H. P., and Cooper, J. (1974) The nonverbal mediation
    of self-fulfilling prophecies in interracial interaction. *Journal of Ex-
    perimental Social Psychology* 10:109–120.
Wortman, C. B., and Brehm, J. M. (1975) Responses to uncontrollable out-
    comes: an integration of reactance theory and the learned helplessness
    model. In L. Berkowitz, ed., *Advances in Experimental Social
    Psychology.* Vol. 8. New York: Academic Press.
Zawadski, B., and Lazarsfeld, P. F. (1935) Psychological consequences of
    unemployment. *Journal of Social Psychology* 6:224–251.

Martin Rein and Lisa Peattie

Problem Frames in Poverty Research

Introduction

This paper does not attempt to examine poverty research by critically reviewing various empirical and theoretical studies that have been done, by indicating their strengths and inadequaties, or by proposing additional and perhaps modified research. Instead, it attempts to locate the intellectual tradition on which poverty research is based to provide an alternative framework for thinking about poverty research, and thereby to sharpen our understanding of the assumptions on which present poverty research rests.

Present conceptions about poverty are grounded in an implicit political theory about the sources of change; these conceptions shape and constrain the kinds of questions that are posed and indicate what points in the system can appropriately be thought of as targets for change.

The institutions and ideas surrounding poverty research seem implicitly to involve conceptualizations in three different realms: the political, the economic, and the social realms. These realms, while separate, interact so that one can in principle start in any one realm and be led naturally to the others. In practice, poverty research starts with the political realm, in which programmatic intervention takes place.

TWO APPROACHES TO POVERTY RESEARCH

Each of these realms can be conceptualized differently and a variety of academic disciplines and professions have historically established ways of looking at each realm. A reciprocal relationship exists between the

[Martin Rein is professor of social policy in the Department of Urban Studies and Planning, Massachusetts Institute of Technology. Lisa Peattie is professor of anthropology, Department of Urban Studies and Planning, Massachusetts Institute of Technology.]

research and the conceptualizations developed through these established intellectual traditions and the design of programmatic interventions; research may stimulate new program designs, and new opportunites for intervention or difficulties arising in the practice of old ones generate agendas for research. However, we believe that there is a general tendency for an established structure of intervention (i.e., government and its policies) to set a framework for conceptualization and research, a framework that to a substantial degree stablizes and bounds them over time. In this way policy leads to research, rather than the other way around.

The distinction made in the political realm between potential clients who are expected to work and those who are not expected to work divides poverty research along lines suggested by two different models of programmatic intervention. The first model of intervention we label the direct distribution approach. (It might also be called the income redistribution approach.) This approach uses programs for distributing income and goods such as food and housing as its main mode of intervention, and it measures the appropriateness and effectiveness of its interventions against an understanding of society in which income is a proxy by which to measure the relative well-being of individuals. In this approach, the political realm is separate from, although related to, the social and economic realms; intervention is not seen as altering the operations of the other two realms, but as correcting for their undesired effects.

The second model of programmatic intervention, which we call the work distribution approach sees the occupational structure as the stragetic point for programmatic intervention, since it is through jobs that the original distribution of resources begins. Other terms by which this approach is identified associate it with "jobs" or "occupations." The approach thus directs itself to intervention in labor markets by increasing individual human capital, by removing barriers to access to labor submarkets, or by creating new jobs. In this approach the political realm sees intervention as altering the economic realm in order to maintain the norms of the social realm. How deeply to intervene into the structure of capitalist society is at issue; in addition this approach searches for points of intervention that will have minimal consequences for the general functioning of both the economic and social realms.

Some of the problems that concern poverty research fall between both models of intervention, but the treatment of such problems and the associated research agenda depend on the model that is used to deal with them. Unemployment is an example of a problem that is dealt with in both the direct distribution and the work distribution models of intervention. When the consequences of unemployment are seen as a problem of the loss of earnings, the remedy sought is a strategy of earnings replacement. The intellectual rationale underlying most social security programs, takes the direct distribution approach. When unemployment is seen as a problem of job loss or (in the cases of youth and housewives) as a problem of labor market entry, the remedy sought may be a strategy of public employment, work experience, or job training programs, which take the work distribution approach. Research about unemployment from the direct distribution approach deals with questions ranging from adequacy to abuse. By contrast, research on unemployment from the work distribution approach centers on such questions as the adequacy of unemployment as a proxy for hardship, the dynamics of unemployment (layoffs, voluntary unemployment) and analysis of alternative strategies (improved job search, training, job creation, etc.). Sickness is another example of a problem that is variously treated: as a benefit in the direct distribution approach or as "sick pay" in the work distribution approach.

The apparent need, in the political realm, to design programs with either a direct distribution approach or a work distribution approach creates distinctions that hardly appear in the study of the economic and the social realms within the academic traditions. The academic disciplines implicitly assume that there is unity between the study of economic institutions and the study of social institutions, because a strong degree of congruence exists between economic rewards and social well-being and satisfaction. The performance of markets in industrial societies binds together the two systems of occupation and of reward. Entering the problem of program design from one or the other approach is regarded as not particularly important, because each puzzle can lead to the other, if pursued far enough. Thus, it does not appear necessary or even useful to make a clear distinction between the study of distributional issues, that is, the reward system or the distributional dimensions of stratification, and the study of relational issues, that is, the occupational system or the aspects of class having to do with an individual's relation to the means of production and the structure of authority, since distributional and relational issues are both aspects of the same question.[1] The bedrock of the stratified or class system depends on one's position in the occupational structure, and the distribution of social and material benefits closely correlates with that occupational position.

Although the direct distribution and the work distribution approaches can be assimilated into a single framework that sets off the political realm from the economic and social realms, within the political realm a choice between the two approaches must be made at the beginning, because the practical implications lead in very different directions. The two approaches, when applied, in turn generate differing research agendas, each of which draws on academic traditions of the study of the economic and social realms but takes new directions shaped by concerns for programs.

Programmatic intervention through the direct distribution approach draws largely on economic research on factor shares: that is, distribution according to major functional groupings such as labor and capital. This approach has generated a substantial body of research more directly responsive to concerns for distributional programs that are thought to increase well-being, and that takes as a unit of analysis the rewards flowing from resources available to individuals and to families.

Programmatic intervention through the work distribution approach draws on structural studies intended to develop understanding of the socioeconomic structure of society: that is, how economic institutions shape the social structure and are, in turn, shaped by it. However, the programmatic concerns of this approach tend to draw thinking away from an interest in the general functioning of the economy on a macroscale, toward a set of studies that takes as a unit of analysis the job, the firm, the occupation, or the industry in which people work.

Through both the direct distribution and the work distribution approaches, studies of poverty have thus taken existing bodies of academic research, drawn from them, and pulled them into lines more responsive to programmatic concerns.

Research on Direct Distribution

The direct distribution approach to research generates a set of conceptual problems around the questions: What should be counted as income? Whose income should be aggregated? Within what unit of time? (Monthly, annually, once a lifetime?) These conceptual problems have been resolved by a convention—subject to challenge— of using annual money income as the official basis for the definition of poverty.[2].

Since income is but a proxy measure for well-being, and since descriptions of income distribution are made in order to identify where in society remediable injustice exists and to which groups and individuals income should somehow be redistributed, a whole range of research issues has come into being involving comparisons of the consequences for people's well-being of different income distributions. In social practice we accept that children have entitlements that are different from those of their working parents, and that income should be expected to taper off in old age; programs to distribute income "better" should reflect these societal practices, as for example, sharing income within families. So research on the distribution of income must decide how to weight social practice, either by ignoring it, by simplifying assumptions about social practice, or by giving major or minor attention to it.

Another unresolved conceptual problem concerns the construction of equivalence scales for comparing families that have the same level of income but that differ in the number of adults and children, the ages of family members (i.e., stages in their life cycles), and the members' participation in the labor force. A per capita approach is difficult to defend because it ignores economies of scale and the obviously different consumption needs of adults and children of different ages. The weaknesses in equivalence scales have led to the search for measures of equivalence other than income. As in the example of the differing entitlements of children, working parents, and the elderly, both the problem and its resolution draw on social practice, mediated through research, although this does not imply that research and social practice are perfectly in tandem.

The problems surrounding the measurement of social equivalence in terms of income come to the fore when we try to define poverty, which is a concept of economic well-being related to a judgment about the quantities of goods and services that families of different sizes and compositions require in order to maintain themselves in society. If we accept interdependent utilities as essential to understanding deprivation, then we must accept the fact that poverty has to be measured in relative terms so as to take account of the pattern of collective consumption that exists in society. The periodic redefinition of absolute measures of poverty suggests that, in practice, interdependent utilities are widely accepted.

These questions of description, conceptualization, and measurement are highly diverse, but as a group they all refer to a concept of programmatic intervention centering around the direct distribution of money. Answers to these questions start with the idea that the existing distribution of resources and/or well-being can and should be improved. They try, first, to describe the distribution and, second, to relate it to social practices and norms bearing on what it should be. While these studies serve a variety of scholarly purposes, their importance is to clarify to whom incomes should be distributed; they have a programmatic referent.

The programs to which such studies potentially refer need to develop principles of distribution that take account of social arrangement and economic constraints. Such principles are other topics for research. The economic and social realms are treated in such programs as natural or given and the political realm must accommodate to them or explicitly try to alter them. The obvious example of accommodation is the precept that income transfer programs must not disrupt the organization of family life in the social realm. Witness the consternation and dismay that follow when welfare is alleged to break up families. On the other hand, income transfers may be judged to have a positive effect, as in the example of efforts to increase the generosity of child allowances in order to increase the birth rate. Programs are at least expected to be neutral with respect to family life. They may fall short of the postive ideal of doing good, but they should not damage valued social institutions. Since the economic realm is assumed to generate all the resources to be distributed, its continued integrity has a special position. Above all, the efforts to improve the distribution of income must not damage the incentive to work. Ideally, income reshuffling efforts should be neutral or positive with respect to work incentives.

The poverty research literature discusses direct distribution in broader terms when it makes a distinction between poverty and inequality. It is in this distinction, some researchers believe, that issues of structure are addressed through the study of distribution; the framework of inequality is seen as providing a vocabulary for describing the arrangement of society. Studies of economic inequality as measured by the size distribution of income—usually divided into arbitrary units such as deciles, quintiles, etc.—serve as summary indicators of the outcomes of structure and process. This approach can be assimilated into a programmatic framework, that is, by looking at the impact of benefits and taxes on what is sometimes seen as the "original" distribution. This framework is useful as an indicator of the impact of programmatic intervention but does not itself yield leverage for intervention. (The arguement used for the distribution of income also applies with respect to the distribution of wealth.)

Research on Work Distribution

An agenda of poverty research issues emerges in the work distribution approach just as in the direct distribution approach. Programmatic interventions from this approach focus on issues such as equalizing opportunity and breaking down the institutional rigidities that inhibit access to jobs, for example, racial discrimination, educational barriers, and discrimination by sex. These interventions start with different premises. On one hand, programs can start with an individual and try to alter his or her motivation, information, skills, and competence to hold and perform jobs. On the other hand, programs can start with the institutional arrangements of hiring, promotion, compensation, working conditions. These aspects of work are related more to the structure of an occupation and industry in labor markets rather than as properties of individuals.

There is also a role for research in this area. The principal issue is not so much how far down is down, but how long the same people remain on the bottom. Interventions that begin with the individual and those that begin with institutional arrangements are both concerned with the degree of openness of society and the extent to which a person's position in the social structure is inherited or shaped by merit or effort. To make the case that intervention in the market is necessary, it is useful to be able to show that mobility is limited, that individuals with talent do not move up within the system, and that the institutional rules governing distribution of occupational status maintain privilege across generations.

Research Issues of Concern

Programmatic interventions concerned with the behavior of individuals generate a research agenda that is both psychological-educational and sociological in character. On one hand, one wants to know about the acquisition of skills, about work motivation, work habits, the use of time, perceptions of the job market—about economic socialization in the broadest sense. On the other hand, one wants to know about the institutions and social networks that structure job search, about career ladders, occupational sorting, and the interactions between commitments to family and work. Interventions focused more narrowly on poverty deal with the problems of disadvantaged workers, how they can be motivated to get the most from available training programs and how they can hold jobs and perform them better.

For those working on the structure of occupations, what economists would designate as "imperfections" in a "labor market" become the center of concern. Such researchers focus on the bounded character of an occupation, on the institutional structuring of such boundaries, and on the social factors that prevent workers from being spatially and socially mobile; instead of treating job creation as a function of the market demand for goods, refracted through the productive structure, they attempt to go outside the market to envision processes by which jobs could be institutionally created or firms could be given incentives to hire workers they otherwise would not hire (e.g., youth, women, welfare recipients), and to analyze what jobs should be created and where.

Sociology-Oriented Issues

A sharply focused concern with particular program interventions through work distribution produces a somewhat paradoxical result in the way in which research deals with the economic and social realms. In the social realm, the study of the sociology of occupations ranges very widely across issues of status and prestige, yet the poverty research concerned with occupations by and large makes selective use of this body of research, because it tends to interpret occupation in terms of the availability and the adequacy of income. In doing so, poverty research omits those aspects of well-being having to do with status, self-affirmation, life-style, emotional support, colleagueship, etc. It also omits those aspects of occupations that indicate how occupations fit into the social realm (political stability, etc.) and the economic realm (how labor markets work). Thus, while poverty research centering on income tends to explore the ways in which income is a proxy for well-being, the poverty research centering on occupations tends to deal with occupations as a proxy for income. Research that appears at first to focus on structure turns out to focus more on income distribution than on relational or structural issues.

Economic-Oriented Issues

Where the programmatic intervention for job training and job creation fits within the economic realm is uncertain. Full employment is an acknowledged precondition for effective intervention, if a jobs program is to be a residual category in a healthy economy. But a new problem of high unemployment combined with high inflation now makes it unclear how to manage the economy. No substantial research is under way on what macroeconomic measures would bring about a "healthy" economy.

Programmatic Intervention and Dual Labor Market Theory

There is a research perspective, identified particularly with dual labor market theorists, that would consider labor market imperfections as not only phenomena of central interest, but also as phenomena essential to the functioning of the economic system as a whole. In this research perspective, the intervention issues have to deal not so much with barriers to individual access as with the differences between "dirty" jobs and acceptable jobs. To this group of theorists, job security as well as earnings are important issues to consider. Such intervention as job training and job creation and the research associated with these intervention strategies are criticized by dual labor market theorists as superficial and unrealistic in the light of the underlying characteristics of economic structure.

With respect to this group, it appears that theory and conceptualization appeared first, as a criticism of both the descriptive formulations and the interventions proposed by advocates of the equal opportunity approach, with its emphasis on human capital and marginal job restructuring as the strategic variables for program intervention. Indeed, much of the work of this group stands as a criticism of the character of industrial society itself, rather than as a contribution to remediation. "Dirty" jobs are seen as making up a "secondary labor market" used by industrial societies to deal with economic fluctuation; since economic fluctuations are an inevitable feature of such societies, it is argued, it seems to follow that to ameliorate one set of "dirty" jobs would be merely to pass on the uncertainty to another group of workers too weak to protect itself. However, the dual labor market theorists have also attempted to derive from their analysis general recommendations for intervention, for example, to reduce the proportion of "dirty" jobs, to improve the work settings and remuneration of the "dirty" jobs that remain essential, and to promote circulation between "dirty" and acceptable jobs so that "dirty" jobs do not become the definer of entrenched status and economic differences.

Once thought moves away from the sorts of intervention represented in existing programs, centering on income streams, and into a perspective that seems to suggest a change in basis economic structure, the implications for intervention become more problematic. The idea of strategic variables implies a strategy of intervention. The kinds of changes proposed by those who follow a dualist perspective are hard to attach to specific institutional and political mechanisms in a society described as requiring the very phenomena that they seek to eliminate.

Discussion

As we stated at the outset, we believe that intervention motivates research rather than the other way around. We need not be too critical of this reversal of the traditional view of how thought and action should relate, because it can open up issues and lead to development that is useful and that may, and often does, turn out to be theoretically interesting. A policy perspective leads to the exploration of problem areas that one conceivably could do something about; it also leads to the neglect of problem areas that appear intractable to intervention. This tendency explains why at the program level the focus is on the individual and the small occupational group, and at the macrolevel the focus is on money rather than on institutional structures. In this apportionment of programmatic concerns, sociology attaches itself to individuals and small groups; economics tends to dominate the large-scale programs of income redistribution.

When the removal of institutional barriers is a politically acceptable strategy then research can follow accepted policy directions. Where there exists critical research that was not programmatically inspired, then intervention-oriented research has something to draw and to build on. For example, once affirmative action against racial and sexual discrimination are on the political agenda, then productive research can be pursued in that arena.

At this point, it would be useful to recapitulate our argument. First, we identify three realms—the political, the economic, and the social—and argue that poverty research springs primarily from the puzzles presented in the political realm. These puzzles are of a special kind because in the political realm, most clearly of all three, the remedies or answers shape the theory and questions rather than the other way around. If one accepts as a remedy a selective income tax, a universal family allowance, or contributory social insurance, the research questions that appear to be in need of attention arise in each case from the proposed answer; we do not examine the question of whether the intervention is the best remedy for poverty.

Secondly, we argue that within the political frame of reference there are two main approaches that we have labeled the direct distribution and the work distribution approaches. Within these approaches ambiguities and doubtful underlying assumptions are almost never subject to critical review. If questions are raised, they usually come from challenge arising elsewhere. For example, some researchers grounded in the work distribution approach are currently trying to uncover weaknesses in the direct distribution approach by showing that its programs tend to break up families. In this way, social practice helps to define programmatic research. What, then, is the contribution to programmatic research of economic and social research? The answer is complicated by the fact that academic research is influenced by practice in the economic and social realms as well as by the conceptual and methodological paradigms of its disciplines. Societal influence is most strongly felt at the margin of a discipline, and the academic researchers at the margin in turn set out to influence the political realm. Academic researchers interested in income distribution and dual labor markets provide an example, as discussed below.

In the process of drawing on academic research for program design it is not so much the research findings that are crucial as the cast of mind of the researchers. They grasp from a discipline an essential insight that is converted into a progam. In the example of academic interest in income distribution, the comprehensive means-tested negative income tax, ideally administered through the tax system, served as a prototype. Whatever its origins in the academic disciplines, the negative income tax is now a reform in the political realm, and poverty research is inspired by an effort to work out the design problems presented by the conception with the analytic tools of economists.

Advice to policy makers then centers on design issues rather than on the study of the economic and social realms. After a decade of experimentation and research, there is some doubt about the assumptions of selectivity on which the negative income tax rests as well as doubt about the further expansion of direct distribution as a remedy for poverty. Those who are disillusioned are searching the work distribution approach for a better remedy.

Dualist studies of the economic realm lead to a radical diagnosis of the poverty problem because dual labor market theorists believe that both fluctuation in the economy and the unequal apportionment of the costs of these fluctuations are inherent features of an industrial (or perhaps of capitalist industrial) society. Hence, any improvement for one group is counterbalanced by increased uncertainty for some other group. Such an assessment has contributed little to programmatic design in the work distribution approach because the diagnosis itself asserts that no fundamental reform within the system is possible.

How then is poverty research, which derives from the programmatic interventions of the political realm, related to the economic and the social realms? It is shaped by the prevailing practices in those realms, which are the context or climate within which problems are set and remedies are accepted. When the context changes because new practices evolve, new issues for poverty research arise in the political realm.

Social movements, such as the civil rights or the women's rights movements, send out ripples signaling a change in the context, stimulating thought and action, and creating a diffused sense of need for a new programmatic agenda for research to address. The implicit assumptions that organized current programs and research are made visible. For example, the direct distribution approach is organized around the assumption of pooled resources. Study and programmatic action have been devoted to unravelling the intellectual and political puzzles posed by the pooling of resources, but the women's right movement has created a climate in which individuals are able to challenge the assumptions of pooling. What is particularly interesting is that this challenge seems to be taking place almost simultaneously in many industrial societies. A new principle of distribution is being sought, for which the individual, rather than some pooled unit (such as kin, household, nuclear family), is the focus. The new challenge assaults the treatment of dependence and the major cash transfer programs on which the foundations of the welfare state rests.[3]

An Alternative Framework for Poverty Research

It is probably no accident that research and intervention both emphasize distributional questions rather than questions about processes and structure in both the direct distribution and the work distribution approaches. This characteristic of the field seems to be related to another issue, which we have not yet addressed. This issue has to do not with the way in which poverty and inequality and the distributional and relational dimensions are conceived, but rather with the conceptualization of intervention itself.

There is an implicit map that dominates programmatic research in both the direct distribution and the work distribution approaches. In both approaches, programmatic intervention is conceived quite differently from the other two realms—the economic and the social. The economic and social realms are thought of as "natural" realms of ongoing processes; these processes generate the problems that are addressed by action in the form of intervention. The economic and social realms are related to each other, and intervention relates to them either by altering their arrangement or by adapting intervention so as to leave them unaltered. Economic and social processes have a sort of prior status as natural and ongoing; the fact that intervention can at times be framed to alter these processes indicates that designing interventions to maintain the status quo also represents a positive choice, not a neutral one.

Considering this map as a whole, one might be struck by the peculiarity of a conceptualization that treats the economic and social realms as natural social processes, but the political realm as a framework of rational activity. Furthermore, this activity is hierarchical in structure: there are actors and those acted upon. The language used to describe it seems to imply the existance of a group of benefactors. Indeed, the history of programmatic interventions starts with charity, and the vocabulary of benefits and benefactors derived from that framework. One might think of modern poverty research as an effort to rise conceptually above that way of viewing the world, just as the concepts of entitlement and universalism are efforts to rise above that view in practice.

This argument leads to a view of intervention that places it outside politics and outside history and construes it as a process by which those who have or control give to or direct those who do not. Benefits are thought of as flowing through the actions of those who initiate programs, rather than through some complex process in which groups accommodate to each other through a struggle in which even those at the bottom—the "beneficiaries"—have a role.

When private and religious charity became transformed into modern social policy, programs carried out on behalf of the poor were regarded as the product of a societal expression of compassion and humanity and not as instruments serving the interest of any particular group. In somewhat the same way, the research associated with poverty issues carries the same assumptions of disinterest. In reality, of course, it is the established groups in society whose perspectives dominate the framing of problems; nevertheless, these problem frames and fields of interest are seen as self-evident and therefore are not themselves subject to question.

Poverty research can be thought of as a component of this process. Research ideas do not merely guide intervention; they also reflect interventions or are a weapon for proposed interventions. The questions at issue are not whether research is dishonest or whether the rules of evidence are improperly applied; the questions are what topics are investigated and how problems are framed. We further note two points: research that is not policy-oriented and that makes critical judgments about values is important to the basic conceptual structure that guides both research and intervention; and programmatic research draws on ideas and evidence that come about as part of an intellectual process more directly responsive to the drive for cognitive orientation than to the wish to act. However, we believe it is a mistake to set as an ideal research that progresses naturally, starting with a description of situations and problem changes and moving through prediction to counsel for action. At this point we are not prescribing a different focus for research, but a more realistic way of understanding what we are doing to solve the problem of poverty.

To look at poverty research in a different light is also to see intervention in a different light—as a natural process in the same sense as economic and social processes appear natural to us now. We believe that a more realistic approach joins economic, social, and intervention processes, operating in their respective realms, into a common framework.

The Claims Perspective

We have found it useful to substitute for the concepts implied by benefits and the welfare system a set of concepts centering around claims and the structures of claims. A claim is based on a principle of distribution. Claims represent what people receive in society. The distributional principles that we call claims are fuzzy around the edges. Each has an element of established right or entitlement, but also a fringe that is less clear-cut, which is open for bargaining, benefaction, pressure, and demand. We assume those elements of claims that now appear as entitlements may have been less established in the past and are the outcome of some historical process of claiming and defining claims.

The usefulness of this conceptualization is that it integrates the three realms of the political, the economic, and the social into a single framework. Each realm may be thought of as a province to which distributional principles apply. The realms are not, however, independent, so that the processes by which distributional principles arise and become established involve all three realms. These distributional principles permit us to join the structural and distributional patterns in society by social conventions rather than by a set of laws in which the economic and social realms are separated. The political realm of programmatic intervention is not only separate from the social and the economic realms, but it is also of a different kind. The difference is that programmatic intervention does not appear to be subject to natural processes and lawlike regularities. The essential idea of programmatic intervention is that it alters performance in the social and economic realms.

Thus, in a claims perspective, we view the output of the political realm not as interventions to give benefits, but as a system of claims derived from an interactive process of claiming and granting.

Another consequence of taking the claims perspective is to focus on the relationships between the claims that arise in the political realm and the claims that arise in the economic and social realms. We see the main claims-managing institution in the political realm as the state. We see the main claims-managing institution in the social realm as the family. We see the main claims managing institutions in the economic realm as business firms and private property. Each of these has its own vocabulary to describe the process of claiming and the principles of distribution that are acceptable in them. In the economic realm the main distribution principles are compensation for work and compensation for the use of capital. In the social realm the organizing principle of distribution is kinship solidarity. In the political realm there are three distributional principles: one based on need, one based on contribution, and one based on citizenship. Underlying and legitimizing all three principles is a conception of common membership in a unit of solidarity. In addition, the state, or government, is an employer itself and therefore subject to the distributional principles of compensation.

While the establishment of claims is a process of pressure, leverage, and bargaining, claims are asserted in terms of normative rationales, which typically include both elements of assertion as to the nature of society (inevitability, efficiency) and elements of assertion as to what is ethical (justice, compassion, right character). Although the claims made against the family, against firms, and against the state interact, they are to a substantial degree separate from each other, in substantial part through the separation of the rationales underlying each. Thus, for example, the rationales for claims against the state are largely found in law and legislation and in political theory; the rationales for claims against firms are found in economic theory centering on concepts of productivity; and the rationales for claims against the family involve loyalty and social custom as well as the sociological and psychological theorizing that attempts to make sense of behavior. (The demand for "wages for housework" has the power to shock, in part because it violates the traditional separations between the rationales of claims.)

Because the various sets of claims against kin, against firms, and against the state and their various rationales can never be completely segregated but are bound to interact with each other, the outcomes of the various historical processes of claiming are a number of distinctive claims systems. These claims systems may then be compared as wholes, not only with respect to the distribution of claims based on economic resources (as in income distribution studies) or security sources (as in divisions between primary and secondary workers), but also with respect to the placing of claims. One might, for example, compare societies in which the dominant claims system is one of claims against firms with societies in which the dominant system is one of claims against the state or against kin. Such a comparison would cross-cut the usual socialist-capitalist division; Yugoslavia, for example, a country that has state-owned factories run by worker councils, would be placed in a category with some capitalist states, in contrast with more centrally managed capitalist and socialist economies.

Claims Systems and Claims Packages

The thrust of this perspective is to see the various systems of claims as both internally negotiable and as culturally variable. A given system of claims appears in this view as a system of social conventions, or an always-evolving system of power relations.

With respect to poverty and inequality, claims take at least two forms: first, a claim for stability and security, and second, a claim for an adequate standard of living. Claims for security against interruptions in economic well-being include seniority rights, severance pay, and pension arrangements. Other claims focus on the issue of adequacy, ranging from a bid for a wage increase to the demands of organized welfare groups to have special grants for school clothing or equipment to furnish a new household. In struggles over such issues, the concept of adequacy is given different content by different participants in the dialogue: changes in the conventional meaning of adequacy are part of the struggle over claims. Even the concept of nutritional adequacy, which might appear to be beyond the realm of political opinion, is part of the process of negotiation.

A claims package is a unique assemblage of claims that a household puts together in attempting to maximize its stability, security, and adequacy. A claims package involves selection from a range of possible alternative income sources. In modern industrial societies, individuals and families can derive income from such sources as earnings by a principal wage earner, earnings by other members of the family, income from assets, income from private retirement plans, income in the form of gifts or recognition of legal obligations (child support), income from relatives, and income from a number of public transfer sources, of which the three major types seem to be contributory social insurance programs, needs-tested programs, and universal citizenship benefits (such as family allowances in most European countries and Canada).

Claims involve more than the dimensions of income; they also confer position and status, and the claims that people can reasonably assert are determined by their position in society. Claims against the state, such as certain licenses to work or rebates on expenditures (e.g., mortgage rebates), can be made only by people who already have some measure of social and economic resources. Such claims against the state constitute a way of multiplying the privileges of position. At the other end of the spectrum, claims against the state such as welfare, food stamps, and public housing also confer status and are determined by prior status.

The claims packages assembled by households today are the product of a long evolutionary process of claiming that parallels the history of industrial development. The political history of the eighteenth through the twentieth centuries in Europe has as its major theme the emergence of new claims against the state and the firm and the redefinition of claims against kin. To cite some conspicuous examples: the legitimizing of labor unions in the hard-fought struggle for the right to organize established a new claiming group with a claiming agenda; the obligation of the United States federal government to provide jobs or, failing that, to provide income for families of long-term unemployed workers represents claims against the state that were inconceivable in previous ages; there has also evolved with time a much less specific, but nevertheless substantial claim against the state that it should manage the economy so as to produce a reasonable level of stable well-being for its citizens. In these and other ways new claims continue to be created: against the state (e.g., day care), against firms (e.g., job splitting, careers for women, etc.), and against the family (e.g., changing sex roles within the family). Of course, new claims generate reactions—for example, backlash against welfare and against the women's rights movement.

But not all claiming arises from this direct process of groups organizing to make the claim on their own behalf. There is also an indirect process by which one group makes claims on behalf of another. For example, social workers who want to make services available to the mentally retarded, the mentally ill, or to the otherwise disabled will lobby and proselytize for the rights of their potantial clients to services of this sort. The motives inspiring such claiming processes are varied, usually combining self-interest and altruism in arguments that conform to the claims rationales accepted in society. Once a claim is established—as, for example, in the entitlement of the elderly to social security benefits—claims managers come into existence to manage this body of claims, and they promote their interpretation of the best interest of the claimants.

Discussion

We have been arguing that poverty research is largely programmatic in its intellectual origins; it starts with a possible or proposed answer and works out the logic of the proposed intervention. The "answers" that generate research at any period come from practice in the economic and social realms. The studies that work out the logic of the proposed interventions also come from practice in the economic and social realms. If our argument is broadly correct, it would be fruitful to make explicit what is now implicit, that is, to uncover the processes in the economic and social realms that shape the poverty research agenda. A claims perspective provides the framework for making a bridge between the two realms and the poverty research agenda.

A Proposed Agenda for Research

CLAIMS AT THE MACRO- AND MICROLEVELS

The issues seem to fall into two broad categories: claims and claiming at the level of the individual and household on the one hand, and the functioning of claims structures as a whole on the other. Within each of these broad categories relational and distributional issues are joined.

At the microlevel, the distributional issues have to do with the way that claims and claims packages vary in space and time and according to social placement. How do individual choices among work, welfare, and leisure vary—between urban and rural areas, between regions, between classes?

We know that claims packages change as people move from one family pattern to another and as their needs and preferences vary over their life cycles. It would be useful, therefore, to study how people reassemble claims packages. Such studies would parallel studies of how people move across the occupational structure. This approach would extend mobility studies not only to occupational mobility, which provides a particularistic description of labor market experience from the perspective of the job and the career path of an individual, but also to claims mobility, as individuals vary their claims packages on the basis of position in the income distribution, stage of the life cycle, and family organization.

Since claims vary not only by their sources but also in their content, there are choices to be made between claims for income and income stability, and claims for status and other aspects of well-being. Thus, it would be interesting to understand the ways in which individuals, families, and collective bargaining units make trade-offs between claims of different content. How do women, in the light of family commitments, evaluate part-time work against the higher earnings and perhaps greater potential for career mobility of full-time work? Collective bargaining may deal with earnings as well as with issues of status and respect; the symbols of access to a telephone or to an executive washroom are examples. What governs such trade-offs?

The study of distribution over time can lead to structural issues when we try to understand how claims packages take account of economic forces, such as the level of economic growth or inflation, and of public policy, such as taxation and welfare. More generally, it is important to know whether claims for income or claims for other aspects of well-being tend to dominate claims packages. A central policy concern in this issue is whether transfer payments displace earnings as a source of income, that is to say, whether financial assistance inhibits work incentives.

The structural context in which claiming takes place influences the claims packages that families put together. The context continually changes as new programs are added and old ones become transformed, occasionally even dropped. At an aggregate level, we want to know how different claims structures influence claims packages—for example in the South versus the Northeast. At a programmatic level, we want to evaluate the intended and unintended effects of deliberate intervention.

Given that not all decisions to fulfill claims are fully honored, we need to know what institutional mechanism of oversight can be called upon to ensure compliance. Since claiming takes place in many settings, there is a variety of localized mechanisms. The courts are the main cross-institutional mechanism of oversight, to which the others may or may not be referrable. An important question for research concerns the capacity of the courts to enforce new claims that are being created in a variety of institutional settings. Many of these claims concern poverty and individuals and families at the low end of the income distribution. We note in particular the claim for equitable provision of facilities such as sewers and streets, claims for equitable services from garbage collection to police and fire protection, claims for access to education and training, access to medical services (abortion, in particular), and access to decent facilities and maintenance in public housing programs.

Another general issue of importance is how sets of claims and the interaction between sets of claims in different realms can restructure institutions. One would want to know, for example, how claims within a family are altered by a woman's entering the labor force and acquiring claims on the economic realm, as well as from the distribution of resources among family members, or by the legal regulation that keeps young people out of the labor force. In turn, such an analysis becomes a way of describing changes in family organization under varying labor market conditions. To take another example, does the growth of governmental intervention eliminate a significant role for intermediary institutions, such as churches or voluntary organizations?

Studying, at the microlevel, how changes in claims restructure particular institutions such as the family leads to some large issues with respect to the organization of society. To what extent is there a drive to consistency within cultures, which leads to competition between legitimizing claims rationales? Does a set of values presented strongly in one sphere of life penetrate into other spheres? Specifically, does the rationale for competition in economic life overwhelm other spheres? The question is general, but in its specific form we want to know if claims against the state, rationalized as the citizen's right to live that obliges the state to provide the means for a livelihood, will come to dominate other claims.

Researchers argue vigorously that the availability of claims against the state has eroded claims against the family, and this tendency in turn has threatened social solidarity. They say that we must attempt to revitalize the intermediary institutions (such as the family, the church, the voluntary association) to prevent the integrative fabric of society from becoming weakened. An alternative argument might suggest that the availability of claims against the state has revitalized claims against kin, especially for low-income families. There cannot be a system of reciprocity without something to exchange. Welfare provides low-income families with resources that can be distributed among kin. Thus public transfers may strengthen the ties of social solidarity rather than undermine them.

Studying the Pattern of Claims

Economists with whom we have discussed this claims perspective immediately raise two macro issues: (1) Claims cannot exceed the total amount of goods produced by society. Since a society cannot for long distribute more than it produces, some mechanism for keeping the two accounts in check is needed. A preferred mechanism is one that is self-equilibrating so that neither a manager nor a political overseer needs to worry about the process. (2) Distributional systems are not neutral; there is a close relationship between the structure of claims and the total amount of goods produced by society. The way we slice up the pie influences the size of the pie. Moves to distribute resources according to criteria of welfare or social justice that fail to take "proper" account of incentives to produce run the risk of undermining the vitality of the economic system and reducing the resources available to all.

With respect to these problems, neoclassical economic theory proposes a solution. The marginal productivity theory of wages proposes a mechanism through which the amount of wage claims and the supply of goods and services against which claims are made will tend to be self-calibrating. Problems remain, however. The usefulness of the theory to explain (and therefore justify) any given system of income claims is reduced by the evident variety across societies of possible workable arrangements yielding different patterns of remuneration, the role of power in the construction of such arrangements, and the nature of the theory itself, which renders it in effect immune to empirical proof or refutation. Furthermore, in the perspective we are adopting one is required to deal also with claims arising in the social realm and the political realm. These realms are not expected to have the same kind of calibration that firms use in hiring practices; in these realms groups use power and pressure to demand benefits in exchange for stability and consensus. While suggestions have been proposed to deal with such claims, no clear and dominant theory now exists.

In the absence of workable theory to guide interpretation, we are confronted with difficult problems in evaluating trends in the claims structure at the macrolevel. We do not have a basis for judgment on changes either with respect to the kinds of institutions within which and against which claims are made, or with respect to the content and amount of the claims themselves.

We are witnessing a growth of claims against the state, which we call the welfare state. At the same time we are also experiencing the growth of claims against business corporations, leading to more job security for some, improved quality of the work environment, and fringe benefits from pensions to medical care to educational grants. We see, therefore, that there are welfare systems in both the economic and political realms, and that they substitute and complement each other. But we do not have the data to compare these systems with each other in a given country, or to compare their varying combinations among countries; even if we did have such data, we do not have the theoretical basis for evaluating them. Shall we interpret these trends as a sign of success, or as a cause of failure? Do these claims erode or nourish productivity? Do they lead to less worker alienation, more collective identification, and hence to larger output, or do they lead to undermining of incentives? If production and growth affect the structure of claims, then is it true that in time the claims arising from the growth of society will erode the structure that made growth possible?

Are we entering a period of overload requiring the retrenchment of poverty programs because the state is coming to have more claims than it can honor, or is there still scope for further development of new redistribution-oriented programs? Specifically, is welfare reform that calls for a large increase in expenditures feasible or, if feasible, desirable?

Within the context of poverty and inequality, one can examine claims packages and claims structures as these concern the individuals and families at the low end of the income distribution. But to do so violates the organizing idea of this paper: that distribution cannot be understood independent of the interaction of groups exercising power, and through the exercise of that power redefining the accepted principles by which institutions distribute resources.

We propose a research agenda that highlights the interaction between distributional and relational issues. In the course of the negotiations concerning claims, the political, the economic, and the social come to be seen as intertwined, or as aspects of a single system with respect to which policy is made. A theory of the economy cannot be separated from a theory of the state and a theory of society.

Thus far, we have reviewed the content of the research agenda, but the claims perspective we have developed also suggests that more than content and methodology must be addressed if we are to grasp an understanding of the problem-setting process. This suggestion leads to the question of the social organization of research. Who frames the problems? To whom are the findings useful? What is the sponsorship of research? Is there an adjudication role for research through which it could rise above particular perspectives on claims and become the instrument of discovering some general interest within which competing claims could be assimilated? Since its inception, social science has yearned for such a role—but we believe it is illusory.

Conclusion

In brief, then, poverty research itself can be seen as part of a political process. Most organizations for poverty research have as their sponsors the federal government and its interest in the administration of the welfare system in the context of political issues surrounding public expenditures. The academic researchers in such organizations accept this framework as not only reasonable but also as obvious and requiring no inquiry as to its appropriateness. As a result, within such organizations an intellectual and political hegemony is formed. If this characterization is correct, then these organizations seem to be an unlikely context in which to raise substantive questions about the framework of research, much less proposals for different frameworks of research.

Without a constituent group or groups to support new initiatives, new frameworks of research have no basis for launching. One could imagine, for example, poverty research being generated by social movements such as civil rights, women's rights, the environment, and the new political conservatism represented by the American Enterprise Movement. In the past, many research organizations concerned with poverty have pushed forward their own programmatic agenda, (the negative income tax reform, the extension of welfare to the working poor, the integration of the tax and benefit system, etc.). In the future, poverty researchers may be called upon to adjudicate the reform agendas created by new movements on the political horizon, some of which seek to expand the welfare state and others to constrict it. The new context of a debate about overload of programmatic intervention will shape the research agenda in ways that are not obvious at the moment. It is possible at any time that one of these movements or a coalition of several might call into question the existing hegemonic structure of problem definition. This possibility seems plausible when we consider how traditions established in the past such as comprehensive planning have been successfully undermined. Only when such an assault is launched is it likely that the social organization of poverty research could be critically examined, and the alternatives explored.

Notes

1. Goldthrope argues (1972, p.344):

    In liberal interpretations of stratification in western industrial societies two distinctive features may be noted. First, there is an emphasis on the *distributive* rather than the *relational* aspects of social class; that is, on differences in economic resources, prestige, education, etc., considered as attributes of individuals and groups, rather than on the ways in which differential power and advantage actually operate in social interaction between individuals and groups, and thus shape the social structure . . . . Secondly there is the assumption . . . that processes inherent in the development of industrialism . . . are working to bring about an automatic secular decline in inequalities of condition and opportunity alike.

2. These measures of family income exclude in-kind income and the value of subsidized commodities such as medical care, food stamps, and public housing. For a challenge of these assumptions, see Browning (1975).

3. The unequal treatment of one-earner versus two-earner families is at issue, because two-earner families now receive the same retirement benefits as one-earner families.

References

Browning, E. K. (1975) *Redistribution and the Welfare State.* Washington, D.C.: American Enterprise Institute for Public Policy Research.

Darity, W. A., Jr. (1978) Policy Advice and the Consensual Framework of the Institute for Research on Poverty. Unpublished paper.

Goldthorpe, J. (1972) Class, status, and power in modern Britain: some recent interpretations. *The European Archives of Sociology* 13(2).

Paul E. Peterson

Federalism and the Great Society: Political Perspectives on Poverty Research

The problems encountered in the implementation of antipoverty programs in the 1960s—Johnson's Great Society—were rooted in conflicts inherent in the structural arrangements of a federal system of government. These programs, with their emphasis on special assistance to the poor and needy, demonstrated a stronger commitment to redistribution by the central government of the United States than was evident at any other time in its history, save perhaps for the New Deal. However, this egalitarian thrust was implemented through a federal system whose local units did not—indeed, could not—share the federal commitment. Research on poverty has repeatedly revealed the limits on the effectiveness of many programs aimed at reducing poverty in the United States. But in general these studies have not appreciated the structural limitations that the federal system itself placed on Great Society programs. To do so would require the reconstruction of a theory of federalism.

We no longer have a theory of federalism. The word has become at once so encompassing and so vacuous that any multitiered decision-making system can be entitled a federation. Even contractual relationships between central governments and private business firms are now considered to be an element of federalism (Elazar et al. 1969). Once the concept of federalism is stripped of any distinctive meaning, we no longer have criteria for the appropriate division of governmental responsibilities among layers of government. Federalism is what federalism does. Even more, we have no orienting concepts that can assist us in explaining the patterns of conflict and cooperation among governmental levels.

In this paper, I shall argue that concepts taken from economics provide the opportunity for reviving a structural approach to the study of federalism, thereby providing a more comprehensive explanation for

[Paul E. Peterson is professor in the Department of Political Science and the Department of Education at the University of Chicago.]

many of the difficulties faced by the antipoverty programs of Johnson's Great Society. Given a federal system of government, central and local governments perform inherently different political functions. The central government is responsible for regularizing relations with foreign countries, for maintaining the nation's prosperity, and for sustaining social welfare and other redistributive services. Local governments concentrate on operating efficiently those services necessary for maintaining a healthy local economy and society. Because of these differing responsibilities, central and local governments often find themselves engaged in value conflicts over matters of domestic policy. Local governments are primarily concerned with the productiveness of their economy, while the central government is more interested in achieving equality.

Decline of Dual Sovereignty Theory

Traditional theories of federalism took as their point of departure the presence of two sovereigns within a single domain. Each sovereign had power over its citizens with respect to the functions for which it was responsible. Neither had power to interfere with the proper role of the other sovereign. A constitution defined the distribution of powers between the dual sovereigns.

Sovereignty was divided between a central state and a local republic in order to avoid both internal and external threats to liberty. Small republics limited the possibility of internal despotism, because citizens knew and understood affairs of state that touched them closely. They could readily be called upon to participate in the defense of their freedoms. However, the small republic could be easily overcome by external enemies. Only through joining together in a federation with other republics could a common defense be maintained. The permeability of the small republic by external forces justified its relinquishing certain powers to a higher sovereign (Diamond 1969).

This dual sovereign theory of federalism linked governmental structure to political processes and policy outcomes. It provided a rationale for the proper division of powers between the central state and the local republics within a federation. It gave federalism a core definition: the presence of a contractual arrangement—a constitution—that divided powers among the sovereigns. Although changing circumstances would require continuous interpretation of that constitution, the theory provided the necessary conceptual apparatus for doing so.

In the United States, constitutional interpretations since the Civil War have regularly expanded the range of powers allocated to the central government so the concept of dual sovereignty, which was somewhat forced even in 1789, has become increasingly difficult to sustain. With the expansion of the Commerce clause in the 1930s and the simultaneous acceptance by the courts of grants-in-aid from the central government to the states, hardly a function remained that could not be exercised as readily by the central as by state and local governments. However valid the dual sovereign theory remained in principle, it had little applicability to a country that had come to believe that its liberties were as safe, if not safer, in the hands of the central government as at state and local levels.

The most creative adaptation in federal theory to these constitutional changes was Morton Grodzins's (1966) metaphor of the "marble cake." Grodzins showed that virtually all governmental activities are affected by decisions taken at national, state, and local levels. Power was both widely diffused and widely shared. The overall pattern had become marked more by cooperation and mutual assistance than by confrontations between dual sovereigns. Drawing upon the emergent behavioral tradition, Grodzins showed that governmental interrelations were characterized by endless processes of sharing and exchange. The resulting formation had, like a marble cake, no discernible structure at all. The metaphor diffused rapidly in the literature of federalism. It fitted nicely with the contemporary process-oriented focus of the political science discipline as a whole (Truman 1951, Greenstone 1975), and it seemed to give point and direction to descriptive studies of intergovernmental relationships. More innovative writers added their own metaphoric variations—picket fence, upside-down cake, harlequin ice cream brick, or what have you (U.S. Senate 1969, Wright 1975).

The impact of Grodzins's work was not limited to the academic scholarship of federalism. His ideas also served to justify the Johnsonian experiment in "creative federalism," a phrase repeated by Lyndon Johnson on several occasions, but endowed with little content. One enthusiastic popular commentator (Ways 1969, p. 620), however, expressed in 1965 the meaning of creative federalism:

> Federalism means a relation, cooperative and competitive, between a limited central power and other powers that are essentially independent of it. In the long American dialogue over states' rights, it has been tacitly assumed that the total amount of power was constant and, therefore, any increase in federal power diminished the power of the states and/or "the people." Creative federalism starts from the contrary belief that total power—private and public, individual and organizational—is expanding very rapidly. As the range of conscious

choice widens, it is possible to think of vast increases of federal government power that do not encroach upon or diminish
any other power. Simultaneously, the power of states and
local governments will increase. . . .

Programmatically, the Great Society epitomized the Grodzins view of
American federalism. Johnson's zeal for reform in American domestic
social policy was accompanied by an equally intense commitment to the
execution of these policies through state and local governments. In 1965,
Congress enacted 21 new health programs, 17 new educational programs, 15 new economic development programs, 12 new programs to
meet city problems, 4 new programs for manpower training, and 17
resources development programs. All were implemented through joint
action between the federal and one or more of the lower levels of government (MacMahon 1972, p. 84). Federal intergovernmental transfers to
state and local governments increased from $7.7 billion in 1962 to $41.7
billion in 1973. In 1962, intergovernmental transfers constituted 27
percent of the budget of local governments; by 1973, these transfers
constituted 37.1 percent (Peterson 1979). The programs were federal:
formulated and financed by central departments but administered and
executed by state and local governments.

The evidence that Grodzins and other political scientists influenced the
shape of "creative federalism" is admittedly only sketchy. In all probability, federally financed social reform was executed through conjoint effort by all levels of government, because ties between Congress and local
officials, together with Johnson's own practical sense of what was
feasible, precluded any alternative. Perhaps both politicians and scholars
were influenced by judicial decisions that no longer treated as significant
the assignment of responsibilities to one or another level of government.
Yet the marble cake metaphor was at least a useful justification for the
burgeoning network of intergovernmental relationships.

This unprecedented network of intergovernmental relationships
rapidly expanded without serious debate about the level of government
appropriate for carrying out specific tasks. Since power was so widely
shared, and since cooperative relationships were already so extensive, it
seemed to make little difference what combination of governments performed social services—as long as the federal government paid the bill.
The specific structural arrangement for any particular program was, like
so many of Johnson's policies, an issue open to bargaining, and a great
range of intergovernmental practices soon came into being. Whether he
had directly contributed to this outcome or not, Grodzins would have
been content with the result.

The Effectiveness of the Great Society

Time has not treated "creative federalism" generously. Many of the Great Society programs proved to be less in practice than they had in principle promised to become, and research on these programs has revealed that the cooperative partnership between the federal government and state and local governments did not carry out Johnson's objectives with flawless precision. Conflict, confusion, and simple abandonment of original objectives occurred in most of the more visible antipoverty programs.

I do not mean that in the aftermath of the Great Society there was any increase in the level of poverty or even that the absolute level of poverty remained constant. Such conclusions depend on the measure of poverty used, and, as on most politically sensitive issues, it is possible to reach diametrically opposite results. On one hand, taking absolute levels of poverty and including estimates of earnings that take into account unreported income and cash and in-kind income transfers, one can conclude that poverty in America has been all but eliminated (Lynn, Jr. 1977). On the other hand, taking earnings of low-income groups relative to those of median and high-income groups, one can conclude that no significant change has taken place, even a decade after the war on poverty was declared (Haveman 1977). Using still another measure, official poverty statistics reach the moderate conclusion that problems of poverty are being steadily, if slowly, ameliorated (Lynn, Jr. 1977).

For the sake of argument, let us simply accept the more optimistic assessments of changes in the condition of the poor. Even if the overall position of the poor has improved in absolute terms, it remains highly problematic how much of this change has been due to the programs of planned poverty reduction initiated by the Great Society. A highly inflated, wartime economy seems to have had the biggest impact on personal incomes in the late 1960s and early 1970s. And the governmental programs that had the greatest impact on the poor were the highly centralized programs of income redistribution administered by the central government, such as social security, the provision of medicare to the elderly, and the food stamp program.

By far the least successful of government programs aimed at the poor were those complex programs of service delivery financed centrally but administered locally. The Economic Opportunity Act, the Elementary and Secondary Education Act, manpower development programs, model city programs, the "New Towns" program, urban economic development programs, health maintenance organizations, juvenile delinquency prevention policies, and a host of similar schemes were the liveliest, most imaginative, and most highly touted of the government's efforts at redistributing social and economic opportunities in the United States. But these antipoverty programs seem to have had the smallest long-range impact on low-income groups in the United States. Robert Haveman, former director of the Institute for Research on Poverty at the University of Wisconsin and a cautiously optimistic evaluator of the poverty policies of the federal government, has concluded that "while poverty was reduced during the decade (after 1965), it is difficult to attribute this result directly to the programs that were an explicit part of the war" (Haveman 1977, p. 2.).

Specific evaluations of particular programs are consistent with this overall assessment. Examining the celebrated community action program, the most visible of the antipoverty programs, one finds little evidence that it had much impact on the socioeconomic well-being of the poor. After studying five California cities, Kramer (1969) reported that "if one . . . seeks to determine the cumulative influences [of various participatory techniques] on redirecting the focus and content of any part of the social service system, one finds relatively little change in the basic orientation of health, education and welfare agencies" (p. 241). John Strange's (1972) summary, after an extensive review of both published and unpublished analyses of community action, is much the same: "In some cases the number of groups participating in the pluralistic contest for power and influence has been expanded. [But] it is generally agreed . . . that no radical redistributions of influence, power, service, rewards, or other benefits has occurred" (p. 660). After reviewing research on a wide range of educational and training programs, Levin (1977) reached even harsher conclusions: "A wide variety of programs were either initiated or expanded during the poverty decade, and the evaluations and relevant research suggest that their effect on the reduction of poverty was minimal" (p. 179). The pattern was little different for housing policy. As Karl Taeuber (1977) has observed, "The gap between planned innovations and actual implementation was as great in Model Cities and other new HUD efforts as in the community action programs. . . ." (p. 362). Even in the area of health care, the one policy area in which the poor seem to have experienced substantially increased access to a valued public service, "those programs with considerable state discretion have not had a . . . record of high performance" (Davis 1977, p. 230).

Some have suggested that these so-called antipoverty programs were never intended to reduce poverty in America. They were only symbolic programs designed to pacify an unruly urban population in a time of social unrest. But this view is contradicted by the evident commitment and capacity of American society to reduce overall levels of absolute poverty. To explain adequately the extent to which antipoverty efforts were singularly unhelpful in achieving their objectives, one must look for more specific sources of goal-displacement and program frustration. In this regard it is notable how little research attention has been given to the fact that almost all of the antipoverty programs were centrally financed and locally administered.

Throughout the reassessment of antipoverty efforts, the premises upon which creative federalism rested have seldom been questioned. The marble cake analogy continues to be the accepted metaphor for the American federal system.

The Substitution of Metaphor for Theory

The practical problems faced by Johnson's creative federalism were rooted in structural relationships not adequately comprehended by the marble cake metaphor. However apt and appealing the analogy may be, comparing federalism to a structureless piece of pastry is not theory. It suggests flux, change, and complexity when the purpose of theory is to identify simplicity, pattern, and order. The metaphor directs attention toward individuals, groups, and processes, when the essence of federalism is a stable relationship among structures of government.

Students of federalism since Grodzins have yet to develop a theory of federalism. Their descriptive analyses, persuasive as they sometime are, have (1) failed to give a distinctive meaning to federalism, (2) failed to preserve any distinctions among functions appropriate to each level of government, and (3) failed to identify any pattern to cooperative and conflictual elements in the federal system. Influenced by the process-oriented behavioralism of the discipline of political science at large, they have all but ignored the structural arrangements of the federal system. Instead, they have concentrated research energy on the activities of groups, elites, constituencies, and bureaucrats at all governmental levels. They have so stretched their energies that they cannot now develop a theory of federalism apart from a complete theory of politics.

First, and most important, their definitions of federalism are so vague that it is impossible to distinguish federalism from relationships between central and field offices in a unitary government. Daniel Elazar's (1966) efforts are more careful than most, but even he defines federalism (p. 2):

> as the mode of political organization that unites smaller polities within an overarching political system by distributing power among general and constituent governments in a manner designed to protect the existence and authority of both na-

tional and subnational political systems, enabling all to share in the overall system's decision-making and executing processes.

By this all-encompassing definition, even the U.S. Forest Service is a federal system. Its decision-making processes are divided between central and field offices, which are united together by a handbook of rules and regulations that protects the existence and authority of each jurisdictional level. From a different perspective, Kaufman (1960) has judged the Forest Service to be a highly centralized agency of the central government. But certainly the concept of federalism, when applied in this way, begins to encompass almost all political relationships. Perhaps that is Elazar's intent, for he goes on to say that federalism "is more than an arrangement of governmental structures; it is a mode of political activity that requires certain kinds of cooperative relationships through the political system it animates" (p. 2). This free-flowing assertion is certainly in keeping with the current emphasis on political process, but it does little to focus the study of intergovernmental relationships. To be sure, modern interpreters of American federalism are understandably concerned not to define federalism in narrow, constitutional terms. To see the essence of federalism as the division of powers among constituent units as defined by a written constitution places the study of federalism in a straight-jacket at a time when intergovernmental relationships are marked by patterns hardly foreseen by the earliest interpreters of the American Constitution. But modern federal theorists have not supplied a sufficiently focused substitute for traditional definitions of federalism in order that a distinctive, middle-range theory of intergovernmental relationships could emerge.

Second, without a definition of federalism, modern writers have been unable to state the characteristic and appropriate function of each level of government. In a fascinating commentary, Martin Diamond (1969, p. 79) observed that Grodzins "was driven by the difficulty of defining localness toward rejecting any standard for distributing functions between state and national government. He came to argue that 'Local Is As Local Does.' " The theory degenerates into sheer description. And, once again, it becomes impossible to distinguish the federal system from a decentralized administrative structure.

Perhaps it is unkind to suggest that modern theorists are also left without a standpoint from which to study intergovernmental relationships. After all, Grodzins (1966), Elazar (1966), and other of Grodzins's students (Elazar et al. 1969) have commented extensively on the federal "partnership" and have given intelligent accounts of a cooperative sharing of power among governmental levels. But even though their em-

pirical studies are lucid and helpful, general theoretical explanau.
the pattern of cooperation and conflict among governmental levels have
not been developed. When the concept of the marble cake was first
developed, intergovernmental relationships were so poorly understood
that sheer descriptive accounts were useful. But the social scientific
studies of the "creative federalism" of Johnson's antipoverty programs
have hardly improved on early efforts. The results of the Great Society
experiment have left many disturbed about the quality of the sharing
among federal partners, but few have expressed their uncertainties at a
high level of theoretical abstraction.

Federal Theory and Poverty Research

In the absence of a federal theory to guide research, political analyses of
Great Society programs, at their most interesting and provocative, have
used other sources for their theoretical power. In the search for an adequate explanation for the limited success of these redistributive programs, three rival hypotheses have been advanced: (1) the power of local
ruling elites, (2) the complexity of intergovernmental relationships, and
(3) the differential constituencies of central and local governments. Each
offers a plausible but, in the end, inadequate explanation for the
regularity with which national programs have been frustrated at local
levels.

LOCAL RULING ELITES

In both popular and academic literature, the favored explanation for the
difficulties faced by Great Society programs is the power of local ruling
elites. Local politics, it is said, has been dominated by power structures
consisting of bankers and businessmen who, together with a few conservative labor leaders and politicians beholden to them, dictate the major
contours of local policy (Hunter 1953).* More sophisticated versions of
this explanation do not claim that the ruling elite makes each and every
local decision but only that its presence precludes redistributive issues
from reaching the agenda of local politics. Its power is used to keep
policies that are of interest to low-income groups and racial minorities
from ever reaching a threshold of public awareness in the local community (Bachrach and Baratz 1962).

*For a collection of readings from this literature and a general bibliography, see
Hawley and Wirt (1968).

A study of Baltimore's community action program provided Bachrach and Baratz (1970) with an opportunity to apply this perspective directly to the implementation of the most visible of the antipoverty programs. In this study, they contend that the politics of community action in Baltimore was marked by "non-decision-making." They concluded (pp. 79–80) that the efforts by black leaders:

> to transform the covert grievances of the black population
> into issues was . . . abortive, in part because they lacked
> arenas where they could practice the politics of conflict as
> distinct from the politics of confrontation, and in part
> because they had no access to key centers of decision-making.
> In short, the prevailing mobilization of bias blocked black
> leaders' attempts to arouse their would-be constituents to
> political action and thereby assured that blacks would remain
> "locked-out" of the political system.

To support this conclusion, they note that Baltimore lacked an open-occupancy ordinance, discriminated against blacks in public and private employment, and funded the antipoverty program only frugally (p. 97).

About some matters Bachrach and Baratz are certainly correct. If Baltimore resembled other local governments, then the civil rights movement and the war on poverty did not dramatically change the course of local public policy to the extent that low-income minorities received greatly expanded benefits from locally financed redistributive programs. On that score, the evidence to the contrary presented below seems conclusive. But the mechanisms precluding achievement of this objective do not seem to square with the "non-decision-making" model. Indeed, the empirical materials in the study testify to the earnestness and persistence with which redistributive issues came to the regular attention of Baltimore's leaders. As the authors point out, "by the end of 1967 the CAA (Community Action Agency), with its black director in the forefront, was operating at full tilt and practically in the open to organize the black poor for political action" (p. 89). Unless one is prepared to accept Bachrach and Baratz's penchant for stretching the concept of "non-decision" so that it coincides with its opposite—the mayor's decision to establish a series of biracial task forces, for example, is labeled "an extremely effective non-decision" (p. 71)—one can hardly claim that a ruling elite excluded issues of race and poverty from the agenda of local politics.

Fundamentally, the ruling elite hypothesis is unable to cope with the signal accomplishment of antipoverty programs: their capacity to open up local political systems to previously excluded groups. Although the socioeconomic impact of the programs was limited, they did improve the opportunities for political participation by blacks and other racial minorities. Led by the "maximum feasible participation" focus of the community action program, most of the Great Society service delivery programs contained features that required the active involvement of representatives of low-income groups and racial minorities in the deliberative process. Although these policies varied by locale and program, the overall impact was greatly to increase both the involvement of minorities as organized supporters of antipoverty programs and their recruitment to positions of administrative responsibility. The war on poverty was most successful in changing the agenda of local politics. Matters of concern to minority groups became regular, if not pervasive, issues in city politics. Even more significant, black leaders and groups representing minority interests became permanent elements in the institutionalized bargaining process through which local policy was formulated (Greenstone and Peterson 1973, Peterson and Greenstone 1977).

Unfortunately, improved access to local politics did not thereby radically alter the socioeconomic well-being of racial minorities and low-income groups (Chicago Urban League 1977). But to attribute this to the power of a ruling elite once again misguides poverty research. If the issue were simply to place on the agenda of local politics the problems of poor minorities, then the programs of the Great Society would certainly have ended poverty and racism in America. But, as we shall see, there are limits inherent in the functions that local governments can perform, and even "maximum feasible" political participation by minorities and the poor does not alter these limits.

ORGANIZATIONAL COMPLEXITY

Quite another interpretation of the Johnson antipoverty programs derives from an understanding of the variety, the complexity, and the changeability of political and organizational relationships in a pluralist system. From this perspective, intergovernmental relationships do not consist simply of encounters between federal officials and local elites; on the contrary, at all levels of government (federal, regional, state, and local) are numerous public and private agencies, with overlapping jurisdictions and competing clientele, that must be consulted in the course of implementing government policy. Any one of these entities can act as a "veto group" to frustrate the execution of policy—or at least to delay its implementation until the original purposes are substantially modified.

As familiar as this pluralist view of American politics has become (Truman 1951, Riesman 1960, Dahl 1961), Pressman and Wildavsky's

(1973) imaginative utilization of these ideas in their analysis of the innovative programs of the Economic Development Administration (EDA) is worthy of special consideration. The study is a detailed analysis of the problems that beset the EDA when it sought to improve minority employment opportunities in Oakland, California by funding a number of public improvement projects in that city. After beginning with high hopes, large projected budgetary outlays, and the appearance of cooperation on the part of both federal and local officials, EDA was frustrated by numerous delays; almost no detectable progress toward the original objective was made. Although the specific problems encountered are discussed in fascinating detail, Pressman and Wildavsky also reach for a more general explanation for the failure of this and other Great Society programs (p. 94):

> What seemed to be a simple program turned out to be a very complex one, involving numerous participants, a host of differing perspectives, and a long and tortuous path of decision points that had to be cleared. Given these characteristics, the chances of completing the program with the haste its designers had hoped for—and even the chances of completing it at all—were sharply reduced.

The problems of the Great Society were thus the problems encountered by any government program in a pluralist political system in which many participants influence policy. Differences must be negotiated, plans must be delayed, and policies must be modified. The solution is either to develop more simple programs, abandon federal efforts to intervene in socioeconomic relationships, or accept that long delays and major revisions are inevitable.

Although the case study is written with incisiveness and energy, in the end the argument cuts too deeply. Inasmuch as it applies to all government programs, it does not provide an adequate explanation for the particular problems encountered by the redistributive programs of the Great Society. In the first place, complexity was not a feature unique to the antipoverty programs of the Johnson administration. Many programs that have become a routinized feature of the federal system—for example, those for highways, rivers and harbors, land reclamation, and airport construction—are equally complex but have nonetheless been incorporated into the ongoing political processes of the federal system. National and local objectives have in these cases been similar enough that, whatever problems they may have encountered in particular cases, few can make the claim that the programs have failed. Indeed, local governments avidly compete for resources for these programs. Complexity is not a sufficient explanation for the diffidence with which localities participated in antipoverty programs.

Second, Pressman and Wildavsky's assertion that programs failed because participants had diverse views with respect to complex phenomena is at best a very low-level theoretical statement (McFarland 1969). In this respect, Pressman and Wildavsky resemble the students of "marble cake" federalism, who find relationships too complicated to identify critical elements patterning the complexity. For example, even though the empirical material in the Oakland study makes it quite clear that the "feds" were concerned primarily with redistribution (e.g., employing minorities) and the "locals" were concerned primarily with obtaining aid for economic development, Pressman and Wildavsky provide no general explanation for this patterning of the differences between the two levels of government. To say that policies fail because they are complex is a beginning, but research on poverty needs to develop more sophisticated tools to help identify the specific complexities that frustrate the effectiveness of redistributive programs.

DIFFERENTIAL CONSTITUENCIES

Constituency theory offers the promise of identifying patterns of conflicts between central and local governments. In its most general formulation, constituency theory argues that political leaders pursue objectives desired by those who select them for office. Regarding the differences between central and local governments, McConnell (1966) has argued that the central government, with a larger constituency, can be expected to serve broader and more diffuse interests. In local government, which has a smaller constituency, it is easier for dominant economic interests to control policy to the exclusion of weaker, less well-organized interests. In governments with a large constituency, the mutual checking of powerful interests and the need to build coalitions of diverse interests permit consideration of weaker, broader, more diffuse concerns, perhaps including even those of the poor. Although McConnell acknowledges (p. 113) that "it should not be expected that a constituency of a given definition will always produce a particular policy," he nonetheless sees essential differences in constituency influences at national and local levels (p. 114):

> Policies generally adhering to maintenance of the status quo
> and favoring the concrete interests of existing elites will tend
> to be associated with organizations [such as states and locali-
> ties] based on small units; alternatively, large units [e.g., the

central offices of the national government] will more probably produce policies favoring change directed to the general, diffuse, and widely shared interests of a broad segment of the population.

One of the best case studies of the failure of a Great Society program is quite convincingly interpreted within the tradition of constituency analysis. In her study of the "New Towns In Town" program initiated in late 1967, Derthick (1972) documents in detail the processes by which a program, originally planned to provide low-income housing through low-cost distribution of surplus federal land, failed to build any new homes for the poor at all. In a thoughtful concluding chapter, Derthick emphasizes the differences in the value commitments of national and local governments and then relates them to their differing constituencies (p. 101):

> In shared programs, both the federal government and local governments have a political function: both play a part in defining the objectives of public action and in responding to differences of value, interest, and opinion. The federal government, being removed from particular and parochial conflicts, is better able to express idealistic and progressive objectives. Local governments, more deeply engaged in these conflicts, are better able to respond to the actual preferences of active political interest.

Although Derthick correctly identifies differing value commitments on the part of national and local institutions, she leaves unstated the exact mechanisms by which local constituencies generate demands that differ from national policies. In Derthick's case study, for example, interest groups and constituency pressures, far from constraining policy choice, were notable for their absence. Although some local officials may have anticipated opposition to a low-income housing program, even that hypothetical opposition does not account for the position of big-city mayors, who could also have anticipated support from sizable low-income and minority constituencies.

The constituency thesis is most helpful in accounting for differential local responses to national policy. But what Derthick, Pressman and Wildavsky, Bachrach and Baratz, and other researchers (Murphy 1971, Pressman 1975) have documented is the consistency of conflict between national and local objectives, including those urban locales where local constituencies have every reason to be most supportive of redistributive programs. Even where the poor constitute the bulk of a local electorate, local governments often frustrated the policy objectives of the Johnson administration.

Toward a New Theory of Federalism

The power of local ruling elites, the complexity of intergovernmental relationships, and the differential constituencies at the national and local levels have all been evoked as explanations for the difficulties that Great Society programs faced when being implemented within a federal system. Although all three hypotheses identify local resistance to redistribution, none provides an adequate explanation for the phenomenon. The problem with all of them is that they are theories concerning the relationships among individuals, groups, and organizations. Influenced by behavioral theories of politics and the marble cake metaphor of federalism, all three approaches try to find explanations for structural differences in government institutions in terms of relationships among elements at the national, state, and local levels. We need instead a theory of federalism that will identify the structural features of central and local institutions and link those features to the processes of intergovernmental policy formation.

There can be no return to a theory of dual sovereignty; the work of Grodzins (1966) has surely laid that moribund notion to rest. But a new theory, like the traditional theory of dual sovereignty, must do three things. First, it must provide a definition that clarifies the way in which a federal system is distinguished from a decentralized administrative structure. Second, it must specify characteristic and appropriate activities of the central and local governments within the federal arrangement. Third, the theory must account for persistent patterns of conflict and cooperation among the various levels of government. Some of the elements that such a theory might contain are presented below. This presentation draws heavily on concepts better known to economists than to political scientists.

Federalism is a system of government in which powers are divided between higher and lower levels of government in such a way that both levels have a significant amount of separate and autonomous responsibility for the social and economic welfare of those living within their respective jurisdictions. Within the federation, the central government assumes responsibility for relations with foreign countries and determines the exchange relationships among the component units of the federation. The central government may exercise numerous additional powers, but for the system to remain a federation, lower levels of government must have at least two crucial powers.

First, lower levels of government must have a significant amount of control over the recruitment of their own political and administrative leadership. If local leaders are selected by officials of the central government, or if recruitment processes are governed by such stringent, centrally determined criteria that the local community has no effective choice, then local government is without power to take responsibility for the well-being of its inhabitants. Second, local government must have the power to tax its citizens in order to provide a range of government services that can enhance the well-being of the community. If local government is totally dependent upon centrally determined grants, it has very limited responsibility for the determination of the well-being of the local community. It will always be dependent on external sources of funds and, consequently, will always feel a need for more such funds. Because such funds do not come directly from the local community's own resources, the monies require strict central government supervision. Once it is no longer dependent on local resources, the local government loses the capacity to act responsibly on its own behalf, and thus becomes simply an agent of the central government.

Federalism is thus to be distinguished from simple decentralization, which can occur without the granting of either recruitment or financial powers to lower decision-making levels. For example, the U.S. Forest Service grants considerable decision-making autonomy to its field offices, though they do not gather their revenues from local sources or act independently in the recruitment of personnel. Were the central administrators of the Forest Service or any other department or agency to lose these two powers to their district offices, the organization could scarcely be considered a single governmental unit. Indeed, these are precisely the circumstances for which the term federalism is appropriately reserved and that at one time might have been characterized as dual sovereignty.

Within a federal system, the objectives of central and local governments stand in contrast to one another. Local governments are particularly concerned with operating efficiently so as to protect their economic base; the domestic policy structure of the central government is more concerned with redistributing values so as to achieve a more egalitarian distribution. These central-local differences are not a function of any particular political movement or any political party or group that happens to be in power at a specific time. Although partisanship and group pressures may aggravate or alleviate somewhat the tension between the objectives of national and local governments, the local emphasis on economic productivity and the national emphasis on equality is a function of the structural relationship of the two levels within the federal system.

Local Government and the Local Economy

When forced to choose between equality and promoting the local economy, local governments in a federal system place greater weight on economic productivity. This choice is not due to a local power elite or to the biases inherent in small constituency politics; instead, it is a function of the external socioeconomic context in which local governments operate. Unlike national governments, local governments have little control over external socioeconomic forces. Just as an individual firm in a competitive economy cannot control its sources of supply or the demand for its products, so local governments cannot control the movement of capital and labor across their boundaries. Local governments are open systems that can be easily permeated by external forces and are therefore particularly sensitive to external changes. In responding to external forces, local governments act to protect an overriding set of interests. Just as a private firm wishes to maximize its profits, so the local community seeks to maximize its economic well-being.

Local leaders can be expected to try to safeguard the economic prosperity of the local community for at least three reasons. First, economic prosperity is necessary for protecting the fiscal base of local government. In the United States, taxes on local sources and charges for local services remain an important source of local government revenues. Although transfers of revenue to local units from federal and state governments increased throughout the postwar period, as late as 1974–1975 local governments still raised almost 60 percent of their own revenue (U.S. Bureau of the Census 1976). Raising revenue from a community's own economic resources requires continuing local economic prosperity. Second, good government is good politics. By pursuing policies that contribute to the economic prosperity of the local community, the local politician selects policies that redound to his or her own political advantage. Third and most important, local officials usually have a sense of community responsibility. They know that, unless the economic well-being of the community can be maintained, local business will suffer, workers will lose employment opportunities, cultural life will decline, and city land values will fall relative to other areas. To avoid such a dismal future, public officials try to develop policies that assist the prosperity of their community—or, at the very least, do not seriously detract from it.

Governments make decisions that maximize this goal within the numerous environmental constraints with which they must contend. As policy alternatives are proposed, each is evaluated according to how well it will help to achieve local economic prosperity. Although information is imperfect and local governments cannot be expected to select the best alternative on every occasion, policy choices will be constrained to those few that can plausibly be shown to be conducive to the community's economic prosperity. Internal disputes and disagreements may affect policy on the margins, but the major contours of local revenue policy will be determined by this larger objective, as shaped by factors in the community's environment.

In attempting to maximize their economic prosperity, local communities are competing with each other. Each must attract productive capital and labor to its area, and to achieve that end the conditions for productive economic activity must be as favorable in one community as they are in competing communities. Otherwise, there will be a net outward flow of productive resources, leaving a community with a declining economic future. Significantly, local governments can do little directly to control the flow of productive resources; for example, they cannot establish tariff walls or control human migration in the same way that nation-states can. Efficiency is all the more important, therefore, in the design of their policies, so that they protect and enhance the productive capacity of the community.

Central Government and Social Equality

Central governments are also concerned about the economic well-being of their society. But by comparison with local governments, central governments are responsible for less permeable socioeconomic systems. The economic constraints on domestic policy choice operate much less restrictively at the national than at the local level, because the national government has at its disposal a range of powers that curb the impact of the external environment on the indigenous society and economy. The most important of these powers is the capacity to issue passports and visas. Through the exercise of these powers, almost all highly industrialized countries have in recent years carefully restricted immigration. Exact formulas vary, but foreigners are allowed permanent residence in an industrialized society only if they either meet highly select personal criteria (marriage or blood relationship to a citizen, for example) or have highly desired skills that will enhance the nation's economy. Without such laws, it would be impossible for these industrialized economies to maintain high wage levels and elaborate systems of social security for their residents. Given the availability of inexpensive transportation, foreigners from less thriving countries would otherwise swamp their social welfare system.

Central governments also protect their economies from worldwide external forces through a host of controls over the movement of capital, goods, and services. Tariffs, quotas, a national currency, control over exchange rates, and the capacity to fund its own indebtedness are among the powers a central government uses to increase its autonomy from external forces. Not all countries can use these devices with equal effectiveness. The United States is particularly fortunate in that foreign exchange amounts to less than 10 percent of its total economic activity. Smaller countries with less self-contained economies have much less scope for autonomous action. But all countries except the smallest and most dependent (perhaps Hong Kong is the limiting case), have less permeable economies than those for which local governments are responsible.

Greater autonomy allows for greater redistribution from the more prosperous to the less so. It may be that even in an entirely self-contained economy, trade-offs remain between efficiency and equality. Too high and too progressive a rate of taxation to finance too elaborate a welfare state may weaken incentives for capital formation. On the other hand, some minimum standard of welfare provision seems necessary to ensure a steady, healthy, capable working population. These are highly debatable issues that are beyond the scope of this analysis (compare O'Connor 1973). But at the very least there is one set of constraints that do not restrict decision-making at the national level. Taxpayers cannot easily flee to other jurisdictions while needy immigrants flood the social-delivery system. Because of their greater control over their boundaries, central governments have much greater capacity to redistribute goods and services than do local governments.

When governments have the capacity to redistribute, political forces in relatively open, pluralist polities will generate demands for redistribution. Political parties that compete for popular favor have every incentive to redistribute income from smaller numbers of high-income groups to larger numbers of lower and lower middle-income groups in the population. Although the surge for redistribution may be episodic, a response to such specific events as the major depression of the 1930s and the mobilization of black discontent in the 1960s, competitive politics in industrialized societies periodically bring redistributive pressures to bear on the policies of central governments.

Once these policies have been promulgated, a governmental agency is charged with the responsibility for implementing a program; the staff then develops a loyalty to the substantive mission of the program

(Greenstone and Peterson, 1973). As a constituent element of the central government's governing apparatus, the agency has a legitimate claim on a continuing—and perhaps slightly increasing—portion of the national budget. To perpetuate its program, its staff solicits the backing of organized elements serviced by its program, who campaign on its behalf in Congress, in other parts of the executive, in the news media, and among the public at large. Quite apart from any short-term political calculus, a structure of power supporting a redistributive program develops a national base.

Differences in Policies in Central and Local Governments

Because the interests of local and central governments are different, the pattern of public policies promulgated by the two levels of government is different. For one thing, central and local governments tend to rely on contrasting principles for raising revenue. The central government depends largely on the ability-to-pay principle, and therefore raises most of its revenues through a progressive income tax, taxes on corporate earnings, and excise taxes on luxury commodities. Local governments, on the other hand, rely more on the benefits-received principle, which specifies that individuals should be taxed in accordance with the level of services they receive. As a result, over one-fourth of local revenues are raised through user charges, and the remainder is collected through taxes on property, sales taxes, and nonprogressive income taxes (Peterson 1979). One need not posit any local power elite to account for this propensity of local governments to favor more regressive taxes. If local communities were to rely on the ability-to-pay principle, there would be a greater disjunction between taxes levied and benefits received, and those paying the most in taxes (who are usually those contributing the most to the local economy) would have strong incentives to migrate elsewhere. Proportional or, preferably, somewhat regressive local taxes come closer to approximating the benefit principle, the principle that is consistent with the economic well-being of the local community.

Second, the expenditures of central and local governments perform different functions. Specifically, the central government assumes the responsibility for financing redistributive policies. As Table 1 shows, 47 percent of the domestic budget of the central government was allocated for redistributive purposes even at the beginning of the 1960s. After the declaration of war on poverty, this percentage increased to more than 55 percent. By contrast, the percentage of local revenues used for redistributive policies was only 12.9 percent in 1962. Significantly, even after the emergence of the civil rights movement and its supposed impact

Table 1.
Percentage Distribution among Functions of Direct and Intergovernmental Expenditures by Local, State and Federal Governments from their own Fiscal Resources: 1962, 1967 and 1973[1]

FUNCTION	Local			State			Federal (Domestic only)		
	1962	1967	1973	1962	1967	1973	1962	1967	1973
	(Percentage of Total Expenditures by Each Level of Government)								
Redistributive									
Welfare	2.5	2.5	2.0	6.2	6.4	11.2	12.2	11.9	12.6
Hospital & Health	6.1	6.7	8.6	7.4	7.2	6.2	3.3	3.7	3.5
Housing	2.4	1.5	0.9	0.2	0.2	0.4	1.5	1.9	3.4
Social Insurance	1.9	2.2	2.3	14.4	9.4	17.0	29.7	34.0	35.6
All Redistributive	12.9	12.9	13.8	28.2	23.2	34.8	46.7	51.5	55.1
Non-Redistributive									
Housekeeping	26.8	26.4	28.5	12.4	12.9	8.4	4.6	4.5	3.8
Utilities	13.2	13.1	11.1	–	–	–	–	–	–
Postal	–	–	–	–	–	–	7.0	7.2	5.1
Transportation	8.1	6.6	5.7	17.8	16.0	11.3	6.2	5.8	4.2
Natural Resources	1.1	1.1	0.7	2.9	3.5	2.3	19.3	9.9	7.8
Interest	4.1	4.4	5.6	2.2	2.3	2.7	12.3	12.1	9.9
Education	33.4	35.2	34.2	33.6	39.5	38.4	3.2	7.2	8.2
Other	0.4	0.3	0.4	3.0	2.6	2.2	0.8	1.8	5.8
Total (%)	100.0	100.0	100.0	100.1	100.0	100.1	100.1	100.0	99.9
Total ($m)	33,591	45,853	77,886	29,356	45,288	89,504	58,960	86,852	186,172

[1]Table adapted from Peterson 1979, Table 3. For sources and other notes see citation.

on local service delivery systems (Piven 1976), this percentage increased over the next decade by less than one percent. The role of the states stands midway between that of the central and local governments. States have contributed somewhat less than 35 percent of their budgets to redistributive programs.

The figures in Table 2 are even more dramatic. This table shows the percentage of all expenditures devoted to a particular activity contributed by each level of government. As the table shows, not only was the local contribution to redistributive programs scarcely more than 10 percent in 1962, but also the percentage has declined since that time. The fiscal role of the federal government, on the other hand, has become especially significant. And if the political pressures for federalizing welfare policy and health care are any sign, this pattern is likely to continue. As the United States continues to become an increasingly integrated political economy, the redistributive function may well become an almost exclusively federal prerogative.

The distinctively redistributive role of the central government is especially evident in programs supported by federal grants-in-aid. Table 3 shows the distribution by function of intergovernmental revenues from the central and state governments to lower governmental levels. The states allocate most of their intergovernmental monies for educational purposes, but the primary role of the central government has been to finance the redistributive activities of states and localities. When local governments do provide welfare, hospital, health, and housing services to low-income groups, these services are generally provided through intergovernmental grants from the federal government. Even in 1973, after the establishment of a revenue-sharing program by the Nixon administration, 40 percent of intergovernmental revenues received by states and localities was specifically designated for a redistributive function. The increase in undesignated revenues in that year came largely at the expense of funds for educational and other purposes, not as a substitute for redistributive activities.

Intergovernmental Relationships

These data on the contrasting functions of central and local governments suggest that the contrasting purposes of the two levels of government affect redistributive policies. But if the two levels of government pursue differing policies, then intergovernmental programs requiring the cooperative action of both levels of government will be subject to considerable tension. On one hand, the departments of the central government will endeavor to pursue a more egalitarian course, seeking to ensure that federal monies are used for

Table 2.
Percentage Distribution among Governments of Direct and Intergovernmental Expenditures by Local,
State and Federal Governments from their own Fiscal Resources, by Function: 1962, 1967, 1973[1]

FUNCTION	Local			State			Federal			Total		
	1962	1967	1973	1962	1967	1973	1962	1967	1973	1962	1967	1973
	(Percentage of Expenditures for Each Function by all Governments)											
Redistributive												
Welfare	8.5	7.8	4.3	18.4	20.1	28.7	73.1	72.1	67.2	100.0	100.0	100.2
Hospital & Health	33.2	32.2	35.4	35.2	34.0	29.6	31.6	33.8	35.0	100.0	100.0	100.0
Housing	46.7	29.3	9.7	2.5	3.8	4.5	50.7	66.9	85.8	99.9	100.0	100.0
Social Insurance	2.9	2.9	2.2	18.9	12.3	18.2	78.1	84.8	79.6	99.9	100.0	100.0
All Redistributive	10.8	9.7	7.4	20.6	17.2	21.5	68.6	73.2	71.1	100.0	100.0	100.1
Non-Redistributive												
Housekeeping	58.7	55.4	60.2	23.7	26.6	20.4	17.5	17.8	19.4	99.9	99.8	100.0
Postal	—	—	—	—	—	—	100.0	100.0	100.0	100.0	—	—
Utilities	23.3	19.7	20.1	45.1	47.3	45.0	31.6	33.0	34.9	100.0	100.0	100.0
Transportation	3.0	4.7	3.3	6.7	14.9	12.0	90.3	80.4	84.7	100.0	100.0	100.0
Natural Resources	14.9	14.8	17.2	6.9	7.6	9.6	78.2	77.6	73.2	100.0	100.0	100.0
Interest	100.0	100.0	100.0	—	—	—	—	—	—	100.0	100.0	100.0
Education	48.9	40.0	34.9	43.0	44.4	45.0	8.1	15.6	20.0	100.0	100.0	99.9
Other	8.6	5.4	2.2	60.1	41.1	15.3	31.3	53.5	82.5	100.0	100.0	100.0

[1]Table adapted from Peterson 1979, Table 4. For sources and other notes, see citation.

Table 3.
Intergovernmental Expenditures by State and Federal
Governments, by Function, 1962, 1967, 1973.[1]

FUNCTION	Intergovernmental Expenditure					
	State			Federal		
	1962	1967	1973	1962	1967	1973
	(Per Cent)					
Redistributive						
Welfare	16.3	15.2	18.4	31.6	28.2	29.0
Hospital & Health	1.8	1.6	2.1	2.2	2.7	4.2
Housing	.3	.4	.4	4.1	4.5	5.1
Social Insurance	–	–	–	6.0	3.8	1.9
All Redistributive	18.4	17.2	20.9	43.9	39.1	40.2
Non-Redistributive						
Housekeeping	–	–	–	.9	.9	2.1
Transportation	12.2	9.9	7.4	36.3	27.4	13.2
Natural Resources	.2	.2	.2	1.8	1.6	1.6
Education	59.4	62.2	57.1	15.1	26.1	20.8
Other and Undesignated	9.7	10.6	14.4	2.0	4.9	22.0
TOTAL	99.9	100.1	100.0	100.0	100.0	100.0
Dollars (millions)	10,906	19,056	40,822	7,735	15,027	41,666

[1]Table adapted from Peterson 1979, Table 5. See citation for sources and other notes.

redistributive purposes. On the other hand, local governments, eager to sustain their local economies, will wish to use federal monies so that those contributing the most to the local economy will benefit most from local expenditures.

Consider the interests of local governments that are offered the opportunity to secure a grant-in-aid for a complex new governmental program. Of course, it is an opportunity to receive "free" federal funds for the benefit of the local community. These dollars, pumped into the local economy from outside, have a short-term positive effect on the community's economy, no matter what the purpose for which they are expended. Yet the short-term effects are dispersed quickly. Because local economies are not self-contained but involve extensive trading with other sectors of the highly integrated American economy, any "shot-in-the-arm" effects that federal grants have on local prosperity do not necessarily cumulate. As a result, any local government considering a federal grant must weigh more heavily the long-term economic impact of the policy objectives for which the grant is expended (Thompson 1965, Forrester 1969).

If the purpose of the grant is to assist in the development of the local community's economic base, local leaders will have strong incentives to respond favorably. Federal funds for highways, sewers, industrial parks, dams, dredging of canals and harbors, and the renewal of downtown business districts are attractive prizes, eagerly sought and won. So are air force bases and defense contracts. These are "hard" federal dollars that build the economy of local communities. The grants are invested in productive resources that generate a continuing source of local revenue, materially adding to local prosperity.

The redistributive programs of the Great Society, however, seldom had this unequivocally positive effect on local economies. By and large, they were "soft" programs aimed at servicing the poorest segments of the local population, either by providing them with better education, more training for industrial employment, more health care, more legal assistance, or more political power. To the extent that a local community faithfully carries out the intentions of federal policy, the community makes itself a more attractive locale for poor people to live. To the extent that excellent schools providing high-quality instruction are provided to poor minorities, poor minority groups have great incentives to migrate to that community. To the extent that inexpensive but attractive homes are provided for those in need, the community becomes a haven for the homeless. The more redistributive the policies of any local community, the more that community attracts those in need of governmental assistance. Unfortunately, in an economy with less than full employment, redistributive policies contribute little, if anything, to the local economy. On the contrary, they only add to local crime rates, the costs of fire insurance, and other demands on local services.

When given the opportunity to participate in redistributive Great Society programs, local governments consequently have every incentive to accept the monies (for their short-term positive effect on local economies) but then to modify any redistributive impact they might have. The classic case, of course, was urban renewal, which began as a program for housing the needy but ended as a program to improve the industrial and commercial capacities of central cities (Wilson 1966, Greer 1965). In many cases, urban renewal funds were used to build high-quality homes for upper-middle classes so as to attract desirable citizens back to the central city. Apart from urban renewal, local communities have generally resisted the placement of low-income public housing in their neighborhoods, and even the availability of low-cost federal land was not sufficient enticement to participation in federal low-income housing programs (Derthick 1972). Rather than build housing for the poor, local communities have used their zoning powers to exclude residents who "cannot pay their own way"—i.e., those who do not pay in local taxes an amount that covers the cost of services extended to them (Babcock 1966, Mills and Oates 1975). And because local governments are especially interested in economic productivity, officials in Oakland were far more anxious to secure federal funds for the extension of the Oakland harbor than to insist that local employers act affirmatively in minority recruitment (Pressman and Wildavsky 1973).

Conclusion

The central government's commitment to reduce poverty and achieve egalitarian welfare distribution has been frustrated by structural features of the American federal system. Numerous studies have documented the difficulties encountered by Great Society programs in the course of their implementation. But most have attributed the difficulties to conservative local elites, to the inherent complexities of intergovernmental programs, or to the differential constituencies of central and local governments. These explanations are incomplete. Local elites seem conservative because the local community must be concerned above all with protecting its economic base. Federal programs become involved in complex bargaining situations, because central and local interests contradict one another. The local constituencies to which local officials listen are those representing the interests of business and property, because they are the interests that must be protected if the economic well-being of the community is to be safeguarded. In sum, the differing functional responsibilities of central and local governments generate value conflicts that impede the implementation of redistributive policies.

Poverty research has not appreciated this important structural element affecting policy outcomes. Future research could usefully address these questions through cross-national comparative studies and through properly designed studies of the process of policy making in the United States. A few suggestions follow rather directly from the foregoing analysis.

Perhaps the most interesting large-scale research would involve cross-national comparative analyses of the policy implications of various types of intergovernmental arrangements. Although research on this issue is virtually nonexistent, redistributive programs among different levels of government in European countries do not appear to encounter the same level of local resistance that they do in the United States. In Great Britain, for example, there is extensive central-local cooperation in the provision of public housing and social services. Although confrontations sometimes occur, the disputes are usually partisan in nature. It is just as likely for local governments, led by Labour leaders, to attempt to thwart a conservative central government policy as it is for conservative local authorities to undermine a redistributive objective. The consistent disjunction between national and local goals, so evident in the United States, does not occur in other structural contexts.

Research on the elements that differentiate the American from European systems could be highly constructive. The most likely differentiating factor is the much greater equalizing role that central subsidies play in local finance in European countries (Griffith 1966). In Great Britian, as in most European countries, local communities raise less than half their local revenues through local taxes; more important, the remainder is distributed among local authorities in such a way as to ensure that all have roughly similar per capita amounts for expenditures, although certain variations in local need are also taken into account. In other words, a decline in the value of local property does not become translated into a substantial loss in local government income. Local policies are therefore not as closely tied to local economies as in the United States.

Other differences may play an important role as well. Local governments service larger, more heterogeneous populations in Great Britain than in the United States. Capital expansion depends not on a local government's capacity to raise revenue in the bond markets but on the approval of a central department. The central government has its own regional policy, which encourages private investment in areas of high unemployment.

Within the United States, one can usefully compare the problems of implementing a policy through a highly centralized administrative structure with the problems encountered in federal arrangements. If the substantive policies are similar but administrative arrangements quite different, the federal theory offered here would have a reasonably clear test.

One might also compare the implementation of redistributive policies with the implementation of developmental policies that promote local economic growth. How do central-local relations differ in the two policy areas? Does one policy seem to be more "complex" than the other? Is central-local conflict greater on redistributive issues and inter-local competition greater on developmental issues?

The collection and routine analysis of data on intergovernmental expenditures are only in their infancy. To what extent is the vastly increasing program of intergovernmental expenditures freeing local governments from a dependence on their local economy? Is resource equalization beginning to occur? To what extent do programs of federal assistance encourage or deter localities from assisting low-income groups in the community? What are the differences among states in state grant-in-aid programs?

The fact that states differ in their relationships with local governments can be exploited for research purposes. Some states have a more "unitary" system, in which substantial state grants-in-aid supplement local budgets, while other states have essentially a "federal" arrangement. What differences do these arrangements make for the implementation of state-initiated programs of redistribution?

There is variation in the degree to which legislation allows flexibility in federal-local relationships. Do local interests have greater scope when the federal mandate is most flexible? The two most substantial studies of policy implementation—the Derthick and the Pressman-Wildavsky studies—both examined programs that had highly imprecise congressional mandates. Can problems of implementation in a federal system be reduced through more detailed legislative enactments?

Without research on these questions, it is possible only to speculate about the precise connections between government structures and redistributive policy. In general, the overriding political problem to which research needs to direct itself is how the federal system can be made compatible with the objectives of reducing poverty and achieving a more equitable distribution of income. Within the marble cake framework, it seemed that any task could be performed by any level of government, or any combination of levels of government. But if the various levels of government have distinct functions, and intergovernmental cooperation is frustrated by their competing interests, then successful efforts to aid the poor through a decentralized social service delivery system may require changes in the structure of government on a scale not seriously considered even among those carrying out basic research in the field.

References

Babcock, Richard (1966) *The Zoning Game*. Madison: University of Wisconsin Press.

Bachrach, Peter, and Baratz, Morton S. (1962) Two faces of power. *American Political Science Review* 56:947–52.

Bachrach, Peter, and Baratz, Morton S. (1970) *Theory and Practice*. New York: Oxford University Press.

Chicago Urban League (1977) The Current Economic Status of Chicago's Black Community. Unpublished report 2.

Dahl, Robert (1961) *Who Governs?* New Haven: Yale University Press.

Davis, Karen (1977) A decade of policy developments in providing health
      care for low-income families. Pp. 197–231 in Robert H. Haveman, ed.,
      A Decade of Federal Antipoverty Programs. New York: Academic
      Press.
Derthick, Martha (1972) *New Towns in Town: Why a Federal Program Failed.*
      Washington, D.C.: Urban Institute.
Diamond, Martin (1969) On the relationship of federalism and decentraliza-
      tion. Pp. 72–80 in Daniel J. Elazar, R. Bruce Carroll, E. Lester Levine,
      and Douglas St. Angelo, eds., *Cooperation and Conflict: Readings in
      American Federalism.* Ithasca, Ill. F. E. Peacock.
Elazar, Daniel (1966) *American Federalism: A View from the States.* New
      York: Thomas Y. Crowell.
Elazar, Daniel J., Carroll, R. Bruce, Levine, E. Lester, and St. Angelo,
      Douglas, eds. (1969) *Cooperation and Conflict: Readings in American
      Federalism.* Itasca, Ill. F.E. Peacock.
Forrester, Jay (1969) *Urban Dynamics.* Cambridge, Mass.: MIT Press.
Greenstone, J. David (1975) Group theories. Pp. 243–318 in Fred Greenstein
      and Nelson Polsby, eds., *Handbook of Political Science II.* Reading,
      Mass.: Addison-Wesley.
Greenstone, J. David, and Peterson, Paul E. (1973) *Race and Authority in
      Urban Politics.* New York: Russell Sage.
Greer, Scott (1965) *Urban Renewal and American Cities.* Indianapolis: Bobbs
      Merrill.
Griffith, J.A.G. (1966) *Central Departments and Local Authorities* London:
      George Allen & Unwin.
Grodzins, Morton (1966) *The American System.* Edited by Daniel J. Elazar.
      Chicago: Rand McNally.
Haveman, Robert H. (1977) Introduction: poverty and social policy in the
      1960s and 1970s—an overview and some speculations. Pp. 1–20 in
      Robert H. Haveman, ed., *A Decade of Federal Antipoverty Programs.*
      New York: Academic Press.
Hawley, Willis D., and Wirt, Frederick M., eds. (1968) *The Search for Com-
      munity Power.* Englewood Cliffs, New Jersey: Prentice-Hall.
Hunter, Floyd (1953) *Community Power Structure.* Chapel Hill: University
      of North Carolina Press.
Kaufman, Herbert (1960) *The Forest Ranger.* Baltimore: Johns Hopkins Press.
Kramer, Ralph (1969) *Participation of the Poor: Comparative Case Studies
      in the War on Poverty.* Englewood Cliffs, New Jersey: Prentice-Hall.
Levin, Henry M. (1977) A decade of policy developments in improving educa-
      tion and training for low-income populations. Pp. 123–188 in Robert
      H. Haveman, ed., *A Decade of Federal Antipoverty Programs.* New
      York: Academic Press.
Lynn, Laurence E., Jr. (1977) A decade of policy developments in the income-
      maintenance system. Pp. 55–117 in Robert H. Haveman, *A Decade of
      Federal Antipoverty Programs.* New York: Academic Press.
McConnell, Grant (1966) *Private Power and American Democracy.* New York:
      Alfred Knopf.

McFarland, Andrew S. (1969) *Power and Leadership in Pluralist Systems.* Stanford, Cal.: Stanford University Press.

MacMahon, Arthur W. (1972) *Administering Federalism in a Democracy.* New York: Oxford University Press.

Mills, Edwin S., and Oates, Wallace E., eds. (1975) *Fiscal Zoning and Land Use Controls.* Lexington, Mass.: D.C. Heath.

Murphy, Jerome T. (1971) Title I of ESEA: the politics of implementing federal education reform. *Harvard Educational Review* 41:35-63.

O'Connor, James (1973) *The Fiscal Crisis of the State.* New York: St. James Press.

Peterson, P. E. (1979) A unitary model of local taxation and expenditure policies in the United States. *British Journal of Political Science* July.

Peterson, Paul E., and Greenstone, J. David (1977) Racial change and citizen participation: the mobilization of low-income communities through community action. Pp. 241-278 in Robert H. Haveman, ed., *A Decade of Federal Antipoverty Programs.* New York: Academic Press.

Piven, Frances (1976) The urban fiscal crisis. In Stephen David and Paul E. Peterson, eds., *Urban Politics and Public Policy.* 2nd ed. New York: Praeger Publishers.

Pressman, Jeffrey L. (1975) *Federal Programs and City Politics.* Berkeley: University of California Press.

Pressman, Jeffrey L. and Wildavsky, Aaron (1973) *Implementation.* Berkeley: University of California Press.

Riesman, David (1960) *The Lonely Crowd.* New Haven: Yale University Press.

Strange, John H. (1972) Citizen participation in community action and model cities programs. *Public Administration Review* 32:655-669.

Taeuber, Karl (1977) Discussions. Pp. 360-63 in Robert H. Haveman, ed., *A Decade of Federal Antipoverty Programs.* New York: Academic Press.

Thompson, Wilbur R. (1965) *A Preface to Urban Economics.* Baltimore: Johns Hopkins Press.

Truman, David (1951) *The Governmental Process.* New York: Alfred Knopf.

U.S. Bureau of the Census (1976) *Local Government Finances in Selected Metropolitan Areas and Large Countries: 1974-75.* Washington: Government Printing Office.

U.S. Senate, Committee on Government Operations, Subcommittee on Intergovernmental Relations (1969) The federal system as seen by federal aid officials. Pp. 331-338 in Daniel J. Elazar, R. Bruce Carroll, E. Lester Levine, and Douglas St. Angelo, eds., *Cooperation and Conflict: Readings in American Federalism.* Itasca, Ill.: F.E. Peacock.

Ways, Max (1969) "Creative Federalism" and the Great Society. Pp. 619-631 in Daniel J. Elazar, R. Bruce Carroll, E. Lester Levine, and Douglas St. Angelo, eds., *Cooperation and Conflict: Readings in American Federalism.* Itasca, Il. F.E. Peacock.

Wilson, James Q., ed. (1966) *Urban Renewal, The Record and the Controversy.* Cambridge, Mass.: MIT Press.

Wright, Deil S. (1975) Revenue sharing and structural features of American Federalism. *Annals of the American Academy of Political and Social Science* 419:100-119.

Walter Korpi

Approaches to the Study of Poverty in the United States: Critical Notes from a European Perspective

Introduction

To a student of social policy bred in one of the European "welfare states," the social policy scene in the United States offers a curious contrast. On one hand, poverty-oriented social science research in the United States is a highly flourishing field, bustling with vital and talented scholars using the most modern and sophisticated methodologies to tackle the problems they have chosen to study. On the other hand, in examining the present social policy agenda in the United States, the European observer finds lively debates on issues that he or she has previously met only in the more or less dusty pages of historical accounts of the development of social policy at home.[1] This reflects the fact that more than in any other advanced industrialized society, social policy in the United States comes close to what Titmuss (1975, pp. 30–31) has termed the residual welfare model, in which the private market and the family are seen as the natural channels through which an individual's needs are met and in which social welfare institutions are regarded as only temporary substitutes that are used when these natural mechanisms have broken down.

The very richness of poverty-oriented social science research in the United States makes selectivity necessary in discussing this research and in comparing it with relevant European research. Since the particular issues focused upon by poverty researchers depend largely on the institutional structures and policy arrangements in their respective countries and since the abundant American poverty research has touched on a much larger number of issues than its European counterparts, it does not appear fruitful to attempt to compare the extent to which researchers on one side of the Atlantic have covered the blank spots on the maps of researchers on the other side. For a European social scientist interested in

[Walter Korpi is professor of social policy at the Swedish Institute for Social Research in Stockholm.]

social policy, the striking differences between American and European poverty research are not related to the fact that researchers on the two sides of the Atlantic have covered different issues. The striking differences are instead related to the basic approaches to research on poverty prevailing in Europe and in the United States and to the terms in which poverty is conceptualized and explained as well as to the choice of criteria for policy evaluation.

I therefore think that it is more fruitful to compare how researchers have approached the problem of poverty—that is, to look for the blind spots in the eyes of the poverty researchers. Such a focus inevitably makes this type of review more controversial. While specific research issues can be added to or deleted from research agendas relatively easily, the ways in which researchers approach their problems are rooted in the contexts in which they work and are therefore much more difficult to change. I am convinced, however, that to the extent that comparisons between European and American poverty research can be of use in evaluating and redirecting research in the United States, the greatest potential gains are to be found in a discussion of the basic issues concerning approaches to poverty research.

Against the perspective of what is prevalent in Europe, I look at three basic aspects of the way in which social science research in the United States has approached the problem of poverty. In so doing I am relying liberally on my subjective judgment of what is typical for research in the United States and in Europe.[2] The first aspect concerns how poverty is to be conceptualized. Widely diverging approaches crystallize around the issues of whether poverty is to be seen as an absolute or a relative condition and of dimensions it is assumed to have. The way in which poverty is conceptualized is bound to have consequences for the poor as well as for poverty research. The second aspect concerns the ways in which poverty is explained, that is, the types of theories, factors, or paradigms relied upon in accounting for the existence of and variations in poverty. The third aspect concerns the terms by which programs and policies to relieve poverty are evaluated, that is, the criteria considered important in judging the outcome of specific policies and in designing new policies. As a background to this discussion I begin by briefly characterizing the development and institutional setting of poverty research in the United States and in Europe.

Institutional and Disciplinary Settings

Poverty-related research can be characterized in terms of the institutional settings in which it is carried out and the ways in which it is financed, factors that are of relevance for the degree of closeness to policy makers. Relatively close to policy makers is research that has been financed and/or initiated by them. It is carried out in research institutes specifically directed to the study of policy-relevant issues in certain sectors of public policy. This type of research, called sectorially oriented research, can be contrasted to discipline-oriented research, which is carried out by academics in traditional university settings and is financed by general research foundations. This latter type of research springs more or less clearly from the concerns within academic disciplines rather than from the concerns of policy makers. Although it may be equally relevant and valuable to the policy makers as the sectorially oriented research, this type of research can be assumed to be relatively insulated from the day-to-day concerns of the policy makers. The distinction between these two orientations is thus based on the institutional setting of the research and on the way in which research is financed. It is a classification of research, not of researchers. The actual research practices or products of these two orientations need not, however, be sharply differentiated.

The flow of funds and personnel into poverty research, generated by the rediscovery of poverty in the early 1960s, shows both similarities and differences between Europe and the United States. Although discipline-oriented research has been of importance in Europe as well as in the United States, increases in research funding in poverty-related areas appear to have come primarily to sectorially oriented rather than to discipline-oriented research. The mandate given to sectorially oriented research, however, appears to have been broader in Europe than in the United States. For instance, new research institutes created in Norway and Sweden were given relatively broad policy areas as their concern, and in Sweden research on labor market policy and research on social policy were combined. In the United States a major part of the new research has been focused specifically on evaluation of policies and programs related to poverty. Sectorially oriented research also appears to have had a relatively strong programmatic orientation toward poverty as indicated, for instance, by the name of the new research institute, the Institute for Research on Poverty, apparently the only major research institute in the world dedicated to the study of poverty.

In terms of the mix of academic backgrounds of researchers involved in the new sectorially oriented research, there appear to be differences between Europe and the United States. In several of the European countries, for instance those of Britain and Scandinavia, there is a relatively even balance between sociologists and economists in sectorially oriented research, with the sociologists not infrequently more active than the economists. In the United States, on the other hand, the economists have clearly dominated sectorially oriented research. This dominance is evident, for instance, in the day-to-day activities of the Institute for Research on Poverty, where the economists have a marked dominance and the representatives of sociology and other disciplines appear to have used the institute primarily as an outlet for publication. Although the directors of the institute have all been economists, the lesser salience of the sociologists at the institute in addition reflects the narrowly academic orientation of American sociology, which tends to consider policy-oriented and politically relevant research of minor relevance for the discipline. In Europe, sociologists have been much more interested in tackling the socially and politically relevant problems of their societies.

Quite irrespective of its type of orientation, social science research in Europe appears to have been relatively homogenous in approaches to the problem of poverty. In the United States, however, there appears to be a tendency to divergence in approaches between sectorially oriented and discipline-oriented poverty research. It also appears that at least some of the discipline-oriented poverty research in the United States has been relatively similar to European research in its approaches, whereas the sectorially oriented research in the United States in some important ways stands out as being different. Here I primarily contrast the sectorially oriented American research, especially that carried out at the Institute for Research on Poverty, with poverty related research in Europe.

Conceptualizing Poverty

The way in which poverty is conceptualized is bound to be of crucial importance for research as well as for policy evaluation and for the development of policy strategies. The main issues confronting us are whether poverty is to be seen as an absolute or a relative condition and what dimensions poverty is assumed to have.

ABSOLUTE VERSUS RELATIVE POVERTY

As is well known, there are two basic approaches to the conceptualization of poverty. One approach searches for an absolute definition of poverty, typically trying to define it in relation to human physiology and in terms of subsistence levels of nutrition. The other, the relative approach, attempts to define poverty in relation to society, primarily in terms of the distance between the poor and the average or median standard of living in society, thereby making poverty one aspect of inequality.

The history of the study of poverty can be described as a continuous retreat of the absolute and advance of the relative definitions of poverty. The attempts in Britain by Booth and Rowntree around the turn of the century to base the definition of poverty on minimum levels of nutrition have gradually yielded to the realization that poverty is relative. The debate between the proponents of these two approaches by now has made clear, however, that there are not two definitions of poverty, between which we can choose according to taste, but instead two different aspects of poverty, which are both important, although in differing ways. One aspect of poverty is the social and political definition of poverty, which relates to the conditions prevailing in a particular society; another aspect concerns the standard of living among the poor, which is reflected in the absolute view on poverty.

Efforts to tie the definition of poverty to nutrition levels have failed, since, in modern industrialized societies, nutrition requirements cannot be defined merely in terms of calories necessary for physiological functioning. The types of food deemed acceptable and the ways of preparing food change with the standard of living in society as does the proportion of income spent on food. As defined for political and practical purposes, "minimum decency" or "subsistence" levels applied in means-tested social or public assistance programs are generally found to increase in real terms and to constitute a relatively fixed proportion of the increasing average standard of living in society. Opinion polls indicate that the perception by the public of the minimum amount of money a family needs to get along in a community tends to increase with increasing disposable family income and to constitute a relatively stable proportion of median family income (Rainwater 1974). These observations underscore the fact that for practical and political purposes, poverty is defined in relative terms and depends on the average standard of living in a society at a particular time.

The fact that in our societies poverty is not defined in absolute terms can be illustrated by an example. Let us assume that in 1944 American poverty researchers had set an absolute definition of poverty equal to about half the median income of that time, to be adjusted only for the rate of inflation and not for increases in real income. By 1964, at the very time of the declaration by President Johnson of the first war on poverty in history, poverty researchers would have found very few Americans who, according to their definition, were living in poverty. Would they then have insisted that the war on poverty was unnecessary, that the enemy already was soundly defeated, and that the Great Society, in which hardly anyone was poor, was already a reality?

When analyzing changes over time in the level of poverty, the distinction between the absolute and the relative conceptualizations of poverty becomes clear as well as important. The absolute view indicates that the standard of living of those at the bottom of the stratification ladder has increased dramatically during the postwar period, a fact that certainly is of significance and is reflected, for instance, in an increase in life expectancy. In spite of this increase in standards of living of people in the bottom layers of society, their condition is still defined by the government as unacceptable and requiring major political action, simply because the standard of living of these people is still far behind that of the majority of the population, a fact that shows that the politically and socially relevant aspects of poverty are defined in relative terms. To chart our progress against poverty in the social and political sense, we much therefore use a relative definition of poverty.

In the postwar years the relative definition of poverty has largely been accepted by European researchers in sectorially as well as in discipline-oriented research (for representative discussions, see, e.g., Coates and Silburn 1970, chap. 2, Kincaid 1973, chap. 1, Sleeman 1973, p. 87, Townsend 1974, Atkinson 1975, pp. 186–191, Robson 1976, pp. 141–143).[3] European governments have also often left it to their bureaucracies to define the "poverty lines" to be used for administrative purposes, primarily in connection with means-tested social assistance. These governments have come to apply a relative definition of poverty, since, although unsystematic, the year-to-year changes in assistance levels made by public authorities have tended to follow increases not only in prices but also in average standards of living in each society.

In the United States, discipline-oriented research has also generally come to view the concept of poverty in relative rather than in absolute terms (e.g. Galbraith 1958, Fuchs 1965, Smolensky 1965, Mencher 1967, Rein 1970, Miller and Roby 1970, Rainwater 1974). On the theoretical level, the government of the United States has also recognized the relative nature of poverty. The U.S. President's Commission on Income Maintenance Programs (1969, p.8) stated:

> As society becomes more affluent it defines poverty as not only the lack of the components of a subsistence level of living, but also the lack of opportunity for persons with limited resources to achieve the quality of life enjoyed by persons with an average amount of resources. The definition of poverty progresses from one based on absolute standards to one based on relative standards.

And a report to the Congress from the U.S. Department of Health, Education, and Welfare (1976, p. xxi) proudly states:

> Poor persons living in the United States in the 1970s are rich in contrast to their counterparts in other times and places.

> They are not poor if by poor is meant the subsistence levels of living common in some other countries. Nor are most poor like their counterparts in this country fifty or one hundred years ago.

In practice, however, the United States government has defined poverty in absolute terms and has drawn a poverty line based on the costs for an economy food basket, adjusted only for price increases. The reasons for this discrepancy between theory and practice are probably largely related to the fact that an absolute measure of poverty is more likely than a relative one to indicate "progress" over time.

Sectorially oriented poverty research in the United States appears to have made uneasy compromises between intellectual demands and strategical as well as tactical considerations of what is possible in the political climates in which this research has been carried out. The result has been that while this research generally recognizes the validity of the intellectual arguments in favor of a relative view on poverty, in practice it has largely come to rely on the absolute definition. For instance, although considerable internal debate has been waged on the merits of relative versus absolute definitions of poverty within the Institute for Research on Poverty, the major research products of the institute have been permeated by the absolute view. The defense for this view was formulated by Lampman (1971, p. 53):

> While income poverty is a relative matter, I do not think that we should engage in frequent changes of the poverty lines, other than to adjust for price changes. As I see it, the elimination of income poverty is usefully thought of as a one-time operation in pursuit of a goal unique to this generation. That goal should be achieved before 1980, at which time the next generation will have to set new economic and social goals, perhaps including new distributional goals for themselves.

The first book from the institute in a series of poverty policy analyses discusses the relative and absolute definitions of poverty and defends the absolute measure, recognizing "that those with low incomes gain benefits from rising income and consumption regardless of their position in the income distribution" (Plotnick and Skidmore 1975, p. 39). The book then goes on to rely more heavily on the absolute than on the relative definition in charting the progress against poverty for the decade 1964–1974.

The view of poverty as a relative phenomenon with a poverty line defined in terms of a fraction of median income does not make it impossible to reduce or to eliminate poverty. In Sweden, for instance, poverty among the elderly has by and large been eliminated in the postwar period (Korpi 1974). But the relative definition draws attention to the difficulties involved in reducing poverty, increasing the realism in attempts to understand the causes of poverty and to design and evaluate programs against poverty. Whereas an absolute definition of poverty tends to limit attention to those below the poverty line and easily confines the study of poverty to a study of the poor, a relative definition tends to make the study of poverty one aspect of the study of inequality.

The choice between the absolute and relative definitions of poverty is of central political relevance because it tends to lead to different answers to politically relevant questions, such as "Is the extent of poverty decreasing?" and "What types of policies affect the extent of poverty?" The choice between an absolute and a relative definition of poverty is of course also of central relevance to the poor. Since the official poverty line in the United States serves significant administrative purposes and is used, for instance, in defining eligibility for some types of benefits, reliance on an absolute poverty definition tends to make the standard of living of the poor slip in relation to that enjoyed by the majority of the population.[4] As long as sectorially oriented research continues to give scientific legitimacy to the absolute view of poverty, it thereby tends to counteract the development of effective programs against poverty. On the other hand, because of the conservative political climate prevailing in the United States, the poverty researchers working with absolute definitions of poverty may have made a first step in the direction of progress for the poor by helping to place the issue of poverty on the agenda of the nation.

THE DIMENSIONS OF POVERTY

The dimensions or variables considered in the definition of poverty are relevant not only for defining eligibililty for public transfers but also for understanding the causes of poverty and for evaluating programs to reduce poverty. In the United States, those involved in sectorially oriented research have generally tended to define poverty in terms of constraints on the resources commanded by a household (e.g., Watts 1968). In my opinion this stress on command over resources is a very fruitful basis for a definition of poverty preferable to definitions in terms of attained consumption or satisfaction. Whereas European researchers have attempted to consider a multiplicity of resources in discussions of poverty, sectorially oriented poverty research in the United States has relied almost exclusively on income, generally cash income, for delineating and defining poverty. Considerable work has, however, been put into efforts to refine the income definition of poverty (Moon and Smolensky 1977). A large part of these efforts has been directed to the problem of including the value of in-kind transfers into the income measures (Smeeding 1975). This latter issue is in some ways relevant but does not consider the negative aspects of constraints on choice introduced by stigmatizing in-kind transfers.

Discussions of the measure of poverty indicate, however, that the definition of poverty cannot be limited to income but that other resources should also be considered. Attempts to include the effects of control over capital (that is, of net worth) on economic well-being irrespective of the money income generated by this capital are a step in this direction (Weisbrod and Hansen 1977). Garfinkel and Haveman (1977) suggest that command over certain other resources, what they call earnings capacity, should be considered in the definition of poverty. The concept of earnings capacity refers to the potential of an income unit to generate an income stream using its physical and human capital to capacity. Earnings capacity includes years of schooling and considers the job opportunities available for the members of a household.

Earnings capacity as a measure of economic position is developed primarily to correct for shortcomings in the measure of current income, especially the potential dependence of this measure on the relative tastes of household members for income and leisure. Since the United States has had one of the highest levels of unemployment in advanced industrialized countries in the postwar period and provides few opportunities for the adequate care of children of working women, the constraints on choice produced by these circumstances strongly limit the extent to which tastes for income versus leisure can affect income. The concept of earnings capacity, however, points to the desirabililty of including command over resources other than income in the discussion of poverty. It is thus a step in the direction of recent developments in Europe in which efforts to measure the distribution and the changes in the welfare of the population have produced definitions of levels of living in terms of command over a multiplicity of resources.

In the pioneering work by Johansson (1970, 1972, 1973) and Erikson (1974, 1975, 1976), an individual's level of living is thus defined as command over resources in money, wealth, knowledge, psychic and physical energy, social relations, security, and so forth, by means of which he or she can control and consciously direct the conditions of life. This definition thus conceives of levels of living not in terms of subjective satisfaction or fulfillment of needs but in terms of control over resources, which are defined in terms of relevant policy areas. The level-of-living concept is broken down into nine components:

1. Health and the use of medical care,
2. Work and working conditions,
3. Education,
4. Economic resources,
5. Political resources,
6. Family background and family relations,
7. Housing and environment,
8. Security to life and property, and
9. Leisure and recreation.

The ultimate purpose of the measurement of levels of living in terms of these components is to provide basic information to citizens concerning the state of their welfare and thus to improve the political decision-making processes in the nation. The information from the different components is not to be pooled into a single measure by the researchers. Instead, the weights of the different components are to be developed through political decision-making processes. The inclusion of political resources gives the measurement a dynamic character. (For an alternative approach to the study of levels of living, see Allardt 1973.)

This multidimensional approach to the conceptualization of the level of living points to the limitations involved in studies that discuss poverty only in terms of income. Although income, of course, is indispensable in delineating those eligible for public transfers, antipoverty programs must be evaluated also in terms of their effects other than the reduction of income poverty. A limitation to income, even if expanded to include the value of in-kind transfers, makes discrimination impossible between, for instance, policy measures intended to enable the poor to earn their way out of poverty through a decent job and programs such as food stamps, which enable them to survive. The discussion of the dimensions of poverty therefore should be broadened to include other aspects and to consider the consequences of command over different types of resources for participation in customary or socially approved activities (Townsend 1974) and for participation in "validating activities," that is, "activities that confirm a person's sense of himself as a full and recognized member of his society" (Rainwater 1974, p.17).

Explaining Poverty and Inequality

In discussing the approaches used in explaining poverty and inequality in various counties, it is of interest to look at the various social and economic settings in which the explanations have been formulated. In Table 1 some characteristics of relevance in this context are given for

Table 1.
Some Characteristics of Social and Economic Structures in France, Germany, Netherlands, Sweden, the United Kingdom and the United States.

	Inequality of post-tax income, standardized for household size		Unemployment 1959-75 (percent)	Economic growth rate 1959–65 (percent)	Increase in real wages 1959-69 (percent)	Increase in consumer prices 1959-69 (percent)
	Variance of logs	Percentage of total income to the two lowest deciles				
France	.136	4.2	2.5	3.6	3.6	4.0
Germany	.087	6.5	1.0	5.5	5.7	2.2
Netherlands	.047	9.1	(1.7)	3.5	3.5	3.8
Sweden	.060	7.3	1.9	3.1	4.3	3.4
United Kingdom	.080	6.1	3.1	2.4	3.2	3.7
United States	.111	4.9	5.2	2.0	2.2	2.2

France, Germany, the Netherlands, Sweden, the United Kingdom, and the United States for the postwar period. In some important respects the United States appears to differ from most of the European countries.

The data in Table 1 indicate that the United States together with France has a high degree of inequality in the distribution of income. The data on income distribution in this table have been published by Sawyer (1976) and the measure of income inequality is the variance of logs, which is the indicator of inequality most sensitive to differences among countries at the bottom end of the income distribution. Other data support the view that the degree of inequality in the United States is relatively high. Wiles (1974) took the ratio of the per capita income after taxes received at the fifth and ninety-fifth percentiles on the income distribution as an indicator of the differences between "the rich" and "the poor." He found that in Sweden the rich receive three times more than the poor; in Britain and Denmark six times more; and in the United States thirteen times more. The difference in life expectancy for blacks and whites in the United States is at present about eight years, a difference that is probably considerably greater than those found between comparable socioeconomic groups in European countries. On the other hand, access to higher education has traditionally been more equitable in the United States than in many European countries.

The data in Table 1 indicate that the United States has had a much higher level of unemployment than European countries. Such a high level reflects a sluggish economy with a lower growth rate and a lower rate of increase in real wages than those of most European countries. On the other hand, the rate of inflation has been lower in the United States.

These differences in the socioeconomic characteristics of the United States and several European countries are not reflected in approaches to the explanation of poverty and inequality in the way one might expect. To begin with, sectorially oriented American poverty research does not convey an awareness of the relatively high degree of inequality currently found in the United States. Historical traditions, founded in the contrast between poor, overpopulated, autocratic Europe and the land of opportunity and freedom that is the New World, still contribute to the highly positive image held by most Americans, including poverty researchers, of social and economic conditions in the United States. Unemployment has also been largely neglected by sectorially oriented poverty research in the United States. Somewhat surprisingly, then, inequality and unemployment have been much more central issues on the political and research agendas in Europe than in the United States.

Sectorially oriented poverty research has included valuable work in tracing the development of income inequality in the United States (e.g., Masters 1975, Taussig and Danziger 1977) and in analyzing the role of the government in redistributing income through taxes and other means

(Reynolds and Smolensky 1977). Efforts to explain poverty and inequality in the United States, however, appear primarily to have been sought in terms of the characteristics of the poor. The culture of poverty theory is a case in point, although it is now intellectually largely discredited and never played any important role at the Institute for Research on Poverty. The work motivation of the poor, however, continues to be a central topic for American research. The human capital theory, which sees poverty as a reflection of lack of occupational skills and education among the poor, remains the dominant approach to the explanation of poverty in sectorially oriented poverty research as well as among American academics in general.[5] American researchers also often tend to see the current degree of inequality in their society as underpinned by widely shared values that accept a large degree of inequality (e.g., Tobin 1970). While it is true that survey studies show a widespread acceptance of inequalities in income (Rainwater 1974), these values, of course, cannot explain the distribution of income.

American poverty researchers as well as other social scientists generally appear to accept as fact that there is a negative relationship between equality and efficiency, something that Okun (1975)—surprisingly enough without supporting empirical evidence—has described as "The Big Tradeoff." A look at the postwar record of income inequality and economic growth in some industrialized western nations indicates, however, that we should take a second look at this assumption. In fact, data for Australia, Canada, France, Germany, Japan, the Netherlands, Norway, Sweden, the United Kingdom, and the United States yield a slightly negative correlation between income inequality and the rate of economic growth for the period 1950–1965.[6]

In sectorially oriented poverty research in the United States there is a striking lack of theories attempting to explain poverty and inequality in terms of conflict theories, in which economic and political power resources play a central role and inequality is viewed as an outcome of conflicts over distribution. This type of approach is more common in Europe, but it is, of course, not unknown in the United States. Thus, for instance, Lenski (1966) has argued that inequality in the distribution of privilege in society is primarily a result of the distribution of power. The dearth of conflict-oriented approaches in the study of poverty and inequality in the United States is somewhat surprising in view of the relatively high degree of conflict manifested in American society. For instance, throughout this century, the United States has had one of the very highest volumes of industrial conflict among western countries, with strikes sometimes still involving a degree of violence. Racial conflicts, of course, have been very serious and coupled with violence.

Although more skeptical views have been set forth (Edelman 1977), the traditional and still pervasive view of the United States as a model pluralistic democracy (Lipset 1961, Almond and Verba 1963) appears to have drawn the interest of American poverty researchers away from a consideration of the consequences of power distribution for poverty and inequality. Wilensky (1975) and Jackman (1975) argue that political factors play insignificant roles in affecting the flow of public expenditures and the degrees of inequality. Their studies, however, appear flawed by methodological weaknesses (for an alternative view see Hewitt 1977).[7]

American poverty researchers have paid relatively little attention to the low levels of collective organization among the less privileged strata of the population. The United States thus has one of the very lowest levels of unionization among the western democracies. As Gunnar Myrdal (1963) observed long ago, the United States has a highly unorganized underclass. Furthermore, among the western democracies the United States has a record low level of electoral participation, about 50 percent compared with the 80–90 percent common in most western European countries. What is more significant, the differences in political participation between the blue-collar and the white-collar sectors of the electorate are much larger in the United States than in western Europe and have been increasing in recent years (Burnham 1974, 1978).

Although occupational skills and education must be assumed to play significant roles in the distributive processes in society, it also appears fruitful for research on poverty and inequality to consider the distribution of power in society and, especially, to ask to what extent the interests of less privileged citizens are articulated and effectively represented in the processes if interest aggregation that take place in the private as well as the public sectors of society.[8] To what extent, for instance, are the interests of workers in getting a living wage represented in large sectors of industry (for instance, service and agriculture) or in regions (for instance, the Southwest) where unions are very weak? To what extent can employees protect themselves against layoffs and occupational hazards? Could an increase in the level of unionization make it easier for the working poor to protect their interests?

A sensitivity to the role of politics in setting the baseline and background to poverty and antipoverty programs would also lead us to ask questions concerning whether the interests of the less privileged citizens of the nation have been effectively represented in policy making on the inflation-unemployment dilemma facing most western governments in the postwar years. In the United States, this dilemma has consistently been solved in a way that has generated high unemployment (for a comparative discussion, see Martin 1973, Hibbs 1977). Poverty researchers have documented that anti-inflation policies leading to high unemployment "have the effect of visiting the greatest hardships on those least able to bear it" (Palmer and Barth 1977, p. 238). The record high levels of unemployment, however, have figured surprisingly little in the efforts of American research to explain inequality and poverty.

The view of poverty as income deficiency has led American poverty researchers to see the remedies to poverty largely in terms of income transfers. The stress on human capital theory has suggested remedies in terms of training, an emphasis that has led to more limited programs. An appreciation of the role of the distribution of economic and political power in the generation of poverty and inequality, if correct, would open up alternative ways of affecting poverty. Such an alternative strategy would give the poor command over resources that they themselves could use for acquiring income and suggests that, for instance, legislation facilitating union organization and voter registration could be a significant long term antipoverty policy. It would also draw attention to the level of unemployment as a crucial variable for antipoverty policy. The fact that the latest period of a marked decrease in inequality in the United States, 1930–1959 (Williamson and Lindert 1977), coincided with increasing unionization, "progressive" government, and (during the war) tight labor markets indicates that this type of approach might be a fruitful one.

Policy Evaluation

In the United States, research to evaluate the consequences of antipoverty programs has been carried out on a relatively large scale. The effects of this evaluation research, however, have been double-edged, since the researchers often appear to have concluded too hastily that the evaluated programs have had insignificant effects (Aaron 1978). American poverty researchers have also pioneered the use of the large-scale social experiment for evaluating the consequences of programs. In this context, the New Jersey Income Maintenance Experiment (Kershaw and Fair 1976; Watts and Rees 1977a, 1977b) has attracted international attention. On the European scene, evaluation research has been something the policy makers have asked for but received little of.

The basic question originally proposed for the evaluation of antipoverty programs "What do they do for the poor?" served a useful purpose in directing attention to the fact that several of the categorical programs (e.g., unemployment benefits), assumed to help the poor, did not achieve this goal to any significant extent (Lampman 1974). The focus on the extent to which public expenditures for social purposes reach those below the poverty line was later strengthened and summarized in the concept "target efficiency," which has served as a major criterion for the evaluation of antipoverty programs (Barth et al. 1974). The extent to which programs reduce the poverty gap between those above and those below the poverty line is another evaluation criterion of the same nature. In the context of a political situation in which antipoverty programs have been under strong attack for wasting funds on graft and bureaucracy, American poverty research has made an important contribution by showing that this has not been the case and that antipoverty expenditures actually benefit those for whom they were intended. From other points of view, however, the above type of criteria appear very doubtful and even counterproductive to the development of long-term policies and programs to improve the relative position of the poor.

The target efficiency and poverty gap criteria for policy evaluation are firmly set within the "residual welfare model," in which the bulk of social policies are intended for those below the poverty line. This selective policy strategy can be effective in the short run and these criteria can measure the extent to which this model is effective. But this approach does not consider the political consequences of the policy strategy chosen, that is, how well the strategy can generate support for continued efforts that will help less advantaged citizens in the society. Since those who directly benefit from the selectivist strategy constitute a small minority of the population largely without political or economic power, support for this strategy depends primarily on the feelings of charity among the great majority of citizens who receive no immediate material benefits from the strategy. This basis for support is a very weak one for the development of effective policies in support of the poor. Selective programs that are "target efficient" limit the benefits of programs and therefore also limit the potential supporters of the programs to those below the poverty line. In the residual welfare situation, antipoverty programs may become the means for social control of the poor.

In order to find the necessary base of support for policies in favor of the poor, it seems reasonable to assume that those below the poverty line must develop coalitions with important segments of the rest of the population. Stress on a universalistic policy strategy appears to be an important part of this coalition-building process. Such a policy strategy distributes the benefits of the policies more evenly within the population, and therefore benefits not only those below the poverty line but also significant groups above this line. A universalistic strategy can be expected to generate support based on the self-interest of substantial segments of those above the poverty line. It is thus a base for building a coalition between the poor and the non-poor, a strategy that is of crucial importance if the poor are to improve their relative position in the long run. Whether a policy facilitates or hinders the building of coalitions between the poor and the non-poor therefore can be seen as an important criterion in evaluating and designing antipoverty policies. The target efficiency and poverty gap criteria are direct opposites of this concern.

The problem of "welfare backlash" has often been seen as an almost inevitable phenomenon. Wilensky (1976, p. 8) suggests that welfare backlash reflects the fact that "people are happy to consume government services but are increasingly restive about paying for them" and attempts to explain variations in welfare backlash primarily in terms of the extent to which "corporatist democracies" manage to close off the channels for this restiveness and to hide the costs for welfare policies by relying on forms of taxation with low visibility. It would appear, however, that this phenomenon can instead be accounted for largely in terms of the rational reactions of citizens to the policy strategies used by governments.[9] Selectivist strategies that rely on means testing and that direct a major part of the benefits of programs to those below a poverty line leave a large constituency for welfare backlash (see Figure 1). Universalistic strategies, on the other hand, imply that most households would benefit from at least some programs. The constituency for welfare backlash is therefore small, whereas the bases for support for the policies are large. In Sweden, for instance, when the Conservative Party proposed in the 1960s that the child allowance be abolished for the first child, the proposal met rather sharp negative reactions from the voters. It was seen as an attack on the welfare not only of the poor but also of the great majority of all households, and as a threat to the network of social programs that in one way or another tended to benefit one or more members of each household.

The problems connected with the narrow criteria for program evaluation inherent in the target efficiency concept have been noted by some poverty researchers. Watts (1977, p. 120) states that "some of the 'off target' programs may represent a wiser choice than would programs aimed narrowly at the small minority counted as poor" and Cohen (1977, p. 193) notes that "the negative income tax or anything that is going to give income to people with low income but not give any income to others . . . is a very difficult idea to sell." Although some sectorially oriented poverty research has discussed the relative values of universalistic versus selectivistic policy strategies (Garfinkel 1978), the political consequences and the consequences for the quality of services provided to the poor of the selectivistic strategy have been for the most part overlooked. Nor do programs for the evaluation of the negative income tax, an income maintenance strategy central in the welfare reform pro-

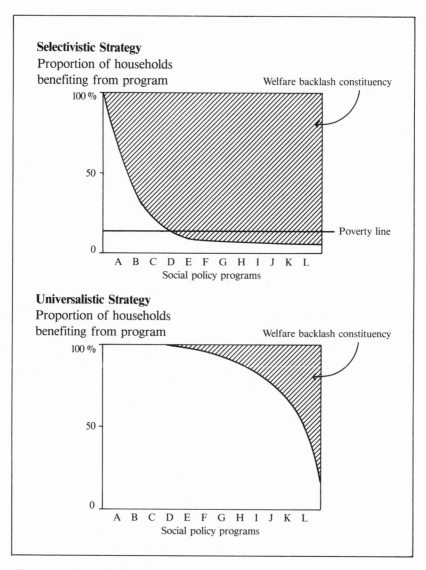

Figure 1. A selectivistic social policy strategy creates a larger constituency for welfare backlash than a universalistic strategy.

posals of Nixon as well as of Carter, appear to have tackled this problem. A significant limitation of the social experiments designed to test the effects of the negative income tax is that they cannot easily incorporate considerations of this nature.

The concentration of the sectorially oriented poverty research on the criteria of target efficiency and the proportion of people below the poverty line in evaluating antipoverty programs also appears to have had the effect of paying relatively little attention to other consequences of these programs. For instance, one can hear poverty researchers state that the war on poverty has been won and support this claim with the fact that the proportion of the population below the poverty line has decreased. But as Lyndon Johnson presented it, the war on poverty was to achieve its goals primarily by providing employment and training. For a foreign observer, it is striking that the expansion of antipoverty programs in the late 1960s and 1970s came not primarily in the areas of employment and training but instead in the form of means-tested programs (AFDC) combined with in-kind transfers (food stamps, medicaid) and work requirements. The decrease in the proportion of people below the poverty line was primarily an effect of cash transfers, not of programs for increasing job opportunities.

American poverty research appears to have taken lightly the recent change of direction in the development of social policy programs in the United States toward the development of a modern welfare state. In the developed welfare states, work requirements are associated with the old Poor Laws, in-kind transfers are nearly abolished, and means-tested programs are seen as necessary but relatively minor complements to the social insurance programs. In Sweden, for instance, only about 2 percent of government social expenditures in the 1970s have been made up of means-tested programs, while other programs are universal or give benefits according to simple information based on income. In-kind transfers and work requirements have been abolished from the public assistance program. In the United States, on the other hand, in 1977 about 25 percent of the expenditures for income maintenance programs were means-tested and somewhat more than 50 percent of the expenditures were given in kind, the most extensive programs being medicaid and food stamps. The use of work requirements has been increasing.

The role that social control has played in the development of recent antipoverty programs in the United States has also been largely neglected in sectorial poverty research, but it has been discussed in the discipline-oriented research (e.g., Cloward and Piven 1971). The stigma attached to the means-tested in-kind programs has received little attention in sectorially oriented poverty research (see, however, Garfinkel 1978 and Steiner 1971, pp. 318–329).

Politics and Poverty Research

Poverty and inequality are traditional areas of potential as well as manifest political conflicts. It is therefore not surprising that research in these areas tends to reflect the political climates prevailing in the countries and the settings in which research is carried out. For a person who moves from one political climate to another, the extent to which poverty research reflects the political situation in the different countries becomes quite striking. For instance, the choice between absolute and relative definitions of poverty as well as the dimensions in which poverty is viewed appear to reflect not differences in the intellectual or moral endowment of the researchers in different countries but rather the fact that a definition acceptable in one political setting is highly controversial in another.

The concerns of researchers also reflect the political climate in a country. How are we to explain, for instance, the fact that the leading question for American poverty research has been the work motivation of the poor? It was the basic question posed in the New Jersey Income Maintenance Experiment, the most important single research project carried out by the Institute for Research on Poverty, and in subsequent experiments of this kind. The question of the effects of income maintenance programs on labor supply has been a central issue in many other studies carried out by poverty researchers (Masters and Garfinkel 1978). This concern has not been shared by European poverty researchers and does not appear defensible on intellectual grounds only. One of the few studies that has investigated the work-related values and desires of the poor indicates, for instance, that the poor do not differ significantly from the non-poor in the value they place on work (Goodwin 1972). The concentration of American research efforts on the work motivation of the poor reflects a conservative political and intellectual climate that has set the issues for poverty research.

On the other hand, American poverty research has largely neglected the consequences for the poor of the extremely high levels of unemployment existing in the United States throughout the postwar period. In fact, after the 1940s (Bakke 1940), few studies have analyzed the consequences of unemployment for the unemployed. In Europe, where unemployment has been considerably lower, the concerns of politicians as well as researchers have been keyed much more strongly to the question of unemployment. It is an intellectual paradox that living in a society that has been a sea of unemployment, American poverty researchers have concentrated their research interests on the work motivation of the poor.

Since poverty is such a politically charged topic, the organization of poverty research becomes problematic. On one hand, it is desirable that poverty research be policy oriented; on the other hand, one would like research to provide critical evaluation rather than legitimation for the policies chosen. Ideally one would also have poverty research discuss and develop alternatives to the policies prevailing in a society. How research should be organized to solve these problems remains a difficult problem. Although the danger that research loses touch with policy concerns has been much discussed, the opposite danger, that poverty research can become too dependent on policy makers, has received less attention. The absence of politically based conflicts between policy makers and sectorially oriented poverty research may mean that the possibility that the sectorially oriented poverty research has avoided working on issues or using approaches for which the risks of political backlash have been high.

A situation in which researchers are economically vulnerable to the decisions of the policy makers clearly increases the risks for political dependency among researchers, for instance, if the existence and budgets of research institutes are subject to annual review by policy makers. One can hardly expect that research done in such situations will provide basic challenges to the prevailing political currents or that it will clearly depart from the dominant intellectual climate in the nation. When researchers spend part of their careers in public policy-making institutions, a practice that is prevalent among American economists but less usual among Europeans or in other disciplines, there are both positive and negative factors for the development of fruitful poverty research. Although such a practice increases the knowledge of the researchers, it also makes them more sensitive to political considerations, since their acceptance in policy-making institutions will depend partly on the positions they take in the scientific arena. In this context, it can perhaps be noted that some of the major discussions of alternative strategies to the antipoverty policies pursued in the United States (Schorr 1977, Furniss and Tilton 1977) have been carried out in more traditional university settings and not in the centers for sectorially oriented research.

Conclusions

A European social scientist engaged in poverty research easily finds much that can be learned from American research. One important area concerns the possibilities of and problems in carrying out large-scale social experiments, in which Americans have led the way. Another area concerns evaluation research, in which valuable experiences have been accumulated in the United States. A third area relates to the methodology of research; in this American social scientists are leading the way in the application of quantitative methods for the analysis of poverty-related problems. There is furthermore a remarkable vitality in American poverty research, evident not only in the enormous productivity of the researchers but also in their combination of creativity and advanced methodology. More than in any of the European countries, poverty researchers in the United States have contributed to the mapping out of the details of the functioning of antipoverty programs in their society. All these achievements are indeed impressive.

Taken one by one, the research concerns of the sectorially oriented poverty studies in the United States appear justified. Viewed as a whole from the perspective as well as the distance across the Atlantic, however, major weaknesses and imbalances are evident in American poverty research. A basic weakness is the reliance on the absolute definition of poverty, which cannot be scientifically justified in studies of changes in the extent of poverty over time. It also appears that the sectorially oriented poverty research in the United States could benefit from a greater pluralism, which should partly be of a disciplinary nature, and the present dominance of the economists should yield to a better balance among different disciplines. The social sciences have important differences in the ways in which they approach and define research problems. For instance, whereas economists see work as a disutility and find it natural to study the consequences of income maintenance alternatives on work motivation, representatives from other disciplines are probably more likely to question this assumption. How research is to be organized so as to combine policy orientation with the necessary independence from policy makers remains a problem on both sides of the Atlantic.

In terms of issues, American poverty research has largely neglected the problem of unemployment, whereas it has concentrated too much on the study of the work motivation of the poor and on the problems of income maintenance. Insufficient attention has been paid to the explanation of poverty and inequality and to the development of alternatives to the prevailing policy strategies. The criteria used in program evaluation have focused too narrowly on target efficiency and have neglected other significant aspects of antipoverty programs, such as their political consequences in inhibiting or encouraging political coalitions in support of continued efforts to reduce poverty and inequality.

How much countries can learn from each other in the development of programs against poverty and inequality remains problematic. To the extent that the conditions for policy development are set by the constellations of economic and political power in a country, the flow of ideas and experiences across borders will be of relatively little significance in affecting the course of policy making. The role of poverty researchers, however, is to be the critics of policy makers—that is, to spell out the assumptions of the present policies, to analyze their consequences, and to develop alternatives to the prevailing policies. Especially in this latter role, poverty researchers in the United States have considerable gains to make by tapping experiences in the development of various types of social policy programs in European countries. If American society is to move from the present "residual welfare model" of social policy to, in the words of Titmuss (1974, p. 31), the "institutional redistributive model" of social policy, it could benefit from the full-scale social policy experiments related to this model that over the years have been carried out in several European nations. Despite attempts at comparative research (e.g., Marris and Rein 1973, Heclo 1974, Heidenheimer et al. 1975, Kahn and Kamerman 1975), it is rather surprising how little European experiences have been utilized by policy makers as well as by researchers in poverty-related areas in the United States.

Notes

Acknowledgment: Prepared for the committee on evaluation of poverty research, National Academy of Sciences. This study was made possible by a fellowship from the German Marshall Fund of the United States and by support from funds granted to the Institute for Research on Poverty by the Department of Health, Education and Welfare pursuant to the provisions of the Economic Opportunity Act of 1964. For helpful comments on drafts of the manuscript I wish to thank Sheldon Danziger, Robert Erikson, Irw Garfinkel, Robert H. Haveman, Sten Johansson, Robert J. Lampman, Alva and Gunnar Myrdal, Alvin L. Schorr and Timothy Tilton as well as members of the evaluation committee. The opinions expressed here are those of the author.

1. Thus, for instance, a Swede reading the Carter welfare proposal presented in 1977, which proposes the creation of public service employment based on minimum wages—not normal or union wages—is reminded of the fact that in the 1920s, two Social Democratic minority governments were forced to resign because of their proposal that public work projects should be created at normal union wages, a proposal that became government policy in the early 1930s. And the issue of national health insurance, which has been debated in the United States in the late 1970s, was settled a generation ago in Sweden as well as in many other countries.

2. Since I am most familiar with poverty research in Scandinavia and Britain, my discussion of European research is based primarily on developments in these countries.

3. This tendency does not mean, of course, that absolute indicators of poverty are never used by European poverty researchers. See, for instance, Fiegehen et al. (1977).

4. In a comparison of the American poverty line with the British social assistance guidelines, Zimbalist (1977) clearly indicates how the absolute poverty line makes the poor slip in relation to increasing median incomes while the British social assistance levels by and large have followed rising average incomes.

5. An alternative theory for explaining inequality has been suggested by Thurow (1975).

6. The measure of income inequality used to calculate the correlation between economic inequality and growth is the variance of logs of income after taxes for "standardized" household size given by Sawyer (1976, p. 19), which correlates -0.28 with the percent of economic growth 1950–1965 in these countries.

7. Both studies are of a cross-sectional nature, including countries with a very wide range of economic development, making conclusions concerning the impact of political efforts on equality exceedingly difficult to draw. Jackman also uses an intersectorial measure of income inequality, which is not relevant to the study of the consequences of politics for inequality.

8. An analysis of health policies from a perspective of political conflict has been done by Alford (1975). Race and local politics have been studied by Eisinger (1976).

9. Wilensky's analysis of welfare backlash is weakened by the fact that his dependent variable includes such a wide variety of political and other phenomena, in practice almost everything that has departed from "normal" developments in various societies. He does not consider alternative explanations to deviating political phenomena. In the cases of the parties of Glistrup in Denmark and Lange in Norway, for instance, it would appear that these protest parties have largely reflected the disillusionment in the electorate over the fact that none of the party blocks could solve the problems related to the "stagflation" of the 1970s, and that the major parties were seriously split and weakened in connection with the fights on the nationality issue in connection with entry into the European Economic Community.

References

Aaron, H.J. (1978) *Politics and Professors: The Great Society in Perspective.* Washington, D.C.: Brookings Institution.

Alford, R.R. (1975) *Health Care Politics. Ideological and Interest Group Barriers to Reform.* Chicago: University of Chicago Press.

Allardt, E. (1973) About Dimensions of Welfare. Report no. 1. Research Group for Comparative Sociology, University of Helsinki.

Almond, G., and Verba, S. (1963) *The Civic Culture.* Boston: Little, Brown.

Atkinson, A.B. (1975) *The Economics of Inequality.* Oxford, England: Clarendon Press.

Bakke, E.W. (1940) *Citizens Without Work*. New Haven: Yale University Press.

Barth, M.C., Cargano, G.J., and Palmer, J.L. (1974) *Toward an Effective Income Support System: Problems, Prospects and Choices*. Madison: University of Wisconsin, Institute for Research on Poverty.

Burnham, W.D. (1974) Equality of voting. In L. Rainwater, ed., *Social Problems and Public Policy*. Chicago: Aldine.

Burnham, W.D. (1978) The Appearance and Disappearance of the American Voter: A Historical Overview. Unpublished paper. Massachusetts Institute of Technology.

Cloward, R., and Piven, F.F. (1971) *Regulating the Poor. The Functions of Public Welfare*. New York: Pantheon.

Coates, K., and Silburn, R. (1970) *Poverty: The Forgotten Englishmen*. Harmondsworth, England: Penguin.

Cohen, W.R. (1977) Discussion. In R.H. Haveman, ed., *A Decade of Federal Anti-Poverty Programs*. New York: Academic Press.

Edelman, M. (1977) *Political Language: Words That Succeed and Politics That Fail*. New York: Academic Press.

Eisinger, P.K. (1976) *Patterns of Interracial Politics: Conflicts and Cooperation in the City*. New York: Academic Press.

Erikson, R. (1974) Welfare as a planning goal. *Acta Sociologica* 17(3):274–288.

Erikson, R. (1975) Livskvalitet—empiri och teori. (Empirical and theoretical aspects of the quality of life). *Plan* 29 (i):6–9.

Erikson, R. (1976) Local variations of levels of living. *Plan* (Special issue prepared for the Habitat Conference in Vancouver, 1976):57–65.

Fiegehen, G.C., Lansley, P.S., and Smith, A.D. (1977) *Poverty and Progress in Britain 1953–73*. Cambridge, England: Cambridge University Press.

Fuchs, V.R. (1965) Toward a theory of poverty. In *Task Force on Economic Growth and Opportunity: The Concept of Poverty*. Washington, D.C.: Chamber of Commerce of the United States.

Furniss, N., and Tilton, T. (1977) *The Case for the Welfare State: from Social Security to Social Equality*. Bloomington: Indiana University Press.

Galbraith, J.K. (1958) *The Affluent Society*. London: Hamish Hamilton.

Garfinkel, I. (1978) Income Support Policy: Where We've Come From and Where We Should Be Going. Discussion paper no. 490-78, Institute for Research on Poverty, University of Wisconsin, Madison, Wis.

Garfinkel, I., and Haveman, R.H. (1977) *Earnings Capacity, Poverty, and Inequality*. New York: Academic Press.

Goodwin, L. (1972) *Do the Poor Want to Work?* Washington, D.C.: Brookings Institution.

Heclo, H. (1974) *Modern Social Politics in Britain and Sweden*. New Haven: Yale University Press.

Heidenheimer, A.J., Heclo, H., and Adams, C.T. (1975) *Comparative Public Policy: The Politics of Social Choice in Europe and America*. New York: St. Martin's Press.

Hewitt, C. (1977) The effect of political democracy and social democracy on equality in industrial societies: a cross-national comparison. *American Sociological Review* 42(June):450–464.

Hibbs, D.A. (1977) Political parties and macroeconomic policy. *American Political Science Quarterly* 71(December):1467–1487.

Jackman, R.W. (1975) *Politics and Social Equality. A Comparative Analysis.* New York: Wiley.

Johansson, S. (1970) *Om levnadsnivaundersökningen* (On the level of living study). Stockholm: Allmänna förlaget.

Johansson, S. (1972) Conceptualizing and measuring welfare: some experiences from the Swedish low income committee. *Statistisk tidskrift* 10(2). English translation available from Swedish Institute for Social Research, S-106 91 Stockholm.

Johansson, S. (1973) The level of living survey: a presentation. *Acta Sociologica* 16(3)211–219.

Kahn, A.J., and Kamerman, S.B. (1975) *Not for the Poor Alone: European Social Services.* Philadelphia: Temple University Press.

Kershaw, D., and Fair, J. (1976) *The New Jersey Income-Maintenance Experiment: Operations, Surveys and Administration.* New York: Academic Press.

Kincaid, J.C. (1973) *Poverty and Equality in Britain.* Harmondsworth, England: Penguin.

Korpi, W. (1974) Poverty, social assistance and social policy in post-war Sweden. *Acta Sociologica* 17:2–3, 120–41.

Lampman, R.J. (1971) *Ends and Means of Reducing Income Poverty.* Chicago: Markham.

Lampman, R.J. (1974) What does it do for the poor?–a new test for national policy. *The Public Interest* 34(Winter):66–82.

Lenski, G. (1966) *Power and Privilege: A Theory of Stratification.* New York: McGraw Hill.

Lipset, S.M. (1961) *Political Man.* London: Mercury Books.

Marris, P., and Rein, M. (1973) *Dilemmas of Social Reform.* Chicago: Aldine.

Martin, A. (1973) *The Politics of Economic Policy in the United States: A Tentative View from a Comparative Perspective.* Beverly Hills: Sage.

Masters, S.H. (1975) *Black-White Income Differentials.* New York: Academic Press.

Masters, S., and Garfinkel, I. (1978) *Estimating the Labor Supply Effects of Income-Maintenance Alternatives.* New York: Academic Press.

Mencher, S. (1967) The problem of measuring poverty. *British Journal of Sociology* 18:1–12.

Miller, S.M., and Roby, P. (1970) *The Future of Inequality.* New York: Basic Books.

Moon, M., and Smolensky, E., eds. (1977) *Improving Measures of Economic Well-Being.* New York: Academic Press.

Myrdal, G. (1963) *Challenge to Affluence.* New York: Pantheon.

Okun, A.M. (1975) *Equality and Efficiency: The Big Trade Off.* Washington, D.C.: The Brookings Institution.

Palmer, J.L., and Barth, M.C. (1977) The distributional effects of inflation and higher unemployment. In M. Moon and E. Smolensky, eds., *Improving the Measure of Economic Well-Being*. New York: Academic Press.

Plotnick, R.D., and Skidmore, F. (1975) *Progress Against Poverty: A Review of the 1964-1975 Decade*. New York: Academic Press.

Rainwater, L. (1974) *What Money Buys: Inequality and the Social Meanings of Income*. New York: Basic Books.

Rein, M. (1970) Problems in the definition and measurement of poverty. In P. Townsend, ed., *The Concept of Poverty*. London: Heineman.

Reynolds, M., and Smolensky, E. (1977) *Public Expenditures, Taxes, and the Distribution of Income: The United States, 1950, 1961, 1970*. New York: Academic Press.

Robson, W.A. (1976) *Welfare State and Welfare Society*. London: Allen & Unwin.

Sawyer, M. (1976) *Income Distribution in OECD Countries*. Paris: Organization for Economic Cooperation and Development.

Schorr, A.L. (1977) *Jubilee for Our Time: A Practical Program for Income Equality*. New York: Columbia University Press.

Sleeman, J.F. (1973) *The Welfare State: Its Aims, Benefits and Costs*. London: Allen & Unwin.

Smeeding, T. (1975) Measuring the Economic Welfare of Low Income Households, and the Anti-Poverty Effectiveness of Cash and Non-Cash Transfer Programs. Ph.D. dissertation, University of Wisconsin, Madison.

Smolensky, E. (1965) The past and present poor. In *Task Force and Economic Growth and Opportunity: The Concept of Poverty*. Washington, D.C.: U.S. Chamber of Commerce.

Steiner, G.Y. (1971) *The State of Welfare*. Washington, D.C.: Brookings Institution.

Taussig, M.K., and Danziger, S. (1977) Trends in Inequality of Well-Offness in the United States Since World War II. Special Report No. 11. Institute for Research on Poverty, University of Wisconsin.

Thurow, L.C. (1975) *Generating Inequality: Mechanisms of Distribution in the U.S. Economy*. New York: Basic Books.

Titmuss, R. (1975) *Social Policy*. London: Allen & Unwin.

Tobin, J. (1970) On limiting the domain of inequality. *The Journal of Law and Economics* 13(October):263-277.

Townsend, P., ed. (1970) *The Concept of Poverty*. New York: American Elsevier.

Townsend, P. (1974) Poverty as relative deprivation: resources and style of living. In D. Wedderburn, ed., *Poverty Inequality and Class Structure*. Cambridge, England: Cambridge University Press.

U.S. Department of Health, Education, and Welfare (1976) *The Measure of Poverty*. Washington, D.C.: U.S. Government Printing Office.

U.S. President's Commission on Income Maintenance Programs (1969)

Poverty Amidst Plenty. Main Report. Washington, D.C.: U.S. Government Printing Office.

Watts, H.W. (1968) An economic definition of poverty. In D.P. Moynihan, ed., *On Understanding Poverty.* New York: Basic Books.

Watts, H.W. (1977) Discussions. In R.H. Haveman, ed., *A Decade of Federal Antipoverty Programs.* New York: Academic Press.

Watts, H.W., and Rees, A. (1977a) *The New Jersey Income-Maintenance Experiment: Labor-Supply Responses.* New York: Academic Press.

Watts, H.W., and Rees, A. (1977b) *The New Jersey Income-Maintenance Experiment: Expenditures, Health and Social Behavior and the Quality of the Evidence.* New York: Academic Press.

Weisbrod, B.A., and Hansen, W.L. (1977) An income-net worth approach to measuring economic welfare. In M. Moon and E. Smolensky, eds., *Improving Measures of Economic Well-Being.* New York: Academic Press.

Wilensky, H.L. (1975) *The Welfare State and Equality: Structural and Ideological Roots of Public Welfare Spending.* Berkeley: University of California Press.

Wilensky, H.L. (1976) *The "New Corporatism," Centralization, and the Welfare State.* Beverly Hills: Sage Publications.

Wiles, P. (1974) *Distribution of Income: East and West.* New York: American Elsevier.

Williamson. J.G., and Lindert, P.H. (1977) *Long Term Trends in American Wealth Inequality.* Discussion paper no. 472–477. Institute for Research on Poverty, University of Wisconsin.

Zimbalist, S.F. (1977) Recent British and American poverty trends: conceptual and policy contrasts. *Social Service Review* (September):419–433.